THE EMERGENCE OF FEMINISM IN INDIA, 1850–1920

D0209844

To my parents:
Kusuma Anagol and Jayakumar Anagol

The Emergence of Feminism in India, 1850–1920

PADMA ANAGOL
Cardiff University, UK

ASHGATE

Published by
Ashgate Publishing Limited
Gower House
Croft Road
Aldershot
Hampshire GU11 3HR
England

Ashgate Publishing Company
Suite 420
101 Cherry Street
Burlington, VT 05401-4405
USA

Ashgate website: http://www.ashgate.com

British Library Cataloguing in Publication Data
Anagol, Padma
The emergence of feminism in India, 1850-1920
    1.Feminism – India – Maharashtra – History – 19th century 2.Women's rights – India
    – Maharashtra – 19th century 3.Equality – India – Maharashtra – 19th century
    I.Title
    305.4'2'0954'09034

Library of Congress Cataloging-in-Publication Data
Anagol, Padma.
  The emergence of feminism in India, 1850-1920 / by Padma Anagol.
    p. cm.
  Includes bibliographical references and index.
  ISBN 0-7546-3411-6 (alk. paper)
  1. Feminism—India—Maharashtra—History—19th century. 2. Women's rights—India—
Maharashtra—History—19th century. 3. Equality—India—Maharashtra—History—19th
century. I. Title.

HQ1744.M33A53 2006
305.420954'09034—dc22

2006000580

  ISBN-10: 0-7546-3411-6
  ISBN-13: 978-0-7546-3411-9

Printed and bound in Great Britain by TJ International Ltd, Padstow, Cornwall.

Contents

Acknowledgements

I have found writing the 'acknowledgements' the most overwhelming aspect of this book, although a pleasurable one. My love of history was kindled during my undergraduate studies in Mysore through Mr Prasanna Kumar, my first history teacher and the flames kept ablaze during my postgraduate days in the Centre for Historical Studies, Jawaharlal Nehru University, New Delhi. I was indeed fortunate to be taught by some of India's finest historians and if Prof. K.N. Panikkar, Prof. Sabyasachi Bhattacharya, Prof. Bipan Chandra, Dr Majid Siddiqui, Dr Madhavan Palat and Prof. Romila Thapar do happen to read this book, I hope they may see that their lessons were not taught in vain.

An early incarnation of this work took the form of a doctoral thesis. I would like to thank The Association of Commonwealth Universities who awarded me the Commonwealth Scholarship that saw the beginnings of a doctorate under the able guidance of Prof. Kenneth Ballhatchet who honed my skills as a 'researcher'. Regrettably, he did not live to see the end product as he succumbed to a stroke soon after the commencement of my degree. In 1988, Prof. David Arnold kindly undertook the task of supervision and I owe him a special word of thanks for encouraging me to bring it to completion. I would like to thank the Department of History, Bath Spa University and the Cardiff School of History and Archaeology, Cardiff University for various reasons: the first for showing enough faith in my abilities to give me a full-time teaching position when I was still a doctoral student and the latter for their trust in a 'freshly' graduated student no doubt, an eager one as I was in 1995. I have availed grants from both institutions, which allowed me to make valuable field trips to India. In addition, my colleagues at Cardiff have provided a congenial environment to work in for which I am grateful.

A work such as this one represents could not have been possible without the large-hearted warmth and generosity of many people in India and Britain. Several friends on whose time and energy I have made countless demands are: Vyankatesh Kulkarni, Naila Khan, Sheila Smith, Andrea Hintze, Jane Buckingham, Satinder Gill and Florence Stratton. The intimate connection between Modern British History and empire is an inescapable one but Laura Nym Mayhall, John Shaw and Adrian Gregory gave these connections new meanings through sharing references and most of all, by offering useful comments on drafts of articles. Further, over the years, Laura Mayhall has been a wonderful friend and sister who capably read the entire draft of the monograph and produced comments within a week. Colleagues who have always been encouraging and giving are Geraldine Forbes, Clare

Midgley, Margaret Ward, Philippa Levine, David Hardiman, Parita Mukta and Barbara Ramusack. I have known Chris Bayly since my graduate days and he has always been very supportive and I would like to take this opportunity to thank him for his many kindnesses over the years.

When I initiated this project Rosalind O'Hanlon gave me several useful references that proved to be a good guide especially as I started out on my first field trip in 1988. The search for primary sources took me to many cities and towns both in Britain and India. In this connection I would like to thank the Chief Librarians of Oriental and India Office Collections, British Library, School of Oriental and African Studies Library, Wellcome Institute Archives, London, Centre for South Asian Studies, Cambridge, Maharashtra State Government Archives, Mumbai, Mumbai Marathi Grantha Sangrahalaya, Bombay, Pune Marathi Granthalaya, Shasakiya Vibhagiya Granthalaya, Pune, Jawaharlal Nehru Library, University Of Bombay, Kalina Campus, Jayakar Library, University of Poona, Kesari and Mahratta Office, Poona and finally Kolhapur University Library. Local historians who are truly gifted and extremely enthusiastic about helping younger scholars and to whom I am grateful are: Prof. Vidyut Bhagvat, Prof. Sarojini Chawalar, Prof. Raja Vora, Prof. Mali and Prof. Ram Bapat. Dr Tikekar, who fortunately occupies the position of both a scholar and an archivist, on several occasions, has gone out of his way to help me track sources. The staff members of Huzur Paga School, Seva Sadan Society and Mukti Mission were extremely accommodating and patient with my queries and I would like to thank them for their cooperation in allowing me to photocopy large amounts of materials from their collections. Despite making many field trips over the last two decades, I have never failed to be impressed by the admirable interest and pride shown by local scholars and ordinary people of Maharashtra in their history, society and culture. The living connections between the past and the present are always brought home starkly during my research trips, when I have learnt much and absorbed the vibrant Maharashtrian way of life.

Many friendships that took root during my doctoral days continue and I count myself privileged in this respect. Among them, I warmly thank Ashok and Chitra Kulkarni who had housed me as a poor doctoral student but continued to shower the same affection on subsequent visits. My extended family members are scattered all over India and the West yet, they have always responded to my calls for help in the last decade. I am especially grateful to those relatives who, by the fact of living in the Northern or Southern Maharashtra belt, have been crucial in providing me the comforts that only a 'home away from home' can give. They are: Dr Shrikant and Dr Manjari Anagol, Prof. Malathi Anagol and Mahavir Anagol, Suresh and Sarita Bahirshet, Shakuntala Ambannavar, Gunadhar and Sushila Anagol, Ratan and Usha Anagol, Chitragupta and Lata Anagol, Dr Sunanda and Dr Dinesh Bargale, Dr Neema, Vinay and Dr Namita Anagol. I believe that no words can repay their unconditional support that has taken many forms. Equally, my sisters Seetha, Meena and Kanthi and my lovely niece, Shilpa, have always been there when I needed them. I owe considerable debt to my brother-in-law, Mr Narasimhlu (Siddharth) and Devaki Jain for persuading my father to send me to Nehru

University for postgraduate work; otherwise I have no doubt that my career may have very well taken a different path. One person who has singularly made this project a realizable one is Patrick McGinn alias *Swataha*, from whom I have taken more than I have given, and without whom I really do not believe this book would have seen print.

Many of the ideas formulated in the various chapters of this book were first tried out on unsuspecting audiences in conferences and seminar series over the last decade and I thank them for giving me the valuable opportunity of dialogue. They are: the Department of History, School of Oriental and African Studies; Series on 'Women and Crime' in Institute of Commonwealth Studies; the Annual Conference of the British Association of Asian Studies; the seminar series on 'conversions' in the Department of Religious Studies, Cardiff University; Centre for Asian Studies, Cambridge University; Conference on 'Britishness' in Centre de Recherches Historique, L' Ecole Des Hautes Etudes en Science Sociales, Paris and Cardiff Historical Association, Cardiff, Wales. Equally, many of my students have risen bravely to the challenge of their ranting tutor especially in my Special Subject 'Gender and Imperialism, India 1829–1929,' and I wish to thank them all for their stimulating discussions.

Erika Gaffney, my commissioning editor, has been extraordinary in many ways: first of all for being a canny reader and spotting potential in my manuscript and patiently waiting for me to turn it into a book. Her generosities are many, especially her empathy through the many illnesses and surgeries I have undergone that have considerably delayed the production of this book. My heartfelt thanks go to her and her team including Meredith Coeyman and Melissa Riley-Jones. A special word of thanks goes to Lesley Stewart who helped me make up my mind in paring an early version of this manuscript which was double the present word count. Two anonymous readers were responsible for generating a contract with Ashgate and I would like to thank them for their wonderful feedback. Their faith in my project as expressed in their reports egged me on during difficult times.

Some subsections of the chapters in this book have formed parts of articles that have been published previously. I would like to thank Oxford University Press for permission to reproduce some material in chapter 5 of this book from the following article: 'The Emergence of the Female Criminal in India: Infanticide and Survival under the Raj', *History Workshop Journal*, 53 (Spring 2002): 73–94. For permission to cite some portions of my article 'Indian Christian Women and Indigenous Feminism', from C. Midgley (ed.), *Gender and Imperialism* (Manchester: Manchester University Press, 1998), in chapter 2 of this book, I wish to thank Manchester University Press. Finally, the last section of chapter 6 of this monograph has drawn upon material used in 'The Age of Consent Act (1891) Reconsidered: Women's Perspectives and Participation in the Child Marriage Controversy in India', *South Asia Research*, 12/2 (November 1992), for which I wish to thank Sage Publications.

A Note on Translation and Citation

A phonetic style that dispenses with the use of diacritical marks has been adopted that allows for a simpler and easier form, which helps the reader to enunciate accurately. In keeping with the normal standards I have translated all the titles of articles and books in Marathi language but not the title of journals or newspapers. In addition, Marathi phrases used in the book are always translated and these appear in square brackets throughout the monograph. The archive or private collection from which the source was derived is mentioned in the bibliography although individual chapters contain the abbreviated form of the name of the archive where official sources are quoted or cited from including the Native Newspaper Reports. Wherever such abbreviations occur it has been indicated for the first time and the full reference has been given followed by the abbreviated form, for example,, Maharashtra State Archives, hereafter (MSA).

Some idiosyncrasies of the language and culture of the Maharashtrian region have posed challenges in translation as well as citation. The term 'Pandita' occurs in the name of a few women pioneers and this refers to the honorific title earned by the lady in a given area of expertise either through an open competition such as with Anasuyabai Pandita or as one conferred by royalty as in the case of Godavaribai Pandita. In the Maharashtrian tradition, the norm was to recognize or address unmarried women by their father's surname and married women by their husbands' surnames, however, learned women were recognized by their maiden names followed by the title. The exception to this rule is the extremely well known Pandita Ramabai, whose international audience anglicized the style of addressing her as 'Pandita Ramabai' instead of 'Ramabai Pandita'. For this reason I have retained the anglicized version and used the full name both in references within chapters as well as the bibliography. Some women writers came from aristocratic backgrounds and had titles attached to their names (for example, 'Shrimant Sagunabai alias Tai Saheb Pant Pratinidhi') whilst others used nom de plumes. These have proved impossible to translate and abbreviate in any form, hence I have used the entire name of the authoress whilst citing them in both the chapters and the bibliography. Quite a few women writers used pseudonyms especially when writing to the 'Correspondence of Readers' columns in the Women's Press. These pseudonyms are retained and wherever possible if the identity of the author is known I have made that clear. The names of women petitioners including prisoners have been considerably distorted in the anglicized spelling adopted in the British records. But, I have resisted the urge to correct them because the referencing system's main purpose is to help other scholars find the original source materials.

Although more recent governments of Maharashtra have changed the names of cities, keeping in mind that older catalogues use the place names as was current in the nineteenth century rather than now, I have favoured the citation of place names such as 'Bombay' and 'Poona' instead of the contemporary 'Mumbai' and 'Pune'—unless of course, the archive or library consulted has shown a preference. Finally, all translations from Marathi to English are mine. Therefore, all errors in translation remain my responsibility too.

Chapter 1

Women's Agency and Resistance in Colonial India: An Introduction

Growing up in a Marathi and Kannada speaking extended family in northern Karnataka, stories of great Kannadiga and Maharashtrian women who had made a major impact on the society, religion and politics of the region were often narrated as part of the evening leisure activities.[1] The achievements of women of recent Indian history such as Pandita Ramabai, Rani Chenamma and Ramabai Ranade were recounted with pride by my women kinsfolk just as much as the female saints and heroines of the myths and legends of older traditions such as Akkamahadevi and Janabai. Knowledge of these women jostled alongside stories of women members of my family drawn from paternal and maternal family history. Women members of my extended family often talked in a tone mixed with admiration, respect, envy or dismay depending on the particular story they were narrating—about the strength of character of a canny grand aunt; the hardy and astute nature of a great- grandmother; the courage and leadership qualities of a widowed female relative who held all the men in her family 'under her thumb'. These tales were the staple diet of my growing years along with the sad anecdotes of many bygone female members of my family—those women who had experienced extreme hardship and who had been deprived of house and home and a living through the machinations of other members of the extended family. This repository of fascinating life-stories drawn from my own family had a powerful bearing in generating my scholarly interest in the subject during my years as a student of history. When I began my research on the topic, however, I found it difficult to reconcile the varied and complex picture that I had been nurtured on with that of the more starkly drawn picture emerging from the contemporary scholarship on Indian women.

The Historiography: Problems of Theory and Method

The enormous and growing body of literature within gender and women's history of India is a testimony to the burgeoning interest in the field from scholars across many

---

[1] My grandparents were practising Jains and hence we ate before sundown leaving a large gap to fill between dusk and bedtime.

disciplines and international locations.[2] The scope and range of the current research, especially in the last two decades, has been in-depth and wide-ranging and distinct thematic concerns are discernible. These include: the marginalization of women in the economy and popular culture;[3] the impact of colonial law and administrative policies on the role and status of women;[4] the reconstitution of patriarchies via the recasting of the concept of 'womanhood';[5] and, more recently, the historical visibility of women.[6] Although these works are significant contributions to gender studies, women's agency, explored through the twin aspects of the issue of consciousness and resistance amongst Indian women in the colonial past, has not sufficiently engaged the attention of scholars working in the field.[7] This is despite the huge increase in publications within

---

[2] Useful historiographical surveys are in Barbara Ramusack, 'From Symbol to Diversity: The Historical Literature on Women in India', in *South Asia Research*, 2 (1990): 139–57, and Aparna Basu, 'Women's History in India: An Historiographical Survey', in Karen Offen, et al., *Writing Women's History: International Perspectives* (Houndmills: Macmillan, 1992), pp. 181–210.

[3] Nirmala Banerjee, 'Working Women in Colonial Bengal: Modernization and Marginalization', in Kumkum Sangari and Sudesh Vaid (eds), *Recasting Women: Essays in Colonial History* (New Delhi: Kali, 1989), pp. 269–301; Dagmar Engels, *Beyond Purdah: Women in Bengal, 1890–1939* (New Delhi: Oxford University Press, 1996), chapter 6. The latter theme is dealt with by Sumanta Banerjee, *The Parlour And the Streets: Elite and Popular Culture in Nineteenth-Century Calcutta* (Calcutta: Seagull, 1989). On Maharashtra see Sharmila Rege, 'The Hegemonic Appropriation of Sexuality: The Case of Lavani Performers of Maharashtra', *Contributions to Indian Sociology*, 29/1, 2 (1995): 23–39.

[4] Among others, see Lucy Carroll, 'Law, Custom And Statutory Social Reform: The Hindu Widow's Remarriage Act Of 1856', *Indian Economic and Social History Review*, 20/4 (1983): 363–89; Janaki Nair, *Women and Law in Colonial India: A Social History* (New Delhi: Kali, 1996); Sudhir Chandra, *Enslaved Daughters: Colonialism, Law and Women's Rights* (New Delhi: Oxford University Press, 1998).

[5] Partha Chatterjee, 'Colonialism, Nationalism and Colonialized Women: The Contest in India', *American Ethnologist*, 16/4 (1989): 622–33; Uma Chakravarti, 'Whatever Happened to the Vedic Dasi? Orientalism, Nationalism and a Script for the Past', in Sangari and Vaid (eds), *Recasting Women*, pp. 27–87.

[6] Recently the trend has shifted to emphasizing the works of well-known and/or lesser-known women who have written unique texts questioning gender relations. For the former see Meera Kosambi (ed.), *Pandita Ramabai in Her Own Words* (New York: Feminist Press, 2000); for the latter see Rosalind O' Hanlon, (ed.), *A Comparison between Women and Men: Tarabai Shinde and the Critique of Gender Relations in Colonial India* (Madras: Oxford University Press, 1994). Several influential anthologies have also been published; the volumes edited by Tharu and Lalitha offer extracts from over 140 texts by unknown or lesser-known women from 13 Indian languages from 600 B.C. to the early twentieth century demonstrating the long tradition of female dissent in India. Susie Tharu and K. Lalitha (eds), *Women Writing in India, 600 B.C. to the Present* (New York: Feminist Press, 1991).

[7] It is relevant to mention at this point that, although women's perceptions and participation in revolutionary movements have been studied, such studies mainly

Indian gender and women's history since the early 1970s. However, if one examines the historiographical concerns of the early social history of India (1960s and the 1970s) and later feminist scholarship (1970s and 1980s), the reasons for the neglect of women's agency become apparent. The position of women in Indian society has been looked at either as part of broader studies in the social and cultural history of India or more directly, in the attempt to trace the changing role of women in colonial India. Such scholars have argued that improvements in the status of women came about from the nineteenth century onwards, not as the product of a process of conscious assertion on the part of Indian women, but through programmes of social reform devised and carried out by Indian men and the colonial state. In many ways the picture, which emerges of Indian women as passive recipients in these processes, has been predetermined by the approaches, which scholars have adopted. In the 'Western impact–Indian response' paradigm that informs their work, there is little room for women as conscious agents.[8] Instead, Indian women are projected as a monolithic and oppressed entity and reduced to mere beneficiaries of the 'awakening' experienced by their men folk because of contact with Western influences.[9]

These problems have been compounded by a Eurocentric bias in charting protest and self-assertion movements in Afro-Asian women's history due to an absence of an alternative approach to define the experiences unique to women in colonial societies. The use of Western models to explain the situation of Indian women has resulted in sympathetic Indianists hesitating to describe even the most radical women as 'feminists'.[10] Meredith Borthwick, for instance, who has greatly enriched our

---

concentrate on what was happening at the height of the nationalist agitations of the twentieth century. A fine illustration of peasant and working women's voices in the Communist party-led Telengana struggle between 1946 and 1951 is Stree Shakti Sanghatana (ed.), *We Were Making History: Life Stories of Women in the Telengana People's Struggle* (London: Zed, 1989).

[8] I have adapted the model of 'impact–response' to modern Indian history that was originally outlined by Paul Cohen in his hugely influential work but, in relation to American historiography on modern China, *Discovering History in China: American Historical Writing on the Recent Chinese Past* (New York: Columbia University Press, 1984).

[9] One of the earliest and most influential works following this framework is Charles Heimsath, *Indian Nationalism and Hindu Social Reform* (Princeton: Princeton University Press, 1964). In many of the works on social reform in the 60s and 70s, Indian historians including those writing in the broad area of women's history follow its approach. See for example B.R. Nanda (ed.), *Indian Women: From Purdah to Modernity*, (New Delhi: Vikas, 1976).

[10] Some exceptions are Geraldine Forbes and Barbara Ramusack, who were amongst some of the earliest pioneers of women's history of modern India alongside Neera Desai, Pratima Asthana, Vina Mazumdar, Kumari Jayawardena amongst others. See Geraldine Forbes, '"Caged Tigers": First Wave Feminists in Twentieth-Century Bengal', *Women's Studies International Forum*, 5/6, (1982): 526–36 and her book *Women in Modern India* (Cambridge: Cambridge University Press, 1996); Barbara Ramusack and Sharon Sievers,

understanding of the changing conditions of the *bhadramahila* ['respectable' middle-class Bengali women] during the period 1850–1905, has utilized approaches originally devised to study the history of women in the West. Following the Western–impact/Indian–response paradigm, she finds that the *bhadramahila* was emerging as a response to the *bhadralok* [middle-class Bengali men], who in turn were reacting to British rule.[11] Therefore, it is not surprising that she finds that the *bhadramahila* did not display any 'feminist consciousness'. She states:

> When I began my study I was interested in locating a 'feminist consciousness'. The possibility still interests me, but as I understand more about the lives of women at that time, the more misguided I feel it is to expect that kind of perception then.[12]

One could argue here that the expectation was misguided, not because such a feminist perception did not exist, but because its absence was already predetermined by Western connotations of feminism.[13] Ghulam Murshid's work on the response of Bengali women to modernization labours under similar problems even though a large part of the vernacular source material he uses are journals edited by women, some of which even include writings by some radical women of the period.[14] Malavika Karlekar in *Voices from Within*, on the other hand, has offered a refreshingly different analysis. By treating autobiographical writings as 'personal narratives', she showed the range of responses made by nineteenth-century Bengali women. While tracing the formation of women's subcultures in the *antahpur* [inner house], she effectively demonstrated how literacy and education enabled at least an elite section of Bengali women to question male constructions of Indian femininity.[15]

Women in Asia: Restoring Women to History (Bloomington and Indianapolis: Indiana University Press, 1999).

[11] Meredith Borthwick, *The Changing Condition of Women in Bengal: 1850–1905* (Princeton: Princeton University Press, 1984).

[12] Meredith Borthwick, 'Looking at Women's History: Nineteenth-Century Bengal,' in Meredith Borthwick et al., *Problems and Methods of Enquiry in South Asian History* (Nedlands: University of Western Australia Press, 1984), p. 22.

[13] Recently, something of a breakthrough has occurred, and orientalist assumptions about non-Western women, which include concepts of veil and *purdah* in Muslim societies and anthropological theories on African societies, and women have been questioned. Some exciting works are Reza Hammami and Martina Rieker, 'Feminist Orientalism and Orientalist Marxism', *New Left Review*, 170 July/August (1988): 93–106; Malek Alloula, *The Colonial Harem*, trans. Myrna Godwich and Wlad Godwich (Manchester: Manchester University Press, 1987); Ifi Amadiume, *Male Daughters, Female Husbands* (London: Zed, 1987). Chandra Mohanty has questioned some of the conceptual frameworks of the Zed series on Third World women in 'Under Western Eyes: Feminist Scholarship and Colonial Discourses', *Feminist Review*, 30 Autumn (1988): 61–88.

[14] Ghulam Murshid, Reluctant Debutante: Response of Bengali Women to Modernization, 1849–1905 (Rajshahi: Sahitya Samsad, 1983).

[15] Malavika Karlekar, Voices from Within: Personal Narratives of Nineteenth-Century Bengali Women (New Delhi: Oxford University Press, 1991).

Even with the growth of feminist scholarship in the 1980s, the idea of 'women as subjects' was far from the chief area of concern. This is best uncovered through the words of the editors of *Recasting Women*, one of the major contributions to the field:

> This anthology has grown out of our need as academics and activists to understand the historical processes, which reconstitute patriarchy in colonial India. We wish to focus primarily on the regulation and reproduction of patriarchy in the different class caste formations within civil society.[16]

Clearly, the 'reconstitution and reproduction of patriarchy' was the determining theme of the volume. Their attempts to understand how the 'reconstitution of patriarchy' has affected present day Indian women's problems has, predictably, resulted in the neglect of recovery of women's voices during the colonial period.

Indeed, the 'creation and re-creation of patriarchy' as a major theme dominates the historiography of gender and women's studies in India. Tracing the historical developments by which patriarchy emerged as the overriding form of societal order and the ways in which it institutionalized the rights of men to control and appropriate the economic, sexual and reproductive services of women has been a major preoccupation of scholarship in this area.[17] The consequences of this, namely, the failure to engage in recovering 'Women's History' (borrowing a term from Gerda Lerner[18]), is one of which the scholars themselves have been aware. The editor of another enormously influential volume, *Women in Colonial India: Essays on Survival, Work and the State*, based on a collection of essays published over the years on gender history in the *Indian Economic and Social History Review*, has commented, 'If the papers have a common weakness—and in this they reflect the existing database—it is that we hear the voices of women at large only rarely...'[19] Many of the original contributors of this volume have now published monographs on various aspects of the subjection of Indian women.[20]

Moreover, I would further argue that the dominance of the 'constitution and reconstitution of patriarchy' paradigm in Indian gender history has created and helped to spread certain myths about women's participation in modern movements in India. For instance, Sangari and Vaid have argued that during the

---

[16] Sangari and Vaid, 'Introduction', *Recasting Women*, p. 1.

[17] Another series of 16 articles emphasizing the regulatory and repressive nature of the colonial state over female sexuality have been recently published; see Patricia Uberoi (ed.), 'Special Issue: Social Reform, Sexuality and the State' *Contributions to Indian Sociology*, 29/1, 2 (1995).

[18] Gerda Lerner, *The Creation of Feminist Consciousness: From the Middle Ages to Eighteen-Seventy*, vol. II (New York: Oxford University Press, 1993) especially 'Introduction'.

[19] J. Krishnamurthy, 'Introduction', *Women in Colonial India: Essays on Survival, Work and the State* (New Delhi: Oxford University Press, 1989), p. ix.

[20] The significance of this volume as well as contributors' works is detailed in the 'Bibliographic Essay' of Forbes, *Women in Modern India*, pp. 255–81.

colonial period, women internalized 'the offered models' of private/public sphere ideologies, with 'varying degrees of conformity'.[21] Their suggestion here is that not only were 'models' 'offered' but also Indian women tended to submit or conform to them. Yet, if one examines Indian women's contributions to the making of modern India in terms of their perspectives and participation in the religious and social reform movement, such a picture is shown to be highly misleading. In fact, if anything, Indian women were not only actively attempting to enter and legitimize their presence within the public sphere, but, more importantly, they were blurring the divide between the two. In Maharashtra, for instance, women ingeniously adapted and modernized many of the institutions of the private sphere, in order to meet the requirements of the colonial world; indeed, if we examine the *halad kunku* ceremonies [women's rituals] or *kirtans* [religious discourses] of Maharashtrian women it becomes apparent that the private and the public are one and the same.[22] A second example that I cite from is the work of a well-known feminist historian of the nationalist period who has argued that

> ... women of the intelligentsia played a mediating role, first publicly demonstrating their acquiescence with the changes promulgated by male social reformers, then disseminating the reform ideals within the female world.[23]

Although this conclusion currently has wide acceptance, it is one based mainly on the study of the twentieth-century Indian women's movement which has grave implications that are similar to Vaid and Sangari's suppositions, for the agency of Indian women. The women's movement of the nineteenth century studied in its own terms shows that not only women were *recasting themselves* rather than *being recast* [24] but also that women were engaged in contesting patriarchal discourses on womanhood and were creating roles for themselves that often differed from male perceptions and aspirations for them. The lack of detailed micro-studies; the application of the 'passivity model' to Indian women derived largely from the Bengal-centric studies;[25] the tendency to treat the nineteenth century as no more than a backdrop to twentieth-century developments combined with the stranglehold of deconstructing patriarchal discourses has resulted in the nonretrieval of Indian women's agency within this period.

Whilst the quest for an understanding of how patriarchy works in the subordination of women is an indispensable project, it is an essentially incomplete one. It obscures the

---

[21] See their 'Introduction', *Recasting Women*, pp. 10–15.

[22] See the development of the assimilation and accommodation strategy of Hindu feminists in chapter 3.

[23] Gail Pearson, 'The Female Intelligentsia in Segregated Society–Bombay, A Case Study', in M. Allen and S.N. Mukherjee (eds), *Women in India and Nepal* (Canberra: Australian National University Press, 1982), pp. 136–54.

[24] The title of Sangari and Vaid's volume is suggestive of the patriarchal mould that women were 'being recast' into by their men folk.

[25] For an elucidation of this issue see 'Arrangement of the Book' later in this chapter.

ways in which women resist patriarchy, construct their identities, assert their rights and contest the hierarchical arrangement of societal relationships between the sexes. Women's agency is subsumed and sidelined in favour of the theme of the 'constitution and reconstitution of patriarchy'. No amount of dismantling of patriarchal discourses is going to reveal what Indian women thought about and made of developments in the social reform era or the nationalist period. Equally, if we do not retrieve women's discourses we will, as Geraldine Forbes says, probably never answer the question, 'why [do] women participate in patriarchal systems?'[26]

The rise of poststructuralism in the past decade has also thrown up different kinds of difficulties with regard to the question of agency.[27] The linguistic turn in Indian cultural history has resulted in scholarship with an understanding of colonial power-relations in which unlimited domination is ascribed to ruling forms of power-knowledge. The application of these discursive tools forecloses any meaningful investigation into resistance or autonomy by Indian men or women.[28] Not only is colonial domination deprived of all complexities and variations, more crucially for the study of 'Women's History', Indian women are stripped of agency.[29] A leading thinker in this field, Gayatri Spivak, has firmly stated that 'the subaltern woman cannot speak'.[30] According to this thesis, imperialism was an essentially destructive project that entailed a violent rupture from the Indian past, with the result that the Indian woman was unable to answer back and therefore remains a historically muted subject.

---

[26] Geraldine Forbes (ed.), *Shudha Mazumdar: Memoirs of an Indian Woman* (New York: Sharpe, 1989), p. xvii.

[27] The questioning has already begun in many of the major disciplines involved especially sociology and history and, to some extent, literary studies as well. Representative examples are J. Appleby et al., *Telling the Truth about History* (New York: Norton, 1994); Anthony Giddens, 'Structuralism, Post-Structuralism and the Production of Culture', in his monograph, *Social Theory and Modern Sociology* (Cambridge: Cambridge University Press, 1987), pp. 73–108. In the context of South Asia/Subaltern Studies see Rosalind O'Hanlon and David Washbrook, 'Histories in Transition: Approaches to the Study of Colonialism and Culture', *History Workshop*, 32 (1991): 110–27 amongst others.

[28] The growing doubts in academia regarding the uses of discourse analysis are currently covered in major journals. Some classic statements are Benita Parry, 'Problems in Current Theories of Colonial Discourse', *Oxford Literary Review*, 9 (1987): 27–59, Nancy Fraser, 'The Uses and Abuses of French Discourse Theories for Feminist Politics', *Boundary 2*, 17/2 (1990): 82–101.

[29] Whilst scholarship in feminist circles in the West has discussed the problems pertaining to using discursive tools, Indian feminist scholarship has yet to deconstruct the halo surrounding it. For the debates in the Western academy see Joan Scott versus Brian Palmer, Christine Sansell and Ansonia Rabinbach, *International Labour and Working-Class History*, 31 (1987): 1–29; Joan Scott versus Linda Gordon, *Signs*, 15 (1990); and Laura Lee Downs versus Joan Scott, *Comparative Studies in Society and History*, 35/3 (April 1993): 414–58.

[30] Gayatri Chakravorty Spivak, 'Can the Subaltern Speak?' in Cary Nelson and Lawrence Grossberg (eds), *Marxism and the Interpretation of Culture* (Hampshire: Macmillan, 1988), pp. 271–313.

Moreover, discourse analysis, which has provided those scholars anxious to dismantle the dominant ideologies of colonialism, nationalism and imperialism with an attractive tool, has resulted in the obliteration of women's voices. If Indian women are studied in scholarship as mere 'representations' or 'sites' for the play of dominant discourses, they are in danger of being completely erased from history. It is certainly ironic that an approach that has done so much to criticize Orientalist essentialism has also reinforced the stereotype of the passive Indian woman.

Even those studies that appear to adopt a less deductive approach to the study of imperialism and nationalism succumb to the poststructuralist notion that power and discourse is possessed entirely by the colonizer. We therefore have scholars arguing that women's perspectives and participation during the colonial period did not matter because they made no difference to the outcome of major legislation affecting women's lives.[31] The dismissal of native male voices as 'shadows of imperial sovereign selves' or 'distorted mimics' goes some way in explaining the disdain towards any form of recovery of women's voices by the adherents of poststructuralist approaches. In a recent article, Sumit Sarkar has perceptively exposed the limitations of the application of such frameworks in the recovery of subaltern histories. According to him, viewing the colonial state as wholly hegemonic raises various problems. He poses the following question: how are we to characterize subaltern women's movements that made use of Western ideologies and colonial law, justice and administration? If reforms such as banning *sati* and legalisation on widow remarriage are read as 'surrender to western values', then he convincingly argues, 'we are really back to the crudest and most obscurantist forms of nationalism'.[32] He goes on:

> Most surprisingly, a fair amount of recent feminist scholarship seems to be falling into this trap, and one hears about nineteenth-century efforts to educate women as being somewhat retrogressive, and even the raising of the age of consent in 1891 from ten to twelve as a Victorian curtailment of feminine sexuality.[33]

Moreover, by not studying women as agents of their own history and viewing them as capable of generating only 'derivative histories', the colonized subject is denied any 'collusion and complicity' in participating and creating the exploitative structures of Indian society and polity.[34]

---

[31] See Sumit Sarkar's critique of feminist scholarship, 'Orientalism Revisited: Saidian Frameworks in the Writing of Modern Indian History', *Oxford Literary Review*, 16 (1994): 204–24 and also Sanjam Ahluwalia's critique of Mrinalini Sinha, *Colonial Masculinity: The 'Manly Englishman' and the 'Effeminate Bengali' in the Late Nineteenth Century* (Manchester: Manchester University Press, 1998), in *History Reviews On-Line*, 4/1 (Fall 1997). <http://www.depauw.edu/~dtrinkle/hrol/curr41.html>.

[32] Sumit Sarkar, Ibid., p. 214.

[33] Ibid., p. 214.

[34] Tanika Sarkar has stressed the need to study the 'agency' of Indians in the colonial period and has examined the complicitous roles of conservative male Bengalis within the context of the Phulmani Dasi case and the attendant rise of militant nationalism. See her

This study, in contrast, places the agency of Indian women as the central focus of concern. It tracks the trajectories of Indian feminism demonstrating that Indian women's quest for civil, political and religious rights arose straight from the belly of the great religious and social reform movements of the nineteenth century. While scholars in gender and women's history have tackled the question of female agency, these have been essentially 'All-India' studies, which have generated a call for in-depth region-based studies.[35] There have also been studies of female agency where individual women resist certain kinds of oppression.[36] However, the need for a fuller study not only of isolated cases of women resisting patriarchy but groups and communities of women asserting, resisting and making sense of their lives during the colonial period is needed.[37] This book provides a necessary shift in scholarship. And, by offering the first in-depth study of Maharashtrian women, it uncovers the history of women's agency in modern India.

The Approach of This Book: Definitions and Concepts

The present study aims to analyze the complexities of an emerging feminism in Maharashtra in the context of the social reform movements of the last half of nineteenth- and early twentieth-century colonial India. The study points conclusively to Maharashtrian women as agents in determining, to a great extent, the course of their lives through the analysis of the key concepts of women's

---

article, 'Rhetoric against Age of Consent: Resisting Colonial Reason and Death of a Child-Wife', *Economic and Political Weekly* (4 September 1993): 1869. She has now extended the study to include women's agency in a religious framework through the first modern autobiography of an Indian woman. See Tanika Sarkar, *Words to Win: Amar Jiban* (New Delhi: Permanent Black, 2003).

[35] Radha Kumar, *A History of Doing* (New Delhi: Kali, 1993); and Forbes, *Women in Modern India*.

[36] As early as 1990, Veena Talwar Oldenburg made a bold case for the courtesans of colonial Lucknow, arguing that their very lifestyles represented both autonomy from and resistance to Indian patriarchy, 'Lifestyle as Resistance: The Case of the Courtesans of Lucknow, India', *Feminist Studies*, 16/2 (1990): 259–87. Rosalind O'Hanlon has outlined a critique of gender relations through an analysis of Tarabai Shinde's treatise. See O'Hanlon 'Issues of Widowhood: Gender and Resistance in Colonial Western India', in Douglas Haynes and Gyan Prakash (eds), *Contesting Power: Resistance and Everyday Social Relations in South Asia* (New Delhi: Oxford University Press, 1991), pp. 62–108.

[37] Two engaging studies emphasizing the theme of women's subjectivity and how structure and agency dovetail have recently been released. See Nita Kumar (ed.), *Women as Subjects: South Asian Histories* (New Delhi: Stree, 1994); and Bharati Ray (ed.), *From the Seams of History: Essays on Indian Women* (New Delhi: Oxford India, 1995). The former emphasizes anthropological studies of North India and the latter concentrates mainly on Bengal but neither have extensive case studies from southern/western India.

identity and autonomy, women's assertion and resistance, and women's power and protest within the wider context of colonial political and social relations.

The approach of the book is informed by a conception of female agency that centres on uncovering the intentions and experiences of Indian women as they asserted their rights, addressed social inequalities and rejected or adapted tradition in an engagement with the world around them in what amounted to Indian feminism. In doing so it moves beyond the rather limited configurations of agency based on issues of 'consent', or 'coercion'[38], 'transgression' or 'subversion' or which reduce autonomy to mere resistance [39] essentially reactive to the interventions of the colonial state or Indian men. This broader conception of women's agency allows for a more composite and dynamic concept that goes beyond 'celebratory', 'compensatory' or 'her-story' histories.[40] By considering women's interaction with the colonial state and indigenous men it is hoped that this study will demonstrate that female agency originates where other forms of agency are present, coexisting and competing with them.[41] It is an approach in keeping with Joan Scott's attempt to see gender as relational, signifying the power relationship between the sexes.[42] For gender to be a useful 'analytic concept', she argues, it must include a notion of politics and hence all social institutions and organizations.[43] Keeping in mind her formulation of 'gender', this work has attempted to construct and interpret the complex shape of women's subjectivities in the areas of religion; education; marriage and crime; and their entry into the public domain via feminist organizations.

The terms 'feminist' and 'feminism' have evoked and continue to evoke strong responses in a variety of settings and incorporate imagery which vary dramatically from the aggressive 'man-haters' to more benign and sober assessments which include individuals and movements that support the goal of women's emancipation. Stereotypes therefore abound and the term has no self-explanatory quality. A major debate has emerged over the question of applying the term 'feminism' in different

---

[38] The historiography on the subject of *sati* [widow burning] provides a good example of the process by which female agency has been reduced to simplistic conceptions of volition. For a trenchant critique on the literature, see Ania Loomba, 'Dead Women Tell No Tales: Issues of Female Subjectivity, Subaltern Agency and Tradition in Colonial and Post-Colonial Writings on Widow-Immolation in India', *History Workshop Journal*, 36 (1993): 209–27.

[39] For a conception of agency as resistance see the introductory statement by Douglas Haynes and Gyan Prakash (eds), *Contesting Power*.

[40] 'Celebratory histories' are defined as triumphalist accounts of women's successes; 'compensatory histories' are those which 'add' women in a mechanical fashion to male histories and 'her-story histories' simply record the presence of women in history.

[41] An insightful account of how and why feminist scholarship should avoid reductive conceptions of female agency is in Janaki Nair, 'On the Question of Agency in Indian Feminist Historiography', *Gender and History*, 6/1 (1994): 82–100.

[42] Joan Scott, 'Gender: A Useful Category of Historical Analysis', *Gender and the Politics of History* (New York: Columbia University Press, 1988), pp. 28–52.

[43] Ibid., p. 43.

chronological periods and contexts in Western traditions.[44] An often-asked question even among historians writing about women in the early modern period of European history ponders: 'Can one write the history of feminism that precedes the invention of these words?'[45] The answer has inevitably been in the affirmative, with the stipulation that we need to ground our response in careful definitions based on historical evidence. Feminism's fortunes in the Western societies have varied a great deal over historical time but they have been carefully delineated and subjected to reassessment quite often over the past century or so. There is a growing consensus amongst historians in the West that, if one takes into account the different historical epochs, geographic locations and factors affecting women's lives, there are a multitude of 'feminisms' rather than one single 'feminism'.[46]

Recently, the necessity of finding a concept that encompasses women's experiences in non-Western contexts has led contemporary women's movements in Asia and Africa as well as the diasporas in Western countries to redefine the term.[47] For the Indian subcontinent, the term is used loosely with no rigorous attempt to extend it to cover the earlier stages of women's resistance to patriarchal ideas. Many varieties of Indian feminisms in the twentieth century have been studied and these studies now form an impressive and rapidly developing critical body of thought in its own right. They range from the feminist nationalists[48] of the national movement to Gandhian

---

[44] For an exhaustive analysis of the controversy amongst the Western tradition see Karen Offen, 'Defining Feminism: A Comparative Historical Approach', *Signs*, 14/1 (1988): 119–57. For an extension and application of the term to European women of the medieval and early modern periods, see Joan Kelly, 'Early Feminist Theory and the *Querelle des Femmes*' in *Women, History and Theory* (Chicago: Chicago University Press, 1984), pp. 65–109; and Moira Ferguson (ed.), *First Feminists: British Women Writers, 1578–1799* (New York: Feminist Press, 1985). Middle-class British women's feminism in the Age of Empire has been termed 'Imperial feminism' by the British diaspora; see Prathiba Parmar and Valerie Amos, 'Challenging Imperial Feminism', *Feminist Review*, 17 (1984): 3–19.

[45] Karen Offen, *European Feminisms, 1700–1950: A Political History* (Stanford: Stanford University Press, 2000), p. 20.

[46] For a discussion of the plural and diverse feminisms see Barbara Caine, *English Feminism, 1780–1980* (Oxford: Oxford University Press, 1997).

[47] The term 'feminism' has now been broadened and applied in various countries and contexts: for Africa see Filomina Chioma Steady (ed.), 'Introduction' *The Black Woman Cross Culturally* (Cambridge: Cambridge University Press, 1981); for Egypt see Margot Badran, 'Dual Liberation: Feminism and Nationalism in Egypt, 1870s–1925', *Feminist Issues* (Spring 1988): 15–34; for Japan see Sharon Sievers, *Flowers in Salt: The Beginnings of Feminist Consciousness in Modern Japan* (Stanford: Stanford University Press, 1983); for African-American women see Bell Hooks, *Feminist Theory from Margin to Center* (Boston: South End Press, 1984).

[48] A classic formulation is in Kumari Jayawardena, *Feminism and Nationalism in the Third World* (London: Zed, 1986). In the 1980s Gail Minault, Geraldine Forbes, Vijay Agnew, Neera Desai amongst others also studied the connections between feminism and nationalism.

feminism[49], eco-feminism[50] and the emergence of the unsavoury 'new woman' viewed through the rise of the saffron sari syndrome of the Hindu Right.[51] Curiously, and despite this phenomenal rise in feminist movements of various hues and shades in the twentieth century, not much attention has been paid to the origins of Indian feminism. This state of affairs exists despite the growing consensus in the field of Indian gender and women's history that feminist thought in India has developed over a much longer period than this modern picture indicates. Equally, the beginnings of the saffron-sari clad 'new woman' can be traced to the cow protection movements of the nineteenth century.[52] In some ways, the legacy of the early twentieth-century women's movement has coloured and confused the perceptions of scholars in the field; indeed, it has forced historians of women to adopt various defensive positions.[53] From the 1920s onwards Indian women active in the nationalist movement vehemently opposed the use of the term 'feminist' as understood in Europe and America on the grounds that it propounded and projected an anti-male ideology.[54] This helps explain the hesitancy and ambivalence of scholars working in the field of feminist/women's studies in pursuing the subject. The often quoted example of Madhu Kishwar, contemporary India's pioneering women's activist, is a brilliant illustration of this caution who has rejected the term 'feminist' both for herself and her ground-breaking journal called *Manushi* on the grounds that it has an 'overclose association with the Western women's movement.'[55] Contemporary feminist scholarship emanating from the so-called Third World has been burdened by 'sanctioned ignorances'—skewed knowledges that have percolated down from the early twentieth century about what

---

[49] Devaki Jain, 'Gandhian Contributions Toward a Feminist Ethic', in Diane Eck and Devaki Jain (eds), *Cross-Cultural Perspectives on Women, Religion and Social Change* (Delhi: Kali, 1986), pp. 255–70.

[50] Maria Mies and Vandana Shiva, *Ecofeminism* (London: Zed, 1993).

[51] Tanika Sarkar, 'The Woman as Communal Subject: Rashtrasevika Samiti and Ram Janmabhoomi Movement', *Economic and Political Weekly* (31 August 1991): 2057–62.

[52] Padma Anagol, Lakshmibai Dravid: The Political Economy of Nationalism and the Birth of the Hindu Right, (forthcoming).

[53] Veena Oldenburg, for example, defends the use of the term 'feminist' by saying that social scientists and historians use other theoretical models from the West such as Marxism and post-structuralism, and hence one ought to be able to use the useful phrase 'feminism'. See Veena Oldenburg, 'The Roop Kanwar Case: Feminist Responses', in John S. Hawley (ed.), *Sati: The Blessing and the Curse* (New York: Oxford University Press, 1994), pp. 102–3.

[54] The stance taken by influential female leaders such as Kamaladevi Chattopadhayaya on the label of 'feminism' has been commented on and negotiated with from the 1970s onwards. See Jayawardena, *Feminism and Nationalism in Asia*; see also Geraldine Forbes, 'The Indian Women's Movement: A Struggle for Women's Rights or National Liberation?' and Barbara Ramusack, 'Catalysts or Helpers? British Feminists, Indian Women's Rights and Indian Independence', in Gail Minault (ed.), *The Extended Family: Women and Political Participation in India and Pakistan* (Delhi: Chanakya, 1981).

[55] See her statement in 'Why I am not a Feminist', *Manushi: A Journal of Women and Society*, 61 (Nov/Dec. 1990): 3.

constitutes 'Western feminism'. Mary John argues persuasively that not being like Western feminists and equating the militant suffragette to a male-hater and not wanting to be like the 'memsahib' is simply reverting the orientalist gaze and freezing Western women into cardboard stereotypes of sensuality.[56] Hence, it is all the more crucial that we study women's ideology and work in the early nationalist era prior to the Gandhian-led movements. In order to understand the connections between past and present forms of feminism, an important task has to be an assessment of the earlier feminist traditions, especially its origins and significance, which includes the reclamation of the terms 'feminist' and 'feminism' and a delineation of the conundrum of the 'anti feminist'.

One of the aims of this book is to uncover these early developments by tracing the development of feminist consciousness before the rise of Gandhi and mass nationalism. Tracking feminist resistance and assertion in the nineteenth century through word and deed, and identifying its crucial connections to the mutations that take place in the early twentieth century which witnessed and facilitated the rise of feminist nationalists, forms the core of this work. In order to fully comprehend the historical range and possibilities of feminism, however, the origins and growth of its gendered critique must be located within the region's cultural and ideological traditions. Equally Indian women's subjectivities were forged within the context of colonialism; and they had a choice now, of selecting from a wide array of discourses on tradition and modernity. The rise of feminism in India was made possible through a combination of factors: the presence of a colonial economy, the new web of modernizing impulses which interacted with the contending circumstances and criteria of sex, race, status and class, caste and religion.

This study suggests three important criteria for identifying a feminist. First, it includes women and men who have exhibited consciousness of injustice towards women as a group either by men and/or other women, religion, or by customs. Secondly, it includes those who have articulated their dissent through word and/or deed either individually or collectively and finally, it is presumed that such women and men engage themselves in confrontational and nonconfrontational strategies either individually or collectively to improve the disadvantaged status of the female sex. This study also emphasizes individual consciousness because feminist consciousness has developed in stages that have no clear continuities and which often take the form of isolated insights. Although these insights, such as Tarabai Shinde's, were worked out in isolation, they had origins in a common set of social and political problems that faced women at that time. I define 'Indian feminism', then, as a theory and practice based on presenting a challenge to the subordination of women in society and attempting to redress the balance of power between the sexes.[57] By the same logic, the

---

[56] *Discrepant Dislocations: Feminism, Theory and Postcolonial Histories* (Berkeley: University of California Press, 1996), endnote 12, p. 127.

[57] I have used the term 'subordination' instead of 'oppression' here in keeping with Offen's clear-cut separation of the two: the former, she argues, is 'verifiable' and can be located historically by examining laws, institutions, practices and customs of any society

act of empowering oneself by treading on or harming the interests of other women is my definition of an anti-feminist.[58]

The terms 'subjectivity', 'agency', 'experience' and 'identity' are hotly debated in feminist theory today. Moreover, the scholarship acknowledges that many of these concepts overlap to a degree. I agree with Chris Weedon that personal 'experience' is a crucial component of 'subjectivity' and hence would extend her definition that 'a woman's self' is 'formed by her observation of and practical engagement with the world,'[59] to the shaping of the nineteenth-century Indian woman's subjectivity. 'Agency' is construed here as conscious goal-driven activities by women that embrace the possibility of *'change'.*[60] Further, I will argue in this book that 'assertion' and 'resistance' are twin aspects of women's agency. Women's will or volition to act in conscious forms to resist, stretch, or overturn structures of power is broadly defined as 'resistance'. 'Assertion' is defined as a form of resistance in which women use legitimized instruments of agitation that have the blessings of the state.[61]

Maharashtrian women resorted to a rich vocabulary in the Marathi language to express ideas that are now considered as feminist terms and enrich the Indian feminist lexicon with concepts and terms such as the following demonstrate: *bhaginivarg* [sisterhood]; *strihak* [women's rights]; *strivarg* [womankind or womanhood]; *strianubhav* [women's experience]; *bandhivasan* [bondage]; *dasyatva* [slavery]; *mokaleek* [independence or freedom]; *stri jati* [female sex]; *purush jati* [male sex]; *purusharth* [manliness and masculinity].[62] These phrases occur regularly in the

---

whilst the latter is a 'highly subjective and psychological response'. See Karen Offen, *European Feminisms*, p. 22.

[58] See chapter 4 for details.

[59] Chris Weedon, 'Subjects', in Mary Eagleton (ed.), *A Concise Companion to Feminist Theory* (Oxford: Blackwell, 2003), p. 112.

[60] This follows the phenomenological feminist perspective encapsulated in Sandra Bartky's work. Phenomenology focuses on the centrality of human subjectivity arguing from the position that our 'reason' and 'theories' emanate from lived human experience. Bartky takes this further through a marriage of feminist philosophy with phenomenology. She argues that there are distinctive ways of perceiving feminist consciousness. When a woman begins to perceive the various oppressions that she and or /other women face this awareness may lead to anger or despair. Even such an awareness, she argues, is an advance over 'false consciousness' because it marks the beginning of an understanding of the origins of women's subordination and 'even beginning to understand this, makes it possible for *change.*' See her classic essay 'Towards a Phenomenology of Feminist Consciousness', in Nancy Tuana and Rosemarie Tong (eds), *Feminism and Philosophy: Essential Readings in Theory, Re-interpretation and Application* (Boulder: Westview Press, 1995), pp. 396–406.

[61] See chapters 3 and 4 for more details.

[62] Almost all the chapters in this book describe how women use these terms within particular historical contexts; wherever possible it is also demonstrated how they differ from men's use of the same terms.

colloquial and formal texts written by Maharashtrian women and the most significant of the magazines within the broader women's press of the time, *Arya Bhagini*, literally uses the concept of 'Bhagini' [Sister] in its title—a telling sign of the times. *Swadeshbhagini* [Indian Sister] is yet another women's periodical which had a long run at the turn of the century. The vernacular use of the terms is retained as far as possible in the book so that readers may appreciate the varied richness of the early feminist thought in colonial Maharashtra.

Arrangement of the Book and Sources

The core argument put forward in this book is that Indian feminism grew out of the women's movements of the late nineteenth century, reaching maturity in the early twentieth century. The pioneering studies of women in India centred on Bengal generated the 'passivity of women' model which in turn led to a generalized representation of the subjugated and repressed Indian woman. It is beyond the scope of the present volume to comment with any kind of authority on the position of women in Bengal. Nevertheless, it is possible that historians of Indian women have been looking in the wrong places. It has been argued that the Indian woman has been silenced by the colonial archive.[63] Pursued in the courts for absconding from brutal or unacceptable husbands, pursued by the courts for killing their spouses, however, using the same legal structures to redress their grievances and assert their rights, rebellious Indian women have left their indelible stamp on the colonial archive. When we combine these sources with the institutional records of women's organizations set up to improve the lives of widows and child brides and when we delve deeper to examine vernacular plays, press and literature, a considerable body of evidence can be amassed to present a case for the emergence of feminism in India. The choice of a different location such as Maharashtra[64] has also been dictated by the comparative lack of a gender history of the region.[65] Turning the lens away from Bengal also helps to demonstrate the heterogeneity of Indian women's experiences especially in attending to the assumption of concepts of *purdah* [forms of seclusion] and practices such as *sati*[widow burning] as being uniformly common to the whole of India.

---

[63] Gayatri Chakravorty Spivak, 'The Rani Of Sirmur: An Essay in Reading the Archives', *History and Theory*, 24 (1985): 247–72.

[64] 'Maharashtra' refers to the Marathi-speaking area of western India that was subsumed in the larger Bombay Presidency, an administrative area of colonial India. The area in question is broadly consonant with the contemporary state of Maharashtra that was created after the linguistic reorganization of states in the Republic of India in 1960.

[65] In 1998, we see for the first time the appearance of a monograph on the gender history of Maharashtra; however, even this book focuses mainly on the life and work of Pandita Ramabai, an influential feminist of the time, and its main concern is the 'reconstitution of patriarchies'. See Uma Chakravarti, *Rewriting History: The Life and Times of Pandita Ramabai* (New Delhi: Kali, 1998).

Chapter 2, 'Discriminating Converts: Christian Women's Discourse and Work', examines the motivations of Indian women in processes of conversion, demonstrating how they approached religion through a woman-centred critique of Hinduism and Christianity. The questions of women's salvation, of personal morality, imbalance of power between the sexes expressed in religious structures and the role of religion as a 'social doctrine' are elucidated by converts as crucial markers for their rejection of Hinduism and their critiques of sectarian Christianity. Further, Indian Christian women's entry into the public arena is analyzed, showing how their adoption of nondenominational Christian work maintained their autonomy, giving them, at the same time, unfettered access to resources not normally available to Hindu women. Chapter 3, 'Beyond Kitchen and Kid: Hindu Women's Discourse and Work', focuses on the creation of the radical and central concept of *bhaginivarg* [sisterhood] amongst Hindu women through the creation of a women's press, separate female institutions, women's networks and subcultures. Their close scrutiny of Hindu customs, especially those which affected the life-chances of young girls, widows and their access to education and professional identities also form a central focus of this chapter.

How women attended to their material security in individual and collective ways is the subject matter of chapter 4, 'Women's Assertion and Resistance in Colonial India'. Informed by definitions of 'resistance' and 'assertion', and drawing a distinction between constitutional and nonconstitutional forms of resistance invoked by women, the chapter shows how women accessed knowledge of state procedures such as 'petitioning' and law courts in claiming their rights to property, livelihood, to remarriage, to mobility and custody of children. The process through which some feminists transformed 'symbolic' to 'open' resistance is also studied through an analysis of women's literature in the form of folksongs and plays. Equal attention is paid to all classes of women asserting and claiming their rights, from the aristocratic *sardar* ladies to the *kalavantin* [female artiste] increasingly redefined as a 'prostitute' in this period due to the operation of the Contagious Diseases Act and the emergence of the ambitious middle class anti-feminists of the late nineteenth century. 'Crime' provides a window onto women's lives in nineteenth-century India and hence forms the topic for study in chapter 5, 'Women, Crime and Survival Strategies in Colonial India'. A gendered examination of crime reveals dual aspects—whilst the state and indigenous men intervened to criminalize the body of the Indian woman through the redefinition of 'criminal castes and tribes' and infanticidal women, Indian feminists themselves were provoked into writing some of the most biting critiques of Indian society and the state as a result of these interventions and listening to the perspectives of the redefined Indian criminal women. Rather than suppressing the agency of Indian women, it is argued here that the repressive acts of Indian men and the state gave fillip to the emerging women's movement. An instance of the maturity of the feminist movement in late nineteenth-century India is provided by women's public participation in the Age of Consent debates of the late 1880s and early 1890s, explored in chapter 6, 'Women as Agents: Contesting Discourses on

Marriage and Marital Rights'. Women's attempts to remain agents of their lives through recourse to the law courts for restitution of conjugal rights, divorce, separation and maintenance and remarriage form the main focus of study in this chapter. Legislation in social matters did not arise from the interventionist ambitions of the colonial state. A veritable rebellion of Indian wives prompted Indian male reformers such as Ranade and Malabari to seek legislation. The reaction of Indian male elites represented a backlash to the vigorous attempts made by Indian women in asserting their rights through the courts in an attempt to shore up patriarchy and meet the threat posed to their masculinity by the actions of their womenfolk.

Since this book makes a claim for seeing the rise of Indian feminism in the nineteenth century as opposed to the current view that it begins with the Gandhian-led nationalist movement I have had to harness new and more imaginative means of recovering Indian women's voice-consciousness. Women's self-authorization programmes and the construction of identities in non-Western contexts can be traced in Indian language collections. For the perceptions of women, I have concentrated on Marathi sources as many women spoke and engaged in dialogues with each other in their mother tongue and conducted their public work in local languages. Thus, I have used wide-ranging materials as diverse as book reviews written by women to the maps created by the earliest attempts of Indian women cartographers as evidence of their agency. The range of empirical material harnessed here includes autobiographies, biographies, periodicals meant for 'women only', women's petitions and memorials to the government, folk writings in the form of collections of women's songbooks, cookbooks, embroidery and sewing manuals written by women, literature (novels, short stories, plays and tracts) and treatises on philosophical, religious or social questions. Women's journals edited by women and indisputably meant for women readers have been used to gauge the opinions of ordinary women. Letters by women to the editors of women's magazines or for important national and regional newspapers have also proved useful as an index of their awareness and dissent. Advertisements of new books and book reviews of women writers by their peers have yielded valuable biographical material that would not have been made available otherwise. Organizational papers have been a rich mine of information for the work done by feminists of the time, and some of these early women's institutions are indeed an enduring legacy of the nineteenth century which continue today.

No work emerges in a vacuum. This study owes an intellectual debt to many. As indicated earlier, my own interest and curiosity in the subject was triggered by family members, among whom knowledge about influential feminists such as Pandita Ramabai and Ramabai Ranade was commonplace. Whilst working on my doctoral thesis, I encountered Gail Pearson's extremely detailed account of Bombay feminists' work during the civil disobedience movement which convinced me that the fiery feminist nationalists she was describing must have inherited or at least benefited from a much earlier tradition of dissent in Maharashtra, and it doubled my enthusiasm to pursue the project. Methodologically, I have tried to surmount the paralyzing effects of deductive approaches drawn solely from the social sciences or poststructuralism by adopting a more inductive historical enquiry. In constructing this historical narrative I have utilized diverse conceptual tools that possessed the potential to explain phenomena and uncover processes. I have freely borrowed and adapted concepts from feminist theory especially from scholars working on American, European, Southeast Asian and African feminisms. I have found the anthropological insights of James Scott, Michael Adas and Lila Abu-Lughod in understanding resistance extremely helpful. Tapping the rich mineshafts of Medieval and especially Early Modern European gender and women's history has proved to be very rewarding especially in interpreting women's 'thought' and 'action' and understanding the nature of women's networks and subcultures. The discerning reader will probably see the imprint of the footsteps of Joan Kelly, Gerda Lerner, Nancy Cott, Karen Offen, Sharon Sievers, Diana Fuss, Susan Stanford Friedman, Julia Kristeva, Maureen Quilligan, Caroline Bynum Walker and Joan Scott on every page of this book.

Finally, it is hoped that this study, which focuses on woman-centred issues but treats them as agents affecting socioeconomic and political processes within the society as a whole, will persuade other scholars to see in this work a case for the more integrated approach to the writing of gender and women's history of India. This would mean that not only is gender history placed in the right perspective, but it will also illumine all aspects of social reality, which involve women and men.

Chapter 2

Discriminating Converts:
Christian Women's Discourse and Work

Introduction

In recent decades, social and cultural historians have identified the nineteenth century as an era of momentous socioreligious reform in India. The reformers tended to belong to different religions, most notably Christian, Hindu, Muslim, Sikh and Zoroastrian movements, who used various forms of religious authority to legitimize their programmes for religious and social change. Whether indigenous in origin or Western influenced, all attempted to address a key issue—namely, the position of women. Standard social histories have traditionally treated the subject as an interaction between missionaries, indigenous men and modernizing forces under colonialism.[1] What compelled socioreligious movements to address the issue of women's status and why the image of Indian womanhood was recast during the nineteenth century by Indian male reformers and conservatives has now received attention from feminist scholars.[2] However, despite the increased focus on the status and image of women in these studies, scant attention has been paid to the central subject of the social reform movements, the women themselves.[3] Issues, such as the motivations of Indian women in participating in the socioreligious reform movements and movements of religious conversion, their views on the male reformist and conservative discourses and their acceptance or rejection of representations of Indian womanhood, are all areas that have not yet received the attention from scholars in the

---

[1] The most representative works are Charles Heimsath, *Indian Nationalism and Hindu Social Reform* (Princeton: Princeton University Press, 1964), and Kenneth Jones, *Socio-Religious Reform Movements in British India* (Cambridge: Cambridge University Press, 1989).

[2] The literature is growing enormously in this field. See, for example, Kumkum Sangari and Sudesh Vaid (eds), *Recasting Women* (New Delhi: Kali, 1989).

[3] Individual women whose immense popularity during the social reform movement brought them to the attention of the British and Indian public have now formed the subject of contemporary studies. Representative of these are Meera Kosambi (ed.), *Pandita Ramabai in Her Own Words* (New York: Feminist Press, 2000); Uma Chakravarti, *Rewriting History: Pandita Ramabai, Her Life and Times* (New Delhi: Oxford University Press, 1998) and Antoinette Burton, *At The Heart of Empire: Indians and the Colonial Encounter in Late-Victorian Britain* (Berkeley: University of California Press, 1998).

field that their significance merits. By examining the way in which women participated in these programmes of socioreligious reform, this book aims to redress this balance by placing women at the centre of their own narrative.

The early feminist movement in western India was intrinsically linked to a gendered approach to issues of faith and belief systems. It seems to be a universal phenomenon that the definition and discourse on the 'nature' of 'woman' originated in commentaries on religious texts, which authorize patriarchal customs. The assumed 'inferiority' of women in the Western tradition, for instance, stemmed from the oldest Biblical stories of the creation of Adam and Eve and the Fall of Man. Contesting negative representations of womanhood has therefore been a preoccupation of Western women, generating a thousand years of feminist Bible criticism.[4] The significance to Western women of their relationship to religion is not unique and particular to them alone, but similar patterns are observable in all parts of the world; for instance, the Bhakti movements in medieval India demonstrate religious revisionism by women.[5] Religion has therefore been the principal arena in which women have fashioned their weapons of opposition, providing them with their chief passage to feminist consciousness.

This chapter not only analyzes the participation of Indian Christian women in the era of social and religious reform movements but also aims to develop a better understanding of the motivations of a certain section of Indian women who became Christians by looking at why Christian doctrines and 'mission Christianity' were so attractive to them.[6] In tracing the growth of feminist consciousness, it will be shown that their feminist critiques came through a process of questioning the 'position of women' in the dominant religion of their birth and time, Hinduism, before rejecting it in favour of Christianity. Neither were their actions, like their male counterparts, prompted by mere intellectual abstractions. Indian Christian women pioneered both nonsegregated educational schemes and the Indian philanthropic enterprise of the nineteenth century through their organizational work in the provision of homes for widows and prostitutes, as well as participating in schemes for famine and plague relief. Most of the women studied here were involved in indigenizing Christianity to suit Indian women's needs and their nondenominational Christian work, although frowned upon and attacked by missionaries, gained national and international recognition. These pioneers were not only significant in their own right but were of

---

[4] See Gerda Lerner, *The Creation of Patriarchy*, vol. I (New York: Oxford University Press, 1986), and *The Creation of Feminist Consciousness: From the Middle Ages to Eighteen-Seventy*, vol. II (New York: Oxford University Press, 1993).

[5] This observation holds true for women in Ancient India too. See Susie Tharu and K. Lalitha (eds), *Women Writing in India, 600 B.C. to the Present Day*, vols I and II (New York: Oxford University Press, 1987); for medieval India, see Vijaya Ramaswamy, *Walking Naked: Women, Society, Spirituality in South India* (Shimla: Indian Institute of Advanced Study, 1997).

[6] Keeping in mind that nineteenth-century Christianity in the colonies embodied certain aspects of cultural imperialism, I use the term 'Christianity' in a qualified way, that is, 'mission Christianity' or 'representations' of Christianity to Indians by missionaries.

great importance in influencing a far larger number of Maharashtrian women, who were inspired to continue the search for an identity and pursue programmes of welfare work specifically for women.[7]

As well as examining how and why Christianity proved so attractive to some Indian women, this chapter has also been prompted by the need to remove the misconceptions of some historians of Indian Christianity, in particular, the idea that converts were mainly recruits from the lowest castes of India or the presumption that female converts were merely following the lead of the menfolk of their households.[8] In fact, Indian Christian women who had formerly been Brahmins, the highest in the caste hierarchy, produced some of the finest feminist critiques of Hinduism, and far from following their men folk, women exhibited a remarkable independence of judgement, whether in resisting or choosing Christianity. Their response to missions and missionary activity are not only important in demonstrating their agency, but hold potential for assessing the degree of social change brought by American and European missions in Asian countries, a question that contemporary scholarship has recognized can only be satisfactorily answered by studying the Asian response.[9]

By treating Indian Christian women as active rather than passive agents, it is also hoped that another serious gap in Indian historiography is redressed—the exclusion of Indian Christians from mainstream histories of India. Discussing the various approaches to the study of Western religion (Christianity) and imperialism, Jeffrey Cox has argued persuasively that South-Asian Christians have become victims of the historical critiques of imperialism and colonialism,[10] demonstrating that, within historical scholarship, missionaries have been portrayed as 'imperialists', reducing Indian Christians to the status of 'collaborators' and Pakistani Christians to 'heretics'. By treating Indian Christian women as agents of their own history, it will be established that rendering Indian Christians as mere 'by-products' of mission

---

[7] At the end of 1900, Pandita Ramabai had 2,000 pupils in four of her institutions and all of them, except a handful, were converts to Christianity. She also spread her work outside Maharashtra after 1900 by opening branches in Doddaballapur and Gulbarga, now in Karnataka. In any one year in the 1890s, Soonderbai Powar's school had 200 female converts. Franscina Sorabji likewise noted with pride that over 400 students had completed their education in the Victoria High School. Shewantibai Nikambe had 120 girls in the Princess High School, all of whom were high-caste Hindu girls. For details on these pioneers, see Appendix.

[8] David Edwards, *Christian England*, vol. III (London: Collins, 1984), pp. 314–45; M.A. Sherring, *The History of Protestant Missions in India* (London: Trubner & Co., 1875).

[9] Several influential works have appeared that focus mainly on Western women's missionary work in Asia and Africa: see Leslie A. Flemming (ed.), *Women's Work for Women: Missionaries and Social Change in Asia* (Boulder: Westview, 1989); F. Bowie, S. Ardener and D. Kirkwood (eds), *Women and Missions: Past and Present* (Oxford: Berg, 1993), and, more recently, Maina C. Singh, *Gender, Religion and "Heathen Lands": American Missionary Women in South Asia* (New York and London: Garland, 2000).

[10] See Jeffrey Cox, 'Audience and Exclusion at the Margins of Imperial History', *Women's History Review*, 3/4 (1994): 501–14.

Christianity is an untenable proposition. As this chapter will demonstrate, their attitudes towards Christianity were much more complex and their rethinking of Christian rhetoric far more than simply 'derivative' phenomena.[11]

Christian Missions and Processes of Conversion

Some of the first missions to India in the 1820s applied themselves rigorously to the education of women. Their programmes rested on the belief that the 'womanhood of India' were 'the protectress[es] [sic] and zealous adherent[s] of traditional heathenism'.[12] Indian grandmothers, mothers and wives, it was held, taught the first lessons of idolatry and ritual to children and, therefore, conversions were unlikely unless the influence of women was combated. By the latter half of the nineteenth century, with the beginnings of the women's movements in Europe and America, the complexion of female missionary activity had changed; revisionist historians have demonstrated that these missionaries were no longer concerned with conveying the Christian message as an end in itself but were increasingly interested in the cause of the 'heathen' women in their own right.[13] Recently Antoinette Burton, Geraldine Forbes and Barbara Ramusack have drawn a more complex picture about the roles of missionary and nonmissionary white women's activities in the colonies. They assert that white women who went to colonies in the nineteenth century constructed and relied on the notion of 'enslaved' Indian women to serve the purposes of their own programmes of emancipation.[14] They argue convincingly that overseas opportunities not only provided space for the surplus 'genteel' population of white women but also empowered them through collaboration in the ideological work of empire.

In the 1860s, the first women's auxiliary units of various missions such as the Society for the Propagation of the Gospel and the London Missionary Society began to arrive. Between 1858 and 1871, there were eight women's auxiliary units of

---

[11] How Indian women approached issues of conversion and rejected Hindu belief systems in favour of an indigenized Christianity in their quest for gender equality was outlined in my article, 'Indian Christian Women and Indigenous Feminism', in Claire Midgley (ed.), *Gender and Imperialism* (Manchester: Manchester University Press, 1998), pp. 79–103.

[12] J. Richter, *A History of Missions in India* (Edinburgh: Oliphant and Co., 1908), p. 329.

[13] Nancy F. Cott, *The Bonds of Womanhood: 'Woman's Sphere' in New England, 1780–1835* (New Haven: Yale University Press, 1977), especially chapter 4.

[14] Amongst others, see Antoinette Burton, 'The White Woman's Burden: British Feminists and the Indian Woman, 1865–1915', *Women's Studies International Forum*, 13/4 (1990): 295–308; Geraldine Forbes, 'In Search of the "Pure Heathen": Missionary Women in Nineteenth-Century India', *Economic and Political Weekly*, 21/17 (1986), *Review of Women's Studies*: 2–9 and Barbara Ramusack, 'Cultural Missionaries, Maternal Imperialists, Feminist Allies: British Women Activists in India, 1865–1945', *Women's Studies International Forum*, 13/4 (1990): 309–21.

Anglican and American missions in India.[15] Such was the enthusiasm in female circles in Britain that the Church of England Zenana Missionary Society alone sent 214 women between 1887 and 1894. According to Leslie Flemming, the highly organized women's missionary movement in North America sent and supported two-thirds of the Presbyterian overseas mission force in the nineteenth century.[16] With the arrival of women missionaries, the old missionary enterprise of conversion acquired a new angle, namely, a concern for the 'plight of Indian womanhood'. Combating *sati* [widow burning] and infanticide, providing refuge homes for deserted wives and widows, educating women in *zenanas* [women's secluded quarters]—all these appeared prominently on missionary women's agendas in the late nineteenth century.

During the nineteenth century, missionaries regarded the Bombay Presidency, especially Maharashtra, as an ideal ground for their conversion programmes. Typical accounts appearing in missionary literature of this period portray the region's history as one characterized by being least influenced by Muslim rule, with women having greater freedom of movement and the unveiled Maharashtrian women providing fewer obstacles to the work of missionary women. By the 1890s, the missions of the American Board, the Free Church of Scotland, the Church Missionary Society and the Society for the Propagation of the Gospel were firmly established in the larger towns of Bombay, Poona, Nasik, Ahmednagar, Belgaum and Kolhapur and were slowly spreading into smaller towns and villages; together, these areas boasted a 'native Christian' population of approximately 60,000.[17] As early as the 1820s, missions from the Scottish Board and the Church Missionary Society had established roots in Bombay and were highly successful in maintaining high schools, while the American Board was firmly established at Ahmednagar. Members of indigenous elites aspiring to a professional education for their children in the 1820s and 1830s had no choice but to send their boys to Mission schools; the fact that some of the first male converts were from influential Parsi and Brahmin families in Bombay and Ahmednagar was undoubtedly due to the fact that they had been educated by missionaries. It should be noted at this point that the earliest missionaries who came to work in India were considered by converts to be liberal-minded, learned and sincere, in contrast to those of the late nineteenth century who are recalled in disparaging terms by converts.[18]

Not surprisingly, the first female converts were the wives, mothers and sisters of the first Brahmin, Muslim or Parsi converts to Christianity. It is therefore useful to analyze the conversion of the first Maharashtrian male enthusiasts in order to compare and contrast them with the female converts—this reveals a valuable gender

---

[15] Richter, A History of Missions, p. 342.

[16] In 'Introduction', *Women's Work for Women*, p. 1.

[17] Samuel Satthianadhan, *Sketches of Indian Christians Collected from Different Sources* (London: Christian Literature Society for India, 1896), pp. 188–9.

[18] Narayan Sheshadri, Dhanjibhai Nauroji, Baba Padmanji and Kharsedji Sorabji, as the first batch of converts to impact on Maharashtrian society, mention their teachers' influences with a respect bordering on reverence. Some of the well-known missionaries of the time were John Wilson, George Valentine, Robert Nesbit and Murray Mitchell.

perspective on conversions, making it clear how a woman-centred approach is applied by those women who chose to convert from Hinduism to Christianity. The Indian intelligentsia that were emerging in the early half of the nineteenth century had to negotiate an eclectic range of influences. On the one hand, there were the missionaries who, in addition to setting up schools, also preached in the busy marketplaces and engaged learned Hindus in discussion, whilst, on the other, there was the reforming zeal of influential Brahmins who criticized the contemporary state of Hindu society and the practises of a corrupt Brahmin priesthood. Secret societies, such as the Paramahamsa Mandali, flourished alongside open societies like the Dnyan Prasarak Mandali. In addition, the vernacular press was also flooded with articles that regularly exposed Hinduism. The radical vernacular press and its effects on nineteenth-century Indian youth has been recorded by Baba Padmanji, whose life story shows how he benefited from this febrile atmosphere:

> The *Dnayodaya* convinced me of the truth of Christianity and the futility of the claims of the *Shastras* (sic) [Hindu prescriptive religious texts] to divine inspiration; the *Prabhakar* destroyed my religious reverence for the Brahmans; and the *Dnyan Prakash* had preserved me from falling into the quagmire of atheism.[19]

In a manner similar to Baba Padmanji, most of the male converts arrived at an acceptance of Christianity after an intellectual struggle with the religious precepts of Hinduism and Christianity, exhibiting a formidable knowledge of the scriptures of the respective religions in the process.[20] In short, to men, conversion was an intellectual exercise, born out of a major questioning of theological issues, whether in relation to questions of 'revealed' religion or the inconsistencies of the *shastras*. Though Baba Padmanji expressed concern at the suffering of Hindu widows in his work, just as the missionary tracts did, the 'women's question' in relation to various religions was not a major point for apostasy and was not a reason for conversion among men.[21] This was despite the fact that the position of women in different religions was taken up as a

---

[19]   Baba Padmanji, *Once Hindu, Now Christian: The Early Life of Baba Padmanji, An Autobiography*, trans. J. Murray Mitchell (London: Nisbet & Co., 1890), p. 71.

[20]   Nilakantha Goreh, for example, was a Brahmin priest who had begun by refuting Christian doctrines and ended as a staunch Christian. He wrote learned treatises exposing Hindu philosophy. See Nehemiah Nilakantha Sastri Goreh, *A Rational Refutation of the Hindu Philosophical Systems*, trans. Fitz-Edward Hall (Calcutta: Christian Tract and Book Society, 1862).

[21]   After his conversion, Baba Padmanji wrote a novel titled *Yamuna Paryatan* [Yamuna's Rambles], in which he highlighted the Hindu widow's problems through the trials of the heroine, Yamuna.

bone of contention by many Hindus, as seen in the great number of tracts of the period that deal with the question of women's salvation.[22]

This brings us to the central question of why women were prompted to change religions. Were they prompted, like male converts, by intellectual abstractions? If not, then what was the difference between their conversion and that of men? By examining the process of conversion of women such as Pandita Ramabai, Krupabai and Soonderbai Powar,[23] and later the conversion experiences of women from less privileged backgrounds, the central reasons behind women's conversions, and how they differed from that of men, can be seen.

First Generation Women Converts' Critique of Hinduism

It is important to ask why women belonging to Hindu orthodoxy were attracted to Christianity since, in addition to Pandita Ramabai, a host of lesser and relatively unknown Maharashtrian women during this period chose to convert. It may be argued that, apart from Pandita Ramabai, such women were merely following the dictates of their husbands. However, this particular category of women were often, in fact, greatly opposed to the process, and often resisted for years after their husband's conversion. Even among those women who followed their husbands, a certain prioritization of aims is evident. Wives of male converts were generally given the choice of living with their parents or their extended family, meaning that they did not have to automatically make the same decision as their husbands. Yet, despite the fact that they had heard of the great persecution converts were subjected to by Hindus, many still chose to follow their husbands, with quite a few of them forced to make dramatic escapes from their enraged kith and kin. Ganderbai Powar, for example, told the court that, after she announced her decision to convert, her natal family prevented her from joining her husband for several years by imprisoning her in her own home.[24] She was, in fact, relatively fortunate; not all women were so successful in resolving conflicts over religious issues, with quite a few cases ending tragically. Lakshmibai, for instance, underwent a period of severe introspection and remained with her parental family. After seven years, however, she decided to rejoin her husband but found that he had given up on her and remarried. She died a year later.[25] Anandibai Bhagat, who accompanied Pandita Ramabai on her trip to Wantage, England in 1882,

---

[22] For a sample of this literature, see Bhagwant Hari Khare, *How Is Woman Treated by Man and Religion?* (Bombay: Nirnaya Sagar Press, 1895); Dewan Bahadur Raghunatha Row, *Women's Right to Salvation* (Madras: Hindu Press, 1887).

[23] See Appendix for more biographical details on these women.

[24] See Helen S. Dyer, 'Preface' in Soonderbai Powar, *Hinduism and Womanhood* (London: Christian Worker's Depot, n.d.), p. 6.

[25] Baba Padmanji, *Once a Hindu*, p. 136.

committed suicide,[26] although, in her case, the anxieties of conversion were accompanied by the tensions brought on by her interaction with missionaries. Nevertheless, despite these hardships, what is significant is that these women, of their own volition, chose to make these sacrifices to embrace Christianity. As the length of time that elapsed between the husband's conversion and the decision of their wives to convert demonstrates, such decisions were not based on considerations such as obedience to their husbands, but represented the result of an independent decision. In other words, such a choice marked the beginning of their struggle to create a social space for themselves, rather than meekly following the lead of their husbands.

As a first-generation convert, Pandita Ramabai's views are significant in providing a key to the growing feminist consciousness of women in Maharashtra.[27] In her earliest analysis of Hinduism's treatment of women, written for the *Cheltenham Ladies College Magazine* in 1885, she argued that Hinduism advocated a personal religion for man wherein he had special privileges and duties. But a woman had no such special favours marked out for her. Her God, according to Manu's Code (Manu is reputedly Hinduism's first law-giver), is her husband and she must therefore worship and obey him, no matter what his flaws. The woman was therefore wholly reliant on her husband's actions to secure her place in heaven, as she lacked the direct authority to appeal to God himself for salvation. This lack of 'personal responsibility' towards God created great dissatisfaction within Pandita Ramabai, as, she argued, there was nothing to sustain a wife who was unlucky enough to be married to an unworthy husband.[28] Robbed of the personal dignity that a Christian woman could claim, Hindu women, she reflected, could not reach the 'true dignity of womanhood', as Hinduism did not respect women as independent human beings as the Hindu notion of duty and worship of one's husband obliged the woman to try and please her husband in any way, irrespective of ethical values. There was also no religious motive for Hindu women to engage in self-sacrifice, as there was no higher ideal than serving her husband and his family. Therefore, even though women may spend their entire lives in a spirit of selflessness, they actually would gain nothing in spiritual terms.

The fact that Hindu women were as pious as men, if not more so, led her to investigate the manner in which the unjust treatment of the sexes evolved in the practice of Hinduism. Comparing and contrasting female benevolence with that of men's, she wrote:

---

[26] Anandibai's letter to the Head of the Mission school in Bombay reveals both her unhappiness and her fear of having displeased her patron, Mrs Mitchell. Her undated letter was written in 1883 during her stay with the Community of St. Mary the Virgin at Wantage in England. In A.B. Shah (ed.), *The Letters and Correspondence of Pandita Ramabai* (Bombay: Maharashtra State Board for Literature and Culture, 1977), pp. 11–14.

[27] See entry on Pandita Ramabai in the Appendix.

[28] Pandita Ramabai, 'Account of the Life of a Hindoo Woman', *Cheltenham Ladies College Magazine*, 12 (Autumn 1885): 143.

I doubt whether charitable institutions could go on at all were it not for women. In our country when women go to hear a Purana [religious legend] or to worship God in a temple, they never go empty-handed. They must place before the Puranika [Hindu scripture reader] some gift, money, it may be, or a fruit or a flower, or, at very least a handful of rice. And yet, in spite of that, Hinduism declares that women are compounded of every evil thing in the universe...[29]

This deep frustration with the perception of women as 'evil thing[s]' who, despite their offerings, were unable to independently find salvation found clearest expression in *A Testimony*, her autobiographical work,[30] where she identified a common strand linking all the Sanskrit texts of the Mahabharata, Dharma Shastras, Vedas, Smritis, and the Puranas right down to the proclamations of the modern poets and popular preachers of the day:

Women of high and low caste, as a class, were bad, very bad, worse than demons, as unholy as untruth, and that they could not get Moksha as men. The only hope of their getting this much-desired liberation from Karma and its results, viz., countless millions of births and deaths and untold suffering, was the worship of their husbands. The woman has no right to study the Vedas and Vedanta and without knowing Brahma no one can get liberation, i.e., Moksha...My eyes were being gradually opened, and I was waking up to my own hopeless condition as a woman, and it was becoming clearer and clearer to me that I had no place anywhere as far as religious consolation was concerned. I became quite dissatisfied with myself, I wanted something more than the Shastras could give me...[31]

For the first time she rebelled against Hindu injunctions that forbid women from accessing the holy language and read the forbidden books, the Vedas, but her discontent was even greater than when she began her investigation. The notion of female salvation was hotly debated throughout the ancient and middle centuries in the various sects of Hinduism, and the same disputes had also transferred to the rival heterodoxies of the time too, namely Jainism and Buddhism. The idea that the woman has to be reborn a man in order to gain salvation (that is, release from endless transmigration and rebirth) was a central point within this polemic, which hinged on biological theories and sexual psychology that conceived a woman's body to be a receptacle of contamination and pollution.[32] This meant that a woman's fate was

---

[29] Cited in Nicol MacNicol, *Pandita Ramabai* (Calcutta: Association Press, 1926), p. 72.

[30] The fact that this book is presented to female children in South Karnataka Christian families to this day when they have learnt to read and write is a poignant reminder to us about feminist legacies. This oral communication is from Saraswathi Bhat, a descendant of Pandita Ramabai. I would like to thank Meena Siddharth for providing this valuable piece of information in the first instance.

[31] Pandita Ramabai, *A Testimony*, 6th edn (Kedgaon: Mukti Mission, 1964; 1st edn 1907), p. 8.

[32] A fine summary of the debates conducted over a millennium in India is in Burton Stein, *A History of India* (Oxford: Blackwell, 1998), pp. 64–72.

effectively decided by what was viewed to be the inherent sinfulness of her own body; a proposition that Pandita Ramabai was unable to accept. She lost all faith in the Hindu religion and converted to Christianity, before carrying out another act of rebellion by marrying a Bengali of *shudra* [low] caste.

The notion of a woman as a sinful creature whose desire for knowledge results in great calamity, is not, of course, exclusive to Hinduism; Eve fulfils a similar role in the Judeo-Christian story, whose dangerous desire to 'grow mature in knowledge'[33] not only leads to her own downfall but that of her husband. However, the nature of Protestantism in late eighteenth and early nineteenth-century Britain and America had altered greatly in the intervening period, and such changes soon had an impact on missions sent to India. As historians have pointed out, Protestantism had become a matter of the 'heart rather than the head' and in the words of Barbara Welter, a certain 'feminization' of religion had begun. The clergy no longer cast women in the role of sensual temptress, but instead built a rationale for the special obligations of women to religion by emphasizing Biblical women other than Eve, identifying traditional religious values with that of 'feminine' values of humility, kindness and meekness.[34] This was a powerful rhetoric, which influenced British and especially American women in taking immense interest in their 'sisters' overseas. Indian Christian women who had close contacts with Western missionary women also came under this influence and began to adopt Christianity as a positive organizing principle of their lives. Most of the Indian Christian women who form the subject of this study acknowledged that they benefited from the teaching of Western missionaries, which often taught them to see the world in a new light. Pandita Ramabai, for instance, described how the Wantage Sisters of Fulham showed her that 'fallen women' (prostitutes) could be brought back into society, contrasting their work with the nineteenth-century Hindu practice of shunning prostitutes as the greatest of all sinners and unworthy of compassion. She questioned the Sisters over why they cared for prostitutes and thus learned from them about Christ's meeting with the Samaritan woman and his teachings on the nature of true worship, which excluded neither male nor female. It was then that she realized that with regard to the position of women 'there was a real difference between Hinduism and Christianity', and was convinced that Christ alone 'could transform and uplift the downtrodden womanhood of India

---

[33] John Milton, *Paradise Lost*, Book IX, lines 803–84.

[34] Women's effective entry in the public arena was often achieved by fulfilling social offices in churches, like Sunday school teaching, working in missions and distributing tracts during the great revivals of this period. For a study of American women's entry see Barbara Welter, 'The Feminization of American Religion, 1800–1860', in Mary Hartman and Lois Banner (eds), *Clio's Consciousness Raised: New Perspectives on the History of Women* (New York: Harper and Row, 1974), pp. 137–57. For a study of English women's entry, see Leonore Davidoff and Catherine Hall, *Family Fortunes: Men and Women of the English Middle Class, 1780–1850* (London: Hutchinson, 1987).

and every land.'[35] Thus, through Pandita Ramabai's works, the modern reader can gain an understanding of what links diverse movements such as feminism and religious movements—the question of women's salvation.

After the transformation of her ideas, Pandita translated them into action by founding the Kripa Sadan [Home of Mercy], probably the first home for the rehabilitation of prostitutes in India. One finds a remarkable similarity between Josephine Butler's approach to Christianity and Pandita Ramabai's,[36] with both women interpreting the sayings of Christ as a social doctrine and the Gospel itself as the embodiment of the principles of social equality. Both placed a strong emphasis on Christ's 'conduct' towards women and how it had special bearing on the status of women, drawing attention to the fact that it was Christ who had pointed to the double standards of morality prevalent at the time. Both applied these principles of the individual soul's capacity to gain salvation as well as the power of 'love' and 'mercy' to communities of women. In fact, Butler and Ramabai's understanding of Christianity as a 'social' doctrine can be seen in their 'rescue' work with prostitutes. To them, the glaring inequalities between the sexes was not only highlighted in the institution of prostitution and society's attitudes towards it, but gave them clarity in boldly accusing governments, military establishments and men for punishing women for deeds that they condoned in men. What appalled them was not just society's disrespect of women but that the might of nations and empires stood behind these conspicuous inequalities, propelling them to attack governments and politics in their moral campaigns, and making the movements against the Contagious Diseases Acts[37] the most momentous and highly successful campaigns the modern world has ever seen.

Pandita Ramabai was baptized in 1883 along with her daughter Manoramabai. She records that finally she felt at peace with herself, having found what she saw as a 'religion which gave privileges equally to men and women; and where there was no distinction of caste, colour or sex in it'.[38] Her rebellion, then, was against a religion that she perceived to preach inequality by counterposing good and evil respectively in men and women. She rejected the Vedantic teachings about the 'unreality' (illusion) of life and showed a preference for a religion that conceived human life to be 'reality' because this philosophy, she claimed, opened a life of possibilities, of a life to be lived intensely and with a purpose.

---

[35]   Pandita Ramabai, *A Short History of the Kripa Sadan, or Home of Mercy* (Kedgaon: Mukti Mission, 1964), p. 2.

[36]   My understanding of Josephine Butler's work and thought is based on a reading of the philanthropic movements of nineteenth-century British women. See in particular F.K. Prochaska, *Women and Philanthropy in Nineteenth Century Britain* (Oxford: Oxford University Press, 1980), and Anne Summers, 'A Home from Home: Women's Philanthropic Work in the Nineteenth Century', in S. Burman (ed.), *Fit Work for Women* (London: Croom Helm, 1979), pp. 32–63.

[37]   For details on the Contagious Diseases Act, see chapter 4 of this book.

[38]   Pandita Ramabai, *A Testimony*, p. 13.

In addition to Pandita Ramabai, a few other Hindu women who were allowed by liberal parents to seek education in mission schools also began a learning process that made Christianity a desirable choice. An interesting instance was Gunabai, who studied in a mission school in Ahmednagar where she was impressed by the 'Christian values' of compassion and mercy. Her daughter, Shewatibai, recollected that John Bunyan's *Pilgrim's Progress* had such an impact on her mother that she lost all traces of hesitancy and reserve about the wrath of her community and ran away to the mission house, never to return to her parents.[39]

Second-Generation Women: Extending the Feminist Critiques of Hinduism

Pandita Ramabai's critiques were improved upon and extended by a second generation of Christian women who concentrated more on the exposition of the role and status of women in popular Hinduism in their efforts to empower Indian womanhood. Second-generation Christian women were much more systematic in their analysis, addressing men as the original culprits in the vilification of women through their coding and encoding of the Hindu religion. Reminiscent of the fifteenth-century French 'Querelle des Femme', these women identified Hindu men as misogynists who essentialized woman's nature as 'evil'.[40]

In keeping with her mentor Pandita Ramabai, Soonderbai Powar also located women's servitude in Hindu religion and social customs, but she elaborated on Pandita's critique by highlighting the role of men with much greater clarity.[41] She described Indian women as 'slaves' who had been forced to merge their personal freedom and individuality in the personality of man. Through an acute observation of Hindu mannerisms, such as the negative expressions used on the birth of a female child and the ribald popular sayings about wives and widows, she demonstrates how a woman is devalued, making it impossible for her to be an inspiring companion to her husband or a wise and responsible mother to her children.[42] Weaving a narrative through the life histories of the students in her Teacher's Training School, she concluded that, if Hindu women were in 'bondage', it was one imposed by selfish men which made them perceive woman 'as nothing more than a soulless animal to be used for the pleasure of man'.[43]

---

[39]   Shewatibai, 'Recollections of Shewatibai, Mistress of the Epiphany School, Poona, on her mother's conversion', *Magazine of Panch Howd* (Poona: St. Mary Convent, 1892), details unknown, Institutional Collection of Mukti Mission, Kedgaon [Hereafter referred as ICMMK]).

[40]   Joan Kelly, 'Early Feminist Theory and the Querelle des Femme, 1400–1789', *Signs*, 8/1 (1982): 4–28.

[41]   See Appendix for a note on Soonderbai Powar.

[42]   Soonderbai Powar, *Hinduism and Womanhood* (London: Christian Worker's Depot, n.d.) She published an earlier version of the book, probably in the early 1890s, titled *The Bitter Fruits of Hinduism* (details unknown).

[43]   Ibid., p. 31.

Dissecting the Hindu customs of early marriage, female infanticide, the seclusion of women, the dedication of girls as temple prostitutes and the dowry system, which she collectively described as the 'bitter fruits of Hinduism', Soonderbai argued that, '…in the name of their religion, Hindus do many wicked things and have many bad customs which cruelly limit or destroy the liberty of the subject, and strangle social and family happiness.'[44] It is certainly fascinating that Soonderbai uses the term 'liberty of the subject' in talking of the rights of women. It is clear from her biographical details that her contact with Christians of various denominations in her many tours of England, Ireland and Scotland were instrumental in shaping her views on the notion of the 'individual' and the liberation of the subject. That each person worked out his or her own salvation (part of the Christian doctrine) was very much in accord with the more widespread *laissez faire* ethos of secular Britain of the nineteenth century. Adapting the ideas that were taking root in Britain at this time to the Indian environment, Soonderbai was not too far from the conclusion that such Hindu customs (which specifically were detrimental to the life of a woman) derived sanction from the inviolable principles of their religion and philosophy. Additionally, she argued that Hindu men would do nothing to alter Hindu customs because they had themselves created such patriarchal conventions that suited men. Taking the argument further, she asserted that only the Christian religion could free women from such bondage because Hinduism was based on inequality and injustice between the sexes.

Soonderbai's writings demonstrate an awareness of the gendered nature of religion and the way in which men were able to use religion for their own ends. However, one of her contemporaries, the early feminist theorist Krupabai Khisti (later she changed her surname to Satthianadhan), went further in her analysis by not only investigating Hindu men's resistance to granting equal rights to women but also showing how Hinduism negatively affected the attitudes and stunted the personalities of Hindu women.[45] Krupabai was interested in showing how knowledge was produced about women, and her feminist critique of Hinduism clearly depicts how and why Indian women came to be represented as inherently sinful and promiscuous, justifying male control of their sexuality. Whilst acutely aware of how knowledge about women was constructed through crude biological theories, she also reveals how acutely 'political' men's agendas were when they vilified Indian womanhood. Her critique of the nature of women's oppression in Hindu society and her arguments for the education of women helped women not only to counteract the onslaught of Hindu vilification and contempt of women but, in a larger sense, also helped them to break through the rigidity of the roles prescribed for them.[46] In the first instance, marriage, according to her, was not the only goal of a woman's life. Secondly, she argued that education led

---

[44]   Ibid., p. 18.

[45]   For a note on Krupabai, see the Appendix.

[46]   Krupabai develops these themes in four consequent essays: 'Woman's Influence at Home', 'Home Training of Children', 'Female Education' and 'Hindu Social Customs', in Krupabai Satthianadhan, *Miscellaneous Writings of Krupabai Satthianadhan* (Madras: Srinivasa Varadachari & Co., 1896), pp. 1–33.

women to develop some freedom of thought and action, to begin to question the social tyranny and injustice they were subjected to, and, as a consequence of this, they could become self-reliant. Thirdly, she argued that this process of women's self-realization was the only way for the Indian nation to progress.

Krupabai began her analysis with the general proposition that the independence of women was anathema to a Hindu male, who could not bear the idea of a clever wife. Because of the high status that a man commanded in Hindu society, the minute a male child was born he was treated like a king. Because of this, he grew up to be a 'petted, spoiled despot, or a selfish ease-loving lord'.[47] To his 'inflated, self-satisfied nature' the very idea of an intellectual wife in any way superior to him 'will be gall-wormwood'. If his wife possessed qualities that he lacked, he would not tolerate it.[48] The second rationale she outlined was a psychological one.[49] Hindus, argued Krupabai, had lost their power as rulers and had been in servitude for centuries, and, therefore, exercising authority at home was an important compensation for the Hindu male that he would never give up unless women themselves rebelled. The third reason she ascribed to the economic necessity of exploiting women's labour to enable the efficient functioning of the large Hindu joint families. Thus, she concluded, if Hinduism advocated an inferior status and rights for women, it was with the willing connivance of Hindu men.

Second-generation Christian women reviewed the contemporary male discourse on female education proposing new theories on women's education and their obstacles. One of the commonest allegations of Indian male reformers was that women were the greatest opponents of education: they preferred ignorance, that their interests could never rise above petty gossip and trifles, and hence they blocked reform work.[50] Women inverted these arguments by placing responsibility for the 'empty' lives of women on the shoulders of selfish Hindu men. Thus, Krupabai pointed out:

> How few of our educated men ever trouble themselves about their women—as to how they spend the whole day, whether or not they find the hours hanging on their hands, whether the leading of an idle existence is hateful to them or not! They only look upon the women as mere appendices to their great selves... They [women] are not to be blamed; they know of

---

[47]   Krupabai, 'Female Education', *Miscellaneous Writings*, p. 18.

[48]   Ibid., p. 19.

[49]   The anxieties created under colonialism and its lasting psychological impact have been studied comprehensively by practising psychologists and social historians. See Sudhir Kakar, *The Inner World: A Psycho-Analytic Study of Indian Childhood and Society in India* (New Delhi: Oxford University Press, 1981); Ashis Nandy, *At the Edge of Psychology: Essays in Politics and Culture* (New Delhi: Oxford University Press, 1980).

[50]   The opinions of influential Hindu reformers were recorded in Cornelia Sorabji, 'Social Relations—England and India', *Pan-Anglican Papers* (London, 1908): 1–4.

no higher mode of existence: there is nothing to occupy their minds; ...they are treated as toys and playthings, and are humoured and pleased with gilded trinkets or any such trifles.[51]

What we observe here is a rigorous contesting of male knowledge about women. Second-generation women gave a cultural explanation for Hindu women's inferior status rather than rooting it in a biological theory of the weakness of the 'gentle sex'. As Krupabai argued, if Hindu women were ignorant and bigoted, the reasons were external to them. Krupabai's analysis of the attitudes of Hindu men and the atmosphere in Hindu homes eventually led her to argue that Christianity alone could liberate Indian women.

Krupabai's literary outpourings saw the popularization of the term 'New Woman' in the late nineteenth-century context of Indian society. What exactly she had in mind regarding this concept can be gleaned from her conceptual framework of the independent/dependent woman and the further binary pairing of Christianity/Hinduism. She presents this conceptual framework through her most famous literary works, namely, the two novels she wrote in the 1890s under the titles *Kamala: A Story of Hindu Life* and *Saguna: A Story of Native Christian Life.*[52] Kamala's life is described as 'dark' and a prolonged sadness permeates it. Kamala is married early to an English-educated man called Ganesh. The couple's love life is fractured by the machinations of a jealous mother-in-law and scheming sisters-in-law, a common plot of novels during this period of social reform. After the premature death of her husband, Kamala rejects the chance to remarry. Here the author interjects, saying 'Her religion, crude as it was, had its victory.'[53] Krupabai's message was that Hindu teachings give women very little consolation and are reinforced by passive models, like Sita.[54] Krupabai argued that, no matter how much a Hindu woman tried to assert and control her life, 'the book of fate would come to pass' no matter what she did to avert it.[55]

Saguna, the subject of Krupabai's second novel, is presented as a complete contrast to Kamala. In contrast to the 'dark' life led by Kamala, Saguna's life is

---

[51]   Krupabai, Miscellaneous Writings, p. 21.

[52]   In recognition of Krupabai's status as the first English writer of an autobiographical novel amongst Indian women, Oxford University Press has reprinted these novels in a series entitled 'Classic Reissue'. See Krupabai Satthianadhan, *Saguna: The First Autobiographical Novel in English by an Indian Woman*, ed. Chandani Lokuge (New Delhi: Oxford India, 1999), and *Kamala: A Story of a Hindu Life*, ed. Chandani Lokuge (New Delhi: Oxford India, 1999). Recently how Krupabai indigenized the 'English novel' to suit Indian needs has been studied by Priya Joshi *In Another Country: Colonialism, Culture and the English Novel in India*, (New York: Columbia University Press, 2002), pp. 172–204.

[53]   Krupabai Satthianadhan, *Kamala: A Story of Hindu Life* (Madras: Srinivasa Varadachari & Co., 1895), p. 207.

[54]   Sita was the consort of King Rama in the epic *Ramayana*. Sita's character and personality are characterized by passivity and resigned to sacrifice and suffering.

[55]   Krupabai Satthianadhan, *Kamala*, p. 58.

described as bright, influenced by the 'new order of things', which Krupabai says is sweeping all over India.[56] The 'new order of things' refers to the introduction of Christianity as a choice for Indians dissatisfied with the old order of life, and we read that Saguna's life was influenced and her character moulded by her own parents' spiritual struggle to overcome the 'bigotry' of their ancestral religion: Hinduism. She describes Saguna's childhood as a time where learning was encouraged and her freedom of speech and action were unchecked. The Christian life portrayed is one of a 'higher culture' than Hindu life, encouraging open-mindedness in those who profess it, and thus Saguna is given complete choice in pursuing a profession, a freedom unthinkable for Hindu girls of her day except in the most radical circles. Furthermore, in the mission school, Saguna meets Christian girls, all of whom had a 'definite work in view' and were receiving training for it, and her female friends are allowed to interact freely with young men and choose their own spouses.[57] The entire narrative focuses on the growth of Saguna through Christian influence into a confident and independent 'new woman'. Amongst all Indian Christian women's writers in this period, Krupabai's work provides the most thorough analysis of the intricate link between religion and a woman's identity and role. Indian women's self-realization, according to her, could only be achieved by accepting Christianity, as Hinduism stunted her self-awareness and stifled her soul.

Christian Feminists on Women's Subordination and the Break with the Past

The more radical feminist position these women occupied is seen in the theoretical premise they arrived at, namely, that the 'essence' of Hinduism depended and was built on an essentialist view of the nature of womanhood that accorded them an 'inferior' status in comparison to maleness which, in turn, was regarded as 'superior'. Yet, it was also clear that this state of affairs had not always been the case and was, in fact, a recent development. Krupabai argued that Hindus in India's past had far more liberal ideas than present-day adherents of the religion, remarking that

> ...they [the ancient Hindus] acknowledged the rights of women, to some extent, and gave them their true position in society. We have many distinct proofs that female education in early times was not neglected...We easily infer also from the writings of the ancient Hindus that the women of that period had a great many privileges which are now denied to them. Women chose their own husbands, or at least, had a voice in the selection of them...[58]

---

[56]   This novel is autobiographical in content; here, one can see Krupabai in the role of Saguna; Krupabai Satthianadhan, *Saguna: A Story of Native Christian Life* (Madras: Srinivasa Varadachari & Co., 1895).

[57] Ibid., p. 166.

[58]   Krupabai, 'Female Education', *Miscellaneous Writings*, pp. 16–7.

Befitting her role as a foremother and founder of modern Indian feminism, Pandita Ramabai proposed a more complex view on the 'Golden Age' and women's rights than the second-generation feminists like Krupabai and Soonderbai. Despite being a first generation Christian convert, her mastery of Sanskrit literature enabled her to take Krupabai's argument further, stating that, in the Rig Vedic times, there were no caste distinctions, no widow-burning, nor were women secluded. 'On the contrary', she wrote:

> It is taken for granted that they are, as well as men, thinking beings, and even in the later Upanishads we find ladies conversing on equal terms with men on subjects of religion and philosophy. I think this may have something to do with the fact that these works are pronounced by modern Brahmans too sacred for us women to read; it is thought undesirable that the high-caste women of to-day, who are utterly secluded and forbidden to speak to any men except to very near relatives, should read in the Aranyaks of ladies conversing with great sages, such as Yagnavalkya, especially of Gargi, who like the English princess S.Hilda [sic], exercized authority over Brahmans, priests and monks.[59]

If women were not subjugated in the 'golden' past of Indian history, when did their subordination begin? Both Krupabai and Pandita Ramabai attributed the subjugation of women to the gradual ascendancy of the priestly class in Hinduism. Nothing, according to them, marked the constitution of Hindu society as much as the power and influence that the Brahmin priesthood commanded over Hindus. In their opinion, it served the priest's interests to keep the Hindu woman as credulous and ignorant as possible because a learned and clever woman, especially a widow, would then manage her own affairs and estates without the aid of the family priest. Therefore, over the centuries, the Hindu priesthood took every opportunity to decry women's learning and made learned women the cause of every misfortune that fell upon a family in India.

In this explanation for the degeneration of the position of women, we see the departure made by Christian women from the dominant revivalist, reformist and early nationalist discourse of their time. The opinions of Vivekananda, M.G. Ranade, or Bankim Chandra, taken as representatives, respectively, of these three strands in male discourse, tended to disavow Hindu responsibility for the downfall of women's position and attributed it instead to Muslim rule in India. The stark difference in the explanation offered by Christian feminists is that they continued to hold Hindu men responsible for the deterioration in the status of women despite their protestations to the contrary. Such representations of the 'break with the past' (that Indian women were once upon a time equal to men, but this was no longer the case) allowed Indian Christian women to contest nationalist and revivalist discourses. An open confrontation took place in the 1890s when Vivekananda, a proponent of Hindu revivalism, attended the Congress of Religions in Chicago. In an attempt to salvage the position of India among world civilizations, he presented a highly romanticized

---

[59]   Pandita Ramabai, *Indian Religion*, p. 115.

view of the Indian womanhood of the past. In his cosmic world view, the Hindu widow cheerfully ascended the funeral pyre of her husband in order to be united with him in the next life; Hindu men secluded women because they held them in high esteem, and their immense respect for women held back a man from letting his wife out of his house.[60] He denied that widows were ill-treated and asserted that Hindu wives inherited the entire property of their husbands and were free to dispose of their *stridhan* [women's property accrued from their natal home] as they wished, [61] a very different representation from that given by Pandita Ramabai in her lectures in America a few years earlier. Ramabai's fund-raisers, the sixty-five 'Ramabai circles' all over America, challenged him directly, with the American Ramabai Association furnishing evidence regarding the authenticity of her accounts by publicizing the letters of distinguished scholars and reformers like Max Mueller, Miss Manning, B. Malabari and D.K. Karve.[62]

Yet, despite this evidence, some Westerners were taken in by the *swamis'* [guru] rhetoric, and Ramabai had to constantly warn Westerners to read between the lines of the prescriptive texts they had recommended. When an American visitor to the Mukti reported to her that Hindu *swamis* had spoken of the superior position granted to women in Hindu religion, she replied that 'it was not so lovely to experience it,'[63] and appealed to Western women to judge Indian society by living among Indians. In her eyes, experience of the material realities that following the Hindu texts created was much more important than comprehending them on a theoretical level alone:

> I beg of my Western sisters not to be satisfied with looking on the outside beauty of the grand philosophies, and not to be charmed with hearing the long and interesting discourses of our educated men... There are many hard and bitter facts which we have to accept and feel. All is not poetry with us. The prose we have to read in our lives is very hard ...[64]

The dangers of endorsing a philosophy without taking account of its practical implications is verifiable through the work of the Theosophists as represented in Annie Besant's rhetoric and work.[65] As a romanticist, Annie Besant defended the

---

[60]   Vivekananda's lectures reported in *Salem Evening News*, 29 August 1893. From Marie Louise Burke, *Swami Vivekananda in America: New Discoveries* (Calcutta: Advaita Ashram, 1958), p. 32.

[61]   Excerpts of Vivekananda's lectures reported in Detroit and Brooklyn newspapers; ibid., pp. 487–8.

[62]   The full texts of their letters are in *Annual Report of American Ramabai Association*, 1894, pp. 27–9 and for 1895, see pp. 31–41, ICMMK.

[63]   Pandita Ramabai, A Short History of Kripa Sadan, p. 31.

[64]   Ibid., pp. 29–30.

[65] The Theosophical Society in India was popularized by Annie Besant, who became its leader in 1893. It started as a movement of socioreligious dissent in the West but, in India, it fused certain Buddhist concepts with the Hindu doctrine of Karma. Soon, it started to support

Hindu injunctions on 'purity' and 'chastity', which led her to advocate the control of a widow's sexuality. Ramabai, critical of Besant's anti-woman stand, wrote sardonically that '...sometimes, it looks as if the world is going backwards, when one hears English women, like Mrs. Besant, declaring that Hindu widows should never marry again.'[66]

Indian revivalist-nationalists opposed the work of Indian Christian women constantly, and their opposition was not based just on cultural grounds but on practical considerations too. Quite aside from the implications that conversion could have on national cultural identity, a moot concern for late nineteenth-century conservatives and reformers, the politics of higher education for girls and women and its control during this period often led Hindu men to take direct action against the Christian feminist reformers.

So far we have examined how and why a section of literate women converted to Christianity and the argument has been made that the 'position of women' in different religions had been a moot point in women's conversion. We will now turn to illiterate and semi-literate women's decisions to convert from Hinduism to Christianity.

The 'God of Widows and Deserted Wives': Illiterate Women and Christianity

A large number of semi-literate women converted to Christianity during this period, notably at Sharada Sadan, the largest school in India for Brahmin widows founded by Pandita Ramabai in 1889. By the1890s, her school had achieved popularity unheard of within Western Indian circles. However, not everyone found the success of the Sharada Sadan agreeable, not least some of the members of its managing committee who also sat on the Board of the Poona Female High School, which had been founded by Hindu reformers in 1883–84. In the 1890s, the fate of this school was looking increasingly precarious, with the Government threatening to withdraw aid if the number of high-caste girls did not show an appreciable increase. In order to save the school, later to become the famed 'Huzur Paga' school in Pune that produced several generations of famous women nationalists who joined the Gandhian movements in the early part of the twentieth century, the reformers began to scrutinize the Sharada Sadan with care. In 1892, the reformers found it convenient to play up the rumours that Ramabai's institution was converting its pupils to Christianity, an action which not only led to the resignation of several members of the Sharada Sadan's Advisory Board, but also to some of the school's pupils being withdrawn from their studies. Not surprisingly, 12 out of 31 girls withdrawn from Pandita Ramabai's institution were immediately placed in the school run by Hindu male reformers.

Hindu tradition and by 1900 felt compelled to defend Hindu orthodoxy and refrained from social criticism.

[66] Pandita Ramabai, Annual Report of the American Ramabai Association, 1904, p. 21, ICMMK.

The Hindu reformers were partly motivated by jealousy of Ramabai's success, a fact later acknowledged by D.K. Karve, the founder of the Hingne Widows Home which later grew into the first women's university in India, who also admitted that, by alienating her, Hindu circles had lost a brilliant woman to their own causes; indeed, without her example, he would not have ventured to open his institutions.[67] It is also possible that Maharashtrian men feared the way in which she represented a model of an independent, self-willed, assertive woman that directly threatened their authority. While Hindu women could be controlled in a manner that suited them, Christian women were not subject to the same authority, and it is this autonomy that may have accounted for their hostility towards Ramabai and her work. Nevertheless, underpinning the Hindu reformers' attempts to boost the popularity of the institution that they had founded can be traced a real fear that the Sharada Sadan was influencing its pupils to convert to Christianity.

Certainly, many of its pupils chose to convert to Christianity despite the fact that The Executive Committee of the American Ramabai Association only awarded its annual grant of about $10,000 a year to the school on the basis that it was operated as a 'secular' institution. In 1892, 12 out of 49 widows and 13 non widows at Sharada Sadan converted to Christianity, interestingly, all of them adult Brahmin women who, as a result of their conversion, faced the possibility of ill-treatment from their relatives or guardians. In 1899 these numbers had increased massively, with only eight out of 108 remaining Hindus, whilst, according to Pandita Ramabai, in 1905 (the year she publicly dropped secular teaching), 1,500 out of 2,000 pupils in her schools were Christians. Such figures caused immense uproar in the urban Maharashtrian Hindu community, with B.G. Tilak's newspaper, *Kesari,* taking the lead in the vernacular press's denunciation of her. The strength of feeling generated by the rumours and allegations about Ramabai's pernicious influence can be seen in the way that she was not only accused of dishonesty but also had death threats issued against her.

Hindu reformers first attempted to try to counter Ramabai's influence within the school itself. Aside from Ramabai, a Managing Committee appointed by the American Ramabai Association, which consisted of six Indian members including M.G. Ranade, R.G. Bhandharkar and Atmaram Pandurang, influential Maharashtrian Hindu reformers, oversaw the running of the school. The rules and regulations listed by this committee contrived to turn the school from 'secular' to 'Hindu', and there were clashes with Ramabai, who refused their request to make Hindu worship, prayer, fasting and other symbolic practices of widowhood compulsory, instead giving the students the choice. The dispute ended in a compromise whereby Ramabai was debarred from entering the kitchen, dining area, and rooms of Hindu girls from orthodox families. The only place where she could now interact with students was the lecture rooms. These restrictions meant it was difficult for Ramabai to directly coerce any of her students into conversion, although she herself admitted that she might have

---

[67]   See D.K. Karve's letter dated 19 April 1958 and titled 'A Living Testimony', in *Pandita Ramabai Centenary Souvenir, 1858–1958* (Bombay: S.M. Adhav, 1958); D.K. Karve, 'Pandita Ramabai', *Young Men of India*, (June 1922): 302–5, ICMMK.

had an indirect influence on the girls through her lifestyle.[68] Yet, even though these conversions were voluntary, their frequency was not only causing anxiety for the Hindu reformers on the school's advisory board but also for the American Ramabai Society, who, in 1893, sent their president, Mrs Andrews, to investigate the matter and report back to them. The report not only served to vindicate Ramabai, with Mrs Andrews describing the rumours and speculation as 'baseless fabrications',[69] but her interviews with the converts provide the historian a valuable source of information on the reasons why so many of the pupils chose to convert.

Unlike Ramabai, who converted on theological grounds, the interviews that Mrs Andrews conducted demonstrate that many of the converts did so on the basis of more practical considerations. The everyday life of a Brahmin widow in this period was a miserable one. They were held directly responsible for their husbands' death, (popular versions of Hindu faith ascribed the premature deaths of their husbands to sins committed by the women in their past lives, especially infidelity), hence they were stripped of all jewellery, were compelled to wear coarse saris, shave their heads, eat sparse meals and fast regularly and were shunned like untouchables. For these women, the teaching at the Sharada Sadan was a revelation. Not only were they taught that they were not culpable for their husband's deaths, but for this first time some of them felt the joy of living and of being treated like other human beings. As early as 1886, Ramabai had mused that Manu's Code of Law and the earliest Hindu scriptures ought to form part of the syllabus in girls' schools in order to make them realize their true position in Hindu religion and society,[70] and certainly the Hindu *puranas* [religious legends] were taught in her school.[71] By getting women to consider the way in which religion affected their lives, these teachings were giving them a means to counter it. Juxtaposed with these oppressive Hindu laws was the image of Christ as a saviour of deserted wives, prostitutes and widows,[72] a representation that had a tremendous appeal to these anguished women. Part of the explanation for the voluntary acts of conversion can certainly be attributed to Pandita Ramabai's instruction. By incorporating Hindu scriptures in the curriculum she helped her pupils to scrutinize the very laws that embodied their subordination and then abandon it.

In addition to providing solace to these distressed women, converting to Christianity also provided a more tangible freedom, with a significant proportion of the widows who were not bound by any kinship tie or guardians quick to see the advantages of freeing themselves from caste restrictions such as those concerning the cooking of food prepared by their own hands. In 1896, only a handful of women in the Sharada Sadan remained Hindus, and even these had admitted to Pandita Ramabai

---

[68]   Annual Report of American Ramabai Association, 11 March 1894, pp. 16–19.

[69]   Ibid., p. 19.

[70]   Pandita Ramabai, 'Account of the Life of a Hindoo Woman', *Cheltenham Ladies College Magazine*, p. 146, ICMMK.

[71]   *Mukti Prayer Bell* (Magazine of Mukti Mission), December 1904 and October 1905. ICMMK

[72]   'The story of Jivi and others', pp. 1–15, ICMMK.

that they remained so only because they were bound to powerful relatives.[73] Ramabai herself was constantly surprised by the behaviour of orthodox Hindu girls, who, only a few days after their arrival, thought of breaking caste rules. Therefore, it is not surprising that many attributed their misery to Hindu religious customs and eventually, in a somewhat naive manner, accepted Christianity, which they felt could provide an escape from some of the hardships of Hindu strictures on the conduct of widows.[74] Missionary representations of Christian principles and values appeared to be helping them to cope with their everyday existence much better than popular Hinduism. Although a functional approach to religion seemed to govern their acceptance of Christianity, it must not be overlooked that their response is a gendered response to religion with a rejection of their source of subjection—namely, Hinduism, in order to rekindle their aspirations and attend to their needs.

One of Sharada Sadan's exceptional students, Nurmadabai, who was removed from the school after the first uproar over the conversion issue in 1893, corroborated the reason for the many conversions. She had attended Sunday school since the age of seven and at the age of 10 she was admitted to the Sharada Sadan. It was in this school that she felt for the first time that there was 'something real about this religion [Christianity]'. [75] She said that neither Ramabai nor the other teachers had pressured her into baptism; instead it was the motherliness and kindness prevalent in the school atmosphere that had prompted her switch in faith. She admitted to Judith Andrews that a large number of girls had previously experienced no happiness in their own homes but in Sharada Sadan, instead of abuse, they were given affection and care. Similar reports were also received from the pupils' guardians, who were also asked by Mrs Andrews to supply their opinions. D.K. Karve, an important Hindu social reformer and founder of the S.N.D.T. Women's University in Pune, had married Sharada Sadan's first pupil, Godubai (later known as Anandibai Karve); he reported that, in her four-year training at the school, she had not only acquired an 'enlarged and enlightened mind', but had also become 'free from many of our degrading superstitions'.[76]

However, the instruction given to pupils at the Sharada Sadan and the Zenana Teacher Training School was not the only factor responsible for persuading some women to convert. As we have already seen in the case of Ganderbai Powar, many married women, despite disapproval from their own families, chose to follow their already converted husbands. Like the widows at the Sharada Sadan, these women

---

[73] Pandita Ramabai to Dr. Donald, President of American Ramabai Association, 13 September 1902, p. 6, ICMMK.

[74] Annual Report of American Ramabai Association, 11 March 1894, pp. 12–25.

[75] In 1893, when Nurmadabai was removed from Sharada Sadan she refused to go to any other school and after two years was allowed to return. See 'Address of Nurmadabai at the Annual Meeting of the American Ramabai Association', in the *Annual Report of American Ramabai Association*, 1903, pp. 40–42.

[76] D.K. Karve to Mrs Andrews, *Annual Report of the American Ramabai Association*, 1894, letter dated 2 February 1894, pp. 27–9.

were not compelled to do so by their husbands but rather because it afforded them a level of respect that they never experienced before their husbands had converted to Christianity. These women had often initially opposed their husband's conversion, and though they had endeavoured to continue to fulfil the requirements of their religion by continuing to serve their husband, they expressed disapproval by keeping a separate house, serving separate meals to their husbands and continuing to follow Hindu rituals for several years. The reasons they gave for conversion are based on the transformation they experienced in their menfolk's attitude and conduct towards them after they underwent the conversion process. Ganderbai Powar, for example, told of how, when her husband was a Hindu, he was hot-tempered, petulant and harsh to her, but he was 'all kindness' to her after he became a Christian;[77] this change in behaviour was not unique, with Radhabai Khisti noting a similar change for the better in her husband when he underwent the same process.[78] In other instances, women, such as Sakubai, felt that Christianity must be a superior religion since her husband had not remarried in spite of her refusal to live with him for two whole years.[79] Thus issues of personal morality had a powerful effect on women's decisions to convert.

The appeal of an alien religion was quite differently perceived and experienced by male and female converts. The category of women converts who turned to Christianity because of the issue of 'morality' approached it from a subjective viewpoint. This is better understood when we contrast women's attitudes to male converts who used the 'morality' argument. A well-known Maharashtrian Christian of the late nineteenth century, Nehemiah Goreh (originally a Brahmin), argued with the Brahmos and Prarthana Samajists that the monotheist god in Hinduism as described in the revered Hindu texts—the Vedas and Upanishads—had sublime attributes yet had no sense of morality and could not distinguish right from wrong. The Hindu God, according to Goreh, was immoral and adulterous. How, then, he concluded, can one worship God, if he claims to be immortal but is full of mortal failings?[80] Goreh does not consider issues of morality from a subjective point of view but as an abstraction. Women, however, arrived at the same conclusion regarding 'personal morality' but from a subjective viewpoint rather than from a philosophical exposition of the doctrines of Hinduism and Christianity. Christianity also had another strong attraction for many women, particularly those belonging to the lower castes. Mission Christianity in colonial India was represented to Indians as a religion of 'duty' that placed 'service' above 'doctrine', with evangelicalism placing a high premium on manners and morals including right conduct, social pity and compassion for the downtrodden, the sick and despised—including and especially women. For less-educated or completely illiterate women who experienced daily the misery of Hindu widows and wives, a religion that

[77] Kate Storrie, *Soonderbai Powar: A Noble Worker for Indian Womanhood* (London: Pickering & Inglis, n.d.), pp. 6–7.

[78] Samuel Satthianadhan, *Sketches of Indian Christians*, pp. 190–94.

[79] A short account of her work is in the *Magazine of Panch Howd* (1884), p. 7.

[80] Nehemiah Goreh, Four Lectures Delivered in Substance to the Brahmos in Bombay and Poona (Bombay: Education Society Press, 1875), pp. 1–11.

tended to be both 'personal' and 'social', whose precepts had to be integrated into daily life and acted upon, had a powerful impact on them. They saw it as a liberating force and, consequently, often failed to identify the close links that existed between the notion of Christian culture and Western imperialism. In British and American missionary teaching, virtues such as industry, morality, sobriety and decency were attributed to the 'Western' religion of Christianity, and 'Western' culture in general. It is therefore unsurprising that, among the illiterate category of women converts, the process of conversion became subtly intertwined with a belief in the imagined benefits of Western culture and civilization.

Gender and the particular location of converts in class and caste positions determined how they perceived and accepted representations of the alien religion. In the transition from disapproval to acceptance of Christianity, semi-literate and illiterate women displayed little or no knowledge of the theological constructs of either religion. But after their baptism, they were given basic training in Christian doctrines. They proved to be some of the ablest workers in the proselytization programmes of the missionaries. As Bible-women and catechists, they were able to relay religious precepts in a simple and comprehensible manner to villagers.[81] Women, in contrast to men, as we have seen, approached religion and religious issues in a different way. The choice of, and move towards, embracing a new religion was a liberating experience for women. The close association between Christianity and Western culture and civilization made by missionaries defined the relationship between Christianity and Hinduism too.[82] It was a power-laden relationship working in an unequal fashion within mission surroundings; however, it indirectly helped Indian female converts to Christianity to forge new identities while providing them with a new ideal of dignity and self-respect.

Interaction with Missions: Conflict Over Belief and Method

When Indian Christian women forged their links with the West, an important mediator was the white female missionary. Missions belonging to different churches befriended Indian Christian women and rendered various services to them, from forming their beliefs to bailing them out in times of distress. Indian Christian women often acknowledged their help in effusive tones. However, in personal belief and organizational work they differed, which manifested itself vividly in approach and methods of action. The various missionary creeds, for example, Catholic, Anglican, Evangelical, had a profound affect on the beliefs of Christian women, yet the more influential among them filtered these ideas and sieved out what did not suit the

---

[81]   Examples of how Bible-women trained by Soonderbai used conversion techniques is in Kate Storrie, *Soonderbai Powar*, pp. 100–101.

[82]   See Brian Stanley's discussion on 'Christianity and Culture', in The Bible and the Flag: Protestant Missions and British Imperialism in the Nineteenth and Twentieth Centuries (Leicester: Apollos, 1990), pp. 157–74.

interests of their enterprises or conflicted with their understanding of the Bible. In an earlier study I had argued that it was Indian Christian female converts' non-denominational activities that clearly distinguished the roots of their Indian feminism.[83] Thus Soonderbai and Pandita Ramabai in particular were severely criticized throughout their careers for their unconventional religious beliefs. Neither belonged to any church nor did they profess any kind of attachment to a particular denomination. Various accusations were hurled against them and they were called mercenaries exploiting Christian sympathy to promote the welfare of 'high caste Hindu women'.[84] Western missionaries [85] attacked them as well as influential Indian Christian men like Baba Padmanji and S.B. Lotlikar.

The careful distancing between Indian Christian women and missionaries represented the formation of a specifically Indian variety of feminism which, although firmly rooted in an alien religion, held women's issues at the heart of its concerns. Indian Christian women indigenized Christianity because of their woman-centred approach to religion. It stemmed from the belief that any compromises with organized Christianity, apart from their own selective borrowing, would undermine their programmes for the advancement of Indian women. It is important to understand why they resisted belonging to any particular creed or sect. It has been shown earlier that all of them believed that in the spirit of Christ there was neither male nor female. Their feminist critique of Hinduism rejected it as a religion that preached inequality between the sexes either as part of Hindu doctrines themselves or through their interpretation by Hindu priests. As new converts, they were pressured gently to accept a particular church in order to carry on their work, but Pandita Ramabai was very critical of divisive tendencies within Christianity. Her correspondence on theological questions clearly reveals why she chose not to belong to any denomination. In a letter to Sister Geraldine in 1885 she expressed her nonconformist views thus:

> I have just with great efforts freed myself from the yoke of the Indian priestly tribe, so I am not at present willing to place myself under another similar yoke by accepting everything which comes from the priests as authorized Command of the Most High.[86]

---

[83] In 1998, I had termed it as 'indigenous feminism' but would like to retract this phrase as less discerning scholars have mistaken it for a 'pure' or 'unadulterated' essence, which is not what I meant then, or now. See Anagol, 'Indian Christian Women'.

[84] A summary of these accusations are in M. Adhav, 'Pandita Ramabai', paper read at Church History Association of India, Western India Branch, 12 March 1978, p. 1, ICMMK.

[85] Her mentor, Sister Geraldine in England, dubbed Pandita Ramabai a 'heretic'. For an analysis of the metropolitan Anglican Church's reaction to her resistance to accept a Creed, see Gauri Viswanathan, *Outside the Fold: Conversion, Modernity and Belief* (Princeton: Princeton University Press, 1998), pp. 118–52.

[86] Pandita Ramabai to Sister Geraldine, 12 May 1885, in A.B. Shah, *Letters and Correspondences of Pandita Ramabai*, p. 59.

According to her, obedience to the law and to the Word of God was quite different from unquestioning subservience to the clergy. Soonderbai also conducted her work on nondenominational lines in the belief that allegiance to a particular church meant subordination to mediating agencies. Neither of them wanted any intermediaries between God and themselves. Soonderbai, on her tours in England, was constantly asked about her denominational status to which she replied 'King's Own'.[87]

Christian women, as we have seen, critically examined the Indian past with a view to understanding the position of Indian women and their gradual decline in status. Krupabai, Soonderbai and Pandita Ramabai attributed this to the gradual ascendancy of the priestly class among Hindus. Nothing, according to them, marked the constitution of Hindu society as much as the power and influence that the Brahmin priesthood commanded over Hindus. Their experience of the role of the Hindu priesthood in women's oppression was at the heart of Indian Christian women's rejection of clerical mediation.

Victorian values were derived at least in part from the Church's views on female sexuality. The clergy reinforced domestic ideology and its constituents too.[88] Accepting allegiance to any particular church meant accepting Victorian beliefs. Among them were sex segregation and the biological determinist theories, which outlined separate spheres: these were prime concerns to Indian Christian women. To someone like Pandita Ramabai, who was teaching women carpentry and masonry, the natural division theory was an unsuitable one.[89] On one occasion when Pandita Ramabai was Professor of Sanskrit at the Cheltenham Ladies College, she wanted to teach British officers preparing for a career in India, but when she sought permission to do so through Dorothea Beale, the Principal, she was told that the clergy would not allow a woman to teach men, seeing it as a transgression of natural laws. In contrast, in late nineteenth-century India—a transitional period—rapid changes had not yet crystallized into rigid rules, allowing women like Cornelia Sorabji to teach for a year in a male college in Ahmedabad while Pandita Ramabai addressed all-male Indian audiences and Franscina Sorabji opened a nonsegregated school for children of mixed descent. Any strict conformity to church laws would mean a curtailment of their freedom of speech and action. Likewise, Soonderbai rejected modern interpretations of the Bible and taught her own version, which she felt was closer to its spirit.

The tensions between Indian Christian women and their Western 'sisters' increased towards the end of the nineteenth century. While bearing the brunt of missionary attacks on their belief and work, Indian Christian women were themselves active in criticizing Western missionary attitudes towards Indian culture and Indians. The earliest commentaries on 'racism' among women were by Indian Christian women. Krupabai at the age of 14 noted the insolence and arrogance of Western

---

[87]   Storrie, *Soonderbai Powar*, p. 45.

[88]   Catherine Hall, 'The Early Formation of Victorian Domestic Ideology', in *Fit Work for Women*, pp. 15–32.

[89]   Pandita Ramabai to Rev. Dr. Pentecost, 6 December 1892, in *Chikat Pustak* [Notebook] of Pandita Ramabai (Rajas Dongre's collection), ICMMK.

missionaries towards Indians. She recalled her humiliation and anger at which her mother attempted to console her by saying '...how can you expect them to be friends. Dont [sic] you see the difference, they are white and we are black. We ought to be thankful for the little notice that they take us.'[90]

Hence even the rather astute Cornelia Sorabji, always cautious in her dealings with European reformers, felt the need to call for a 'certain change in the attitude of the mind' if Westerners wanted a genuine interaction with Indians.[91] Indian Bible-women also observed the differences between 'old' and 'new' missionaries. The 'new' ones they felt were 'cold, unemotional and kept barriers with supercilious airs', and they predicted that with such attitudes Western missionaries would not convert a Hindu in a thousand years![92]

Indian Christian women were among the first to criticize 'orientalist' notions by marking out Western missionaries as a vehicle for them. Indian women brought into sharp focus the missionaries' inclination to address Indians as 'benighted heathens' and their tendency to constantly classify them. They felt that the contempt and unjustified arrogance of Western missionaries arose through such classifications and ignorance of India. To combat their ignorance, Pandita Ramabai suggested that all missionaries who embarked on a voyage to India should learn about the history and ancient literature of the Hindus. In addition, they should admit what was good and true about the Vedas and thus show fairness and love of truth.[93] She was convinced that Western missionaries were alienating Indians and thus harming the cause of Christianity in India.[94] She saw no rationale in decrying everything in the Indian scriptures, and expected missionaries to argue with Indians on an intellectual level regarding the particularities of each religion.

This explains why Indian Christian women were constantly stressing 'Indianness' and maintained an Indian diet, dress and etiquette. In describing the dress codes of Indian Christians, Lakshmibai noted that Indian Christian women rejected the trailing gowns and skirts of Western women and instead wore a modified form of the Indian sari and a blouse.[95] Manoramabai went to the extent of telling missionaries eager to work in Mukti that they ought to be aware of the fact that Mukti was a 'thoroughly Indian mission' and if they were not prepared to accept this fact, then, they should not come at all![96] A characteristic of Indian Christian women was to enforce their notion of 'Indianness', and in many a 'Foreword' influential dignitaries invited to say a few words about the author would carefully stress how the writer had

---

[90] Krupabai, *Saguna*, p. 108.

[91] Cornelia Sorabji, 'Social Relations', *Pan-Anglican Papers*, pp. 1–4.

[92] Krupabai Sattianadhan, *Saguna*, pp. 132–40.

[93] Pandita Ramabai, 'Indian Religion', *Cheltenham Ladies College Magazine*, 13 (Spring 1886): 106–18.

[94] Ibid., p. 107.

[95] Lakshmibai Tilak, *From Brahma to Christ*, ed. Stacy Waddy (London: Lutterworth Press, 1956), p. 168.

[96] Manoramabai to a would-be-worker abroad, n.d., ICMMK.

not 'denationalized' herself. It is very likely that Indian women felt the need to distinguish themselves from Western missionaries in order to be able to work ably in their welfare schemes for women without the negative connotations that Westerners were rapidly acquiring with their racist approach. Underlying the anxiety of Indian Christian women in making Western missionaries realize the importance of 'Indianness' in mission matters was their perception that emancipation for women in India was still a fragile project which needed nurturing. Towards this end, they adopted wholly tried and tested 'Indian' methods of evangelical work that proved more successful.

Indian Christian men, too, were critical of the radical departures made by some of the Christian women in their methods. Pandita Ramabai had once delivered a *kirtan* [religious discourse in verse usually accompanied by musical instruments] in a temple to a female audience. She defended her action on the ground that women in small towns were not only timid but also had no concept of modern-day notions of lectures and meetings. Therefore, she had used the *kirtan* to communicate practical lessons on social philosophy.[97] When she was attacked by the Indian Christian community, she defended her methods by pointing out that missionaries, too, employed means such as the 'magic-lanterns shows' and *tamashas* [Maharashtrian folk entertainment] to convey their message and so she felt justified in doing the same. The 'Indianness' Christian women represented lay also in the method of worship, which they consciously adopted from Hinduism and retained as good practice.[98] Lakshmibai, Soonderbai and Pandita Ramabai believed in the *bhakti* form of worship, an emotional expression of love of God. In the 1900s a great 'Revival' was reported with large numbers of girls and women embracing Christianity in Maharashtra.[99] When Western missionaries sharply rebuked these forms of worship as expressions of paganism, Indian Christian women defended them as legitimate forms of female worship forming a crucial part of women's lived realities.

So far we have seen how a certain section of Maharashtrian women broke away from the inherited Hindu past and found a new sense of freedom of thought and liberty of action in a new religion. In the next section we will examine whether this break meant a break with the traditional roles of Indian women too.

---

[97]   See Pandita Ramabai's letter in the Marathi newspaper, *Dnyanodaya*, 25 July 1889.

[98]   Leslie Flemming recounts the tale of a rare example of a German missionary woman, Christine Belz, who adopted Indian methods of worship and claimed to be successful in her evangelical work among North Indians in the nineteenth century. 'New Models, New Roles: U.S. Presbyterian Women Missionaries and Social Change in North India, 1870–1910', in Flemming (ed.), *Women's Work for Women*, pp. 43–5.

[99]   Women in Mukti were reported to have fainting spells and trances while they witnessed God during this 'revival'.

Women's Entry into the Public Arena

By breaking with the Indian past through the rejection of Hinduism, Christian women converts turned to other radical programmes. Apart from creating new roles for themselves, the late nineteenth century was also marked by the unique way in which they attempted to drop caste distinctions and overcome race and class barriers too.

One of the most enduring projects they embraced was female education. Educational schemes differed widely in the nature of the curriculum, and the degree of segregation they proposed depended on the ideological convictions of individual women. For example, it was Soonderbai Powar's sincere belief that until the Gospel had been absorbed no Hindu woman could be emancipated, however liberal an education she might have acquired. Therefore, in spite of Pandita Ramabai's protests she left Mukti to start a Zenana Teacher's Training School aimed exclusively at the training of Christian women for a career in gospel preaching.[100] Unlike Soonderbai, Pandita Ramabai believed that the most oppressed class among women were widows and therefore her first institution, Sharada Sadan, was exclusively meant for high-caste Hindu widows. It aimed to train and equip them for a profession that would make them independent of their families and relatives. In the beginning Sharada Sadan admitted nonwidows, especially young, single girls until 1892, because widows had not taken up the available places.[101] Pandita Ramabai, however, made an exception in the case of deserted wives. In 1892 Sharada Sadan had seven Marathi standards and four Anglo-Vernacular standards. The matriculation exam was added in 1895. The curriculum consisted mainly of English, Marathi language and literature; history, geography and mathematics were also taught in the higher standards.[102] This was broadly in line with the curriculum in the state-run boys' schools. Pandita Ramabai sent her most promising students after their matriculation to America for higher education right up to 1910. The reason is unclear though it is likely that funding abroad was more readily available. Women who were not inclined to intellectual activities were trained for a vocation in the weaving, dairy, oil pressing and printing industry that had been started in Mukti by 1900.

In 1895 Pandita Ramabai made a radical departure in her policy of recruiting girls by including prostitutes. As we have seen, the process began when she observed the work of the Wantage Sisters in England. In 1895, she heard stories about the pitiable state of abandoned high-caste Hindu widows in North India and visited Brindavan. Here she 'rescued' 200 prostitutes who did not want to follow the profession. In 1899 she formally inaugurated a rehabilitation centre for prostitutes called Kripa Sadan. Convinced that they needed special care and a different kind of instruction, she segregated them from the Sharada Sadan girls. Here we may note that Pandita Ramabai was perhaps equally prompted by the opportunity of direct evangelization as much as humanitarian concerns for the well-being of the prostitutes.

---

[100]   Storrie, *Soonderbai Powar*, p. 67.

[101]   Annual Report of American Ramabai Association, 2 February 1894, p. 15.

[102]   *Mukti Prayer Bell*, 1906, pp. 6–7.

Although the schools offered different types of emancipation for women, both achieved the common aim of Indian Christian feminists' goal of greatly increasing the self-esteem of Indian females. Krupabai, whom we had mentioned previously, observed in her essay, 'Women's Influence in the Home', that women had only wielded power within the domestic sphere, and only when they had grown older and become the most senior women in the household. This meant that the only opportunity women had to exercise power over their menfolk was by enforcing rituals at home and extracting submission from family members.[103] Such limited power, she had argued whilst making a case for mass education, did not just damage self-esteem but also led, in some instances, to women allowing themselves to be ill-treated and abused. For instance, in her novel outlining the everyday life of a high-caste Hindu woman of Bombay,[104] published in 1895, Shewantibai Nikambe shows the way in which the belief that widows, through sins committed in a previous or this life, were responsible for their husbands' deaths, often gave the deceased's family a legitimate excuse to ill-treat even child-widows.[105] It was not only in the household sphere that beliefs could lead to ill treatment and exploitation. Soonderbai Powar highlighted the way in which Maharashtrian women who had prayed to Khandoba (a local deity) and had their wish granted would, as thanks, hand over the girl-child to the priests for 'dedication to God', which, in practice, meant prostitution.[106] Dispelling ignorance and superstition amongst women not only benefited them but also sometimes benefited their husbands in unexpected but very welcome ways. According to Pandita Ramabai, Hindu daughters-in-law believed that the only way to win the love of a wayward husband was by administering love-potions given by wandering mendicants, which in a large number of cases turned out to be poisonous substances.[107] By dispelling female ignorance, these women were not just aiding womenfolk but also, in some cases, their husbands and families as well.

For although, as we shall see later in the chapter, the schools run by Ramabai and Powar gave women the knowledge and confidence to enter the public spheres of education, preaching and literature, both firmly believed that 'God's ideal is family life'. Pandita Ramabai, in particular, encouraged all her students, whether unmarried girls, widows or abandoned wives, to marry and raise a family and, to this end, invited Christian men from all denominations to join her Industrial Schools and even opened a boy's school after 1900.[108] Far from destroying the institution of marriage and

---

[103]   Krupabai, 'Women's Influence in the Home', in *Miscellaneous Writings*, pp. 1–7.

[104]   Sevantibai Nikambe, Ratanbai: A Sketch of a Bombay High Caste Hindu Young Wife, (London: Marshall Bros., 1895).

[105]   The same argument is repeated in her 'Address of Shewatibai Nikambe', *Annual Report of American Ramabai Association*, 17 March 1897, p. 29.

[106]   Soonderbai Powar, *Hinduism and Womanhood*, pp. 47–8.

[107]   Pandita Ramabai, *Stri-Dharma Niti* [Prescribed Laws and Duties on the Proper Conduct of Women] 3rd edn (Kedgaon: Mukti Mission, 1967; 1st edn 1882), pp. 74–5.

[108]   Manoramabai reported that, in a single year, 22 girls from Mukti were married. *Mukti Prayer Bell*, September 1906, n.p.

children, Christian women leaders wished to reinforce it, albeit with alterations to the established model. Instead of arranged marriages, for instance, they advocated a midway arrangement between that and a 'love' marriage, that is, a self-chosen partner in marriage. Pandita Ramabai had publicly pronounced on Mukti's policy on the matter, and soon reform-minded young Hindus wrote and requested suitable brides from the many female students from her institutions. Surprisingly, given the importance that they placed on marriage and family life for others, in their own personal lives, many of the Christian women pioneers did not practise what they preached.[109] Nevertheless, they provided women within marriage a freedom of action and thought that they did not previously possess.

Franscina Sorabji was one Christian feminist whose ideology differed radically from her contemporaries, and her educational enterprise reflected it.[110] The Victoria High School, founded by Franscina Sorabji in 1876, was not only unique in providing education to both boys and girls. Schools at this time were also divided along racial lines, so a school providing education primarily for Eurasian children was a genuinely groundbreaking venture. Franscina's institution started out with seven children, but soon it underwent a massive increase and, by the 1880s, over 400 students belonging to the Indian, European and Eurasian communities were enrolled as pupils. In order to accommodate their different religious requirements, she devised a kindergarten system that was a forerunner of the Montessori schools, catering to each of the child's individual needs. In addition to this, she provided an education that was Indian in character, using Indian symbols and metaphors instead of the usual English primers that were full of imagery that was alien to Indian children.[111] Yet, although Sorabji was unique in that her personal convictions were strictly divorced from her public schemes, her adoption of an Indian curriculum is just one demonstration of the way in which Indian Christian women during this period were not turning their back on their culture, but rather modifying it to fit their own beliefs.

Women, who had no clear ideological slant but were motivated by a desire to serve 'Indian womanhood', were guided more by circumstances in the way they entered the public sphere. A good illustration of this pragmatism is Shewantibai Nikambe.[112] When Pandita Ramabai shifted the Sharada Sadan from Bombay to Poona in 1889, a large number of girls from high-caste Hindu families in Bombay who were attending her school were stranded. Seeing the reluctance of the parents of these pupils to send their children to a different town created an opening for Shewantibai, who took the opportunity to start an independent school in Bombay.[113] Both Pandita Ramabai and Soonderbai took an interest in the careers of their students after the completion of their education. The more promising and enterprising of them

[109] Manoramabai, Soonderbai Powar, Cornelia Sorabji and Mary Bhor remained single.

[110] See Appendix for details on her.

[111] Cornelia Sorabji, *"Therefore": An Impression of Sorabji Kharshedji Langrana and his Wife Franscina* (London: Oxford University Press, 1924), especially pp. 42–60.

[112] See Appendix for details on her life and work.

[113] 'Preface' by Lady Harris to Shewantibai Nikambe, *Ratanbai*, pp. v–vii.

opened schools for girls in the towns where their husbands resided or entered into professions as matrons, teachers, catechists, nurses and Bible-women.[114] Many other women from the second generation gained personal satisfaction in furthering their own careers and in playing the hitherto unknown role of being 'breadwinners' for their families. Malanbai Kukde, for example, is said to have educated four of her younger brothers from her earnings as a teacher.[115] More ambitious women like Mary Bhor cut out a niche for themselves in Indian society, and at the same time gained the respect of the colonial elite too.[116] This category of women made use of their educational qualification and training, not from a 'mission' point of view but from a professional outlook alone.

Indian Christian women's entry into the literary professions is an understudied subject awaiting research.[117] Apart from the better known Christian feminists, a host of lesser known women entered the field of print literature, taking advantage of the invitations given by the great religious publishing houses of the time such as the Bombay Tract and Book Society, the American Marathi Mission at Ahmednagar and by Baba Padmanji's Victoria Printing Press. Fiction, especially the novel and short story collections, appeared regularly, as did domestic magazines for women.[118] Much of the content of this literature, although explicitly evangelical and didactic, were expressions of women exhibiting a sense of self and confidence, entering a new age where they were able to fulfil their aspirations. Equally, they depict the new found sense of adventure and excitement of embarking into philanthropic works, and for many this came as a deliverance from the *chool va mool* [kitchen and kid] routine of Maharashtrian female existence.

Philanthropy and Conflict with the State

Another important area of public activity which Indian Christian women pioneered was philanthropy. In a period when 'social work' and 'welfare' were barely comprehended by the Indian masses, Christian women not only legitimized but also popularized the emergence of women in this role. Social historians have barely

---

[114]   Annual Report of American Ramabai Association, 11 March 1895, pp. 29–30.

[115]   Cited in Yashodabai Joshi, *Amchi Jivanpravas* [Our Life Together] (Poona: Venus, 1965), p. 49.

[116]   See Appendix for details on her.

[117]   Much of this literature in terms of its literary value was ephemeral because its content was highly relevant and pressing only in the great religious upheavals of the nineteenth century which gave birth to it in the first place.

[118]   A few examples are: Kashibai Sadashiv Desai, *Aichi Malini* [Mother's Beloved, Malini] (Bombay, 1891); Mrs S. Savarkar, *Grace Dermott, or Help for the Afflicted* (Bombay, 1894); Mrs. S.B. Adhav, *A Piece of Advice for Women* (Bombay, 1894). I was unable to trace any of the above but useful summaries appear in the *Catalogue of Books Printed in the Bombay Presidency Starting from Quarter Ending 30 September 1867*.

touched the social and economic processes which impacted on women's lives, such as the plague and famine outbreaks of the late nineteenth century. In this section, the different ways in which these crises affected women and women's own efforts at coping with them will be charted. To an extent, not hitherto recognized, Indian Christian women were active in plague and famine relief works. But were they prompted solely by social service ideals imbibed from Western Christian discourse or were there other reasons besides religious zeal? As women entered social work they were enmeshed with the economics of opium, drink and the traffic in prostitution associated with the Contagious Diseases Act. In doing so, they also clashed with the colonial government over these issues. It is all the more necessary to consider how and why women opposed the government on these issues when the majority, in the normal course of things, considered the metropolitan state as a harbinger of good for Indian women.

Soonderbai Powar's philanthropic zeal and her confrontation with the government can be traced to the late 1860s. Soonderbai was working in Bombay between 1868 and 1888 as a zenana teacher in high-caste Hindu homes, but she was also regularly called on to supervise Sunday schools and address lunchtime factory meetings where hundreds of mill-hands gathered to listen to her. This brought her into close contact with the working classes of Bombay, and she heard firsthand from the female labourers how the *kunbis* had migrated from their rural villages to Bombay in search of employment in order to clear their debts. Once they had obtained employment, both men and women were forced to work long hours, and the men in particular developed addictions to opium and alcohol in order to relieve the stress of an urban life of continuous toil. However, although they initially provided relief, their long-term effects were much less benign. Through her work in Bombay and visits to other cities, such as Lucknow, where two hundred Muslim women met her and detailed their suffering,[119] Madras and Calcutta, Powar obtained a picture of how these addictions impacted on the lives of the poor, with the increased poverty, unemployment and crime that they caused further exacerbating their misery.

In Britain, the rise of alcoholism and its attendant social problems had prompted both nonconformist and established denominations to found temperance movements to promote abstinence among the working classes, and these organizations provided the template for the anti-drink organizations that Indian Christian women founded in the late 1880s and early 1890s. One such group was the Striyanchi Madhyanishedhak Sabha [Women's Anti-Drink Society][120] in Bombay, which had approximately fifty women members and was chaired by Shevantibai Canaren, with Mrs Shewantibai Nikambe as its secretary. Holding lectures on the subject in factories and schools, they urged women to gently persuade their menfolk to abstain from alcohol. However, although alcoholism was a problem common to both countries, the opium problem was much greater in India than it was in Britain and, in 1889, the London Office of the *Bombay Guardian*, a Christian weekly, approached Soonderbai Powar to enlighten the

---

[119] Storrie, *Soonderbai Powar*, pp. 38–9.

[120] Reported in the Marathi newspaper *Dnyanodaya*, 14 and 21 August 1890.

British public on the matter and present papers on the opium trade. Taking up their offer, she travelled all over Britain in 1888 and 1889, working under the direction of the secretary of the Women's Anti-Opium Urgency League. Her campaign was widely publicized by all the leading papers,[121] and her tour was so successful that she was invited back in 1892–93. On her first tour of Britain alone, Powar addressed 116 meetings, telling her audiences of how opium destroyed the strength of men and led to the ruin of their families, how infants were freely dosed with it to enable their mothers to work in factories, and how unhappy women resorted to it to put an end to their suffering. She also dispelled a great number of 'orientalist' myths about how well opium was suited to the Indian constitution, challenging her audience to administer six grains to her and watch how well it suited her! At another meeting, there was an argument that Indians used it as a medicine, to which she replied, 'when they know that five or six grains is a fatal dose, and yet any one can buy 1,600 grains without any questions asked, how can government claim that it is sold as medicine?'[122] Unlike Britain, where there were strict regulations controlling its sale, the 'so-called Christian' government did not place any limits on the sale of opium in India because of the revenue it gained every year from the trade. From this she concluded that the government's policy indicated no concern for its subjects. Powar was probably the only Indian woman to take an openly confrontational stance with the imperial government over the opium issue, but her cause was not the only instance where a desire to achieve social justice brought her into direct conflict with the British government.

The operation of the Cantonment Acts and plague and famine relief works instituted by the British Government in India had a direct impact on the efficient management and administration of Pandita Ramabai and Soonderbai Powar's educational institutions. For instance, Powar's Zenana Teachers' Training School was situated in the cantonment area of Poona, meaning that she and all members of her establishment could be potentially evicted with only 24 hours notice. When the plague reached Poona in 1897, a few of her girls contracted it meaning that, under the Cantonment Act, she had to vacate the house with the remaining ones. She experienced great difficulty in procuring another large house for her students; a problem further compounded by rocketing food prices and difficulty in finding drinking water. It was only with the help of missionaries that the school was able to survive.[123] The plague regulations also forced Ramabai to move out of Poona for five years, from 1897 to 1903. Like Powar, the move had an adverse affect on her

---

[121] See the article on Soonderbai Powar in *The Woman's Herald*, 14 January 1893, n.p. This newspaper was formerly known as the *Women's Penny Paper*.

[122] Storrie, *Soonderbai Powar*, pp. 39–40.

[123] The American Methodist Episcopal Mission lent her a huge *shamiana* [tent], which she turned into a home for a while. Helen Dyer's 'Introduction' to Soonderbai Powar, *Hinduism and Womanhood*, p. 9.

institution's finances, and eventually the colossal expenditure in energy and money led Pandita Ramabai to shift to Kedgaon permanently.[124]

In 1897, 20 of the girls from Ramabai's institution were classified as suffering from 'fevers' and were taken to the plague hospital. Eighteen were returned back and two were reported dead. Ramabai was not convinced by the death certificates and went to investigate and verify the police statements. She soon found that the 'dead' girls, lured by promises of marriage, had in fact become the mistresses of two Indian officials, one of whom was a policeman. The girls voluntarily went back with Ramabai, who accused the hospital authorities of being negligent and irresponsible, and called for an inquiry.[125] She managed to force the Government of Bombay to inquire into the matter, but it did not find in her favour. The episode illustrated the way in which the act was open to abuse by those in authority. Neither did these acts just affect the pupils at the school; they also had a direct impact on the well-being of the prostitutes in Ramabai's Kripa Sadan. Just like Josephine Butler, whose work with prostitutes in the UK had inspired Ramabai to begin her own rescue work, so too her involvement eventually led her into the more seamy side of the operations of the Contagious Diseases Act.[126] Their campaigns had some success, with the Act being repealed in Britain in 1886, with India following two years later. Yet, despite the fact that the Act had been repealed in India in 1888, the military authorities continued to make provision for the use of prostitutes by British soldiers through the system of registering, inspecting and detaining them in lock hospitals until they were cured of venereal diseases under the Cantonment Acts.[127] Moreover, soldiers prevented female missionaries from starting their own segregation units within the mission compounds, despite the fact that the government camps were cramped and unhygienic. This led her to conclude that the government was sponsoring 'legalized vice'.[128] She publicized the matter through the press in the firm belief that 'The BIRTHRIGHT OF INDIAN WOMEN HAD BEEN TRAMPLED [sic] long enough,' and wrote to her friends and

---

[124] Pandita Ramabai's report to the Executive Committee of The American Ramabai Association, 1903, p. 23.

[125] Pandita Ramabai's letter, *The Bombay Guardian*, 27 January 1897.

[126] For the agitation led by English women against the Contagious Diseases Act, see Judith Walkowitz, *Prostitution and Victorian Society: Women, Class and the State* (Cambridge: Cambridge University Press, 1980).

[127] The Cantonment Acts were amended in 1897 after missionaries and English reformers conducted a sustained campaign against them. Even so, the new Acts allowed prostitutes to live in the camps and compulsory examinations continued to be practised until 1900. For these Acts and the agitation surrounding them, see Kenneth Ballhatchet, *Race, Sex and Class under the Raj: Imperial Attitudes and Policies and their Critics, 1793–1905* (London: Weidenfeld & Nicolson, 1980), especially chapters 2 and 3.

[128] Recently Philippa Levine's work suggests that the whole debate over the Contagious Diseases Act and its functioning in the colonies is symptomatic of a crisis in the metropolitan state itself. See Philippa Levine, 'Rereading the 1890s: Venereal Disease as "Constitutional Crisis" in Britain and British India', *Journal of Asian Studies*, 55/3 (August 1996): 585–612.

supporters in England and America about the atrocities committed against Indian women under the Cantonment Acts for the 'benefit of the British soldiers'.[129] She correctly argued that the Contagious Diseases Act was being brought back under a different guise.[130] She also foresaw the collapse of British rule in India if such iniquities continued. It is significant to note here that, while prominent Indian male leaders such as V.N. Mandlik argued against the Contagious Diseases Act because community lifestyles and women of 'respectable classes' were impacted upon, Christian women reformers argued for the protection of the rights of 'all women', irrespective of their class.[131]

Over famine relief works, too, Pandita Ramabai came into direct confrontation with the government. Her famine relief work in Itarsi and around Poona in the late 1890s brought her in close contact with the management of poor homes and relief works, where she soon discovered that only able-bodied men met their requirements. Women with a delicate constitution or debilitated through lack of food for a long time were unable to break up the twelve baskets of stone required to secure one meal a day and were therefore, according to Pandita Ramabai, forced to 'sell their virtue' to the works officials in order to survive.[132] After conducting her own investigations with the help of some of her trusted female workers in the relief camps, she came to the conclusion that there was an 'organized vice trade' operating within the poor houses and relief camps. Her workers reported that *mukaddams* [low-ranking Indian officials], in the form of cooks, storekeepers, and overseers, were exploiting young orphaned female famine victims, and this was compounded by the apathy and indifference of higher officials.[133] Ramabai argued that the least the government could do to improve the situation was to relax the rules for the employment of women on roads and railways to ensure better protection for them. Instead, when she arrived in Poona with 120 emaciated girls, the City Magistrate debarred her from entering the town, even though she gave him an assurance that she would hire several houses for their welfare. She was forced to take the girls to Talegaon where many of them perished, as the village had no adequate medical facilities.[134] She found that the government obstructed rather than assisted the efforts of private institutions and individuals in famine work.

---

[129] Pandita Ramabai's appeal to 'The Friends of Mukti School and Mission', March 1891, pp. 7–11, ICMMK.

[130] Her letter, *Bombay Guardian*, 6 May 1897, 12.

[131] See Ballhatchet, *Race, Sex and Class*, pp. 48–64.

[132] Pandita Ramabai's experiences in the famine-struck areas were recorded in two articles that were reprinted in two issues of the *Bombay Guardian*. The first article, entitled, 'Famine Experiences in India' appeared on 20 January 1897, 6–9; the second, entitled 'Pandita Ramabai's Second Famine Tour', appeared on 6 May 1897, 10–13.

[133] When Pandita demanded an enquiry, the Deputy Collector admitted to her in the course of the discussion that he was aware of such happenings in the poorhouses but was not in a position to remedy them. Ibid., *Bombay Guardian*, 6 May 1897, 11–12.

[134] Ibid., p. 13.

Yet, even though Christian women were critical of certain aspects of British rule, as their agitation against the Contagious Diseases Act and the drug (opium) and drink movements demonstrates, most of them continued to believe that a *ma-bap* or 'parent–child' relationship between Britain and India was the best one in order to safeguard the interests of Indian women.[135] This belief meant that, in the early twentieth century, Indian Christian women began to be marginalized rapidly both within the women's movement as well as in the broader national campaign that still engaged with social reform activities.[136] In addition, more radical solutions to problems than those offered by the liberal politics of Indian Christian women were now pursued, and it was no longer held that improving the position of women alone would lead to progress in India. It was now widely believed among reformers that the only way for India to progress was to achieve independence, and there was an upsurge in national feeling. Movements such as the *swadeshi* [self-help] not only encouraged nationalist feeling but also the rejection of foreign ideas, including Christianity.[137] They also promoted the boycott of foreign goods and, by 1910, Christian women like Pandita Ramabai and the Sorabji sisters had become completely alienated from Indian society by openly opposing the methods of the nationalist agitation such as the picketing and burning of foreign cloth. Given their lack of public support, Indian Christian women completely lost their previously influential voice and gave way to Hindu female leaders such as Ramabai Ranade, who led the women's movement in India until 1920. It is this movement that we will turn our attention to in the next chapter.

---

[135] Krupabai Satthianadhan, *Miscellaneous Writings*, pp. 32–3; Cornelia Sorabji, *'Therefore'*, pp. 58–61.

[136] Both the English and the vernacular press regularly carried reports on the work of Christian female leaders in the late nineteenth century, but between 1900 and 1920, they are hardly mentioned in the press.

[137] Pandita Ramabai's answers to the questionnaire of Mr Mott and others, World Missionary Conference, n.d., ICMMK.

Chapter 3

Beyond Kitchen and Kid[1]:
Hindu Women's Discourse and Work

Introduction

This chapter charts the trajectories of Indian feminism during the course of the social reform movement and the early nationalist period, turning its attention from Christian women to Hindu women. It will be argued that both the awareness by Hindu women of the 'condition of Indian women', and its extension to consciousness-raising programmes, are critical to any consideration of how nineteenth-century Indian feminism evolved through women's personal experiences, the building of separate female institutions, the growth of the Women's Press and through the development of women's subcultures—female networks, rituals and interpersonal relationships. Hindu women realized slowly that an important precondition for this was their own access to male spheres of influence, as the latter formed a vital source of support for them. This chapter will show that many Hindu women considered Hindu customs and practices the chief culprits for the lowly position of women rather than the religion itself, although a discerning few did argue that women's subordination was a man-made situation. Hindu women's critiques examined women's oppression within Hinduism, but unlike their Christian contemporaries, did not extend to rejecting it.[2]

Approaching Indian history, particularly women's history, through a framework that prioritizes the contest between nationalism and imperialism has led to distortions. Partha Chatterjee, for instance, remarks on the 'relative unimportance of the women's question in the last decades of the nineteenth

---

[1] 'Kitchen and Kid' is an idiomatic rendering of the popular Marathi expression *Chool ni mool*.

[2] Some women embraced various reforming sects emerging within Hinduism during the socioreligious upheavals of this period. Ramabai Ranade, Annapurnabai and Shantabai Bhandarkar were Prarthana Samajists, while Anandibai Joshi's views came close to those of the Brahmo Samaj. Kashibai Kanitkar was a confirmed Theosophist. However, in the public eye, they continued to be regarded as practising 'Hindus'. Rebecca Simeon, on the other hand, a feminist from the Jewish, community had co-founded a new reforming sect with her husband Benjamin called the 'Nitiprasarak Mandal' whose central tenets resembled closely Jyotiba Phule's Satyashodhak Samaj.

century.'[3] Furthermore, he goes on to note that there is a 'seeming absence of any autonomous struggle by women themselves for equality and freedom,'[4] leading him to ask the question, why did the 'women's question' disappear altogether in India at the close of the nineteenth century? His conclusion is that, in the absence of an autonomous women's movement, nationalist discourse 'resolved' it by creating a sharp divide between the public/private spheres and by relegating women to the latter. Chatterjee's assumptions are based on a reading of the situation in Bengal and ignores the crucial works on the tensions between the women's movement and the nationalist movement of scholars such as Geraldine Forbes, Gail Minault, Vijay Agnew, Neera Desai and Pat Caplan to name a few. This chapter will show that his fundamental premise that there was no autonomous women's movement in India, whilst perhaps a more accurate reflection of the situation in Bengal, was not true for all India. As will be shown, in nineteenth-century Maharashtra in particular, women were not only engaged in an autonomous struggle for equality and better treatment but also continued to campaign, even after the arrival of Gandhi and the development of a supposedly all-encompassing nationalism. Further, throughout this period, the women's movement was characterized by tensions between those women who wished to concentrate on women's issues alone and those who saw national independence as a necessary step in the path towards equality. As will become clear, in Maharashtra at least, women were not banished to the 'inner world' of the home, but engaged openly in the public sphere to improve their status.[5] Although women's tactics varied from strategic accommodation to outright hostility towards men, common to all was an awareness of women's subordination as a specific group, *stri jati*, and hence, the creation of the concept of sisterhood, *bhaginivarg*. Prominent feminists formulated theories that Hindu men had created new forms of subordination that could be attributed to different causes.[6] To quote Kashibai Kanitkar, '...when we see the present degraded state of our *bhagini* [sisters], the mind is overcome by anger and displeasure and hence we retort back saying that this condition was brought about because men see us as inferior and harbour mean views about us.'[7] This chapter will therefore include an analysis of the politics of

---

[3] 'The nationalist resolution of the women's question', in Kumkum Sangari and Sudesh Vaid (eds), *Recasting Women*, 2nd edn (New Delhi: Kali, 1993; 1st edn 1989), p. 237.

[4] Ibid., p. 250.

[5] In another article, Chatterjee argues that early nationalists and reformers created a sharp divide between the inner/outer (corresponding to home/external world), whilst women increasingly came to be identified with the former; see Partha Chatterjee, 'Colonialism, Nationalism and Colonized Women: The Contest in India', *American Ethnologist*, 16/4 (1989): 622–33.

[6] Notable amongst them were Kashibai Kanitkar, Tarabai Shinde, Yashodabai Joshi and Lakshmibai Deshmukh.

[7] Kashibai Kanitkar's speech for the 'Women's Society' entitled 'Purvichya Stri ani Hallicha Stri' [Indian Women of the Past and Present], *Subodh Patrika*, 8 May 1882, 7.

the women's organizations of the age and their influence on feminist activists of the time.

Finally, an attempt will also be made to examine the nature of Hindu women's feminism. There were certain common preoccupations among women that served to bind them together, irrespective of caste and class differences. The chapter draws on women's perceptions on a range of issues in order to show the commonalities that existed between them, as well as using them to demonstrate how the women's movement existed as a distinct feminist entity within the wider socioreligious reform movements of the nineteenth century. Their woman-centric approach set them apart from other participants, a difference that will come under examination throughout this chapter. Commencing with an analysis of the growth of Hindu women's consciousness on the issue of women's subordination and their desire for their rights to be recognized, this chapter will demonstrate how it led to the consequent development of separate female organizations that possessed a distinct identity within the nationalist movement.

The Growth of the Women's Movement, 1870–1920: Feminist Strategies and Women's Subcultures

The first generation of Hindu female reformers came from the religious reform organization, the Prarthana Samaj.[8] The founders of this organization were influential men, including Mahadev Govind Ranade, who was a key figure in the movement. Ranade sought a popular base for the mass acceptance of the Prarthana Samaj by adopting the principle that social and religious reform could proceed unhindered on different paths and neither of them need involve a sharp break with the past. More significantly, these self-styled 'Hindu Protestants' regarded most social institutions, such as widowhood and early marriage, as areas that could be reformed without affecting the essential character of Hinduism; by doing this, they hoped to bridge the social gap between the Prarthana Samaj and the general population.[9] As part of their social reform programmes, male reformers also started to educate their wives, sisters and daughters. Women were taught to read and write Marathi informally at home, as well as being instructed on science and other subjects at the Prarthana Samaj in Bombay.

---

[8] *Prarthana Samaj* [Prayer Society] was 'Western India's original contribution to modern Indian theism.' Founded in 1867, its main doctrines were belief in a single God, opposition to authority of priests and idolatry and denial of ideas of Karma and transmigration. For details see Charles Heimsath, *Indian Nationalism and Hindu Social Reform* (Princeton: Princeton University Press, 1964), pp. 72–112.

[9] Some cultural historians cite this strategy of the Prarthana Samajists for explaining the success of the social reform movement in Maharashtra unlike their counterpart, the Brahmo Samaj that remained exclusive and did not reach the average Bengali. Ibid., pp. 104–8.

By the early half of the 1870s, around 50 to 70 women were gathering in the hall of the Prarthana Samaj every Saturday to listen to lectures given by prominent reformers. However, not only did they listen but they also learnt the art of oratory in their own right, leading to the formation of the *Striyancha Sabha*, or 'Women's Society', in the 1880s.[10] This organization conducted weekly meetings for women only, where educated women would read essays, give public lectures and impart instruction in various subjects to other women. The content of the lectures and essays reveal an overriding desire to combat popular prejudices against female education in Maharashtra,[11] whilst simultaneously making women understand the advantages of learning the disciplines of history, geography and science. By the 1880s, as the movement grew stronger, women in other areas such as the towns of Dhulia, Poona, Nasik, Akola, Amravati and Sholapur were forming similar groups, and the process of women instructing their fellow women gathered pace. While the women read the glories of ancient Hindu literature, they also read western literary, philosophical and explicitly feminist texts that dealt with the position of women, with Kashibai Kanitkar, Rukhmabai, Anandibai Joshi and Ramabai Ranade revealing their admiration and influence of the writings of George Eliot, Jane Austen and Mill's *Subjection of Women*.

These women's networks were further strengthened by the transformation of older social events and ceremonies that predated the feminist movement such as the female-dominated *halad kunku* ritual held mainly in western and southern India, and other social gatherings, such as *kirtans,* where learned men and women delivered sermons from religious books or from ancient myths, usually accompanied by musical instruments. These rituals and ceremonies provided a framework which the women's movement could build on to bring their new message about the need for female education and to a wider audience too. The main purpose of the *halad kunku* ritual, for instance, was to honour senior married women, who received offerings of arecanut, flowers and coconuts and had their foreheads dabbed with dots of vermilion and turmeric powders,[12] but it fulfilled a social purpose too. It was here that women could exchange social pleasantries, as well as giving them a forum to publicize their daughters' puberty rites, marriage negotiations and announce new arrivals in the family. The ritual probably originated from a desire on the part of women to relieve themselves of the monotony of household chores, and female reformers, like Annapurnabai and Ramabai Ranade, now expanded the participants' horizons even further by incorporating educational schemes within

---

[10] *Subodh Patrika*, a Marathi weekly and the literary mouthpiece of the Prarthana Samaj, regularly reported the proceedings every week from the 1880s onwards.

[11] See Gangutai Bhandari's speech, *Subodh Patrika*, 6 February 1881, 163; Durgabai Joshi's essay, *Subodh Patrika*, 13 February 1881, 167 and 171.

[12] The quest for *saubhagya* (the blessed state of being married) among Hindu wives is constantly enhanced through fasts and rituals. See Mary McGee, 'In Quest of Saubhagya: Roles and Goals of Women as Depicted in Marathi Stories of Votive Devotions', in Anne Feldhaus (ed.), *Images of Women in Maharashtrian Literature and Religion* (Albany: State University of New York Press, 1996), pp. 147–70.

them, such as readings, lectures and essay contests.[13] Lakshmibai Kirloskar[14], the co-founder of the prominent women's organization of Sholapur, called Saraswati Mandir, recorded the functionalist approach to women's rituals and Hindu festivals thus:

> The programmes of interest to women were *kirtans* and particularly the ritual of *Haldi Kumku* [sic] held on Fridays. A religious flavour always pervaded such ceremonies and therefore persons of traditional as well as modern ideas, old and younger women assembled in large numbers. We eagerly grasped these opportunities to explain some of our erroneous religious beliefs and harmful customs and vows that acted as obstacles to the well-being of our *bhagini* [sisters]. These modern ideas were explained so effectively and playfully that most women who came to these gatherings were convinced quickly. Thus, the *Haldi Kumku* [sic] function was used by us to propagate our views and for organising the activities of the Mandir. Had we decided instead, to hold public meetings, women would certainly not have gathered in such large numbers as the concept of attending meetings was a new one. In those days, following the beaten track was the done thing with most Indian women abiding by age-old customs. Therefore we had to come up with a new method of impressing on them the gains of women's education. *Haldi Kumku* [sic] proved to be a useful strategy.[15]

Kirtans also offered an opportunity for feminist leaders to bring their message to a wider audience. In Maharashtra, there appears to have been a tradition of female Kirtankars, and this effectively made it easier for women's organizations, like the Saraswati Mandir and Seva Sadan, to reorganize them to suit their own new needs. As well as reformers, both 'traditionalists' who followed established practices and customs, and 'conservatives' who had taken a decisive stand against reform, attended these gatherings, and astute female leaders took care to cater to these women in an effort to win their support for the new enterprise of female education.[16] On several occasions, Western women also joined these parties, further breaking down some of the prejudices held by some of the more traditional and conservative women, as well as facilitating the exchange of ideas.[17]

Greater political capacities began to be expressed by women, and this period saw the establishment of the first independent women's organization, the Arya Mahila

---

[13] Sarojini Vaidya, *Shrimati Kashibai Kanitkar: Atmacharitra ani Charitra* [Mrs. Kashibai Kanitkar: Autobiography and Biography] (Bombay: Popular Prakashan, 1979), see p. 14 for *halad kunku* and pp. 89 and 177 for *kirtans* and its new use. Also Ramabai Ranade, *Himself: The Autobiography of a Hindu Lady*, trans. Katherine Gates (New York: Green and Co., 1938), p. 116.

[14] See Appendix for details on her life and work.

[15] Cited in Saraswatibai Kirloskar, *Amrita Vruksha: Saraswati Mandir, Sholapur (1895–1970)* [The Nectar Tree: Saraswati Mandir, Sholapur 1895–1970] (Pune: Kirloskar Press, 1970), p. 37. Hereafter [The Nectar Tree].

[16] Even minute details like food preparation and dining arrangements were supervised personally by female reformers due to the notions of pollution prevalent at the time.

[17] Ramabai Ranade, *Himself*, pp. 116–17.

Samaj,[18] which specifically highlighted women's needs and aspirations. The founding of the Arya Mahila Samaj was Pandita Ramabai's brainchild, but women like Ramabai Ranade and Kashibai Kanitkar worked hard to popularize it among Hindu women. Furthermore, not only did they carry out door-to-door canvassing in order to persuade women to attend the group's meetings, but also, when Pandita Ramabai departed for England in 1883, they became President of its Poona and its Bombay branches respectively. However, just as in the private world of the home and society gatherings, such as the *halad kunku* rituals and kirtans, female reformers faced opposition and encountered great hostility from traditional established forces. The vernacular press were viciously anti-woman and, indeed, the anxieties of these commentators about the growth in women's self-determination in Maharashtra led to the development of a new and sinister literary genre called *stricharitra* [portrait of women].[19]

The response of Hindu women reformers was not to oppose these views outright but to adopt the same methods of accommodation and assimilation that they had previously used when confronted with orthodox women at social gatherings. In order to retain their newly found freedom, and ensure its continuation, these women reformers developed and sharpened a feminist strategy for survival by accommodating Hindu views on Indian womanhood. An analysis of Ramabai Ranade and Parvatibai Athavale's public speeches during this period demonstrates how anxious reformers were at this time to attend to the fears of those who opposed them.[20] Addressing a women's gathering at Tasgaon, Ramabai Ranade stressed that the only way to counter the public opposition to women's education was for educated women to demonstrate that their learning would not, in any way threaten domestic life. Indeed, an educated woman was under an obligation to carry on household work perfectly, and maintain the virtues of obedience and loyalty to the men of the family, in order to demonstrate that education did not erode traditional conceptions of modesty and humility.[21] Parvatibai Athavale went further and strove to accommodate conservative opinion by conforming to many of the symbols of a good widow. She records in her autobiography that even though she believed that no widow should cut her hair (referring to the *keshavapan* or tonsure ceremony) against her will, she herself waited nearly eighteen years before she put this into practice.[22] Nevertheless, although doing much to alleviate the plight of widows, as a principal fundraiser for the Hingne Widows' Home founded in 1902, she

---

[18] Pandita Ramabai had brought various women's groups under the umbrella organization of the Arya Mahila Samaj.

[19] An erudite discussion of *stricharitras* is in Tarabai Shinde, *A Comparison Between Women and Men: An Essay to Show Who's Really Wicked and Immoral, Women or Men?* trans. and intd. Rosalind O'Hanlon (Madras: Oxford University Press, 1994), pp. 38–47.

[20] For biographical details on their life and work see Appendix.

[21] Ramabai Ranade, *Himself*, p. 105.

[22] For details on the tonsure ceremony see the section 'The Question of Widowhood and State Intervention' in this chapter.

had been convinced that if she rebelled too openly against the traditional symbols of widowhood, her work for the widows' cause would suffer.[23]

Ceremonies such as the tonsure one were not only public displays but obviously had a great impact on the individual participants and their familial relationships. There was a great deal of conflict in the home between reformers and more conservative or traditional forces within the family unit. Neither were these divisions wholly split down gender lines, with reformist husbands often clashing with orthodox in-laws, leaving the woman trapped in the middle of a fierce conflict, and bearing the brunt of attacks from both sides. For instance, a young Brahmin widow, writing from Satara to seek the advice of the female audience of *Arya Bhagini* [Indian Sisters], a remarkable women's magazine, told of how her father-in-law (a reformist) would not let his wife (a conservative woman) subject his reluctant daughter-in-law to the horrors of the tonsure ceremony. However, her mother-in-law waited until the men folk left for Pune on business, and seized the moment to begin preparations for the ceremony. Her daughter-in-law immediately wrote to her uncle, informing him of these developments, and he rushed back to deal with the situation.[24] The anxieties they created for women ensnared in the middle of such conflicts were discussed at length in the correspondence columns of the women's press of the nineteenth century, as well as in semi-fictional writings, such as 'Gulabbai ani Shevatibai yancha bodhpar samvad' ['Instructive debates between Gulabbai and Shevatibai'].[25] Just as in social and political situations taking place in the outside world, Hindu female reformers advocated a policy of negotiation and reconciliation with more traditional and conservative factions in the household; indeed, Kashibai Kirloskar, for example, considered 'accommodation' as the most important role of the 'modern' housewife. It was her firm belief that Kashibai Kanitkar's tremendous success in the public arena was because she had learnt this new role of appeasing the old without rejecting the new.[26] This view is reinforced by Kashibai Kanitkar's biographer too, who notes that, due to Kashibai Kanitkar's shrewd assimilative policy, even a conservative leader like B.G. Tilak, who ran the *Kesari*, an influential Marathi newspaper, and generally kept a close eye on female leaders, would often report on her activities in a favourable tone, holding her up as an example, in sharp contrast to his treatment of Pandita Ramabai.[27] Kashibai Kanitkar, in turn, modelled her conciliatory methods on those of Dr Anandibai Joshi who, to quote Kashibai Kanitkar:

---

[23] Parvatibai Athavale, *My Story: The Autobiography of a Hindu Widow*, trans. Justin Abbott (New York: G.P. Putnam and Sons, 1930), especially chapters 7–12.

[24] The girl-widow requested anonymity and consequently the letter appeared titled 'Ek Vidhawa Mulgi' [A Widowed Girl], *Arya Bhagini*, May 1892, 34–5.

[25] Letters by women to the *Kartri* [woman-editor] are also expressive in this regard. See letter dated 26 July 1890 from Majali-Karwar signed by 'Ek Kulvadhu' [A Respectable Housewife] and letter dated 28 July 1890 from Thana by Champubai Nadkarni, *Arya Bhagini*, August 1890, n.p.

[26] Kashibai Kirloskar, 'Striyanchi Kartavya Karmen' [Women's Duties], *Maharashtra Mahila*, October 1901, 174.

[27] For details on Kashibai Kanitkar's life and work see Appendix.

... continuously fought the obstacles in her way for the betterment of the *bhaginivarg*; she reconciled the old and the new views with great foresight and wisdom; she humoured the new impatient reformers without hurting the feelings of the old; having lived for 3 years in a totally Christian nation she did not embrace it but preserved one's own customs without offending the foreigners from whom she gained so much. Where men have failed, she succeeded.[28]

Whilst this section has highlighted how women attempted to achieve reform by a strategy of accommodating to mainstream Hindu beliefs and customs, the next section will demonstrate the rise of new women's institutions that were precisely empowered by this strategy of feminist leadership.

The Rise of New Women's Institutions

Cooperation with Hindu men of both factions, liberal and conservative, as well as attempting to achieve accommodation with women who, despite their traditional or conservative outlook, often had a great deal of influence in the household, had therefore become the defining features in Hindu women leaders' ideology. Such an assimilative tendency marked the conduct of the women's organizations opened by women for the welfare of women.

Many study groups and several women's societies were already operating under female leadership in the late 1870s including Ramabai Ranade's Hindu Ladies Social Club. However, mainly due to a lack of organizational structure, none of these early organizations functioned in a stable manner.[29] The Arya Mahila Samaj was the first organization to demonstrate an ability to thrive with a proper structure and ideology. It had two main objectives, namely

a) To free the gentle women of Bharat (India) from being subjected to blind traditional injustice (viz. child-marriage, dependency due to ignorance and down-right slavery), and

b) To uplift them from their present regrettable state in religion, and virtue and custom, etc.[30]

However, this organization opened its doors only to women belonging to 'respectable' families, thus creating an essentially middle-class women's movement that tended to

[28] Kashibai Kanitkar, *Sou. Dr. Anandibai Joshi Yanche Charitra ani Patre* [Biography and letters of Mrs. Dr. Anandibai Joshi], 2nd edn (Poona: Kanitkar and Mandali, 1912; 1st edn 1889), n.p.

[29] For the fluctuating fortunes of these societies see Sarojini Vaidya, 'Vegvegli Sadye ani Pragat Marga' [Differing Methods and Paths of Progress], in *Ramasmriti* [In Memory of Ramabai Ranade] (Poona: Seva Sadan Society Press, 1984), p. 51.

[30] D.G. Vaidya, *Prarthana Samajacha Itihas* [The History of Prarthana Samaj] (Bombay, 1950), Appendix III, n.p.

campaign only on issues that directly affected its members. Consequently, the popular participation of women under the leadership of various women's organizations began as early as the 1890s over the Age of Consent debates, contrary to what feminist scholarship assumes as beginning in the child marriage controversy over the Sarda Act of 1929.[31]

In 1892, Yashodabai Joshi[32] launched a similar venture, the Vanita Samaj [Women's Society] in Amravati. As with the older society, at first, in order to attract women of all shades of opinions (traditional and modern), they held only *kirtans*, but soon lectures given by prominent male reformers were also organized.[33] In addition to these activities, the women were also encouraged to discuss topics that concerned them, namely, education, widowhood and marriage customs. By 1897, Yashodabai learned more about managerial skills and the Vanita Samaj's programmes grew in scope. She firmly believed that not enough had been done for the qualitative improvement of women's lives and so the Vanita Samaj incorporated two radical principles: (1) no daughters of members of the Samaj should be married before the completion of their first degrees and (2) women should be given a professional education to make them independent.[34] The Vanita Samaj promoted adult literacy classes for women, but enhancing practical knowledge was also an important ideal, as recorded in the child care, nutrition and postnatal care classes that were for wives and mothers. To make widows' lives bearable and useful, she also advertised the newly opened D.K. Karve's Anathbalikashram [Orphaned Widows' Home] at Hingne.

Elsewhere in Maharashtra, the women's movement adopted 'separatism' as a strategy and formed their own organizations;[35] although sympathetic men were allowed to join these organizations, they were normally barred from executive and managerial positions. By 1896, four such female institutions were flourishing in Dhulia, Mehekar-Varhad, Jalgaon and Sholapur. Very little detail is available regarding the Women's Societies of Mehekar-Varhad and Dhulia, although we know that around 250 women were involved in the Women's Sabha of Dhulia under the leadership of Annapurnabai Apte whilst, in Mehekar-Varhad, under the leadership of Tulsabai, about 40 to 50 women were involved.[36] In addition to these societies, around the turn of the twentieth century we also hear about the activities of another women's organization in Jalgaon called Bhagini Mandal [Association of Sisters]. Founded by Girijabai Kelkar, it largely catered to the needs of Brahmin

---

[31] For details, see chapter 6.

[32] For details on her life and work see Appendix.

[33] Yashodabai Joshi, *Amchi Jivanpravas* [Our Life Together] (Poona: Venus, 1965), p. 59.

[34] Ibid, p. 60.

[35] From a comparative perspective, I have found Estelle Freedman's concept of separate institution building useful here. See her 'Separatism as Strategy: Female Institution Building and American Feminism, 1870—1930', *Feminist Studies*, 5/3 (1979): 512–29.

[36] Manoramabai Mitra, 'Striyancha Unnatisambandhichi Prayatna' [Schemes and Efforts made in The Direction of Women's Progress], *Maharashtra Mahila*, August 1901, 52–9.

women;[37] Anandibai Shirke, a Maratha woman, claimed that, only after her arrival in 1925, did the organization throw its doors open to other Hindu women like Pathare Prabhus and Marathas.[38]

A great deal more is known about the women's organization at Sholapur, known as Saraswati Mandir [Home of Learning], whose actions demonstrated the importance of separate female institutions in this period.[39] Separate female institutions normally put the entire executive and managerial aspects in the hands of women with men given non-policy making roles of 'helpers'. Originally founded to train women in those pious and homely traits that were seen as ideal in a woman, the female reformers subtly altered the school's agenda to achieve a more compassionate and equal society through the efforts of women, who they saw as society's moral guardians. The philosophy pursued at the Saraswati Mandir was therefore one that subtly blended traditional and modern ideas. Founded on 27 September 1895, the organization explicitly stated that its aims were 'to make women wise, religious and cultured through *continuous* [my emphasis] education.'[40] The seemingly innocuous objectives included in real terms, more dynamic and radical goals clearly seen in their programmes for the education of girls and mature women over and above the Fourth standard (provided by government schools) and towards a vocational training; hostels run for girls and widows; evening classes for adult women wishing to continue their education; essay competitions and fund-raising for scholarships for the higher education of girls; participation in cottage industrial exhibitions and fairs all over India; sports and library facilities for women and a special school and hostel for orphaned girls. Aside from the fact that it declared itself an all-female institution, with an Executive Committee and Steering Committee chaired only by women, it stressed professional education for women in the traditional roles of *kathakaar* [story-tellers], *puranikas* [religious scripture-readers] and *kirtankars* [religious discourse-givers on public platforms],[41] employing the famous Puranika, Anasuyabai Pandita, as an instructor and fund-raiser.[42] However, although this formed the core of its curriculum, its Fifth Annual Report also mentions how the activities of the institution had extended to incorporate the modern idea of physical exercise for women, providing 'leisure centres for women outside the home' in the form of gardens and parks and a club to play badminton and tennis. In addition to these changes to the curriculum, two trained teachers from the Poona Female High School were also employed to teach in the newly started girls' school, in addition to teaching older female learners, and the institution also supervised the introduction of kindergarten classes in Sholapur.

---

[37] For details on her life and work see Appendix and also chapter 4.

[38] Anandibai Shirke, *Sanjvat* [The Evening Lamp] (Bombay: Mauj Prakashan, 1972), pp. 224–5.

[39] The history and activities of this organization from its inception in 1895 to 1970 is available in Saraswatibai Kirloskar, [The Nectar Tree].

[40] Ibid., see Foreword, p. vi.

[41] Ibid., p. 225.

[42] For details on the life and work of Anasuyabai Pandita see Appendix.

In common with female reformers operating in the personal, social and political spheres, educational reformers, such as Saraswati Mandir's founder, Lakshmibai Deshmukh,[43] followed a policy of assimilating traditionalists' concerns whilst simultaneously initiating a process of subtle change. Although stressing the importance of education for girls well after puberty and marriage, she was also quick to emphasize the lack of education on the questions of *dharma* [Hindu concept of religious duties] in educational schemes for girls.[44] The easily accessible religious tone of its public rhetoric,[45] combined with the Steering Committee's decision to renovate an old disused temple found in the grounds bought by the organization, served to further endear them to the traditionalists. This policy of negotiation rather than confrontation with the Hindu patriarchy was extended to its fundraising methods, which were specifically designed not to alienate traditional opinion but, at the same time, allowed the female reformers to decide where the money would be spent and formulate their own policy. For example, fundraisers had to ensure that women only made donations in their own names, with those dependent on the income of the man of the household advised to convince them to allow the donations to be made in the name of the woman.[46] Their rhetoric allayed the fears of the orthodoxy, and their organizational methods, especially the freedom from male interference in the working of their institutions, meant that they achieved greater autonomy in formulating policy and making decisions. The constitution of the Saraswati Mandir allowed executive positions to be held by women only, with men given merely 'advisory' or 'helper' roles, and this was faithfully followed throughout its career until Indian independence. The Saraswati Mandir was unique in other ways too. It is the only example of a late nineteenth-century women's organization which broke caste, religious, regional and class boundaries, incorporating women belonging to the Brahmin, Maratha, Lingayat, Jain, Gujarathi, untouchable and Kunbi communities.

However, despite its achievements, the Saraswati Mandir's influence on the women's movement in Maharashtra paled into insignificance next to the Seva Sadan [Mission to the Women of India[47]] in Poona, the largest of all the separate female institutions. A branch of this organization had originally been established under the direction of male reformers under the leadership of G.K. Gokhale and G.K. Deodhar, who had founded the school with the intention of training poor women as social workers geared towards national service in the same manner as men were being trained

---

[43] See Appendix for details on her life and work.

[44] Editorial, 'Shri Saraswati Mandir: Nibandhmala' [An Essay on the Women's Institution, Saraswati Mandir], *Maharashtra Mahila*, October 1901, 70–71.

[45] Even the choice of a name for the organization was taken from Hindu scriptures. Literally translated 'Shri Saraswati Mandir' means 'Temple of the Goddess of Learning and Wealth'. The name highlights two revered goddesses of the Hindu pantheon—*Shri* or *Lakshmi* [goddess of wealth] and *Saraswati* [goddess of learning].

[46] Parvatibai Degaonkar, [Saraswati Mandir], *Maharashtra Mahila*, May 1901, 228–9.

[47] Seva Sadan literally means 'Social Welfare Society'. The 'Mission to the Women of India' seems more apt as this was how the Society's members described it officially and it appears to be a more appropriate commentary on their overall objectives and work.

in the Servants of India Society. In 1908, Dayaram Gidumal asked Ramabai Ranade to take over the school; under her leadership, it grew into a premier women's organization in western India, playing a pioneering role in the Maharashtrian women's movement. Gaining control of the Seva Sadan also gave Ramabai Ranade the opportunity of fulfilling her dream, first expressed in her Presidential Speech at the All India Women's Meeting at Bombay in 1904, of '…providing a varied scheme of Adult Women's Education and a professional training or vocational education for adult women taking into consideration the 'wants of grown-up women''[48] particularly to those who were in the category of abandoned wives or widows.[49] Its pioneering philosophy attracted a great deal of interest, and the number of students soon began to rapidly increase. For instance, the branch that was established in Poona on the 2 of October 1909 started with six female students in the first month, reported an increase of 260 by 1910, and, by the end of 1920, had a roll of over 1000.[50] In addition to this, the immense popularity of the institution led the management to open eight other branches in urban areas of Maharashtra between 1909 and 1920 alone.[51] When the Poona Girls' High School was founded by male reformers in 1885, Ramabai Ranade's assistance had been sought by on a purely 'informal' basis; now the all-female council of the Seva Sadan would 'occasionally' seek advice from the 'Gentlemen's Helpers' Committee', consisting of eight leading men from Poona.[52] In order to fund this expansion, it sought donations from elite Hindus, mainly women belonging to the Hindu aristocracy,[53] using the money to employ 40 female teachers on regular salaries.

However, despite the fact that it was founded with money from the aristocracy and run by a managing committee that was largely middleclass, with almost every woman on its Managing Committee drawn from the professional Brahmin families of Maharashtra, the Seva Sadan worked consistently for the welfare of working-class women. Unlike the other educational institutions, which mainly focussed on the provision of education for middle-class women, the Seva Sadan recognized the need for working-class women to be able to work outside the home, and therefore inaugurated the first women's co-operative in western India. Although its beginnings were relatively modest, providing training in domestic or cottage industries like *papad*

---

[48] *Silver Jubilee Album of the Seva Sadan Society Containing Review and Reports of the Varied Activities of the Society at its Headquarters in Poona and at its Outside Branches, 1935* (Poona: Seva Sadan Society Press, 1936), p. 19, 34–5, hereafter *Silver Jubilee Album*.

[49] Indirabai Deodhar, 'Progress of Indian Women', *Diamond Jubilee Souvenir, Poona Seva Sadan Society, 1909—1969* (Poona: Seva Sadan Society Press, 1970), p. 19.

[50] Extracts of various annual reports of *Seva Sadan* in *Mahratta*, 16 October 1909, 496, and 25 May 1913, 165.

[51] These were at Satara, Sholapur, Ahmednagar, Nasik, Alibag, Girgaum, Bhamburda and Bombay. *Silver Jubilee Album*, p. 39.

[52] *Mahratta*, 16 October 1909, 496.

[53] The President of the Society was the Ranisaheb (Princess) of Sangli, Lady Sarasvatibai Patwardhan, and of the six Vice-Presidents, three were princesses of the Indian princely states of Jath, Jamkhandi and Kolhapur. *Silver Jubilee Album*, p. 3.

[pappadum], pickle making, cane work, basket weaving and toy making,[54] it was nevertheless successful in attracting the type of student it aimed to assist. In 1911, the management reported that 40 percent of the students were from very poor families who were eager to earn a decent livelihood, while another 35 percent came from families of modest means and were interested in bettering their circumstances.[55] This desire to work received further assistance by the opening of Crèches and Infant Welfare Centres, which meant that they were no longer constrained by their childcare responsibilities.[56]

As well as being revolutionary in the provision of education in basic crafts for working-class women, the Seva Sadan also pioneered the medical education of women, with Ramabai Ranade and her female staff going to great lengths to break down the prejudices against medical work by women.[57] Indirabai Deodhar, a colleague of Ramabai Ranade, attributed part of this success to Ramabai Ranade's personality and the great respect accorded to her being an exemplary wife and daughter-in-law, but the main reason for her success lay in her extremely ingenious adaptation of the contemporary discourse on motherhood. A predecessor of Gandhi, she was extremely skilful in using traditional Indian notions of 'duty' and 'motherhood' in order to convey a modern idea.[58] She saw 'ideal motherhood' as not necessarily bearing and looking after children well but as a general concept of 'love' for others and 'service' to society. Given this definition, 'motherhood' was, in her eyes, not just a duty but 'women's chief right'.[59] Indeed, far from being unsuited to the role, the fact that the female sex was endowed with these attributes meant that it was important to find ways of harnessing them to promote societal welfare.

Therefore, for the first time in western India, medicine became a socially acceptable and even respectable profession for high-caste Hindu women.[60] Although it mainly trained nurses, training, on average, 25 annually and building two purpose-built hostels to accommodate them,[61] women were also trained as doctors, health visitors and midwives. The curriculum also included short-term courses on subjects such as first aid

---

[54] Female reformers who led the programme were Tarabai Patwardhan, Malathibai Gharpure, Bhinabai Lele and Indirabai Deodhar. Ibid., pp. 27–8.

[55] *Mahratta*, 25 May 1913, 165.

[56] For example, the crèches run by the Seva Sadan in Sholapur could accommodate 300 infants and were meant solely for the children of female mill workers. *Silver Jubilee Album*, p. 12.

[57] In order to convince and assure them the Seva Sadan staff personally visited pupils' parents or guardians eager to train in medical work. Ibid., pp. 35, 47.

[58] For Gandhi's use of traditional Indian symbols to convey a sociopolitical message to women, see Madhu Kishwar, 'Gandhi on Women: Part I', *Economic and Political Weekly*, 5 October (1985): 1691–702.

[59] Umakant, *Kai Shri Ramabai Ranade* [The Great Ramabai Ranade] (Bombay: Hind Mahila Pustak Mala, 1925), pp. 110–11.

[60] Due to the nature of the profession, nursing was associated by Hindus with notions of pollution and hence had been a stigmatized occupation considered fit only for Christians or lower-caste Hindus.

[61] 'Visitor's Remarks', from *Silver Jubilee Album*, p. 35.

and hygiene and home nursing, sanitation and public health, which were popularized by conducting examinations and awarding 'Certificates of Proficiency'. Neither did the Seva Sadan solely focus on teaching practical skills. Hindu tradition meant that many female nurses were reluctant to make physical contact with male patients. In order to encourage them to overcome this fear, Ramabai Ranade asked them to consider all male patients as their fathers or brothers and spoke of nursing as a 'sacred duty'.[62] Moreover, she invested caring for the sick and needy with godliness, a theme easily understood by Hindus, which lessened the opposition to women in nursing roles. In this way, Ramabai Ranade was able to break down conservative opposition to women's entry into medicine.

As well as training health workers in a way that was acceptable to Hindu traditionalists, the Seva Sadan also administered a public health education programme that taught women of all classes practical ways of preventing illness. This meant giving free advice to expectant and parturient mothers on matters of feeding and care of sick infants at various maternity homes, dispensaries and hospitals, as well as providing poor women with supplies of milk, clothing and medicine. They also introduced 'Annual Baby Competitions and Children's Week', an entirely novel concept, to promote the cause of infant welfare even further. The scale and variety of the work that they undertook during this period appealed to a wide variety of interest groups, including Indian eugenicists, nationalists and the colonial elite. Although designed with the primary aim of serving the interests of Indian womanhood, its social programme was built on a broad base of support from a variety of political factions and hence, to a broad spectrum of beliefs.

Yet, although appealing to a wide variety of political interest groups, the Seva Sadan, like the other women's organizations, was apolitical. They believed that eventual political reform could only come about through changes to society; indeed, far from helping their programme, political debate could hamper it. This was not an abstract fear, as the struggles between Indian male leaders over whether it was best to pursue reform by social or political means, such as Gokhale versus Tilak in Maharashtra, demonstrated. Nevertheless, the Seva Sedan's desire to stay outside the sphere of political debate was given a great impetus by the women's press of the time, with some far-sighted female writers, such as the editor of *Maharashtra Mahila*, Manorama Mitra, urging female reformers to take on the mantle of leadership '...when the widow's interests and the woman's cause are being shoved in the corner by male leaders it is imperative for leaders like Mrs Ramabai Ranade to take the lead in this sphere.'[63] As time passed, these sentiments not only appeared in the columns of the women's journals but were also being voiced, not only by some of the older women's organizations, like the Shri Saraswati Mandir,[64] but by members of the Seva Sadan itself. Seeing its role as facilitating the interests of

---

[62] Indirabai Deodhar, 'This I Remember', *Silver Jubilee Album*, p. 33.

[63] Editorial, 'Mahilecha Uddhar' [Women's Welfare], *Maharashtra Mahila*, August 1902, 68.

[64] Ibid., May 1901, 197.

women in society and providing humanitarian aid in times of crisis, such as famines, it was reluctant to affiliate itself to a political cause and actively discouraged its members from participating by imposing regulations on political participation. Such actions did not find favour with many of its members, and, by 1915, many, such as the prominent female nationalist, Indirabai Deodhar, were in disagreement with the Managing Committee's policy of preventing members of the institution affiliating themselves to one particular party. Their actions in dissuading Indirabai Deodhar from joining the nationalist programmes of *swadeshi* [self-help[65]] not only demonstrates a fear that politics would interfere with their work but also a failure to recognize the way in which women aspired to be political beings. They failed to critically evaluate and comprehend the early Congress's rhetoric and Gandhi's propaganda on the inclusion of women's programmes in nationalist discourse, and their refusal to engage with the Legislative Councils led many women to grow increasingly dissatisfied and disgruntled with the Seva Sadan.[66] Although admiration for Ramabai Ranade meant that they continued to support the institution during her lifetime, after her death in 1920 large numbers of women chose to respond to the popular call of the Congress and Gandhi and abandoned the separate female institutions.

However, although they chose to follow the political road to reform, the roots of their attraction to the nationalist movement lay in the fact that it used the same language regarding bold and independent women that had been previously used by the Hindu feminist leaders. Like Ramabai Ranade, Gandhi invoked figures such as Sita, Draupadi and Damayanti as ideals of womanhood, with the added incentive that they could now be men's equals in the hitherto forbidden arena of politics. Therefore, far from being passively absorbed by the nationalist movement, as Partha Chatterjee argues, women who already possessed a distinct identity as female reformers *actively chose* [my emphasis] to join the nationalist movement in order to gain the political power that they felt the social reform movement denied to them. What they failed to foresee was that, as the nationalist movement gathered strength in the twentieth century, their hopes and aspirations would be subsumed within a wider agenda for political reform and the nebulous goal of national liberation. Nevertheless, despite the fact that the identity of the female reformers blurred into the nationalist movement to the extent that it almost disappeared, the distinctly woman-centred programmes of the Hindu women's movement undertaken so far show the way in which women were increasingly carving out an identity for themselves during the late nineteenth and early twentieth century. The 'woman-centric' social reformist ideology and separate institution building of this period are a physical manifestation of this change, but underpinning it is the development of an ideology that did not accept the traditional notions about a woman's role being in the 'home' alone. The notion that women had to step beyond the 'kitchen and kid' routine had already been spearheaded by dynamic Hindu feminist leaders, and intrinsic to the development

[65] 'This I Remember', *Silver Jubilee Album*, pp. 30–31.
[66] Ibid., p. 37.

of this ideology is literature (including journals) and education, and it is to these areas that we now turn our attention.

On the Question of *samajik sudharana* [social reform]: Creation of a Women's Press

A great deal of effort has been expended in seeking explanations for male reformist motivation for social reform in the nineteenth century, including the recreation of a past 'Golden Age' of Hinduism, the threat posed by Christianity and the attempt to reclaim political power over the country.[67] However, through all these disparate explanations runs a common thread, an increased awareness of national identity, a theme that is also evident in the increased artistic and literary output of material in the vernacular during this period. Far from being theoretical abstractions, the art and literature produced reflected the hopes and concerns of both the reformers and those who opposed them. Yet, although this phenomenon has been considered in detail by scholars, they have paid rather less attention to whether the experiences of the male reformers during this period were mirrored by their female counterparts. To what extent did women welcome social reform, and did the debates lead to a comparable increase in literary and artistic output?

Certainly, the issues surrounding the often quoted phrase—*samajik sudharana*, or 'social reform', aroused many shades of opinion amongst women, necessitating an outlet for the expression of their views. An ideal medium for them to communicate with one another was through the mode of print periodicals, which provided a place where they could discuss their problems in letters, either published in their original form or in quoted excerpts, and solicit solutions from the journal's readers. Journals, such as those created by the 'women's press' in Maharashtra, conducted wholly by and meant only for women in the Marathi language, allowed for the development of the notion of *bhaginivarg* [sisterhood] within a larger women's collective. [68] By providing a space where women could freely discuss the issue of social reform and its implications on every aspect of women's lives,

---

[67] Heimsath, *Indian Nationalism*, and more recently Kenneth Jones, *Socio-Religious Reform Movements in British India* (Cambridge: Cambridge University Press, 1989).

[68] I have identified 10 Marathi journals run by *kartris* or 'women-editors' that collectively encompass the women's press of the late nineteenth and early twentieth centuries. The periodicals were meant for an audience of women and came from different parts of Maharashtra. They are: *Arya Bhagini*, edited by Anandibai and Manakbai Lad; *Saubhagya Sambhar*, edited by Sarubai Goa from Kolhapur; *Swadesh Bhagini*, edited by Tarabai Navalkar from Bombay; *Subhodini*, by Godubai Shinde from Nipani; *Strisaundarya Latika*, by Mrs Penkar from Bombay; *Bhamini Prakash*, by Chimabai Kadam from Poona; *Maharashtra Mahila*, by Manorama Mitra of Bombay; *Grihini Ratnamala*, by Sitabai Sawant in Bombay; *Striyanchi Maithrini*, by A.A. Abbott, a female missionary; and finally *Simanthini* for which I have no details. The runs vary greatly but their life-span approximately begins in the late 1870s and ends in the 1920s.

including education, domestic economy, religious and national identities, urban versus rural life, the conduct of religious rituals and widowhood, as Susie Tharu and K. Lalitha have previously asserted, the 'women's periodicals' were a key instrument in the transformation and progression of the women's movement in India.[69] Indeed, such was the importance of the issue to many of its female readership, that many of the women's journals devoted whole issues to the subject.

This is not to say that all correspondents to the journal welcomed reform; indeed, many traditional and conservative women were vocal in their opposition to them, believing that the old ways were far superior. Far from dismissing these viewpoints, women's journals took a nonpartisan stance that allowed their readers to hear voices from both sides of the debate, as the publicity page of the *Saubhagya Sambhar* from the town of Kohlapur demonstrates:

Let Dialogue be our Teacher

Dear sisters! 'Social Reform'—now this is a topic on which we sisters, express a range of opinion—and no matter how different it may be to our own—is solicited here! 'Halad kunku' (another name for the same journal) wishes to inaugurate a debate on the topic and opens up a single portal through which contrary views are made available so that our readers can form their own opinions from this dialogue. All opinions, be it progressive or of a traditionalist hue will find a place here. However, your views must be free of slander and prejudice. The Marathi language used to compose the pieces should be fluent. These are our only conditions.[70]

It provided a forum for women belonging to both sides of the debate to discuss the reforms and develop a better understanding of the fiery issues of the day. By doing this, they created an environment that allowed women to freely express their views and develop their own distinct identity. Unlike those women's magazines edited by men, which were didactic in nature and usually intolerant of discussion and dialogue, the journals produced by women for women created an environment that allowed them to express their views unmediated by the menfolk that retained control over many other aspects of their lives.

As well as facilitating dialogue between opposing factions of women within India, columns such as *Jagojagachi strivrit* [Worldwide News on the Woman's Cause] in the women's press, such as *Arya Bhagini* and *Maharashtra Mahila*, provided Indian women with an insight of the progress of the women's movements in other countries, including Britain, America, Russia, China and Japan. The achievements of courageous and career-orientated European women, ranging from medieval figures, such as Joan of Arc, to their own contemporaries, such as Miss Manning, Florence Nightingale and Elizabeth Garrett Anderson, alongside those of local women were described, and women readers were encouraged to aspire to them.[71] Yet, although Indian women were encouraged to

---

[69] *Women Writing in India* (New York: Feminist Press, 1991), pp. 167–9.

[70] December 1905.

[71] The life and works of these women regularly appeared in women's magazines.

see these individual Western women as role models, Maharashtrian feminists, like Anandibai Joshi and Parvatibai Athavale, warned them against blindly adopting Western values. On their tours of America, they had seen how conjugal relationships in the West had broken down, and sought to safeguard Indian families from the same fate. Indeed, some Indian women went further and argued that Western feminism did not just pose a threat to the family unit but posed a threat to the very identity of women themselves. Girijabai Kelkar argued that the provision of higher education for women in the West had led to them developing undesirable competitive traits;[72] their 'natural tenderness and soft nature is replaced by individualism, hatred and harshness', along with the 'avoidance of maternal responsibilities'.[73] Indian feminists did not wish to adopt an equally alien masculine persona but rather the freedom to express their identity in their own right. The ideas of women reformers were not built on Western foundations; instead, as Girijabai Kelkar argued, 'The concept of equality is a new phrase that Indians have learnt from the West and applied in politics alone, but as far as practice is concerned, equality between male and female has been in our country from ancient times onwards.'[74] Far from renouncing their national identity in pursuit of reform, female reformers saw themselves as patriotic by reviving concepts of gender equality that belonged to the 'Golden Age' of Hinduism. Indeed, Anandibai Prabhu Desai protested that the use of terms such as *bandhivasan* [bondage] and *dasyatva* [slavery] in describing the condition of Indian women, in contrast to terms such as *swatantra* [freedom] and *mokaleek* [independent], which were used to describe the position of Western women, were an injustice to Indian women,[75] arguing:

> Some people amongst us hold the view that the concept of education for Indian women has been borrowed from the West. But in a country where there are female deities for learning, wealth, and justice etc., and where jewels amongst women like Leelavati, Gargi, Kani and Ahilyabai Holkar have lived, to express such an opinion is indeed an erroneous and preposterous statement.[76]

By appealing to nationalist sensibilities, Indian female reformers were, at the very least, able to neutralize some of the objections to the idea that the Hindu orthodoxy could have raised. Indeed, in some respects, they made *samajik*

---

[72] Girijabai Kelkar, 'Hindu Samajatil Strishikshanache Pudil Dyaya' [The Aims of Women's Education in Hindu Society], in *Grihini Bhushan: Pushpahar, Bhag Dusra* [Guide-books for Women, Part Two] (Jalgaon: Babaji Press, 1921), pp. 10–17.

[73] Ibid., p. 14.

[74] Girijabai's speech as the Chair of the Eighth Women's Conference, held at Wardha, 27 October 1934. In *Shri. Sou. Girijabai Kelkar Yanchi Adhyakshiya Bhashane* [The Presidential Speeches of Mrs Girijabai Kelkar] (Dhule: Magh, Prakashan, 1957), p. 40.

[75] Anandibai Desai, 'Which is the Most Appropriate Curriculum for Women?' *Maharashtra Mahila*, August 1901, 74–5.

[76] Ibid., p. 74

sudharana or social reform a patriotic duty, giving them a powerful weapon in breaking down the resistance of traditional and conservative women, such as mothers-in-laws, who had been conditioned to oppose their daughter-in-laws' education.[77] In the eyes of many Hindu female reformers, although Western feminism provided them with a key to access their feminist identity, the core of this identity had, in fact, been formed in the 'Golden Age' of Hinduism, as this extract from Gulabbai illustrates:

> I feel that as women realize and learn and educate themselves, Western ideas will seep into their minds. Then the transformation will take place amongst women who will just go back to our own pristine and glorious past and consciously revive the custom of choice in marriage and the evil custom of child marriage will die away...[78]

Thus, the notion of gender equality, a highly controversial subject for Indian men, was reinterpreted and recast by Hindu women of the nineteenth century as one that was 'Indian' and 'Western' at the same time, an idea reflected in the pages of the school magazine of Poona's earliest High School for Girls, now called the Huzur Paga School. This school produced some of the most influential Maharashtrian nationalists between 1910 and 1947;[79] throughout the essay, a consistent theme is that rights, equality and self-reliance are not new concepts but ones that had existed in the Hindu past. According to their arguments, Indian women were simply striding back into the past to reclaim their rights, and thus such ideas as self-reliant and educated women that use their degree to progress beyond the 'kitchen and kid' routine and those who work for a cause or mission should be celebrated rather than condemned.[80]

Instead of dismissing nationalism embodied within the 'Golden Age' debates, the female reformers were instead taking it and using it as ballast to give weight to their appeals for equality. Yet, as the articles written by women in this period also demonstrate, such nationalism did not involve an unquestioning acceptance of the concepts of 'nation', 'nationality', 'religion' and 'worship' that constituted their identity. Indeed, Heimsath has argued that Indian discourse on social reform typically involved a revolt against prescribed ways of behaving, customs, institutions, and that the movement was rooted in a rationalist and egalitarian framework. To many women, ritual had obscured the true nature of religion, with Parvatibai Athavale arguing in a speech that:

> Whenever a question is posed to women such as: 'Which is your nation? What is your religion?' The answer inevitably is: 'Satara is my nation.' 'Wai is my nation.' 'Dharwad is my nation.' And, circling the Tulsi plant and the Peepal tree is my

---

[77] Semi-fictional works in several women's journals carry these notions.

[78] 'By an educated lady', 'Instructive Debates', *Arya Bhagini*, June 1891, 52.

[79] Vidya Bal, *Kamalaki* [Aunt Kamala] (Bombay: Mauj Prakashan, 1972), especially chapter 6.

[80] Indumati Kelkar, 'Adarsh Hindi Striyanchi Kartavya' [Duties of the Ideal Indian Woman], *Balikadarsh*, April 1936, 30–32.

religion, making offerings to God is my religion, burning of oil lamps is my religion. Really, I am serious when I say that no one knows any longer what true religion is.[81]

Rethinking issues of religion, custom and beliefs were integral to the women's movement of late nineteenth-century Maharashtra. From within the belly of this re-examination of Indian religions and their philosophical underpinnings came a novel view of the whole concept of *dhandharma* [philanthropy], which was separated from traditional ideas of Hindu Dharma. To continue with the example of Parvatibai Athavale, she argued that rituals that involved expensive ceremonies at temples should be abandoned, with the funds instead diverted to supporting institutions such as the Hingne Widows' Home in Pune. Charity itself came to be redefined by the premier women's organization of Sholapur, Saraswati Mandir, as gifting to the needy without discrimination of caste or sex rather than gifting to religious institutions such as temples. The novel concept of the *Mushti* Fund [Fistful of Charity] was the brainchild of Mrs. Lakshmibai Kirloskar.[82] In 1898, Saraswati Mandir incorporated hostels for girls and widows seeking a vocational education in Sholapur but the funds were inadequate. Although the girls could be housed in buildings donated by wealthy families for the same purpose, meals could not be arranged so easily. At this time, Lakshmibai invented the concept of the *Mushti* Fund, understood popularly as a 'fistful of charity'. Women organizers went collecting fistfuls of grains from residential homes in Sholapur. Lakshmibai herself explained this innovative concept as one that would not exclude any human as: 'an act of charity should include everyone despite his or her caste, religion, sex or status' and indeed, the rich metaphor of the 'fist' captured the idea brilliantly.[83] The model of charity embodied in the *Mushti* Fund had caught the imagination of philanthropic-minded Maharashtrians and remains highly visible and popular to this day. The topic of *dhandharma* [philanthropy] was constantly revisited by women in this period, who, in the process, radically transformed its meaning from the traditional one of supporting the priesthood and temple-going to a modern one of assisting social causes. By undertaking a process of critically evaluating the function of religious ceremonies, they were not attempting to destroy religion but rather modernize it and, in the process, reconstitute their social institutions.

The temple rituals reflected the public face of religious observances, but equally important in the Hindu calendar were the fasts and feasts held in the home to mark festivals, and the rites of birth and death. With their prominent position in the domestic sphere, it is unsurprising that women played, and continue to play, critical roles in handling food, cooking and dining arrangements; indeed, their role as guardians of Indian culture over the centuries has been widely studied

---

[81] 'Dipushtachi Ghaan' [Stench from Temple Lamps], *Saubhagya Sambhar*, November 1905, 76.

[82] Saraswatibai Kirloskar, [The Nectar Tree], p. 45.

[83] Ibid., p. 44.

by sociologists and anthropologists of the subcontinent.[84] Given the importance of the woman in the household, it is therefore predictable that the subject-matter of women's literature in this period is typically focussed on devotional works[85]; women's rituals[86]; entertainment and pleasure pursuits for women[87]; culinary skills[88]; the arts of embroidery, knitting and crocheting[89]; home improvement and embellishment.[90] Yet, despite their traditional themes, they are not attempting to preserve the old situation where women (particularly widows) became trapped in monotonous ritual but rather to enhance the quality of life for the average Indian woman of the nineteenth century. They saw women's powerful position in the household as something to be cherished and, to this end, sought to protect and elevate domestic work to a 'respectable' status rather than its abolition, as Godavaribai Pandita's Preface to her treatise on culinary skills demonstrates.[91] Godavaribai's aim was not just to produce a cookbook, although this was indeed the first Maharashtrian book on the subject, but aimed to provide remedies that would stem the supposedly deteriorating physical health of the nation. She argues

---

[84] R.S. Khare and M.S.A. Rao (eds), *Food, Society and Culture: Aspects in South Asian Food Systems* (Durham: North Carolina Press, 1986).

[85] Representative are Anandibai, *Anandibaikritpancharatnageet* [Composition of Anandibai on Hindu Theology, Philosophy and Devotional Subjects] 2nd edn (Bombay: Ganpat Krishnaji, 1896; 1st edn 1870?); Kashibai, *Sangita Sitashuddhi* [The Purification of Sita in Verse], (Bombay: Nirnaya Sagar, 1897); Lakshmibai kom Dattatreya Bhave, *Ganapatiche Ganen va Striyanche Nashibacha Dakhala* [Songs in Praise of God Ganapati and Musings on the Fate of Women] (Poona: Siddhi Vinayak, 1895).

[86] Among others see, Shrimant Sagunabai alias Tai Saheb Pant Pratinidhi, *Vatasavitri Akhyan* [Legend of the Divinity Savitri] (Satara: Pandurang Sakharam Kashikar, 1888); Ambabai alias Lakshmibai Siddhaye, *Padya Sangraha* [Collection of Hymns] (Bombay: Indian Printing Press, 1888).

[87] Ramabai Indukarin Inamdar, *Striyakarita Manoranjak Ganyacha Pustak* [Poetry for Women's Entertainment] (Pune: Shivaji Press, 1884); Bhagirathibai Madgavkarin (comp.), *Muli va Striyansathin Fugadya, Kombada, Jhima, Pinga, Ithyadi Manoranjak Ganen va Khel* [Fugdi, Kombada, Jhima, Pinga and Other Entertaining Songs and Games for Women and Girls] (Bombay: Jagadishwar Press, 1885).

[88] Parwatibai and Shripatirao Kondoji Yelwande, *Mausa Paka Nishpatti* [Cookery Manual on Meat Dishes] (Poona: Chitrashala, 1883); Godavaribai Pandita, *Pakdarpan athava Maharashtriya Swayampakashastra* [Cookery Manual or Maharashtrian Culinary Science] (Poona: Dnyan Chaksu, 1893).

[89] Mainabai, *Urnavyuti athava Lonkarichi Vina* [Manual on Knitting Woollen Clothes] (Poona: Shivaji Press, 1886); Yesubai Dharadhar, *Sutachya Vina Kamachen Pustak* [Manual on Weaving Cotton Clothes] (Bombay: Nirnaya Sagar, 1898); Rukminibai Sanzgiri, *Sutachi Veenkam Shiknache Pustak* [The Art of Crochetting], 2nd edn (1st edn 1891), (Bombay: Gopal Narayan, 1902).

[90] Godavaribai Panditina *Rangavallika athava Rangoli ani Leni Kadnyachi Pustak* [Art Of Rangoli and Drawing Figures Using Coloured Powders and Dyes] (Bombay: Bombay City Press, 1889).

[91] For details of her life and work see the Appendix.

that the contemporary habit of visiting hotels and resorting to restaurant food should be discouraged as it led to ill-health because of the unsanitary conditions prevalent there, and by treating culinary skills with disrespect, it had contributed to the declining science of cookery. She argued that male hoteliers, whom she described as 'talentless and dirty people given to opium and tobacco chewing habits,'[92] had caused cooking to be unfairly relegated to the status of an 'inferior' art. By reviving the traditional science of cookery, Godavaribai Pandita hoped to restore it to a position where it was once more 'respectable' for middle-class Maharashtrian housewives to practice it, allowing them to contribute to an improvement in public health. Far from dismissing the domestic sphere, we can therefore see that many female Indian reformers apart from the agenda of re-empowering womanhood also saw it as a way of effecting change in the public sphere as well.

Outside the home, another area where there was increasing demand for books was for the instruction of the pupils of the girls' schools that were beginning to proliferate in the late nineteenth century. The need for textbooks on subjects such as drawing, embroidery, biographies of great men and women, geography, and home decorative arts provided educated Maharashtrian female writers an entry route into the commercial world of publishing; their success can be judged by the number of editions that some of the school textbooks underwent.[93] Chimabai kom Lakshman Kadam is an excellent example of the way in which many educated women supplemented their husband's income by utilizing their skills to serve the burgeoning school textbook market. Before she became a cartographer, it appears that she was a copyist of some sort; however, the demand for maps in Maharashtrian schools meant that she instead switched to cartography from the 1880s to the 1900s.[94] This strong business sense is not only demonstrated by their awareness of what the market wanted but also reflect their awareness of the value of the work they were producing; indeed, many promising women writers including the 'isolated' Tarabai Shinde held the copyrights to their own works, indicating a much higher level of alertness in business and public ventures.[95] In this area of publishing at least, women were able to assert themselves in a way that would have been unthinkable in the past. Although very different forms, the campaigning journalism of the women's press, the domestic science treatises and the school textbooks are notable, therefore, in demonstrating an increased self-confidence in building a distinct women's identity.

---

[92] Godavaribai Pandita, [Cookery Manual], p. 4.

[93] Books on embroidery, weaving, women's rituals and home arts ran into several editions and were printed in batches of 500 and sometimes over a 1000 copies in the late nineteenth century.

[94] For details on her life and work see Appendix.

[95] This information is culled from *Catalogue Of Books Printed in the Bombay Presidency Starting from Quarter Ending 30 September 1867 To Quarter Ending 31 December 1896.*

Literary scholars of western Indian languages have attributed the transformation of the literatures of Gujarati and Marathi to the impact of British rule and introduction of European education on India.[96] This finding is supported by Ian Raeside, who cites the introduction of Western style schools and colleges, the founding of debating and literary societies, and the adoption of Shakespearean theatre in Marathi drama groups as contributing factors to the 'creation of an entirely new literature in the years between 1830 and 1870.'[97] Although the period of the Maharashtrian women's renaissance was slightly later, between 1860 and 1920, their writing demonstrates this strong Western influence, as they utilized genres such as essay writing, novels and short stories to disseminate their message of reform. The massive growth in publication during this period gave them new ways of expressing themselves and communicating that had never been open to them before. Although more traditional Indian genres, such as the ballad and religious poetry (Bhakti hymns), continued to exist, the new forms allowed women to create 'resistance' literature, in the form of treatises and tracts which used inversion techniques and role reversals to explore gender relations, aimed at suggesting a different, a more egalitarian world.[98]

Yet, despite their relative success in this area, women still had to tread carefully. Most Hindu women who entered the world of publishing did so on topics that were regarded as respectable and appropriate for female consumption, with manuals on cookery, rites and fasts, embroidery, lace-making and cotton clothes weaving all coming into this category. Rather less well received were female forays into the field of novel writing, with those women who attempted the form often facing criticism that bordered on ridicule. An example of this are the comments that followed the publication of one of Salubai Tambwekar's[99] attempts to merge the fantasy-based themes of Marathi literature with the newer forms of romantic comedy borrowed from the English novel, with critics describing it as a 'very foolish and absurd story ... wretched both in matter and manner'.[100] What is clear from a survey of the Marathi literary scene is the enthusiastic entry of women in appreciable numbers: many of them welcoming the 'condition of women' as a moot question posed within the social reform movement, which they adapted and wrote about in their literary ventures. Writing had thus given women the opportunity to *recast themselves* as modern women, preparing themselves for

---

[96] M.K. Nadkarni, *A Short History of Marathi Literature* (Baroda: Luhana Mitra Press, 1921).

[97] Ian Raeside, 'Literature, Regional Languages: Marathi, Gujarathi, Konkani', in F. Robinson, (ed.), *The Cambridge Encyclopaedia of India* (Cambridge: Cambridge University Press, 1989), p. 437.

[98] This style is discussed in length in the next chapter.

[99] See Appendix for details on her life and work.

[100] See remarks of the critic entered on the 30th June 1873. From *Catalogue Of Books Printed in the Bombay Presidency Starting from Quarter Ending 30 September 1867 To Quarter Ending 31 December 1896.*

the rapid changes brought by the colonial world, but the critical reaction to Salubai Tambwekar's work shows also the vitriol shown towards those who went beyond the boundaries of what general society at this time regarded as acceptable. Nevertheless, despite these limitations, the Maharashtrian literary renaissance allowed female voices to be heard for the first time. Indeed, by the early part of the twentieth century, even the advice manuals run by men were soliciting articles from 'traditionalist' women that would support their argument.[101] We can therefore not only hear the voice of female reformers in the literature of this period but also their female opponents, allowing us to reach a greater understanding of what women in this period thought about the changing society around them.

Debates between 'Traditionalist' and 'Progressive' Women on Female Education

It should at this point be emphasized that these developments wherein women took part in literary and educational ventures in their own right seems to be unique to Maharashtra during this period and are not paralleled elsewhere in India.[102] Indeed, Maharashtra seems to have had a much more liberal attitude towards women than elsewhere in India during this period, with Maharashtrian women who travelled to parts of Bengal and Punjab struck by the differences in the way women dressed as well general attitudes towards women. Anandibai Joshi, for instance, describes how, when living in Calcutta in 1881, she was pelted with stones whenever she went to the bazaar on her own, commenting:

> This country [referring to Bengal] is not a good one for us for we are living in a manner not warranted by its customs ... There is so much of the Zenana [women's secluded quarters] system here that a woman can scarcely stand in the presence of her relatives,—much less before her husband. Her face is always veiled. She is not allowed to speak to any man,—much less laugh with him. Even the baboos, [Bengali middle classes] who have spent years in England, will not drive here, with their wives, in open carriages.[103]

This impression is echoed in the experiences of Ramabai Ranade who, when she saw groups of Bengali female pilgrims in Mathura and Pushkar, asked them why they were not wearing *cholis* [blouses]. They responded sharply, asking her if the

---

[101] See for example the six-month run from May to November 1916 of *Grihini Ratnamala* which contains a minimum of two pieces by women.

[102] Scholars have shown how even the more independent-minded among Punjabi and Bengali women during the same period could not break free from the ideological straitjacket of the male intelligentsia. Madhu Kishwar, 'Arya Samaj and Women's Education: Kanya Mahavidyalaya, Jalandhar', *Economic and Political Weekly*, 26 April 1986, WS: 9–24; Malavika Karlekar, 'Kadambini and the Bhadralok: Early Debates over Women's Education in Bengal', *Economic and Political Weekly*, Ibid., WS: 25–31.

[103] C.H. Dall, *The Life of Anandabai Joshi* (Boston: Roberts Brothers, 1888), p. 40.

women from her region enjoyed walking about rudely with their heads uncovered in the presence of men?[104] Maharashtrian women reformers were proud of recounting to strangers that except in aristocratic families, the custom of *purdah* [forms of seclusion] was very rare in the provinces ruled by the Marathas, regardless of what religion was practised.[105] Hence, Maharashtrian female reformers were generally hostile towards it, regarding it as a form of oppression. Indeed, some feminists were able to use the custom of non-veiling to empower women better, with Pandita Ramabai quoting it to exclude unaccompanied men from attending her lectures, as *purdah* was not a Maharashtrian practice. Yet, although they would not have tolerated this practice in their own schools, when they heard about their feminist sisters' educational ventures in northern and central provinces of India, they turned a blind eye to it. Like Athavale, who continued to allow her widowed students at the Hingne Widow's Home to be subjected to the tonsure ceremony even though she was personally opposed to it, the female reformers believed that progressive changes in the lives of women would only be achieved through the strategy of accommodation of certain customs, even when they were injurious to women.[106]

Yet, although Maharashtrian society was depicted as being more liberal than elsewhere in India, there were deep divisions over what shape reform should take and its purpose, leading to the emergence of two broad camps of opinion; the 'traditionalists', who believed in physiological or biological theories of difference between the sexes, and 'progressives', who believed that both sexes were equal.[107] The traditionalists did not necessarily oppose reforms per se. Indeed, they agreed with the progressives that primary education for girls was crucial in ending practices that endangered society—ranging from the administration of love-potions to neglectful husbands (which were actually poisonous substances), hiding children from vaccinators and branding recalcitrant children for not attending school—that were a direct result of a lack of education.[108] Moreover, traditionalists also concurred with the progressives that the only way to prevent a breakdown in conjugal relations between highly educated husbands and illiterate wives, was to ensure that women were given the education to enable them to relate to their husbands. This point of view was indeed, very well-expressed by one middle-class housewife who expressed her fears in a women's magazine thus,

---

[104] Ramabai Ranade, *Ranade: His Wife's Reminiscences*, trans. Kusumavati Deshpande (New Delhi: Government of India, 1963), p. 122.

[105] Sarojini Vaidya, *Mrs Kashibai Kanitkar*, p. 88.

[106] *Maharashtra Mahila*, October 1901, 146.

[107] Two prominent leaders, Ramabai Ranade and Kashibai Kanitkar illustrate the existence of two 'camps' within the women's movement. Ramabai Ranade, *Ranade,* p. 105; Sarojini Vaidya, *Mrs. Kashibai Kanitkar*, p. 80.

[108] Manoramabai Mitra, 'Naval Vishesh' [Special News], *Maharashtra Mahila*, April 1901, 174; Anon., 'Mulana Devi Kadnyachi Avashyakata' [The Necessity of Vaccination for Children], Ibid., April 1901, 170–73.

'... modern lifestyles have resulted in compartmentalising the thoughts of illiterate wives and educated husbands. It has brought a rift between the thought processes of men and women ...'.[109] In fact, in a departure from the conservatives, traditionalists accepted that, in some circumstances, economic necessity and the idea of *seva* [social service] meant that certain categories of women, particularly those of lower and upper class origins, could venture out in the public sphere. Sharing the general conviction that the female sex possessed finer sensibilities, the traditionalists often recommended a literary career for the upper-class women, unencumbered by housework,[110] an elevated career that was in sharp contrast to those of household management they recommended for middle-class women to follow and, as an economic necessity, menial jobs for lower-class women.

The ideal education for middle-class women, according to the traditionalists at any rate, should focus on equipping them with the skills to manage a household on a budget that was often extremely limited due to the meagre earnings of husbands and fathers in the service professions. In order to alleviate the situation of making ends meet on a salaried income, traditionalist women recommended that women were skilled in the science of *katkasar* [thrift], with Krishnabai Malvadkar, who edited a women's magazine, commenting:

> People have been defining women's education in ways that suit them, but considering the present-day situation of women, I interpret the word education as follows, 'Learn everything which is necessary for the efficient maintenance of a household', which means learning to read and write Marathi ... and any skill that contributes to domestic matters.[111]

Teaching them to take pleasure in reading and writing was an integral part of diverting their attention from desiring expensive trinkets and other material goods that could prove a drain on household finances. Instead, with an education in domestic management, the skills in thrift that they learned meant that they became an asset to their families, and, indeed, society as a whole.[112] This traditionalist view of women as nurturers, providing the family with security and care within the home (i.e., nursing the elderly and the proper care of children) was reinforced by the 'Advice Manuals' that male publishers, distributors and editors produced for housewives in the nineteenth

---

[109] Anon., 'Eka Brahman Striyen Stri Shikshanavar Vyakhyana' [A Brahmin Woman's Essay on Women's Education], *Arya Bhagini*, February 1891, 20.

[110] Anon., 'Garib, Madhyam, va Shrimant Striyani Apaplya Yogyate Pramane Upayogi Asave' [Appropriate Occupations for Lower, Middle and Upper-Class Women], *Arya Bhagini*, April 1890, 33–4; Anandibai Prabhu Desai, 'Which is the Most Appropriate Curriculum for Women?', *Maharashtra Mahila*, September 1901, 122–8.

[111] *Simantini*, August 1893, 1–3.

[112] Radhabai Sheti, 'Stri Shikshana Sambandhi Matbhed' [Difference of Opinions on Women's Education], *Arya Bhagini*, August 1890, 96; Anandibai Prabhu Desai, 'Striyas Uttam Shikshan Kontha? Bhag Dusra' [Which is the Most Appropriate Curriculum for Women? Part Two], *Maharashtra Mahila*, September 1901, 122–3.

century. [113] Even a cursory glance at them reveals that they believed in a certain kind of passive femininity; the advice they gave to women on 'correct' behaviour included, among other things, subservience even to wayward husbands and an uncritical acceptance of one's culture and heritage.[114] They believed that the proper place for such an education was in the home or, at the very least, in girl's schools that would bring out the caring and organizational qualities in girls that the traditionalists saw as crucial to the effective running of the household.

Progressive women, on the other hand, believed that there were no significant differences between males and female, and that the curriculum had to be the same in order for women to be equipped to enter professional life. Additionally, even those women's organizations that had successfully fudged the divide between 'traditional' and 'modern' insisted that even adult women who could possibly be educated privately at their own homes ought not to do so but instead, seek out schools because 'home education is of inferior quality in comparison to public institutions.'[115] To a certain extent, institutions like the Seva Sadan were able to recruit middle-class girls without incurring the approbation of the traditionalists for they offered an education based on tackling 'need' and 'social welfare'; a philosophy that the traditionalists readily sympathized with. Its social service ethos therefore imbued it with respectability in the eyes of the traditionalists, despite the fact that it was simultaneously implementing radical policies, such as not requiring their students to gain their husband's permission before undertaking a course. Moreover, the women who attended the institution were aiming to improve society by becoming practitioners in areas of *seva* [social service], such as medicine and teaching; it was in these roles, not in that of dutiful housewives that the progressives believed they would be of greater utility to the nation.[116] Unlike the obedient housewife that represented the traditionalist ideal, the progressives argued that initiative, enterprise and ambition should all be regarded as praiseworthy virtues in a woman; qualities that were certainly displayed by middle-class women such as Umabai Kelkar, Anandibai Shirke and Anandibai Karve. In their memoirs, these women describe how they compensated for the precarious nature of their husbands' job situations, not only by practising thrift, but also by undertaking a professional education that allowed them to earn and directly contribute to the household. Indeed, Sagunabai Deo and her daughter, Kashibai Herlekar, earned

---

[113] Radhabai, 'Difference of Opinions', *Arya Bhagini*, August 1890, 90–96.

[114] The literature is vast but the earliest example is *Stri Dnyan Pradip*, in the year 1869 edited by Lakshman Abhyankar; *Grihini*, from 1887 onwards edited by Balwant Rao Nagarkar, *Stri Sadbodh Chintamani*, from 1881 edited by Ankush Ramchandra Gadekar. Of these I was unable to trace the first advice manual by Abhyankar.

[115] See the essay 'Stri Shikshanache Avashyakata' [Necessity of Women's Education], in the series 'Granthamala', reprinted in [The Nectar Tree], p. 27.

[116] Tulsabai's lecture on the uses of women's education reported in 'Schemes and Efforts', *Maharashtra Mahila*, August 1901, 53.

handsome salaries of Rs. 60 per month in their jobs as Headmistresses of Schools in Baroda State and together they acted as the main providers for their families.[117]

Yet, despite the difference in approach, it is perhaps worth noting that these women were ultimately undertaking the training for the good of the other members of their household and not necessarily for themselves. Indeed, it was only at the turn of the century that women expressed the need for a professional education on the grounds of equality. In her Presidential Speech at the founding of Saraswati Mandir, Lakshmibai Deshmukh argued that the debate between traditionalists and progressives on the necessity or otherwise of women's education could be settled by considering the end-product of knowledge itself. Knowledge, she argued, led to the broadening of one's horizons, allowing women to imbibe humility, self-control, inculcate a charitable disposition and learn about the proper care of children, countering conservative opinion which regarded the effects of knowledge on women as an adverse one. She reasoned thus:

> But, if education was like nectar then why argue that only men should drink it and not women? Further, why drink only a little and not to one's heart's content? There is no substance in this argument. The horizon of women's knowledge today extends only to topics of ornaments, household articles, kith and kin and children. This is not their fault. Their ideas are formed by their circumstances or more appropriately their ideas are confined by their confinement to the home. These days, no one would object if I described a woman's position within a home as that of a glorified maidservant and outside the home, she acts as the windowpane through which the family exhibits its wealth and status.[118]

Similarly, in 1901, while praising the efforts of women in educating themselves on a self-help basis and imparting this ethos to their children, Tulsabai, a Maratha female leader of the Mehekar-Varhad's women's organization, urged them to go beyond the roles of being better wives and efficient mothers, arguing, 'Education leads to fame, honour and respect in society. The time has come for women to gain these three fruits of education too.'[119] Whereas the traditionalists had argued that women should stay in the domestic sphere, with their own identities subsumed by the image of the dutiful wife, the progressives' campaign had created a new breed of women who, whilst recognizing her obligations to her family, also wished to carve out an identity in her own right. Women in this period no longer necessarily undertook an education in order to serve her family or society; she worked in order to earn her own income, allowing her greater control over her own destiny. Signs of this growing feminist consciousness were apparent as far back as the 1880s, when Christian women, such as Mary Sorabji, entered the teaching profession, whilst Hindu women, such as Anandibai Joshi and Rukhmabai, overcame the barriers placed in their way by male opponents to females

---

[117] Leela Pande, *Maharashtracha Kartrutvashalini*, [Able Ladies of Maharashtra] (Pune: The Teacher's Ideal Publishing House, 1953), pp. 36–52.

[118] Reprinted in [The Nectar Tree], pp. 13–14.

[119] 'Schemes and Efforts', *Maharashtra Mahila*, August 1901, 53–4.

receiving a medical education by pursuing their courses abroad.[120] However, these had been a few singular women, whereas now women were seeking entry into the professions in much greater numbers, leading to them coming into conflict with other, more powerful, groups in the public sphere who saw them as a direct threat.

Racial and Sexual Discrimination in the Public Sphere

As men felt increasingly threatened by the greater numbers of women entering the professional sphere, prejudice against women training for a profession increased considerably. They argued that, when pursuing public power, women lost their feminine qualities and turned into heartless tyrants, citing the example of the notorious Anandibai of the Peshwa period in order to justify their argument. Such prejudice was not only felt by progressive women at several levels to damage their own claims to self-determination but also threatened the entire social reform movement. Many 'progressive' women not only believed that higher education was important for woman on the grounds that, unless a woman attained a sufficiently advanced level of critical reading no one could convince her of the efficacy of letting her own daughter remain in school after the age of twelve. Moreover, they believed that only a scientific education would allow women to recognize the advantages of adult, instead of child, marriages.[121] The custom of *hunda,* or dowry, meant that women were often married off by their families as young as possible, as the minimum (albeit already substantial) sum of four or five thousand rupees increased greatly as the woman got older.[122] This caused great anxiety to many families, and Lakshmibai Dravid records how they would therefore arrange for their daughters to be betrothed or married off whilst they were still children.[123] Thus, not only was *hunda* placing a great financial burden on the nation's population, leading to greater poverty, but it also prevented the girl from receiving a proper education, whilst their youth meant that they were

---

[120] Anandibai Joshi's public statement seeking a medical education abroad is in Anandibai Joshi, *A Speech by a Hindu Lady* (Bombay: A 'Well-wisher', 1882). Rukhmabai received death threats after her legal action against her husband, over the restitution of conjugal rights, and it convinced her to pursue a medical education in London. See Mohini Varde, *Dr Rukhmabai: Ek Arth* [Saga of Dr Rukhmabai] (Bombay: Popular Prakashan, 1982), pp. 101–2.

[121] Sagunabai Dev's speech reported in 'Schemes and Efforts', *Maharashtra Mahila*, July 1901, 12; Tarabai Nabar, 'Bal Vivahache Dushparinam' [Evil Effects of Child Marriage], *Maharashtra Mahila*, May 1901, 234–6.

[122] Anandibai Lad, 'Lagnyachi Chali' [Marriage Customs], *Arya Bhagini*, March 1886, 1–3.

[123] For a brief note on her see Appendix.

more likely to bear weak progeny.[124] In addition to this, the men that they were often married to were often approaching their dotage, a feature highlighted in anguished articles in the journals of the women's press, who asked their readers to:

> Consider the case of a sixty-year-old frail man and his ten-year-old wife! The man has lost all his teeth, salivates all the time, his body is putrid with decay and emits a foul odour, and one wonders if he is going to live today or not! What can a bride do in such circumstances? How can one expect her to be an obedient wife?[125]

Quite aside from the revolting spectacle painted by Kanthabai of 60-year-old men attempting to rekindle their youth by using false teeth, dyeing their hair and eating the kind of food that was supposed to have aphrodisiac effects,[126] it also trapped women in a cycle of poverty. Not only were they more likely to be widowed, but also their lack of education prevented them from ameliorating their situation by earning a salary, which, in turn, meant that they were more likely to follow their parents' example and marry their own daughters off early. The female reformers believed that the only way to break such a cycle was to encourage such families to allow their daughters to follow a vocational degree, which would turn her from an economic liability into an asset.[127]

The ability of women to pursue a profession was therefore not just a product of the social reform programme but integral to its continued success, meaning that it was vital for women to try to combat male hostility that could potentially impede their progress. An illustrative case is Rebecca Simeon, one of western India's first midwives.[128] Rebecca was an unusually gifted woman who after gaining a professional qualification on midwifery and obstetrics from Grant Medical College began an extremely successful career as a private practitioner and gained fame, wealth and status very quickly. Along with her equally successful husband, Benjamin Simeon, she was well known in Bombay's elite circles. When she published books on midwifery and a medical manual to act as a first aid primer in Maharashtrian homes her works attracted accolades as well as a hostile audience, with male reviewers accusing her of plagiarism and having gone beyond her expertise.[129] Clearly the figure of the confident 'New Woman' of the

---

[124] Lakshmibai Dravid 'Lahanpani Lagne va Strishikshan' [Child Marriage and Women's Education] in *Deshseva Nibandhamala*, [Essays in the Service of the Nation] (Pune: Vijayanand, 1896), pp. 22–8.

[125] Kanthabai, 'Condition of Women', *Maharashtra Mahila*, April 1892, 29.

[126] Tarabai Shinde, *Stripurushtulana athava Striya va Purush Yant Sahasi Kon he Spasta Karun Dakavinyakarita ha Nibandh* [Women and Men: A Comparison, or an Essay Showing Who is More Wicked], S.J. Malshe, (ed.), 2nd edn (Bombay: Mumbai Marathi Grantha Sangrahalaya Publications, 1975; 1st edn 1882), pp. 10–11.

[127] Anandibai Prabhu Desai, 'Which is the Most Appropriate Curriculum for Women?' *Maharashtra Mahila*, September 1901, 80.

[128] For her life and work see Appendix.

[129] Most of the Maharashtrian newspapers of the time reviewed her works. See Mohini Varde, *Dr Rukhmabai*, p. 11.

late nineteenth century was a new phenomenon, which Indian men had not yet learnt to accept gracefully. Rebecca herself remained undeterred as she continued her philanthropic causes in bettering the lives of ailing women. Neither was the hostility confined to traditionalist men, as the dispute that occurred over the appointment of school inspectors for girl's schools in Bombay illustrated. In 1900, Bombay's male inspectors supervised all the girls' schools in the Marathi, Urdu and Gujarati medium run by the Municipality. When a member of the Corporation proposed that they be replaced by female inspectors, a large number of municipal councillors vetoed the move, claiming that there was a great paucity of qualified women and, at any rate, even if there was, women could never be as efficient administrators as men. Such arguments carried little weight with progressive females, with the journals of the women's press arguing:

> The real reason why women are not given such responsible jobs is due to the male sex's desire to reserve the entire job sector for themselves. They are further made bold, to jealously guard it by the powerlessness of women to change the situation.[130]

Female progressives were increasingly aware of the methods that men were employing to preserve their own position; even if a woman surmounted all the obstacles and gained a position in a profession, they were constantly reminded of their inferior status by lower salary scales, the lack of retention incentives and transfers, and poorer working conditions. As Manoramabai Mitra stated:

> Why should women take the responsibility of arduous jobs on a beggarly salary of Rs. 15 or 20? Instead of questioning unequal scales of pay, men turn around and heap false accusations of incapability on women ... If they want to attract women to serve the cause of education they have to pay bigger salaries, hold out incentives and treat them with respect, honour and dignity just as men who serve in these capacities.[131]

Far from accepting the male view that ambition in a woman was somehow ignoble, the female reformers saw it as a positive trait, with one female respondent to an article written by a man against higher education for women published in a Poona newspaper, *Karmanook*, arguing:

> The saintly Ahilyabai Holkar took on the role of the protector of her subjects and proved to be a true patriot. Donning the robes of a warrior, Lakshmibai, the Rani of Jhansi, fought and died for her country...So also Joan of Arc and one can give countless examples of brave, good and ambitious women. My opinion is that ambition is a positive trait. ... If we take the example of men alone, was not Shivaji an ambitious man? Was it a heinous crime for him to have built and defended the country of

---

[130] 'Women's Welfare', *Maharashtra Mahila*, August 1901, 49.

[131] Ibid., p. 50.

Maharashtra? ... Thus it is unwarranted and irresponsible to argue that ambition is a negative quality amongst women alone.[132]

This ambition is reflected in the way in which women belonging to the progressive group did not agitate for entry into the all-male arena of clerical employment but instead concentrated their attention on the teaching and medical professions that would provide them with the necessary financial and social clout to combat male opposition more effectively. This, of course, greatly assisted the cause of social reform but it also greatly enhanced the quality of life for individual women as well. They were just as susceptible to the benefits that employment in the profession brought as men; for instance, many female teachers were reported to have preferred jobs in government schools rather than in philanthropic institutions because of the higher salaries and greater benefits like housing.[133] The beginning of the twentieth century in India therefore heralded the rise of a professional class of women in India, innovative, assertive and ambitious, who, by their actions, not only hoped to assist their less-fortunate sisters but also improve their own position within society.

However, by the 1910s, Maharashtrian women also faced opposition in the professions of medicine and education from a relatively new faction. British women had encountered a great deal of sexist opposition at home when they had attempted to enter the medical field, and many of them therefore decided to export their skills to the colonies. India was an especially popular destination, due to both the opportunities it offered in the field of 'native women's health' and the Dufferin Fund. Their entrance to the medical profession was directly at the expense of Indian women in these fields; a situation exacerbated by the way in which the Dufferin Fund's rules directly discriminated against Indian women. From Yashodabai Joshi's description of the working of the Dufferin Committee in Amravati, who had enlisted her organization (Vanita Samaj's) support in helping to find suitable nurses to be trained at the local hospital, it is apparent that such prejudice was endemic within the organization since its inception:

> Whenever Hindu women came forward to apply, the Committee put forward all sorts of criticisms so as to reject them. Therefore the Vanita Samaj withdrew from the Dufferin Committee. Only I stayed on for sometime hoping things would change but eventually I too withdrew.[134]

Although it accepted applications from Indian women, the organization continued to frame its regulations in such a way that excluded Indian women from actual appointments. One of the main conditions of the Central Committee of the Dufferin Fund for medical posts, for instance, was that candidates, '...must possess a medical qualification registrable in the U.K., under the Medical Act or

---

[132] Rumi Killedar, 'Strivargavar Khota Arop' [False Accusations against Womankind], Ibid., September 1901, 110–11.

[133] Parvatibai Athavale, *My Story*, p. 144.

[134] Yashodabai Joshi, *Our Life Together*, p. 61.

an Indian or Colonial qualification higher than the L.M.S. (Licentiate in Medicine and Surgery).'[135] These criteria obviously immediately excluded the vast majority of female Indian applicants, but even when enterprising women with the appropriate degrees did apply, they were turned down. Dr Nagutai Joshi, for instance, had three medical degrees, two of which were from British universities, yet was rejected for a post in the Dufferin Fund medical service. Predictably, she regarded this as unjust and publicized her grievance widely,[136] pleading, 'Let there be fair play. To import Lady Doctors from foreign countries when Indian talent is available would be a gross injustice not only to the Indian Lady Doctors but also to the country that pays for their services.'[137] Indeed, she argued, not only were Indian female graduates equally competent, if not more so, than those imported from European universities, but they also possessed knowledge of local languages and social customs that European women lacked.

Similar problems were experienced by women operating in the field of teaching, with the earliest recorded instance occurring in 1889 when Mary Sorabji was denied promotion to the post of Lady Superintendent of the Female Training College by the Educational Department. She protested by petitioning the government showing how, despite her seniority and superior qualifications (she held a teacher's certificate from London, had 10 years' experience and knowledge of several Indian languages over that of Laura Brooks, her rival), she had been unjustly overlooked.[138] Neither was her experience unique. As more women joined the teaching and medical services, the discrimination against Indian women on both racial and gender grounds was an increasingly common occurrence, and it became increasingly apparent to them that the only way to combat it was to orchestrate protests against those who would otherwise block their progress. For instance, when Maharashtrian women found that suitably qualified Indian women were being overlooked when applying for jobs at the Female Training College of Poona, instead of meekly accepting the decision, they organized meetings to discuss their grievances. Under the leadership of Kashibai Kanitkar and Yashodabai Bhat,[139] they appealed for justice, arguing that the College, the only one of its kind in Maharashtra, was conducting itself in a manner inimical to the sentiments and feelings of the very people it intended to benefit. Although they had initially tried to avoid being confrontational, their encounters with others operating in the public sphere meant that they were becoming increasing politicized.

---

[135] 'Women's Medical Service in India', *Mahratta*, 9 November 1913.

[136] She wrote about her experience with the colonial authorities in newspapers. See her letter dated 6 October 1913 in *Mahratta*, 12 October 1913.

[137] Ibid.

[138] Petition of Mary Sorabji, First Assistant to Lady S.P. High School for Native Girls, Poona, to Lord Reay, Governor of Bombay, 15 July 1889, (Education Department), 1889, vol.13.

[139] Reports of the meetings are in *Mahratta*, 2 July 1916.

On the Oppression of the *stri jati* [female sex], *hunda* [dowry] and Domestic Reforms

Whilst the struggle for women's rights was taking place in the public sphere, Maharashtrian feminists were also working to lessen women's oppression within the private or domestic sphere. A chief component indeed, some scholars would argue, the defining feature of a 'feminist' is an awareness and articulation of how and why women are downtrodden in society; by providing an analysis of the reasons of women's subordination, they therefore hope to find ways of achieving parity with men. Just as discrimination radicalized the female reformers operating in the public sphere, the autobiographies of Yashodabai Joshi and Gangutai Patwardhan show how sexual harassment, the battering of their mothers-in-law and the harsh lives of their own sisters or friends gradually turned women towards seeking the sources of their oppression in order to find ways of combating it.[140] A similar motivation operated in Tarabai Shinde's case, who states in the 'Preface' to her book that she was aroused to defend the honour of her '*deshbhagini*' [Indian sisters] because she witnessed everyday how they were solely blamed for crimes that were, in fact, largely perpetrated by men. She states emphatically in her 'Preface' that her intention was not to limit her study to a caste-based analysis or a family one but to make a 'comparison between *stri* [women] and *purush* [men].'[141] By reaching an understanding of the causes of their oppression, such women hoped to dispel the erroneous prejudices that existed regarding females in Hindu society and, in doing so, redress the unequal marital relationship, bring more respect and dignity to the life of a female and lessen the miserable condition of the child-wife and the widow.

When examining the growth of feminist consciousness in nineteenth-century Indian women's writing, it is important to have a full understanding of the nuances of the term, *stri jati*. The term is frequently used by female writers of the period, and literally means 'caste of women', although, in many contexts where it is employed, it would be more accurate to translate it as 'female sex'. Nevertheless, even when women writers are utilizing it in this way, the connotations of 'class' or 'category' remain, giving feminist writers, such as Tarabai Shinde,[142] a powerful tool when writing their comparative studies of the *stri jati* and the *purush jati* [male sex].[143] Furthermore, from the wider use of the

---

[140] Yashodabai Joshi, *Our Life Together*, and Gangutai Patwardhan, *Chakoribaher: Ek Atmakathan* [Beyond the Courtyard: An Autobiography] (Poona: Sadhana Prakashan, 1974).

[141] Tarabai Shinde, 'Prastavana [Preface]', [Women and Men, A Comparison], see the first and sixth paragraph.

[142] For notes on her life and work see Appendix. For a detailed consideration of her work see the next chapter.

[143] Tarabai Shinde, [Women and Men, A Comparison]. For the use of the term *stri jati* [female sex] see paragraph 6 of the 'Preface' and pages 6, 7 and 8 of the main text. For the comparative use see pages 10 and 32.

term 'jati' [caste] in modern Marathi literature, it is clear that the phrase can also be used in describing the physiological and cultural evolution of species; indeed, one can see the expression being used by feminist writers in relation to other species, such as 'pashu jati' and 'prani jati' [animal and birds]. The various meanings that can be ascribed to it therefore not only give it force as a description of the status of women in comparison to men, but also show the growth in the feminist writers' awareness of their own distinct identity and speak volumes regarding the realization of 'selfhood' and the formation of women's subjectivities. *Stri jati* was, however, much more than an abstract term to describe the condition of women; for many, the material conditions that their status generated had a direct impact on their material reality. Even the most conservative women recognized the need to improve the economic conditions of women and discussed reform as a means of improving this, but Indian feminists were more radical than this. Instead of blaming prevailing economic trends caused by colonialism, they blamed the low status occupied by the *stri jati* in society on the economic burden women were viewed as placing on their families. Not only were women not earning salaried incomes, as household work was unrecognized and unpaid, but obligations, such as *hunda* [dowry] and *khandani* [tributes of cash and kind demanded by the priestly class during marriages], placed the finances of many families under great strain. This burden meant that many were often reluctant to bring up a female child, and they were often mistreated, both in the natal home and, more frequently, in the marital home. In the words of Kanthabai Tarkhadkar:

> And it is because of this if a daughter is born in any family, the head of the family is instantly dejected and immensely displeased. Because our Aryan people do not yet know that women are equally capable of doing hard labour just like men. [144]

Although this situation could partially be alleviated by providing routes into salaried employment, such as teaching and medicine, for women, the reformers recognized that the large sums of money that priests extracted from families in order to carry out religious rites for the women in the household was also a source of hardship for many people. The misery that it caused for many households fuelled the misogynistic atmosphere that tolerated such abuse; in order to prevent it, the female reformers therefore had to demonstrate that the fault lay not with women themselves but with the greed of the Hindu priestly class. Due to the exorbitant amount of money spent on weddings, which could last two weeks or more and involved countless rituals, priests extracted as much money and gifts in kind as possible from the family of the bride. Such were the profits that could be made from such marriages that many women were convinced that the priests would cunningly persuade a man to marry three or four wives, meaning that women were consigned to the miserable status of co-wives.

---

[144] Kanthabai Tarkhadkar, 'Striyanchi Sthiti, Lagnatil Khandani va Bhat Mandalicha Paise Upatnyacha Thata' [The Condition of Women: Punitive Exactions of the Priestly Class during Marriages and their Methods of Extraction], *Arya Bhagini*, May 1892, 36–9.

Furthermore, the high costs not only increased the chances of a female being murdered by her family in infancy or being subject to abuse, but it also lessened their chances of being educated, as the money would be diverted to meet the expenses of the wedding. Neither were the effects confined to the upper or middle classes nor indeed to women; the plight of the *kunbi* [cultivator] was often described by female reformers as one of eternal bondage. A *kunbi* might not have to pay as much money to priests during a daughter's wedding as an upper-class man, yet the burden of even a small debt drove him from the comforts of his native home to industrial towns such as Bombay. In fact, the female reformers concluded, the priestly class were worse than the usurious *marwari* [money-lender] because, even though the *marwari* charged high rates of interest, the loans had actually been incurred in the first place to feed the priests.[145]

The priest's influence on the lives of women was far-reaching, even extending to their absolute power, in their capacity as astrologers, in deciding whether a girl was born under a lucky star.[146] An indication that her fate would be an unhappy one could potentially become a self-fulfilling prophecy, as her relatives would believe the priest and think even less of a daughter likely to bring bad luck to the family. Given the impact that the priest's judgement could have, it was therefore unsurprising that women reformers set about warning their adherents that the priests were engaged in an act of deception and it was a false science.[147] It was only by disabusing people of their unthinking belief in the power of the priests that the reformers could hope to improve the lot of women. This is not to say that the female reformers condemned and dismissed all the customs and rituals associated with Hinduism; indeed, they advocated the retention of certain rituals, such as *dohale* [cravings during pregnancy] and *vratas* [fasts and vows], both of which, they believed, fulfilled a practical purpose. The *dohale*, for instance, was redefined as having a scientific basis, which allowed its purpose to be retained, but the expensive ceremony surrounding it was discouraged, while prominent vows and fasts surroundings the contentious issue of prolonging the state of wifehood were reexamined and some functional reasons for continuation of these votive expressions of women was sought.[148] What they were arguing for was reform of these practices to ameliorate the suffering of women and ensure resources were available for their education.

Reform was obviously urgently needed, with graphic examples appearing in the women's press illustrating how the costs of lavish puberty and pregnancy rites had meant that many families had ended in debt and having their properties repossessed. Moreover, some of the customs were of dubious worth, both in terms of wasting money that could otherwise be spent on educating the daughters of the family and what it said about a woman's function in life. For instance, the rites carried out for a girl at puberty

---

[145] Ibid., 36–8.

[146] Ibid., 57–8.

[147] Manakbai Lad, 'Jyotish ani Shakun' [Astrologers and Omens], Ibid., July 1891, 57–9.

[148] Anon., [Some of Our Foolish Traditions], Ibid., October 1901, 157; Anon., 'Dohale' [Cravings during Pregnancy], *Strisadbodhachintamani*, September 1881, 32–3; 'Shriharitalika' [Shriharitalika Ritual], *Saubhagyasambhar*, 1 (1902): 14–17.

were considered to be a waste of money that harmed women by reducing them to the sum of their reproductive function, with one correspondent complaining:

> When a girl menstruates for the first time, friends and relatives are informed and letters are written to kith and kin who reside outside the village, the girl is dressed in fine clothes and paraded round with a band of musicians playing various instruments and sweetmeats are distributed to everyone. It is indeed a ridiculous and shameful display...[149]

The profits that priests derived from the traditional rituals meant they had no reason to reform them; indeed, self-interest demanded that the status quo was maintained, so it was necessary for another group to formulate potential reforms. Many women in the reform movement held the view that they were the 'custodians of Hindu culture' and, therefore, by examining the propriety of all customs, rituals and ceremonies within the home, they would then be in a position to weed out what was harmful, retain the good, and make the necessary innovations. Women thus put themselves in the forefront of redefining 'custom', 'morality' and 'tradition' and the creation a new style of living and behaviour.[150]

The rationalism and thrift of the reforms extended to a consideration of secular habits, with habits, such as accumulating gold and silver ornaments, being scrutinized according to the same principles. Women were advised that jewellery could be stolen but, if the money were invested in 'Promissory Notes and Post Office Savings', it could earn interest.[151] Neither were the female reformers afraid of importing customs from other cultures if it enhanced women's welfare. Wearing shoes outdoors, for instance, a recognizably Western custom was promoted as a sanitary habit for Indian women to emulate, whilst another Western habit, physical exercise, was promoted as a way of improving health.[152] Women reformers were not promoting reforms for its own sake or as part of some kind of 'civilizing mission' (which their male counterparts were doing) but rather as a way of achieving tangible improvement in women's lives.

One of the most radical reforms advocated by Maharashtrian women, however, was that of the custom of *hunda* [dowry] and the expectation of gifts from the bride's family, a practice unquestioned even by male reformers elsewhere in nineteenth-century India.[153] Quite aside from the female reformers' argument that it reduced marriage—a supposedly holy union—to the level of a transaction, an interpretation

---

[149] [Some of Our Foolish Traditions], Ibid., 156–8.

[150] Editorial, *Maharashtra Mahila*, May 1901, 13; Also Sundarabai Shirur's speech at the second social conference of Bombay Presidency, reported in 'Schemes and Efforts', Ibid., October 1901, 156.

[151] Manakbai Lad, 'Dagine' [Jewellery], *Arya Bhagini*, September 1891, 80.

[152] Lakshmibai Phadnis, 'Striyanchi Durbalata' [Women's Physical Weakness], *Maharashtra Mahila*, September 1901, 131–4.

[153] Even the more radical male reformers of the Arya Samaj in Punjab never attacked the custom of dowry. Kishwar, 'Arya Samaj and Women's Education,' *Economic and Political Weekly*, WS–14.

that directly challenged those views expressed by leading male reformers during the Age of Consent debates. The utter devaluation of the female sex made obvious to them in the arranged marriage set-up was a common concern in women's writings.[154] A much quoted example was that of an intelligent, good looking and industrious girl who could not secure a suitable match unless her father had a great deal of money while an illiterate old man, with the reputation of a gambler and wastrel, could still manage to marry as many women as he desired.[155] Such undesirable marriages were described as rising from the inhuman basis of these marital contracts and the desire to rise in social status.

In order to remedy this situation they advocated that wealthy parents should not include *hunda* as part of marriage transactions but to give gifts of money and ornaments to their daughter after she was fully integrated in her in-laws home.[156] Writings from the nineteenth century on *hunda* suggests that the old Indian custom of gifting clothes and ornaments to the bride as a part of her trousseau called *stridhan* [women's property] was slowly being substituted by the gift of cash made directly to the in-laws.[157] Women realized how significant this change was for the new bride, whose access to wealth that was 'her own' was considerably reduced by this direct monetary transaction. Maharashtrian women aware of the changes in the dowry system of the time considered *stridhan* as an essential and indispensable part of the young bride's assets and hence advocated the continuation of the custom or its revival (where it had died out) by seeking to revise it. In an essay published and read out in the lecture series of the late 1890s at the Saraswati Mandir, Sholapur, on 'The Hindu Marriage Ceremony', a student had noted that the custom of dowry was a recent one with the term *hunda* being a recent invention.[158] The feisty female student argued that many held the view that it was an age-old custom but hotly refuted it through examples of *stridhan* from the past ages. The article ends with the plea that just as customs were not dropped from the sky and were indeed man-made, likewise it was time to recognize the equal rights of women and eradicate unequal rites within the ceremonial rituals of marriage. It should be noted here that the solutions suggested by the feminists of the time have a resonance and canny resemblance to some of the present-day solutions being sought by the Indian law courts and women's support groups, which are still seeking ways and means of combating the rampant dowry problem.

Another solution that women reformers formulated for dealing with the problem of dowry-seeking families was to encourage wealthy families to marry their daughters to educated young men, regardless of class. Nineteenth-century feminists hoped that

---

[154] For details on the participation of Maharashtrian women in the enactment of the Age of Consent Act, 1891, see chapter 6.

[155] Anandibai Lad, 'Marriage Customs', *Arya Bhagini*, March 1886, 2.

[156] Anandibai Lad, 'Lavkar Lagna Karnyache Chal' [The Custom of Early Marriage], Ibid., 3–4.

[157] Narayan Hari Bhagvat, *Hunda Prahasan* [A Farce on Dowry], 2nd edn (Poona: Sudhakar, 1887).

[158] Reprinted in [The Nectar Tree], pp. 28–34.

enlightened men, exposed to modern lifestyles and conjugal relations, would seek qualities accompanying an educated girl rather than the goods and cash that accompanied her.[159] They argued that only the reformation of the process of marriage negotiation would liberate women from having to enter the unhappy marriages that the constraints of *hunda* often placed upon them. By releasing families from this obligation, it was not only the bride and her immediate family that stood to benefit financially but society as a whole; the funds instead could be used to educate women to allow them to become useful members of society in fields such as teaching and medicine.

The Question of Widowhood and State Intervention

If customs often led to wives facing a lifetime of ill treatment and servitude, the fate that potentially faced widows was far worse. Not only did they face the horrors of the *keshavapan* [the tonsure ceremony] but they also had to endure a miserable quality of life and the general opprobrium of society. The tonsure ceremony, for example, graphically illustrates the pitiful condition of the nineteenth-century Indian widow. This was a spectacle where the widow was dressed up in her wedding finery before all her bangles were systematically broken, the vermilion dot that marked her status as a married woman was wiped off and a barber shaved her head. The experience was undoubtedly traumatic for those who underwent it, with one Hindu feminist describing a thirteen-year-old girl-widow's helplessness undergoing the display as one who was 'mooing like a cow in distress'.[160] Neither was the process merely symbolic; with her shaved head, the widow gave a physical indication of her status that caused the rest of society to shun her as widows were stereotyped as bad omens for those in the process of carrying-out important business. Indeed, not only were widows ostracized but their status as objects of ill-omen often led to them being confined to the windowless centre of the Maharashtrian house, the *mazghar*.

Predictably, there was unanimous agreement amongst Hindu women that the plight of Indian widows was lamentable, and that steps should be taken to try and alleviate their suffering. In recent years scholars working on the gender history of India have explored how discussion among indigenous elites on reform issues centred on the sanction or nonsanction of the *shastras* [Hindu prescriptive texts]. A particular point of contention was the legalization of widow remarriage, with Uma Chakravarti recently demonstrating how *shastric* norms became the key argument in the discourse of both those Maharashtrian male reformers who

---

[159] Anandibai Lad, [The Custom of Early Marriage], *Arya Bhagini*, 3–4.
[160] 'By An Educated Lady', [Instructive Debates between Gulabbai and Shewatibai], Ibid., July 1891, 86–7.

argued against widow remarriage and those who supported it.[161] However, whereas Chakravarti focussed on the male response to the problem, the comparative method adopted here, which studies women's perceptions on the subject and contrasts it with male discourse, brings into sharp focus the differing discourse of women and, more importantly, demonstrates how their perceptions were based on a feminist viewpoint.

Many of the everyday hardships that widows endured could be traced back to the fact that they were prevented from re-marriage. Whereas men argued on an abstract level over whether or not the custom was legitimized by the *shastras,* the female reformers argued for remarriage of widows on humanitarian grounds, with a woman protagonist arguing that, 'Even if a custom is non-conformable with the shastras, if that particular custom is bringing sorrow to large sections of the population, then such a custom should be cast away.'[162] For female reformers, the issue of whether or not widows should be allowed to remarry ought not to be centred on scriptural sanction but rather on a consideration of the plight of the widow, whose ignoble state made her life one of agony and misery. Indeed, many women argued that the way in which the *shastras* legitimized misogynistic views and actions meant that it was justifiable, in some instances, to disregard its edicts. Tarabai Shinde, for instance, concluded that it must have been very convenient for the writers and creators of the *shastras* to invent these rules because they knew how to take good care of their own kind—the *purush jati* [male sex]. She drew attention to the fact that a thoroughly unequal state of affairs existed as the *shastras* did not forbid widowers from remarrying; some woman must have surely angered a *shastra* writer by burning down his house, she speculates, for him to have invented such drivel about womankind.[163]

Women therefore argued that the *shastras* on this topic should be disregarded, and widow remarriage should be permitted on the basis of equal rights. Another male argument that they demonstrated to be flawed was that the widows themselves did not wish to remarry[164] so there was no point in changing the law. By interviewing widows themselves, female reformers obtained very different results, as the extract below demonstrates:

> There are many people who are of the view that until women are able to take advantage of education they will not desire any reform. This is probably true but a large proportion of them who haven't received even elementary education do think in a progressive manner. If you ask them about a topic like widow re-marriage they

---

[161] *Rewriting History: The Life and Times of Pandita Ramabai* (New Delhi: Kali, 1998), chapter 2.

[162] Anon., 'Saraswat Gaud Brahmanache Swami ani Stripunarvivaha' [The Leader of The Saraswat Gaud Brahmin Community and Widow Remarriage], *Arya Bhagini*, October 1891, 81; See also Editorial, 'Samajik Sudharana' [Social Reform], *Arya Bhagini,* June 1891, 51.

[163] Tarabai Shinde, [Women and Men, A Comparison], pp. 9–10.

[164] See chapter 6 for details.

immediately say, just as it was in ancient days, widow re-marriage should be revived as a custom and the sooner it is done the better. Many make subtle enquiries and a lot of women are aware of the laws.[165]

This led female reformers to conclude that only elderly women in Hindu households were opposed to widow remarriage, although prevailing notions of female propriety meant that younger widows could only make 'subtle enquiries' about remarriage. This realization prompted them to suggest that the state should pass laws making it compulsory for child widows to remarry and allowing choice for elderly widows, with one housewife they canvassed asking:

> What is wrong in marrying again after being widowed? When a 50 or 60-year-old frail and sickly old widower marries a 12-year-old girl, that act is completely acceptable to our society. Sometimes a man does not even wait for a while after his wife dies and immediately marries another girl. What sin have women committed to deserve such treatment?[166]

The interminable link between child marriage and widow remarriage was recognized by women, and some radical female reformers asked the government to intervene and enact a law that would force a girl's parents, if they married her very young, to re-marry their daughter if she was later widowed. The element of compulsion was regarded as necessary as child widows were invariably illiterate due to their young age at marriage, and their lack of education would mean that they were too terrified or would even fail to understand that it would benefit them to marry again. In addition to this, it was also believed that it would deter conformist parents from marrying their daughters too young,[167] giving young women the chance of obtaining an education. Given the benefits that such legislation promised, it is therefore unsurprising that the poetry, letters, short stories and articles written by women make constant reference to it, with the women's press of the late nineteenth and early twentieth centuries saturated with the topic. It was in areas of extreme hostility faced by Indian women from men such as the question of remarriage that women welcomed and sought the intervention of the government. The intervention of an alien government was actively encouraged by Indian women in order to combat the indigenous male opposition to women's equal rights. This gendered approach to the state and its functions therefore cannot be read as acquiescence to foreign rule or as some kind of naiveté but is comprehensible if seen from the point of view of the use of the state by a minority group as a major resource for bettering women's life chances.

---

[165] 'A Gaud Saraswat Brahman Lady', 'Remarriage', *Arya Bhagini*, July 1891, 53.

[166] 'Ek Gaud Saraswat Brahmani Stri' [A Gaud Saraswat Brahman Lady], 'Punarvivaha' [Remarriage], Ibid., July 1891, 64.

[167] 'By an Educated Lady', [Instructive Debates Between Gulabbai and Shewatibai], Ibid., July 1891, 63.

It is worth noting at this point that, apart from a handful of male reformers, male discourse during this period was vehemently opposed to widow remarriage;[168] a difference starkly illustrated by the opinions expressed by both sides in the wake of the remarriage of R.G. Bhandharkar's widowed daughter in 1891. After the ceremony, some members of his Gaud Saraswat caste filed a suit against him with their *panchayat*, a council that consisted of powerful and wealthy caste leaders.[169] However, whilst male members of his caste asked the *panchayat* to ostracize him and his family, some of the Gaud Saraswat Brahmin women wrote scathing letters to their opponents, refuting their arguments against widow remarriage. In common with many of the other female reformers, they did not make any reference to the *shastras* but appealed for the marriage to be accepted on humanitarian grounds. They dismissed the spiritual head of their community as illiterate and conservative, in addition to being power-hungry and acquisitive, but reserved particular vitriol for the younger generation of the Saraswat community, who had pretensions to modernity but had aligned themselves with the conservatives on this issue, as the correspondence of a Saraswat woman demonstrates. According to her, these men were the ones

> …who raved about knowing English, staying in a large city like Bombay, assuming superior airs constantly by referring to all other people outside of Bombay as boorish and vulgar and laughing at them. How is it that over a reform issue your intellect has left you?[170]

She calls such men who acquired a Western education merely to gratify the needs of their senses, and not for self-improvement *potepurte shiklele lok*, a highly derogatory term, and argues that, in comparison to them, women were definitely superior in every way. Similar attitudes towards male reformers can also be found in the works of other female writers of this time, with Tarabai Shinde, for instance, describing them as 'fake' and as worthless as a 'spare tit on a goat'.[171] The lack of support from male reformers in important issues meant that women were becoming increasingly self-reliant in the development of campaigns to oppose those traditions that were degrading to women. Male reformers may have provided many of the initial institutions that provided education for women but increasingly, it was the female reformers who were ensuring that they could access them and the opportunities that they offered, no matter what their situation.

---

[168] The male discourse is analyzed in chapter 6.

[169] Pathare Reform Association, *Marriage of Hindu Widows, Advocated By the Pathare Reform Association of Bombay*, 2nd edn (Bombay: Indu Prakash Press, 1869; 1st edn 1863); See also Frank Conlon, *A Caste in a Changing World: The Chitrapur Saraswat Brahmans, 1700–1935* (Berkeley: University of California, 1975).

[170] 'Ek Saraswat Gaud Brahmani Stri' [A Saraswat Gaud Brahman Lady], 'Saraswat Gaud Brahmanachya Swamiche Prakaran' [Public Announcement of The Head of Saraswat Gaud Brahman Community], *Arya Bhagini*, October 1891, 85.

[171] [Women and Men, A Comparison], p. 6.

A high degree of awareness was present among women on the driving forces and the sources of the origin of the *keshavapan* [tonsure ceremony] that widows underwent soon after the death of their husbands. Here too, women traced the constraints put on the widow's mobility and assertion as a mechanism invented by men to control her. Hence, Hindu feminists were keen to ban the *keshavapan* ceremony, described earlier in this chapter. Like the ceremonies surrounding marriage, the female reformers argued that it had no religious basis, but could be entirely ascribed to the avarice and acquisitive nature of the priestly caste that benefited greatly from the fees and gifts given in return for their services. Kanthabai condemned these men in the strongest possible terms, asking them, 'Is it just to live off the proceeds of such an evil custom? Isn't it shameful and despicable to think that a slab of butter placed on a corpse before the cremation would make a delicious meal?'[172] In order to tackle this custom, female reformers suggested possible lawsuits against priests and barbers and encouraged widows to rebel, pointing out that they would not be excommunicated if they refused to have their hair cut, although they would be prevented from joining in certain ceremonies. Moreover, by making sure that Maharashtrian women were aware that this heinous custom was not prevalent in northern India, female reformers were able to argue that it was not authorized by the *shastras*; women, such as Parvatibai Athavale, spent their entire adult lives campaigning for a ban on this custom and spreading awareness amongst women.[173] They argued that such acts did not reflect well on the *purusharth* [manhood] of the other sex as it only served to demonstrate their vulnerability and utter mental weakness. Interestingly, both Indian Christian and Hindu women's critiques of gender relations in this period incorporate a similar strand of thinking on the issue of manhood and masculinity. In their discussions of the meaning of *purusharth*, it not only consisted of a narrow conception of physical traits, such as virility and prowess, but also extended to mental expressions of courage, endurance, and the ability to be humane in unusual circumstances. This consensus regarding the meaning of *purusharth* can be seen in the writings of Pandita Ramabai and Tarabai Shinde who, despite their marked differences in religion, background and influences, ultimately imbue the term with the same meaning.[174]

The female reformers also found an unlikely source of support from another group of women: the 'traditionalists' (described earlier in the chapter) in their attempts to provide a professional education for widows. Wherever widows could afford it, they were encouraged to enter boarding schools and colleges, wherein they would not only gain an atmosphere where they could study without the distraction of everyday household chores, but would also be afforded dignity

---

[172] Kanthabai, 'Condition of Women', *Arya Bhagini*, April 1892, 28.

[173] See the Appendix for a brief note on her life and work.

[174] For the former see 'Pandita Ramabaicha Vyakhyana' [Lecture of Pandita Ramabai], *Subodh Patrika*, 4 June 1882, 18, and the latter, [Women and Men, A Comparison], p. 7.

denied them at home.[175] Women constructed an ideology of 'work' for widows as being extremely rewarding both physically and mentally, arguing that the stimulation that paid jobs offered would protect the widow from evil influences and she would find life less loathsome and tiresome. As Venubai said:

> We can be given socially beneficial work, unlike only that of circling round and round the Tulsi plant or making cotton wicks. We do not want to spend our entire lives with a downcast face circumabulating the Tulsi plant and rolling cotton wicks for Pooja [worship] and bowing to God to help us.[176]

The sheer monotony of this ritual is brought home to the reader who cannot fail to sense their frustration at being locked away inside the home with rituals, which gave them cold comfort. The stress laid by this particular writer on 'socially useful work' shows her pragmatism as well. Moreover, writers such as Venubai argued, the good works that she was able to carry out as a result of her education would not only benefit society, the nation and, by extension, God, but it would also help the widow persuade her own family that she was not a burden, adding to her self esteem. Interestingly, even conservative woman editors who did not necessarily agree with the curriculum or the nature of education imparted to girl-widows in institutions such as the Hingne Widows' Home run by D.K. Karve felt that it was appropriate to give them publicity in their journals.[177] The rhetoric of providing a social service to society as a whole, a significant weapon in the Seva Sadan's arsenal in the 1910s to justify the professional education of widows who formed almost half of their student population,[178] was obviously effective in legitimizing the entry of widows into society in the eyes of more conservative and traditionalist women.

Widows themselves argued that they could serve the society and nation better than anyone else, as they were not tied up by familial obligations and the trials and tribulations that they had undergone, it was argued, gave them the necessary patience and tolerance for professions like nursing. In addition to this, widows were also particularly suited for careers such as midwifery, whereas other Indian women were barred from entering this area due to the prejudice attached to the polluting nature of women undergoing labour and parturient mothers. Although there was also a great deal of resentment at the usurpation of the role of midwives and indigenous female Vaidyas by Western medicine,[179] their status meant that widows could practice these

---

[175] Venubai Namjoshi,'Sushiksit Bandhuna Anath Bhaginichyavatinen Vignyapathi' [An Appeal from Helpless Sisters to Their Educated Brothers], *Maharashtra Mahila*, August 1902, 85–6.

[176] 'An Appeal From Helpless Sisters', *Maharashtra Mahila*, August 1902, 86.

[177] Sarubai Goa, 'Anathbalikashram' [Orphanage for Girls], *Saubhagyasambhar*, 2 (1904): 33–6.

[178] *Silver Jubilee Album*, p. 38.

[179] Kashibai, 'Women's Duties', *Maharashtra Mahila*, October 1901, 178.

new methods without too much opposition from their families.[180] Their argument for the inclusion of widows was not one based on equal rights but a nationalistic one of 'social service', an argument later utilized by Gandhi.[181] Given the strength of opposition, Hindu widows functioning in a Hindu family and society did not consider it strategically advisable to demand jobs on the basis of equal rights, and their entry in the public sphere was therefore cloaked in the rhetoric of the more acceptable concept of service to the family, society and nation. Nevertheless, despite this mask, by the end of the nineteenth century, the desire for reforming the lives of widows had led to a group of women reformers emerging that were clearly distinct from their male counterparts.

Solidarity among *Bhaginivarg*

The Hindu women's attack on the *shastras* is the most important marker in their progression towards feminism binding them into a community of women with common interests caused by peculiar disadvantages not shared by their men folk. Although they did not reject Hinduism in the way that the Christian female reformers did, their common struggle to understand the sources of knowledge production about woman and womankind and the hostility of men to many of their reforms meant that a concept of sisterhood was gradually building among women that cut across caste and religion. The almost relentless targeting of women by male conservatives led to the coinage of the term *bhaginivarg* [sisterhood], an important step in the formation of Hindu women's consciousness of themselves as a 'collective'. The clearest example of this in operation is the manner in which Hindu women rallied round Pandita Ramabai when powerful Maharashtrian politicians like B.G. Tilak spread scandals about her institutions. At the height of the opposition to Pandita Ramabai, Hindu women leaders, like Ramabai Ranade, visited her with gifts for her pupils, as well as ensuring that they personally escorted widows that wished to study at her institutions.[182] Hindu female leaders were willing to forgive her radical action of abandoning the faith of her birth and converting to Christianity on the grounds that her institutions were alleviating the miseries of countless widows and deserted wives and female orphans. They sharply rebuked Hindu reformers and conservatives for persecuting her and questioned the *purusharth* [manhood and masculinity] of men who were good only at condemning the actions of well-intentioned women while perpetuating women's sufferings.[183] At a time when very few people had sympathy for Pandita Ramabai, Ramabai Ranade continued to encourage girls and

---

[180] Jivutai Mantri, 'Striyanchi Prasuti ani Tatsambandhi Upchar' [On Delivery and Related Subjects], Ibid., February 1901, 70–85.

[181] For Gandhi's views on the utility of the widow to the nation, see Kishwar, 'Gandhi on Women', p. 1693.

[182] Pandita Ramabai's Report in the *Annual Report of the American Ramabai Association*, 1894, p. 27.

[183] Manakbai Lad, 'Pandita Ramabai', *Arya Bhagini*, August 1891, 68–9.

widows to attend Pandita Ramabai's schools, an action that served to forge strong links between Hindu and Christian feminist leaders.

Hindu women also kept a close check on the magazines and journals targeted at women but published by male editors. A case took place in 1888 when Balwant Rao Nagarkar, a self-styled reformer and editor of a well known women's magazine titled *Grihini* [Housewife] published a one-act play in which a character named 'Pandita Ramabai', is vanquished in an intellectual tussle with her fictitious and conservative opponent, Umabai.[184] The play portrays the personality of 'Pandita Ramabai' as a one-dimensional, diehard man-hater, who exhibits absolutely no 'womanly skills', a depiction that greatly angered his female readership who flooded his magazine with demands for an 'Open Apology' which was duly printed.[185] One female reader argued that Pandita Ramabai was not, as he claimed, 'de-sexed' and 'unfeminine', justifying her arguments by copiously quoting from Ramabai's advice manual for women titled *Stridharmaniti*, whilst others stressed her untiring work on behalf of Indian women. Such solidarity not only illustrates the advanced nature of feminism in nineteenth-century Maharashtra but also demonstrates the enlightened attitudes that female reformers had towards women leaders who followed religions other than their own.

Another issue that developed the bond between Maharashtrian women of different religions was the uproar over the appointment of Lady Superintendents and Inspectresses to Municipal Schools in the city of Bombay in 1901. Many argued that only European women could properly carry out the kinds of tasks that men could perform, a view that Maharashtrian women saw as a slur on 'Indian womanhood'.[186] Communal politics among men led them to argue that to secure Hindu female inspectresses for Hindu girls' schools was difficult and therefore it was best to appoint Hindu men. However, among women the solidarity was much stronger and allowed them to adopt the attitude that until Hindu women came forward, women of other faiths such as Parsis should be allotted to the post of inspectress or headmistress.[187] Although, as Partha Chatterjee correctly states, Indian male nationalists acted to try and prevent encroachments by the colonial state into the 'inner' spiritual world of India so that they could maintain control of it themselves, their solution hardly helped the Hindu women's cause as it excluded them altogether. Women's nonconfrontational attitude towards other faiths paid dividends with Indian Christian women providing support to young Hindu women entering a society that had hitherto been dominated by men.

Indian Christian women, too, returned the affections demonstrated by Hindu women in equal measure. More experienced women, like Pandita Ramabai and Mary Bhor gave encouragement to Hindu women who were just starting their careers

---

[184] 'Varishta Pratiche Shikshan: Pandita Ramabai va Umabaiyancha Samvad' [Higher Education: A Debate Between Pandita Ramabai and Umabai], *Grihini*, February 1888, 169–76.

[185] 'Patravyavahar' [Letters to the Editor], Ibid., March 1888, 181–4.

[186] Editorial, *Maharashtra Mahila*, October 1901, 147.

[187] Ibid., 147.

through favourable book reviews. One example of this strategy in practice is Rukmini Sanzgiri, whose works on knitting and crocheting were publicized by Mary Bhor and Pandita Ramabai in the journals and adopted in their schools.[188] The birth and development of the unique women's press in Maharashtra as shown earlier in this chapter allowed women to develop passionate friendships and express unabashed admiration for the work done by their favourite female leaders.[189] They reviewed each other's books, wrote biographies of famous contemporary women in the belief that 'a biography of a woman should be written by women', housed each other in times of need,[190] and thus created interpersonal bonds comparable to those developed between British and American feminists during the early nineteenth-century feminist movements.[191] In Maharashtra, women were often encouraged to find inspiration and courage by reading about the women's movements taking place in far-flung countries as remote sometimes as China and Mongolia, let alone Britain and America, or through the example of local women who had been heroic and faced society's opprobrium.[192]

Many women's journals functioned like counselling bureaus. Women communicated their problems through letters, and the editor either published them in their original form or respected their wish to remain anonymous by only quoting excerpts from them and left it to readers to send in their suggestions. Encouragement in times of adversity and solutions to many knotty problems were found through the women's press, binding women into what Kristeva aptly calls a 'community of dolphins' who stayed close to each other and provided vital support networks. Many of the headmistresses of girls' schools were quick to grasp the advantages of such journals and subscribed to them in large numbers.[193] Besides providing moral support, they were acutely sensitive to the lack of funds for their projects. There is an instance when women condemned the acts of wealthy women who donated large sums of money to the *Gayan Samaj* [Music Association] instead of institutions which were engaged

---

[188] Review by Mary Bhor in *Karmanook*, 21 November 1896, and excerpts of Pandita Ramabai's review is published in Rukmini Sanzhgiri, *The Art of Crochetting*. n.p.

[189] Rametabai Bhujangarao Mankar's poem on Manakbai Lad, 'Dindi' [Torch-bearer], *Arya Bhagini*, September 1890 n.p.; Manoramabai's editorial in praise of Savitribai Bhatwadekar's work, *Maharashtra Mahila*, August 1902, 66–9.

[190] Kashibai Kanitkar's book review of Parvatibai Chitnavis, *Amchya Jagacha Pravas* [Our Travels Around the World], in *Vividhadnyanvistar*, March 1916, 20–26; Kamalabai Kibe's book review of Kashibai Kanitkar, *Dr Anandibai Joshi Yanche Charitra* [The Biography of Dr Anandibai Joshi], in Ibid., 14–20.

[191] For bonding among women in Victorian England see Philippa Levine, *Victorian Feminism: 1850—1920* (London: Hutchinson, 1987); Carroll Smith-Rosenberg, 'The Female World of Love and Ritual: Relations Between Women in Nineteenth-Century America', *Signs*, Autumn 1975, 1–29.

[192] Between 1880 to 1920 Maharashtrian feminists such as Pandita Ramabai, Ramabai Ranade, Anandibai Joshi and occasionally European feminists too were regularly the focus of articles by women writers in the women's press.

[193] Radhabai's letter to the editor of *Arya Bhagini*, August 1890, 92.

specifically for women's welfare.[194] This 'coming-together' of women is particularly striking when we consider the revivalist context in which this particular music association was founded.[195] As seen above, a sense of common commitment bound Parsi, Christian and Hindu women on several issues that were gender specific. Equally we see the bonding between women of all communities expressed over the agitation of the Age of Consent debates in the 1890s.[196]

Therefore, by the beginning of the twentieth century, a distinctive feminist movement was emerging from the social reform movements of the nineteenth century. Although retaining their identity as Hindus, and cloaking their ideology in the less-contentious language of social reform, there was nevertheless a growing awareness of a feminist consciousness that crossed lines of caste and religion. As this consciousness of their own position within society developed, it was becoming increasingly clear that women had to develop alliances across traditional boundaries if they were to succeed in reforming attitudes towards women. It was increasingly clear that a policy of accommodation and assimilation was no longer sufficient to achieve further gains in achieving parity with men, and it is to the study of various forms of assertion and resistance by all classes of women that we turn in the next two chapters.

---

[194] 'Schemes and Efforts', *Maharashtra Mahila*, August 1902, 67.

[195] Part of the religious revivalism/nationalism had inspired Indian art critics like Ananda Coomaraswamy to conduct a crusade about Indian art's superior spiritual. Several music societies sprang up funded by revivalists. The Poona Gayan Samaj was one of the most notable ones. J.N. Farquhar, *Modern Religious Movements in India* (New York: MacMillan, 1915).

[196] See chapter 6 for details.

Chapter 4

Women's Assertion and Resistance in Colonial India

Introduction

This chapter analyzes the various forms of individual and collective assertion and resistance by women in late nineteenth- and early twentieth-century colonial India. These initiatives, it is argued here, arose when women were caught up in negotiating with various kinds of power relations in an everyday context.

Women's resistance in India remains a little explored area. Hence, it seems appropriate to begin with conceptual clarifications. The term 'resistance' is a wide-ranging term, encompassing many acts extending its sweep from the private sphere of the home to the public/political arena. By 'resistance' we mean the ability to limit, nullify or overturn structures of power. As such, resistance is an inherently conscious act and is characterized by intention. From within the broader concept of resistance emerges 'assertion'. Assertion is a mode of resistance in which women try to safeguard their interests and rights through an arbitration process such as seeking the law-courts and petitioning the state.[1] Assertion by its very definition is a more positive form of resistance that allows the woman appealing to state authorities to do so, within recognized and legitimized forms of agitation.

The first section is an exploration of women's role as agents in bettering their lives through their use of a variety of state apparatuses, specifically petitioning. This mode of resistance as 'assertion' contested the kinds of power relations that worked to restrict their economic independence, limited their ownership of property and productive resources, controlled their sexuality and restricted their mobility. In their use of petitioning, they at once actively responded to, and resisted, situations that threatened to restrict their agency. Moreover, when appeals and memorials failed to satisfy their demands, certain classes of women adopted more aggressive forms of resistance. Such instances usually occurred when forms of assertion, in which women attempted to safeguard their interests and rights through negotiation, failed, and covered acts as diverse as defying authority, refusing to comply with rules and regulations and finding loopholes in the legal structures and working them to their advantage. In addition to these, women were also increasingly turning to the written word to combat the misrepresentations of femininity and to curb the trend of apportioning blame for

---

[1] Women's recourse to law courts is discussed in more detail in the next two chapters.

contemporary social maladies on womanhood in misogynistic literature. The strategies and sites of resistance that the women employed were extremely diverse and varied in accordance with the caste/class locations of women. For example, upper-caste and upper-class women were more likely to have the self-confidence and self-assurance to use 'appeals' as a way of registering their complaints. These forms of resistance tended to be based on more favourable allocation of power or resources. On the other hand, a prostitute's or middle-class woman's cause of complaint and mode of protest may have differed vastly from those of her upper-class counterparts, as they not only had different concerns but also lacked the access to the grievance procedures that were perhaps more open to wealthier women. Bearing these facts in mind, it has proved useful in this chapter to distinguish 'assertion' from other forms of 'resistance' in Indian women's strategies of opposition and confrontation.[2]

The second section examines a specific form of symbolic resistance adopted by women in their use of a particular genre of literary writing. Women's folk songs, novels and plays written during this period recreated a world that turned social reality upside-down. In them, we find a world ruled by women administrators who are intelligent and able, and a just female police upholds law. In short, this is an equitable world where, they believed, the deceit and cunning practised by men in public and private affairs would be entirely absent.[3] It is shown here that resistance was, and

---

[2] This section has profited from the methodological and theoretical advances in understanding women's resistance in recent feminist scholarship. Specific works are: Toril Moi (ed.), *The Kristeva Reader* (New York: Columbia University Press, 1986); Diana Fuss, *Essentially Speaking: Feminism, Nature and Difference* (New York: Routledge, 1989); Eugenia DeLamotte, Natania Meeker and Jean F. O'Barr, *Women Imagine Change: A Global Anthology of Women's Resistance, 600 B.C.E to Present* (New York: Routledge, 1997). Anthropological work, especially in the 1970s and 1980s, demonstrated the various forms of women's resistance and power in peasant and tribal societies. My work has benefited from two important feminist scholars working in this area. They are Susan Carol Rogers, 'Female Forms of Power and the Myth of Male Dominance: A Model of Female/Male Interaction in Peasant Society', *American Ethnologist*, 2/4 (1975): 727–55 and Lila Abu-Lughod, 'A Community of Secrets', *Signs*, 10 (1985): 637–57; also, 'The Romance of Resistance: Tracing Transformations of Power Through Bedouin Women', *American Ethnologist*, 17/1 (1990): 41–55, and her monograph *Veiled Sentiments: Honor and Poetry in a Bedouin Society* (Berkeley: University of California Press, 1988).

[3] Some scholars of Asian societies have provided rich insights on the cultural resistance of subordinated peoples, and also widened the definition of resistance. Alongside the well-known works of Michael Adas and James Scott have appeared more recently a monograph containing a collection of essays depicting a variety of nonconfrontational resistances in Asia whose importance lies partly in its inclusion of women's resistances. See Veena Oldenburg, 'Lifestyle as Resistance: The Case of the Courtesans of Lucknow', pp. 23–61 and Rosalind O'Hanlon, 'Issues of Widowhood: Gender and Resistance in Colonial Western India', pp. 62–108, in D. Haynes and G. Prakash (eds), *Contesting Power: Resistance and Everyday Social Relations in South Asia* (Berkeley: University of California Press, 1991).

indeed has remained, an important aspect of everyday relations of ordinary women and was a general phenomenon. The process by which symbolic resistance as exhibited through a text is transformed into actual resistance is demonstrated. The ways in which 'symbolic' acts, such as the literary genre of role inversions in 'plays' precedes and informs consciousness, is revealed here. The patterns of women's assertion and resistance uncover distinctive behaviours that are purposeful with specific goals. Thus, in contrast to some current theoretical formulations on resistance, this book reveals that women as resistors were almost always conscious agents of resistance— intention and deliberation is invariably present—either to subvert immediate authority or in the promotion of larger agendas such as feminist consciousness raising.[4] Seeing women as conscious resistors and their acts of resistance as purposeful also sheds light on their ambiguous attitudes towards the colonial state, which was sometimes seen as a benevolent force whilst, at other times, viewed with disapprobation. Collectively, perhaps recovered from the repositories of Indian history for the first time here, these writings therefore provide a valuable perspective from a subordinated group on colonial rule.

The Right to Property: Petitioning as an Instrument of Assertion

Several scholars have noted the importance of petitions and memorials in Indian political life long before the formation of the Indian National Congress.[5] Jim Masselos, for instance, argued that early public associations were excluded from decision-making but impressed their views on the state through petitions and meetings; indeed, even significant agitations, such as the one that adopted the American revolutionary motto of 'no taxation without representation', had their beginnings in petitioning.[6] This section examines the ways in which Indian women learnt to use appeals and complaint procedures will argue that, in the hands of women, petitioning became a sophisticated instrument of assertion, especially when it became evident to them that male-dominated public associations would not allow them entry and that often, the true oppressor was, in fact, their own men folk.

An area in particular that prompted Maharashtrian women to assert themselves was when their control or ownership of property was challenged by others. This ranged from houses or businesses to agricultural land, and even farms and livestock. The

---

[4] In contrast to Haynes and Prakash, who argue that 'consciousness need not be essential to its [resistance] constitution'. 'Introduction' to *Contesting Power*, p. 3. Such a formulation I would argue empties women's resistance of meaning, making their protests against structures of power either accidental or at best incidental.

[5] For example, see Jim Masselos, *Towards Nationalism, Group Affiliations and the Politics of Public Associations in the Nineteenth-Century Western India* (Bombay: Popular Prakashan, 1974); S.R. Mehrotra, *Towards Indian Freedom and Partition* (New Delhi: Vikas, 1979).

[6] Masselos, *Towards Nationalism*, pp. 147–55.

nature of the conflicts meant that these women tended to come from wealthy, and in many cases, upper-class backgrounds. In the early part of the nineteenth century, the establishment of colonial courts of law, as well as the right to appeal to executive authorities, created a forum for the successful assertion of women's property rights. In 1880s, the numbers of daughters and widows of *sardars* [landed elites] administering *watans* [revenue yielding lands] was substantial, with a total of 61; a figure that included first-, second- and third-class *sardars*.[7] The three classes of sardars were classified according to the size of the estate as well as the revenue yield from it, with the first being the highest. These numbers are indicative of the substantial participation of women in administering property well into the nineteenth century, as well as possibly explaining why these women came to be targeted by Maharashtrian men. The statistics are all the more revealing when we consider the highly discriminatory policies of the state in excluding females from inheritance rights of *watans*. Regulation XVI, issued by the government in 1827, declared that a female could not inherit a *watan,* claiming that such a ruling was in 'complete harmony with the feeling of the *watandars* themselves'.[8] Such a policy was motivated, not only by the discriminatory notion that '*watan* property ought only to be found in the hands of males, they alone being competent to perform the services required by the state', but also by the state's drive to achieve uniformity and efficiency in the administration of revenue.[9] Clearly, the pressure that Maharashtrian *watandars* had applied on the colonial state, as well as the officials' own perceptions of a woman's duties derived from the conservative Victorian notions of the proper place of women in society, were creating a hostile environment for Indian women to continue to operate in outside the home. The happy marriage between various forms of patriarchies—Indian and Victorian—is clearly visible in the land administration policies of nineteenth-century Maharashtra.

However, between 1827 and 1868, women, especially widows, were successfully able to defy this ban, mainly by choosing to take one of two possible courses of action. One popular method was adopting a son to inherit the land on their behalf. Widows in Maharashtra could adopt much more easily in comparison to those in Bengal as

---

[7] Out of 52 Sardars belonging to class I, 9 women managed the estates themselves with *zamindari* rights; out of 64 Sardars of class II, 22 widows are listed under various jurisdictions while, out of 91 Sardars of class III, 30 widows are mentioned. None of them were listed as exercizing civil jurisdiction within their *jaghir* and *inam* villages. Government resolution No. 2363, 23 July 1867 in 'List of the Three Classes of and Widows of Sardars', vol. 84, comp. no. 1150, Judicial Department, (hereafter JD), 1890. Maharashtra State Archives, (hereafter MSA).

[8] Cited in the Second Reading of the Bill No. 2 of 1885, *A Bill to Amend Bombay Hereditary Offices Act III of 1874*, vol. 24, Bombay Legislative Council Proceedings (hereafter BLCP), 1886, V/9/2802, p.91 [Oriental and India Office Collections (hereafter OIOC)].

[9] Ibid., p. 92. Prem Chowdhry's excellent monograph on the question of revenue settlements in colonial Haryana indicates similar processes in operation in Northern India too; *The Veiled Women: Shifting Gender Equations in Rural Haryana, 1880–1920* (Delhi: Oxford University Press, 1994).

customary law permitted it.[10] The second method was by figuring out a loophole within the provisions of Act XI of 1843, which allowed females to control *watans* by appointing deputies to perform estate management services. The number of successful cases in the High Court that were instigated by women in order to gain control of the *watans* was so great that case law led to the government in 1886 further amending the Hereditary Offices Act (1874).[11] Realizing that 'the probability of lapses to the State is remote whilst *watandars* and their widows could freely adopt sons', the Select Committee appointed to report on the Bill appeased members of indigenous elites by vesting the rights of *watans* in such a way that females could only inherit if there was no male heir.[12] During the passage of the Bill, some *watandars* made blatant, though ultimately unsuccessful, attempts to return *watans* back to male family members after they had fallen into the hands of women by default. While indigenous elites made use of the colonial machinery to dispossess women of landed rights, they also successfully manipulated various representations of womanhood and employed Indian tradition in order to try and achieve their goal of reasserting their control over land that they believed to be theirs. An illustration of their methods can be seen in their emotive argument that the system of appointing only one representative *watandar* increased the crime of female infanticide as the lack of male *watandars* meant that the daughters born to those who bore the prestigious title of *sardar* could no longer marry men belonging to the same or higher rank, meaning that *watandar* female lives were endangered.[13] These arguments, which harnessed the irresistible sanction and use of tradition and custom in Indian male discourses, were neither new nor original—they were also apparent in the debates over *sati* and female infanticide in Gujarat in the early part of the nineteenth century. Their deployment in debates over Watandari rights simply shows how customary usage and tradition were successfully deployed by Maharashtrian elites in forging new forms of domination over women.

In 1904, the Bombay government tried to place stricter control over female successors of estates and revenue-yielding villages by establishing a Court of Wards on the grounds that women practising *purdah* could not manage their own affairs. Although it was pointed out by Indian members of the Council that not very many Maharashtrian women were in fact in *purdah* and females who were landholders had often proved to be able administrators in the past, the state insisted that 'a female subject to the customs which prevail in the country (in this case *purdah*) [sic] may be

---

[10] For a more general discussion of adoption and inheritance laws as they affected women's rights, see Sandra Rogers who, in an analysis of property disputes in Bombay city between 1875 and 1884, claims that 'Hindu widows were pioneers of property rights in Bombay city'. 'Hindu Widows and Property in Late Nineteenth Century Bombay', in Gail Pearson and Lenore Manderson (eds), *Class, Ideology and Women in Asian Countries* (Hong Kong: Asian Studies Monograph Series, 1987), p. 61.

[11] Bill to amend Bombay Watandari Act III of 1874, BLCP, 1886, pp. 59–94, OIOC.

[12] Ibid., p.93.

[13] Bill No. 2 of 1881, to amend Bombay Hereditary Offices Act III of 1874, BLCP, 1881, V/9/2801, vol. 20, pp. 24–34, OIOC.

on that account unable to manage her estate with any efficiency'.[14] The same Bill empowered the District Collector to declare a female landholder incapable of managing her property 'on grounds of sex', and this was 'to apply mainly to *purdah* ladies'. The right to appeal was also withdrawn and such women could not adopt or make wills after their disqualification. What is clearly evident in the successive amendments of the Watandari Act is how the erosion of women's power took place firstly by the colonial invitation to indigenous groups to represent the proper sphere of Hindu women's duties and then by the empowerment of the state on the basis of these representations of womanhood.

In spite of the alarming restrictions on their powers, women from the landed classes were still able to protest successfully against the arbitrary decisions of the state, especially when it concerned the day-to-day management of their estates. In pre-colonial times, *watandars* had their own military retainers to guard standing crops.[15] After the Rebellion of 1857, the government ruled that, for security reasons, no *watandars* could possess arms beyond a certain limit. Several *sardar* women argued against this regulation, and were successful in getting a dispensation for more arms. Umabai Saheb Purandhare, the widow of a class I *sardar*, for instance, complained that she was obliged to take out licenses for certain old arms that were family heirlooms, and were there for purely decorative purposes.[16] Like other members of aristocratic families, she resented both the curtailment of such privileges and, more significantly, the fact that the Act operated as a tax on family property of this nature. Following complaints from several widows in similar situations, the Governor-in-Council exempted *sardars* of all classes from the necessity of taking out licenses for old family heirlooms.[17]

Other petitions by *sardar* widows that were granted were also usually concerned with tax relief or the provision of facilities that would substantially help them to better the administration of their estates.[18] A fine illustration of the success of the petitioning method is the case of Umabai Bivalkar, the widow of a class I *sardar* of Deccan, who stated that her estates produced a revenue of Rs. 10,002 a year, of which she paid Rs. 6,000 in taxes to the state. In order to protect and guard her standing crops, she employed 43 sepoys, each armed with a weapon. When the District Magistrate of Thane seized 35 of these weapons, she requested them back on the grounds that she

---

[14] Bill No. 1 of 1904 (A Bill to establish a Court of Wards in the Bombay Presidency), BLCP, 1904, V/9/2806, vol. 23, p. 139, OIOC.

[15] H. Fukazawa 'Maharashtra and the Deccan: A Note', in T. Raychaudhuri and I. Habib (eds), *The Cambridge Economic History of India, c.1200–1750* vol. I (Cambridge: Cambridge University Press, 1982), p. 194.

[16] Appeal by Umabai Saheb Purandhare, 25 August 1880, Bombay Judicial Proceedings (hereafter BJP), 1880, vol. P/1591, no. 2254, OIOC.

[17] Resolution of the Governor of Bombay, BJP, Ibid.

[18] For tax refunds, see petition of class I Sardar, 6 April 1881, BJP, 1881, vol. P/1796, no. 858, OIOC.

could not administer her estates efficiently with unarmed guards.[19] The government allowed her to reclaim 16 of the weapons. However, with the restrictions on the claims of aristocratic women continually being tightened, not all appeals were answered satisfactorily; indeed, quite a few petitions that related to subjects of inheritance and adoption were rejected. Where there was conflict between the aristocratic claims of indigenous men and women, as the highly publicized cases of Anandibai Daphle and Bayjabai demonstrated, the state was always likely to side with the interests of men.[20]

Nevertheless, although the interests of Maharashtrian men and the collusion of the state with indigenous elites restricted their autonomy, women belonging to the propertied classes in the late nineteenth century began a process of self-help to help alleviate the difficulties of others in the same situation. One of the main vehicles that they used to express problems that were peculiar to their class and also make suggestions for resolving them were works of literature. One of the more famous literary figures amongst women, Kamalabai Kibe, an aristocrat for instance, used many of her shorter works of fiction to address the problems of upper-class women who had been betrayed or deceived over property.[21] Journals edited by women also advised women against signing documents without knowing the contents and to refrain from investing in commercial transactions without proper guidance from trustworthy people. During this period, women belonging to the aristocracy also enhanced their public image, as well as courted the approval of the government, by participating in state-run enterprises for 'women's welfare', such as projects for girls' education and medical relief for women,[22] with many of the earliest women's magazines and organizations receiving generous grants from upper-class women. An often-quoted early feminist among the aristocracy was the Maharani of Baroda, Chimnabai Saheb whose entire staff, including a secretary and doctor, consisted of women.[23] Tarabai Shinde, a member of the declining gentry (the Maratha elites), and a descendant of the old eighteenth-century Shinde family, raged precisely against the disempowerment of Maratha women when she talked specifically of the imposition of *purdah* and the ever-tightening restrictions on women's freedoms, such as the adoption of the upper-caste injunction against widow remarriage by subordinate castes.[24] The importance of

---

[19] Memorial by Umabai Bivalkar, 24 September 1881, BJP, 1881, vol. P/1796, no. 2682, pp. 1016–17, OIOC.

[20] Lakshmibai and Anandibai Daphle's petition to adopt an heir to the throne of the state of Jath was turned down in favour of a male relative. In *Bodh Sudhakar*, 17 September 1892, *Native Newspaper Reports*, (hereafter NNR); see too the case of Bayjabai, the wife of an Inamdar who lost her entire estate in Kolhapur to Appa Saheb Jadav, *Induprakash*, 31 January 1881, NNR.

[21] Kamalabai Kibe, 'Samaj Chitra Number Ek: Balavriddhavivaha' [Picture of our Society Number One: Marriage of an Old Man with a Young Girl] *Vivadhadnyanvistar*, September 1911, 113–19.

[22] See chapter 3.

[23] 'Naval-Vishesh' [Special News], *Maharashtra Mahila*, March 1901, n.p.

[24] Tarabai Shinde, *Stripurushtulana Athava Striya va Purush Yant Sahasi Kon he Spasta Karun Dakavinyakarita ha Nibandh* [Women and Men, A Comparison or an Essay

Tarabai Shinde's treatise lies in its elaborate plea to contemporary men to share the benefits that British rule had brought equally between men and women. Pointing to the trappings of modernity symbolized by the new lifestyle of the Maharashtrian men, which found expression in the colonial architecture of their homes, furniture, dress and diet and Western lifestyles, she draws attention to the fact that the same men excluded women from these advantages, especially in regard to the issue of widow remarriage.[25] Reading her work as a tract of resistance, especially within the context of the assertive claims made by other aristocratic women that has also been seen, allows us to distinguish it as a self-help treatise perhaps aimed at an erudite audience of titled women, rather than just a solitary foray by an isolated feminist.

The women of the aristocratic class therefore saw their property rights continually eroded over the course of the century. Women that came from less wealthy backgrounds, however, achieved greater levels of success in this area, although it is true that the nature of their claims tended to be matters such as suing for damages caused to their houses or belongings, reclaiming *stridhan* [women's wealth], the initiation of special appeals for the maintenance of agricultural land, or the reclamation of stolen goods from their property. In addition, several women belonging to this class successfully sued the municipality of Bombay for damages caused to their property through illegal orders of the municipal authorities. Janubai and Pilubai, for instance, were awarded Rs. 2,120 as compensation for land confiscated under the City of Bombay Improvement Act of 1898 and were able to reclaim a further Rs. 897 from the Court of the Tribunal of Appeal, Bombay, that had been taken from them as agricultural tax,[26] whilst Mulibai was awarded Rs. 501 by the Municipality for damages caused to her home.[27] There were also cases when women successfully intervened in the management of their property, an example of this being Gangubai Shinde's appeal to the High Court to prevent her father's creditors from demanding a lump sum payment by the sale of her father's property. The Court awarded her the right to administer the estate, enabling her to deal directly with the creditors; as she announced in a 'notice' in local newspapers, she 'alone ha[d] the right of effecting a settlement of the claims of the mortgagee and redeeming the property'.[28] Likewise, Danawa, a widow deprived of her moveable and immoveable property by the illegal actions of village officers who had allowed her husband's property to pass on to her husband's sister's son in her absence, appealed successfully to the government to file a suit in the name of the state on the ground that the village officers' conduct was

---

Showing Who is More Wicked], S.J. Malshe (ed.), 2nd edn (Bombay: Mumbai Marathi Grantha Sangrahalaya Publications, 1975; 1st edn 1882). Hereafter [Women and Men, A Comparison].

[25] Ibid., pp. 12–16.

[26] Proceedings of the Court of the Tribunal of Appeal appointed under section 48(3) of Bombay Act IV of 1898, BLCP, 1907, P/8032, no.40, OIOC.

[27] *Gujarati*, 9 June 1883, NNR.

[28] *Vritt Sudha*, 23 September 1893, NNR.

irresponsible.[29] This was just one of a large number of petitions by widows during the latter half of the nineteenth century over landed property that ended up being settled in the High Court.[30] In many instances, women who felt threatened by intrigue and duplicity from members of their extended family or friends over property disputes sought the protection of the government; in cases that came from princely states, the government normally directed these petitions to the Political Agent or to local authorities for redress.[31] Neither was it only widows who felt vulnerable; there were also several instances when women protested against the removal of their personal property, like *stridhan* [women's property] or items which provided means of livelihood, by their husbands or by agents acting to repossess their husband's property. Jijabai of Islampur, for instance, refused to hand over her ornaments to her husband's creditors as the law recognized them to be *stridhan*, or the property of the woman alone, meaning that their maintenance and disposal lay entirely in her hands. Jijabai petitioned the government to intervene to help her retain her jewels but was told to try the courts.[32] On the other hand, women like Nathbai were entirely successful in regaining property that had been taken from her illegally; the government decreed that the livestock that was stolen from her farm and sold by the culprits should be purchased back by the state and restored to her.[33]

Therefore, although the colonial state acted as an oppressor in some instances of women's property rights, especially in its enforcement of the Watandari Act, which eroded upper-class women's ownership rights, even further, less wealthier and non aristocratic women attended to their diverse grievances by continually accessing new channels of redress. The number of petitions that women brought is indicative of a greater self-confidence, with women involved much less accepting of the situations that they found themselves in than they would have been previously. The law provided one outlet for asserting their rights, but Indian women of this time were also finding other ways of asserting themselves, and over issues other than property, as the following section demonstrates.

The Right to a Livelihood: Economic Deprivation and Women's Agitation

The forging of the Indian middle classes took place against the backdrop of British rule in India, which required the urban professional class to administer

---

[29] 19 Dec. 1884, BJP, 1884, P/2423, no. 3485, OIOC.

[30] BJP, 1884, P/2423, no. 3366 and BJP, 1884, P/2423, no. 2248, OIOC.

[31] Petition of Assa, 12 August 1870, BJP, 1870, P/442/4, no. 194, OIOC. Such cases were regularly reported in the vernacular press too. See *Hitechchu*, 6 December 1879, NNR.

[32] 28 June 1883, BJP, 1883, vol. P/2178, no. 2906, OIOC, and petition of Laxmibai Kelkar from Dapholi, n.d., BJP, 1881, vol. P/1796, no. 1042, OIOC.

[33] 3 February 1870, BJP, 1870, vol. P/442/4, no. 53, OIOC.

their policies and serve the population.[34] Aware of their responsibilities, these elites soon began to possess a heightened sense of awareness of their roles as model citizens and participated in upholding civic consciousness in the social and cultural settings of urban India. Middle-class women's writings of the period, however, tended to focus more sharply on the middle class imperative to actively seek an income rather than expect to live off rents and landed property. These narratives reveal different anxieties that can be gauged by their insistence on instructing their readers that their children's inheritance was not land but a sound education and moral values. Genteel women's petitions to the government reveal the vulnerability of middle-class families dependent on single incomes and pensions, the efforts that they made to stave off debts and retain some independence and the depredations of illness and accident that they potentially had to face without the cushion of the extended families that they had left behind in the villages. These writings and petitions illustrate the precariousness of middle- and lower middle-class urban life at the turn of the century, and the difficulties that such families could face if even the slightest thing went wrong.

Given the fragility of the situation, it is therefore hardly surprising that one of the more assertive forms of women's agitation during the late nineteenth century arose out of the economic situation of the middle and lower classes. The 1850s was a period of rising prices, especially for agricultural goods.[35] Moreover, while it was true that prices of nonagricultural goods, like salt, kerosene and coal, remained stable, the value of the rupee fell rapidly from 1873 and continued to fall until the end of the century, causing wages to depreciate in real terms. The hardest hit in this period were those in the middle-classes who had to manage on a small income, a concern reflected in the printed literature produced by women during the last half of the nineteenth century, which is marked by an overwhelming concern with the problems of the wage earners and the peasantry. In common with the Marathi male press, almost every issue of journals produced by the women's press carried articles on *katkasar* [thrift] that highlighted the need for minimizing household expenses and improved household management.[36] The science of home budgeting began to acquire some sophistication as contributors to women's magazines on *katkasar* began to devise tabular columns in which areas of home spending could be divided. Their call for reducing expenditure

---

[34] B.B. Mishra, *The Indian Middle Classes: Their Growth in Modern Times* (London: Oxford University Press, 1961).

[35] Michelle McAlpin, 'Price Movements and Fluctuations in Economic Activity (1860–1947)', in D. Kumar (ed.), *The Cambridge Economic History of India c.1757–1970* vol. II, (Cambridge: Cambridge University Press, 1983), pp. 878–904.

[36] Representative amongst them are: 'Katkasar [Thrift]', in *Strishikshanchandrika* [Journal of Women's Education], May and June 1900, 131–5; a series entitled 'Grihinicha Anubhav' [Experiences of a Housewife]' that appeared throughout 1888 and 1889, with subsections on '*Katkasar*' [Thrift] in *Grihini* [Housewife]; see also 'Prapanchikas Shahanpanachi Avashyakata [Prudence and Wisdom as Essential Attributes of Domestic Life]', in *Strisadbodhachinatamani* [Women's Advice Manual], September 1881, 2–4.

over ceremonies held to celebrate rites such as marriage, puberty and pregnancy, analyzed in more detail in the previous chapter, was partly due to their concern over the impoverishment of the middle and lower classes. Middle-class women confronted this issue by challenging older lifestyles, demanding that they be replaced by an ethic that instead celebrated the dignity of labour, an idea that would manifest itself in inexpensive and simpler modes of dress, behaviour and diet. Women were told to stop wishing for gold ornaments and expensive saris and instead invest their money in promissory notes and post office savings deposits. Sewing and embroidery were also encouraged to reduce dependence on more expensive tailor-made goods. Neither were these ideas confined to remain between the journal covers, with women holding meetings in places as diverse as temples, plague camps and *kirtans* [religious discourses] to disseminate the new middle-class ethic.[37]

An analysis of a piece of fiction written by women illustrates well how this theory operated in practice. 'A Story of a Home', a semi-fictional account, depicts the middle-class home of Narayan Rao, whose two daughters and sons were all receiving education.[38] His wife dies but he has no problems bringing up his children as his daughters (who are being educated) are mature and responsible children and take the mother's place. However, when Narayan suddenly faces a Rs. 5 reduction in his monthly wage, a shadow is cast over his home, and there is a probability that his oldest son will have to stop attending College. However, his eldest daughter, Yamuna, who is living with her family whilst her husband studies in Bombay for a law degree, takes action to reduce their other outgoings by getting rid of the servants and curtailing home expenditure, meaning that her brother can continue his education. She also advises her father to sell their house, which is old and unmanageable, and move to a smaller home. Her father finally takes Yamuna's advice and solves their problems. Such a story demonstrates the way in which women's practice of prudent household management could allow middle-class families to survive and flourish. Even though there is no radical change in the role Yamuna plays in the household, her education allows her to assume a new and indispensable position of 'house manager', a title which, in form and content, dignified her housewifely status.

This assumption of a new type of authority was also important in restoring some domestic authority back to those women who had lost it when they had accompanied their husbands to the city. In the predominantly agricultural households of rural Maharashtra, women not only attended to the work of a housewife but also actively participated in agricultural work. A typical example was Anandibai Karve's mother, who is described as one commanding much influence within the home, a position that Anandibai herself attributed to her mother's grasp of various agricultural operations; indeed, the fact that Anandibai herself learnt the art of harvesting and marketing grain from her mother and mother-in-law gave her a certain amount of autonomy and a

---

[37] Kashibai Shingane, 'Plague Campatil Hakeekat' [What Took Place in the Plague Camp], *Maharashtra Mahila*, February 1901, 86–91.

[38] 'Arya Mahila', 'Samsaarathlya Goshti [A Story of a Home]', *Maharashtra Mahila*, July 1901, 16–18.

means of independent income.[39] However, as Yamuna's story demonstrates, within the confines of the town and city, the only way a middle-class woman could achieve an equivalent level of power was to enhance the traditional role of housewife. Such attempts, however, had a moral rather than an economic value, although such women could help to preserve the family's position. The real test, however, arose in those situations where the family suddenly lost a breadwinner.

The utter helplessness of families where the head of the household had died or faced redundancy due to chronic illness is recorded in women's petitions to the government. Between 1880 and 1890, hundreds of petitions were sent by women to the government pleading for compassionate allowances, gratuities or employment. The nature of the problems differed from case to case but the overriding link was destitution created by the dependence of urban-based professional classes on single-salaried incomes. For example, in 1884 Mai explained how her husband, a constable working for the Satara police, was discharged from service due to sickness with a gratuity of Rs. 50. Despite taking a job as a domestic help, she 'has struggled since then to maintain herself, her sick husband and four children with difficulty, but is now quite broken down by her hard labour to support her family.'[40] She requested employment for her eldest son 'who knows to read and write Marathi and is quite willing to do any menial work'.[41] Doolumbee, on the other hand, whose husband had died after 23 years service in the Satara police department, petitioned for an allowance because she was 'childless, and alone and quite destitute for the means of support'.[42] Quite a few petitions were by women demanding compensation for the loss of their husbands' lives in the execution of public duties—for example, while trailing rebellious *Bhils* [tribes] or *dacoits* [bandits] or in incidents where they were accidentally killed by European soldiers.[43] These cases speak volumes about the ways in which women asserted themselves and demonstrate that they were aware of their rights to compensation. Compensation was usually demanded either in the form of money or employment for one of the family members who had agreed to look after the widow in return. There are several instances when the state granted up to Rs. 300 as compensation or agreed to employ the eldest son in the department where the widow's husband had worked.[44]

The economic hardships of middle-class women are also starkly demonstrated in their attempts to claim pensions for the services of their husbands who had died a few months before becoming eligible for pension rights. In many cases, the Magistrate forwarded the petitions to the Governor, recommending the 'case as a hard one', and making them special exceptions, especially in instances where the widowed mother or

---

[39] Anandibai Karve, *Maze Puran* [My Autobiography] (Bombay: Keshav Bhikaji Dhavle, 1944), p. 32.

[40] Petition by Mai Bor, 4 June 1884, JD, 1884, vol. 96, comp. no. 1201, MSA.

[41] Ibid.

[42] Petition by Doolumbee, 21 February 1884, JD, 1884, vol. 96, comp. no. 1433, MSA.

[43] For example, n.d., BJP, 1883, vol. P/2177, no. 158, OIOC.

[44] Petitions of Premabai, 11 April 1885, BJP, 1885, vol. P/2651, no. 97, OIOC, and Thukoobai, 22 April 1871, BJP, 1871, vol. P/483, no. 154, OIOC.

wife had a large family of children, although claims were also dependent on the number of years served by the petitioner's son or husband.[45] Many middle-class men in professions like teaching had left their villages for good and in times of distress their wives could no longer depend on either the natal or marital home. The family of Kero Lakshman Chhatre, a well-known Professor of Mathematics of Fergusson College at Pune, was a good example. His widow's appeal was successful in securing a pension worth Rs. 100 per month, which prompted other widows to quote her case in arguing their own.[46] Many of the cases outlined above demonstrate the way in which women viewed the colonial state as a 'resource' and who approached it in times of hardship. In this context, the state was not viewed as an alien ruler or an oppressor; rather, the Raj was seen as the embodiment of the classical 'ma-bap' [paternal] government.

If economic recession and the falling value of wages had a severe impact on the middle-classes, it had even more serious implications for the lower classes. As economic historians have shown, machine-made goods coming from Britain impacted adversely on indigenous handicrafts. Such imports had a dual impact on the lives of the women of this class, who had worked alongside men as cotton spinners and weavers since the family had formed the unit of production.[47] Not only were they left with skills that were now obsolete, but they also often had to contend with a completely new urban environment as poverty forced their families to move to the cities; in Sholapur in 1896 alone, two thousand weavers with their wives and children were reported to have left in search of new jobs.[48] What is remarkable about these women is the tenacity that they displayed in confronting the new challenges that they faced. The harassment of female vegetable vendors, mat-makers or fish-sellers by police officials is well-documented by the vernacular press of the time[49]; what is striking about some of these accounts is that the women were not necessarily passive victims but actively sought the help of the vernacular newspapers in publicizing their plight. Parvati Navar, a fish-seller, for instance, wrote a letter to *Vengurla Vritt* that requested protection from the Patel, a policeman who oppressed vendors like her who did not sell their goods at the prices he dictated.[50] Such cases made regular appearances in the press; a mat-maker complained that a police constable had threatened her on a trifling issue and extorted a bribe of Rs. 10 from her, while a newspaper from Chikodi carried a complaint from a vegetable vendor who was assaulted by two police officials when she had refused to leave her wares in a spot that they had directed.[51] Both the corrupt practices and harassment of

[45] Petition of Gajah Mannugiri, n.d., BJP, 1883, vol. P/2177, no. 1899, OIOC, and petition by Parbutee, n.d., BJP, 1884, vol. P/2423, no. 3161, OIOC.

[46] For example Parvatibai Kunte's petition, 22 December 1888, Bombay Education Proceedings (hereafter BEP), 1889, vol. 3559, no. 164, OIOC.

[47] V.D. Divekar, 'Western India', in Kumar, *The Cambridge Economic History of India*, pp. 346–9.

[48] *Sholapur Samachar*, 31 October 1896, NNR.

[49] For example, *Dnyanodaya*, 10 February 1877, NNR; *Dnyan Prakash*, 21 April 1877, NNR.

[50] *Vengurla Vritt*, 17 November 1883, NNR.

[51] *Samsher Bahadur*, 17 February 1877, NNR; *Chandrakant*, 24 November 1894, NNR.

the police officials were everyday experiences for lower-class women, a situation that partially arose from the speedy introduction of new tax-raising legislation and partially from the lack of awareness of the illiterate masses. A great number of vendors in towns and cities, for instance, were unaware of the fact that licenses were required for practising their trade by municipal authorities and of new taxes on trades such as wood-gathering or salt-making. For instance, in 1878, in the town of Nandgad, a uniform levy was introduced on wood-fuel, the chief source of income for workers in that area.[52] Collection was strictly enforced, and many women who defied the new taxes were fined for their lapses. However, as time progressed, there were instances when such acts of defiance by women were not only noticed but their cause fought for at higher levels of the administration. In 1887, the constant complaints of female hawkers and vendors reported in the vernacular press were finally taken seriously by Indian elites and the efforts of Maharashtrian social reformers, K.T. Telang and Pherozeshah Mehta, finally led to subsection (2) of section 314 of the Municipal Law, which prohibited 'hawking articles of human food without a license from the commissioner', being revoked.[53] In addition to this, in conjunction with other social reformers, such as M.G. Ranade, K.T. Telang and Pherozeshah Mehta were also able to use their influence on legislative bodies to bring about change in the laws governing urban civic life and alleviate the hardships that the lower classes endured.

The Right to Remarriage and Custody of Children

During this period, women were also increasingly asserting their rights as mothers or wives, a process which could take the form of fighting for custody of children, for the right to remarriage or for the release of imprisoned husbands. Despite the diversity of their aims, all these cases reflected the way in which women were taking responsibility in their roles as mothers or wives to attain individual happiness, comfort and security. The petitioning method of redress that women pursued also demonstrates the way in which they viewed the Raj as a humanitarian resource, to the extent that their writings describe it as 'deliverance'; indeed, Tarabai Shinde describes the Raj as the 'real Pandavas' [heroes].[54] Her faith in the Raj stems from her view that it was the Raj that had outlawed *sati* and provided the means of education for women; in her eyes, they alone could rescue the widow from her miserable plight. Nevertheless, although

---

[52] *Native Opinion*, 9 March 1878, NNR.

[53] See the proceedings of Bill no. 4 of 1887, 'A Bill to Consolidate and Amend the Law Relating to the Municipal Government of the City of Bombay', BLCP, 1887, vol. 25, pp. 44–5; the final reading and passing of the Bill is outlined in BLCP, 17 March 1888, vol. 26, pp. 133–4, OIOC.

[54] The 'Pandavas' are the heroes of the Indian epic *Mahabharata* who quell the evil in the land represented by their cousins, the 'Kauravas'. Tarabai Shinde, [Women and Men, A Comparison], p. 14.

women placed great faith in the Raj, they were prepared to engage in hidden and confrontational resistance to achieve their aims if petitioning failed.

In 1880, for instance, Khutizabee pleaded for the release of her stepson from the Sassoon Reformatory, where he had been committed for stealing two bunches of bananas. In the absence of his father, she asserted her right as his natural guardian and was allowed to take her son home on the condition that she would ensure that he would not misbehave again.[55] In a similar case, Sai argued that her son's health was deteriorating in the Juvenile Reformatory and offered to guarantee his future good behaviour and train him as a farmer.[56] However, although women in these situations enjoyed some degree of success, those who asserted their maternal rights in instances where third parties were involved were less successful. For example, when Heerabai, whose son, whilst still a minor, was, she alleged, lured away from home by the manager of a dramatic company and requested the government to issue a warrant for the manager's arrest, the government, as was common in such instances, directed the petitioner to resolve the matter in the courts.[57] Nevertheless, despite the fact that their actions were not always successful, these instances show that women were increasingly unwilling to accept challenges to their maternal authority, and were willing to take over male roles in this sphere if necessary.

As shown above, sometimes women took over roles normally associated with male heads of households. A more interesting shift is their assumption of roles which extended to taking responsibility for ensuring the good behaviour of those who were supposed to be responsible for the family's well-being and morality, namely, their husbands. There were many petitions where women agreed to look after their husbands if the state reduced their prison sentence, and there are quite a few cases where the sentences of convicted men were reduced on the basis of statements made by their wives.[58] Begum Bebee's petition, for instance, attempted to rehabilitate her husband's reputation by drawing attention to his exemplary behaviour in jail, which included saving the life of the jailor at the risk of his own.[59] In response, the government instituted an inquiry to verify her statements and, finding them true, reduced Abdul Hamid's sentence. Not only were women more self-confident in bringing petitions but

---

[55] 31 May 1880, BJP, 1880, vol. P/1491, no. 1575, OIOC.

[56] N.d., BJP, 1885, vol. P/2651, no. 723, OIOC.

[57] Petition by Heerabai Davar, 21 January 1880, BJP, 1880, vol. P/1591, no. 527, OIOC.

[58] Umanaik's wife was able to convince the government to release her husband from the Colaba Lunatic Asylum when she promised to ensure that steps would be taken to see that he would not harm others or himself in future: 30 June 1871, BJP, 1871, vol. P/483, no.155, OIOC; Petition of Rangabai Deshmukhin, who got her son's sentence reduced from 7 to 5 years, 30 July 1885, BJP, 1885, vol. P/2652, no. 2049, OIOC.

[59] 8 July 1871, BJP, 1871, vol. P/483, no. 182, OIOC; See also Jumnabee's petition, 22 November 1870, in which she enclosed a report of her husband's good conduct from the Superintendent of Port Blair that meant that his sentence was reduced drastically from transportation for life to 7 years imprisonment, BJP, 1870, vol. P/442/4, no. 195, OIOC.

the state's response also demonstrates that the authorities of this period were increasingly willing to listen to them.

Nevertheless, although women were increasingly able to take control of the welfare of their families in exceptional circumstances, such as the ones outlined above, in most instances, where their own individual well-being was concerned, the colonial authorities, instead of assisting women, proved even more conservative than traditional forms of authority. This was particularly true in cases where women who had either been abandoned for seven years or more or whose husband had been imprisoned for life wished to regain some status by remarrying. Whereas, previously, caste councils had often shown leniency in such instances and allowed women of non-Brahmin castes to marry again, the British courts of law enforced an extremely strict version of codified Hindu and Muslim personal law, based on consultations with learned Pandits and Muslim, Parsi and other digests, which made no allowances for individual circumstance.[60] Such strict laws applied even in instances when there was clear evidence to show that the woman had been badly treated by her husband. For instance, Bhagi, a Hindu woman, was convicted and sentenced to three months' imprisonment for marrying whilst her first husband was still alive, despite her argument that she had good reason to do so because her first husband had not only ill-treated her but had left her and remarried, thus depriving her of support.[61] Similarly, despite the fact that Ganga, a Hindu woman, converted to Islam before marrying Kasim, the court ruled that Hindu law did not consider a marriage dissolved merely by apostasy. This meant that, without the consent of her Hindu husband, her second marriage was illegal, leading to Ganga being imprisoned for three years for her actions.

Neither did the Courts recognize the authority of a caste to declare a marriage void or give permission to a woman to remarry in the absence of the consent of her husband.[62] Many women, who on the authority of a caste panchayat had obtained permission to divorce and remarry, faced various sanctions for repudiating British laws. Indeed, in one case, a woman was convicted of bigamy even though she argued that she had the authority of her caste-panch to re-marry after she had produced reasonable evidence to show her husband's inability to fulfil conjugal duties.[63] Despite the fact that it recognized that Hindu women could take responsibility for the behaviour of her children and even, in exceptional circumstances, the male head of the household, its reliance on and adherence to scripture-based legal texts in this area meant that

---

[60] David. A Washbrook, 'Law, State and Agrarian Society in Colonial India', *Modern Asian Studies*, 15/3 (1981): 649–721 and C.A. Bayly, *Indian Society and the Making of the British Empire* (Cambridge: Cambridge University Press, 1987), p. 115. For a social history of colonial law and its operation in India see Janaki Nair, *Women and Law in Colonial India: A Social History* (New Delhi: Kali for Women, 1996).

[61] *Bombay Chronicle*, 22 July 1882, NNR. A very similar case was that of Abai, *Jame Jamshed*, 9 August 1884, NNR.

[62] See the case Regina vs. Bai Rupa and Regina vs. Shambhu Raghu, quoted in judgment of Imperatrix vs. Ganga, 29 January 1880, JD, 1880, vol. 17 and 18, MSA.

[63] *Subodh Patrika*, 17 November 1894, NNR.

British law, in effect, upheld the theory that a Hindu woman could not be considered a responsible individual with her own wants and needs. This attitude is also shown in the way that the Courts treated women trapped in loveless and unfulfilling marriages. Benibai, for instance, had been married to Ranchhod at the age of eighteen months but, when they grew up, he turned out to be a simpleton who did not understand his marital responsibilities and obligations. Caste rules said that a woman in such a situation should be allowed to remarry but the refusal of her father-in-law to give consent meant that she had to turn to the colonial authorities. She appealed twice; once to the District Magistrate and then to the Governor, asking them to recognize her youth (she begins her petition by saying that she is 'only twenty six years old') and her need for physical fulfilment:

> There is not the least chance of receiving a bit of worldly enjoyment from Ranchhod ... Now I leave it for His Lordship to consider how am I to pass the bloom of my life with a lunatic who can afford no sort of worldly enjoyment. I request His Lordship to relieve a distressed, wretched woman ordering Ranchhod to divorce me, his wife and allow me to perform a Natra [a second marriage but of lower status than the first] with another man according to our caste custom.[64]

Benibai's situation during this period was not unique. In a period where the lower castes were imitating the higher castes by adopting the former's injunctions and restrictions on widow remarriage, many women found themselves trapped in situations where their physical and emotional needs went unmet. As Tarabai Shinde argued in her treatise on the central concepts of Hinduism, namely *dharma* [right conduct of men] and *stridharma* [women's duties], the fact that religious dogma did not recognize such human needs often resulted in these women seeking refuge in the arms of married men, which in turn could lead them to give birth to illegitimate children. The women were often driven to murder the babies born from these liaisons in order to try and avoid scandal, even though they faced imprisonment, transportation or even death if they were caught.[65] Yet, as Benibai's situation demonstrates, in the absence of caste authority to annul the marriage, she had to petition the government in order to avoid breaking the law by committing bigamy. In an attempt to try and circumvent the restrictions that were imposed on them, abandoned or neglected wives or child wives whose husbands were on life terms petitioned for the annulment of marriages on grounds of 'unnatural widowhood' but they had little success.[66] Nevertheless, their actions demonstrate that women themselves were prepared to use 'petitioning' the state authorities by adopting the role of agents to try and resist the circumstances that could lead to them ultimately being drawn into illicit relationships that could have potentially devastating consequences. Where the state failed them, more aggressive forms of

---

[64] 19 April 1883, JD, 1883, vol. 115, comp. no. 683 MSA.

[65] [Women and Men, A Comparison], especially pp. 1 and 18–19.

[66] Petition of Yemmenne, 17 November 1880, JD, 1881, vol. 48, comp. no. 305, MSA; Jaya's appeal, 11 December 1887, JD, 1887, vol. 49, comp. no. 112, MSA.

resistance could be discerned amongst married women or widows, as will be demonstrated in the next chapter, when they realized the state was not willing to antagonize Indian men in marital matters which were deemed as 'indigenous' male prerogatives.

'Respectability' Movements and Women's Rights to a Profession and Mobility

The increase in women's assertion during this period, coupled with greater educational provision for girls, which allowed them to enter public areas previously closed to them, was, in many respects, liberating for women but also led to other developments that threatened to derail the progress that they made. One of the less pleasant ones that women had to endure was the Indian phenomenon popularly known, and indeed officially recognized, as 'Eve-teasing', which is still in existence today. Originally of Indian–English origin,[67] the phrase is almost unknown outside of India, but basically covers a range of acts that could be construed as sexual harassment, from wolf-whistling at a passing woman on the street to actual physical assault.[68] Vernacular newspapers of the period contain lengthy accounts of indecent assaults and obscene remarks and jokes made against women in bathing-ghats, temples and pilgrimage centres, and on trains and buses.[69] Unsurprisingly, women, in their turn, refused to accept such abuse and often made direct representations to the authorities about the way in which they had been treated whilst going about their business.

A remarkable change that came through the acts of assertion of women to their right to travel was the improvement in transport services. Female travellers using the Western Indian Railway services were particularly vociferous in their complaints about the sexist behaviour of guards, ticket-examiners and male passengers. The government took such complaints seriously; for instance, in 1880, when a European guard was found to have assaulted a Parsi woman travelling from Neemuch to Bombay, he had his salary reduced, was demoted within his grade and transferred from passenger to freight services.[70] Moreover, some railway companies also took pro-active measure to prevent such incidents happening in the first place, with the Bombay railway authorities employing women to issue, examine and receive tickets from female passengers and introducing segregated compartments to ensure women's safety.[71] School and college-going girls were provided with horse-drawn carriages as

---

[67] For a definition of the term see Paroo Nihalani, R.K. Tongue and Priya Hosali, *Indian and British English* (New Delhi: Oxford University Press, 1979).

[68] For a detailed study of the historical context of the origins of Eve-teasing in modern and contemporary India, see Padma Anagol-McGinn, 'Sexual Harassment in India: A Case-Study of Eve-Teasing in Historical Perspective', in C. Brant and Y.L. Too (eds), *Rethinking Sexual Harassment* (London: Pluto, 1994), pp. 220–34.

[69] *Hitechchu*, 11 November 1876, NNR; *Guzerat Mitra*, 21 April 1877, NNR.

[70] 21 Dec. 1880, BJP, 1880, vol. P/1591, no. 3335, OIOC.

[71] *Bombay Samachar*, 11 February 1882, NNR; *Satya Mitra*, 15 February 1896, NNR.

conveyances and often the government met the expenses of such costly travel arrangements.[72] Unfortunately, segregated educational institutions were deemed necessary and formed part of the state and Indian male elite's responses to counter the growing urban phenomena of Eve-teasing.

Paradoxically, however, whilst the authorities were increasing protection to those women becoming more prominent in the public arena, they were also colluding with the Indian middle classes in placing restrictions on the ability of certain 'classes' of women to enter them in the first place. The growth of the 'respectability' movement amongst urban middle classes in Western India was to place insidious limits on some women entering the public sphere. Individuals belonging to the growing Indian middle classes, as yet an under-studied phenomenon, found themselves increasingly anonymous in the crowded settings of huge metropolises, such as Bombay, and therefore sought to assert their identity in new ways. This was partially expressed through displays of their economic status, derived from gainful employment following the acquisition of a Western education. However, a more stable indicator was their emphasis on 'respectability', a concept that had moral purpose and civic-minded responsibility at its core. Although conventions of respectability differed from place to place, certain indicators were common to all classes, whether they were reformists, revivalists or traditionalists: participation in socioreligious reform and revivalist movements; the maintenance of a certain propriety and decorum in speech and bearing[73]; abiding by the law; and keeping homes neat and tidy, both externally and internally.[74] Such tenets demanded that 'respectable' families would educate their daughters to run a household rather than operate in the world of work, meaning that they received a minimal formal education. In return, it was expected that their husbands would treat them with care and affection, which, in practice, meant an end to the practice of married men keeping mistresses and attending performances of dancing girls. The obsession with the notion of being custodians of 'morality' is demonstrated in the number of complaints made in the newspapers and pulp literature regarding the 'Shimga' festivals.[75] The traditionally sanctioned licentious behaviour between the sexes during the Holi festival was now frowned upon and condemned roundly by the

---

[72] *Annual Reports of Poona Female High School*, 1880–90.

[73] Hence the move to discourage what were traditional Indian and Hindu social practices and customs such as 'breast-beating' and loud remonstrations of grief during cremation ceremonies, and the public parading of girls who had reached their menarché (some of these themes are discussed at greater length in chapter 3).

[74] Vernacular print literature is full of advice to middle-class grihinis [house managers] on topics such as hygiene and sanitation, the practice of which, they promised, would bring good fortune to the family.

[75] Gangadhar Balkrishna Gadre *Shimga* [Holi festival] (Bombay: Subodha Patrika Press, 1884).

urban middle classes,[76] who also targeted and damned theatrical entertainments that had elements of risqué humour or playfulness.

The women who suffered most from this clampdown were the *kalavantins* [accomplished women or female artistes] or *kulavantinis* [women of genteel birth].[77] There were four divisions among them—*naikins* and *bhavins*, who originated from Goa and the surrounding villages, *kasbins* (also known as *kunbins*) and *murlis*.[78] Aside from their geographical origins, *naikins* usually placed themselves under the protection of one man, where they passed the greater portion of their time in entertaining their sole employers with their accomplishments in singing and dancing. However, in addition to these attributes, *naikins* were also well-educated women who could read and write Marathi and compose poetry. Moreover, like the other women of this group, records of their property rights indicate them to be a matrilineal society; indeed, Sumit Guha has noted that the Peshwas in the eighteenth century regarded *kalavantins* as 'professional entertainers' and recognized them as 'female-headed households'.[79] Contemporary Indian ethnographers have recorded that Hindus held them in high esteem, and records show that some of the women belonging to this group were wealthy enough to hire Brahmin priests in their service as well as give generously to charitable causes. The second group, *bhavins,* were married women who had forsaken their husbands to serve idols in temples. They were expected to live as ascetics but often they combined temple duties with having a single master. *Kasbins* [professional entertainers] came from agricultural castes, hence the term *kunbins,* and were purchased by wealthy men to perform the duties of ordinary wives. However, unlike women in official marriages, if they conducted themselves well, they sometimes were freed from their bond and allowed to occupy a separate house and cultivate their own land. *Murlis* came from the pilgrimage site Jejuri and, like the *bhavins,* were dedicated to the temple-gods.[80] They were trained in the arts of singing and dancing, and sometimes also played musical instruments.

---

[76] For an analysis of the growing importance of the Ganapati festival over Holi, see Richard Cashman, *The Myth of the Lokamanya: Tilak and Mass Politics in Maharashtra,* (Berkeley: University of California Press, 1975), especially chapter 1.

[77] In the eighteenth century, *kalavantins* were identified as 'professional entertainers' but, by the nineteenth century, I have found that their status had altered considerably. I have therefore used the term 'accomplished women and female artistes' along with 'professional entertainers' interchangeably. My definition also incorporates the wide range of services they offered in contrast to the category of *randis* [prostitutes]. For a brief discussion on the eighteenth-century *kalavantin*, see Sumit Guha 'Wrongs and Rights in the Maratha Country: Antiquity, Custom and Power in Eighteenth-Century India', in M. Anderson and S. Guha (eds), *Changing Concepts of Rights and Justice in South Asia* (New Delhi: Oxford University Press, 1998), pp. 14–29.

[78] Several accounts are available on their professions but the most detailed is in K. Raghunathji, 'Bombay Dancing Girls', *Indian Antiquary,* 13 (June 1884): 165–78.

[79] Guha, 'Wrongs and Rights', p. 22.

[80] Ibid.

The women of these groups had initially prospered in Bombay, whose status as a major industrial and commercial centre with a large textile industry built by the mercantile Parsi and Gujarati communities[81] had led to the creation of a prosperous, cosmopolitan metropolitan elite with contemporary nineteenth-century accounts outlining the affluent and fabulous lifestyles that they led.[82] In order to demonstrate their new-found wealth, many Bombayites hired *kalavantins* to entertain guests with their dance performances, leading to an upsurge in the demand for their services. Aided by a buoyant economy, many of the accomplished women and female artists in this field grew wealthy and, correspondingly, also became very status-conscious.[83] However, under colonial rule, the lives and professional pursuits of these classes of women were to become increasingly precarious as, in addition to state-imposed limitations, they also faced increased hostility from Indians.[84] During the social reform period, those belonging to aspiring middle-classes started a 'respectability' movement that strongly frowned on practices like the *nach* [visiting the houses of professional entertainers], which were increasingly seen as immoral.[85] Whereas, in pre-colonial times, these women had been invited to house-warming, birthday, and thread ceremonies (the ceremony of 'twice-born' castes for young boys) in ordinary households, they were now shunned. Raghunathji notes that Hindus used to hold the *naikins* in such high esteem that she was requested to string the *mangala-sutra* [a black bead necklace symbolizing Hindu woman's married status] at weddings;[86] following the respectability drive of the Maharashtrian middle classes, however, *kalavantins* were regarded as little more than 'prostitutes'[87] and were treated accordingly. Indeed, residents of various towns and cities often sent complaints to the police authorities to remove *kalavantins* from what they considered as 'respectable

---

[81] Raj Chandavarkar, *The Origins of Industrial Capitalism in India* (Cambridge: Cambridge University Press, 1994), chapters 1, 2 and 6. Also Miriam Dossal, *Imperial Designs and Indian Realities: Planning of Bombay City, 1845–1875* (Bombay: Oxford University Press, 1991).

[82] Meera Kosambi, 'British Bombay and Marathi Bombay: Some Nineteenth Century Perceptions', in S. Patel and A. Thorner (eds), *Bombay: Mosaic of Modern Culture* (Bombay: Oxford University Press, 1996), pp. 3–24.

[83] Describing the resplendent public ceremonies and displays of the Naikins, the author says that commentators who watched these pageants said that they were reminded of the 'Rule of Women', the tales told in the epics and myths of India. Govind Narayan Madgavkar, *Mumbaiche Varnan* [An Account of Bombay], N.R. Phatak (ed.) (Bombay: Mumbai Marathi Granthasangrahalaya, 1961, 1st edn, 1863), chapter 13.

[84] An excellent study of the changing lives of prostitutes in Bengal during the colonial period is in Sumanta Banerjee's monograph, *The Parlour and the Streets: Elite and Popular Culture in Nineteenth Century Calcutta* (Calcutta: South Asia Books, 1990).

[85] Vernacular newspapers are full of reports which urge police authorities to convict Naikins and prevent them from bringing up their children in the same profession: see *Kaside Mumbai*, 21 August 1878, NNR; *Dnyanodaya*, 16 December 1876, NNR.

[86] 'Bombay dancing girls', pp. 167–8.

[87] *Subodh Patrika*, 24 May 1884, NNR; *Bodh Sudhakar*, 1 October 1887, NNR.

neighbourhoods', and house them outside the city or town limits.[88] In her treatise, Tarabai Shinde discusses the institution of prostitution and clearly indicts the role of men in the creation of prostitutes. It is true that, in her delineation of the semi pornographic Marathi genres of the time, she does distinguish between a *rand* [prostitute] and a *kasbin* but it is nevertheless clear from her tract that, by the late nineteenth-century, many of these performers and artistes were regarded as little more than 'prostitutes'.[89]

It is unsurprising that middle-class women were part of the respectability movement that led to the *kalavantins'* downfall; indeed, they added to its momentum and contributed greatly to further clarifying its aims. If social ascendancy was lauded among Maharashtrian urban classes and a man was encouraged to seek fortune and fame through talent, he was equally advised to seek recreation and pleasure in domesticity. He was to search for quiet bliss in the enjoyment of domestic affection, and the home was redefined as a great haven of private comfort. By condemning *kalavantins* as ordinary prostitutes, the women belonging to this movement were able to secure two objectives: preventing men from engaging in the practice of keeping mistresses by making the practice socially unacceptable and improving the status of their own role as *grihinis* [housewives] by assuming attributes traditionally associated with *kalavantins*, such as the ability to sing or play musical instruments such as *veenas* [a *sitar*-like instrument]. They argued that, when their menfolk came home tired from the weary business of the public world, the women could soothe their minds by putting on performances that would provide a means of forgetting their cares, meaning that they did not have to seek alternative sources of solace outside the home, an idea explored at length in Sundarabai Shirur's speech to the Second Social Conference of Bombay Presidency in 1901:

> Considering the fine arts and skills, we notice that in our society, they prevail amongst women of the lowest caste and that makes a very unfavourable impression of our society. The status of such arts should be raised in society. A man is not an animal that is satisfied with plenty to eat and drink. That man has a rare gift, which we call his mind. Beauty, sweetness of speech and elegance are experienced by him and he enjoys it ... And if such qualities are unavailable in his home then he automatically is inclined to seek them elsewhere...[90]

She begged that these skills should be taken away from the 'practice of individuals of low mentality', and instead vested with middle-class females, a view echoed in many magazines and journals edited by middle-class women. They believed that female children should learn Indian classical dance and music, an idea that, as the

---

[88] *Nagar Samachar* carried a complaint by Ahmadnagar residents against prostitutes. Reported in 23 February 1878, NNR; and *Dandio*, 22 March 1879, NNR.

[89] For a broad discussion on *rands* [prostitutes] and *kasbins* [professional entertainers], see Tarabai Shinde, [Women and Men, A Comparison], especially pp. 26–9.

[90] 'Schemes and Efforts', *Maharashtra Mahila*, October 1901, 154–5.

preparations preceding arranged marriages show, has persisted well into the twentieth century.[91] In any case, by the end of the nineteenth century, the demolition of the *kalavantins'* status as professional female entertainers, which had begun to crumble as soon as the appraising eye of an East India official had reduced their complex identity of accomplished artistes to the fixed and frozen one of 'dancing and singing girls',[92] was now completed by the anti-feminists of the nineteenth century; following the respectability drive of middle class women, she was now regarded by society as a plain 'prostitute'. The way in which the *kalavantins* were so comprehensively undermined clearly demonstrates the way in which many Hindu women were more concerned with enhancing their own status rather than showing solidarity with other women.

If the 'respectability' drives amongst the Maharashtrian middle classes conspired to usurp her skills and vest them in middle class girl's preparation for marriage, the final seal of opprobrium was hammered by the colonial state. The lives of the *kalavantins* were made even more unbearable by sanitary legislation that was initially designed to counteract the spread of venereal diseases amongst British soldiers stationed in India. The necessity of retaining operation efficiency to ensure the continued stability of imperial rule in the country[93] led to the introduction of legislation such as the umbrella Cantonment Acts (1864), which meant those deemed to be involved in the vice trade (brothel keepers and prostitutes) operating in army cantonments were now subject to compulsory regulation, and the Contagious Diseases Act (1868), which extended similar provisions to major Indian towns and ports. Whilst the proposals were welcomed by many Indian middle-class women, who had challenged the Orientalist assumption that prostitution was a hereditary caste profession in India and that it had a tradition of providing recreation through the provision of *nautch* [cabaret conducted by singing and dancing girls] and courtesans, an argument commonly used to justify the provision of Indian prostitutes to soldiers,[94] other sectors were much more hostile. The Contagious Diseases Act in particular had a large impact on the Indian urban population, leading to a spate of protests from groups as diverse as ordinary Indian men to the prostitutes themselves. However, the loudest voice in this protest was the actions of *kalavantins* who often were subject to the same restrictions and intrusions imposed on prostitutes. Not only did they resent the complete lack of privacy and continual intimate intrusions into their personal lives, but their ability to practice their profession

---

[91] The contemporary matrimonial advertisements for aspiring middle-class brides-to-be list their accomplishments in the fine arts, ranging from classical dance to vocal training in classical music and playing the sitar or veena along with their professional degrees.

[92] The Kalavantin's identity as the 'dancing and singing girl of the nautch' as perceived by the nabobs and later European commentators is evident in many books written on their lifestyles. A flavour of these writings can be obtained from Percival Spear, *The Nabobs: A Study of the Social Life of the English in the Eighteenth Century* (London: Oxford University Press, 1963).

[93] See chapter 2.

[94] Philippa Levine, 'Venereal Disease, Prostitution and the Politics of Empire: The Case of British India', *Journal of the History of Sexuality*, 4/4 (1994): 568; Ronald Hyam *Empire and Sexuality* (Manchester: Manchester University Press, 1990), p. 125.

were threatened by the medical checks and detention in lock hospitals. This was particularly true of *naikins*, whose status had traditionally correlated with that of their protector. Lapses could result in sanctions, and associating with a *mlechcha* [foreigner][95] could harm their standing within their own society; indeed, when they had been forced to cater to the Portuguese rulers in Goa earlier in the century, some *naikins* had faced ostracization and excommunication by other members of their caste, forcing them to emigrate to Bombay to escape the stigma that had become attached to them.[96] Their horror of being examined by European doctors was therefore well founded, and it was clear to many of them that some sort of action was necessary.

Their response was to launch a multifaceted protest against the rules and regulations that the sanitary legislation had imposed on them. A large number of them made collective petitions, arguing that the Act made no distinction between concubines reliant on a single Indian employer and prostitutes plying their trade with European soldiers.[97] Chima, a *kusbin* from Belgaum, for instance, argued that she was not a 'common prostitute' but an accomplished 'singer of ballads by profession', which, she argued, meant that she should be exempted from the Cantonment Act.[98] They pleaded for a more accurate definition of terms like that of 'prostitutes' and the exclusion of those amongst them who did not cater to non-Indians due to rigid caste rules and who lived outside the cantonment area. The vernacular press in India at this time also argued that Indians should be entitled to continue to practice time-honoured customs and social practices, including the retention of *kalavantins,* with some of them pointing out the difference between 'mistresses', who they referred to as 'respectable women', because they had only one master throughout their lives and hence were unlikely to spread contagion, and ordinary prostitutes, who practised their trade indiscriminately.[99]

Despite the support of some of the press, however, the *kalavantins'* petitions failed to elicit a satisfactory response, obliging them to adopt other forms of resistance. The most effective strategy that they employed was 'avoidance protests' whereby the prostitutes avoided checks by the City Police by using the tram services to leave Bombay during the day for nearby villages, returning only at night to ply their trade.[100] This method of avoiding being subject to the checks under the Act was so

---

[95] K. Raghunathji, 'Bombay Dancing Girls', p. 165.

[96] Ibid., p. 167.

[97] Petition from Myboobajee Naikin and others, Professional dancing and singing girls of Poona, contained in a letter 13 December 1871 to the Commissioner of Police, Poona, BJP, 1871, vol. P/483, no. 158, p. 55, OIOC.

[98] 12 February 1870, BJP, 1870, vol. P/442/4, no. 41, p. 15, OIOC.

[99] *Karnatak Mitra*, 18 June 1881, NNR.

[100] For similar protests in radically different contexts, see Eugene Irschick, 'Gandhian Non-Violent Protest: Rituals of Avoidance or Rituals of Confrontation?', *Economic and Political Weekly*, 21 (1986): 1276–85; Michael Adas, 'From Avoidance to Confrontation: Peasant Protest in Precolonial and Colonial Southeast Asia', *Comparative Studies in Society and History*, 23 (1981): 217–47.

successful that, out of 4000 entertainers in the city, only 600 were registered.[101] Strategies of open resistance were rather less successful, with Cantonment officials all over the Bombay Presidency acting swiftly and brutally to contain such acts. Open acts of defiance by *kalavantins* often resulted in indiscriminate force being employed against them, and instances of police officers abusing their powers in their treatment of them were often observed. Unbowed, spectacular cases of defiance by the *kalavantins* reached the daily newspapers and filled their columns. Normally the target of cheap tabloid headlines, *kalavantins* earned a modicum of respect from even the vernacular press, which often wrote in admiration of their brave escapades and the acts of insubordination that they had committed.[102] Nevertheless, the press were unable to prevent many of those women who defied the rules being arrested, convicted and fined for not presenting themselves for medical examination under the terms of the Cantonment Act of 1868. The strict penalties of the Act are demonstrated by the treatment of 27 singing and dancing girls in Bombay in 1871, who, after they were arrested, were not only jailed for a week, but also fined Rs. 25 each.[103]

The *kalavantins* were fighting a losing battle. Not only was the state making their lives intolerable but the indigenous elites who had traditionally patronized them and provided them with their income were deserting them as they heeded the disapproval of the 'respectability movement'. This, coupled with the fact that many of the skills and routines that they had traditionally employed had now been usurped by middle-class wives, forced them to seek new avenues of employment. They found it in Marathi theatre[104] which, following the success of performances by English drama troupes in the 1840s, was undergoing a rapid expansion to meet the demand for drama by local people in Bombay, Pune and other cities. However, the few theatre groups that sprung up in the late nineteenth century were opposed by many members of the new urban professional classes, who feared that the desire for fame would lure their children into the acting profession. Unsurprisingly, the 'respectability movement' denounced the theatre, with Madgavkar, a contemporary observer, commenting 'to work as an "actor" is an immoral occupation and is strictly prohibited in the Hindu shastras; and people from respectable families desist it and scorn it.'[105] Moreover, its popularity among factory workers meant that it came to be seen as a poor man's recreation, which further contributed to the middle classes' decision to shun it.[106] Nevertheless,

---

[101] *Indu Prakash*, 11 September 1880, NNR; *Kaside Mumbai*, 25 September 1880, NNR.

[102] *Dnyan Prakash* reported how a Naikin in Poona single-handedly defied six mounted police and three foot soldiers, 7 June 1879, NNR.

[103] BJP, 1871, vol. P/483, no.30, p. 10, OIOC.

[104] *Kaside Mumbai* carried an article on how Naikins were being employed in dramatic companies as actresses, 13 August 1881, NNR.

[105] Madgavkar, [An Account of Bombay], p. 299.

[106] Shanta Gokhale, 'Rich Theatre, Poor Theatre', in Patel and Thorner, *Bombay*, pp. 194–209.

despite their continued persecution by members of the respectability movement and a loss of status, the theatre provided a refuge that allowed female artistes to continue to exhibit their talents.

Women's Resistance in Literature

Although women accessed many forms of protest during this period, perhaps one of the most potent ways that they had of registering their dissatisfaction was through writing. Using novels, plays or folk songs, female authors were able to take the familiar plots and literary devices that traditionally ran through these genres and mould them to their own ends; a process known as 'symbolic inversion', which is defined by Barbara Babcock as 'any act of expressive behaviour which inverts, contradicts, abrogates, or in some fashion presents an alternative to commonly held cultural codes, values, and norms be they linguistic, literary or artistic, religious, or social and political'.[107] The reasons for the adoption of existing traditions rather than the creation of a totally new form of writing were twofold; by cloaking repressed desires in fantastic forms that only appeared to exist in utopian worlds, they were able to present their ideas without raising the ire of the male censors whilst simultaneously highlighting the everyday injustices and exploitation that women of this period commonly faced.[108]

One of the plays that most effectively inverted traditional forms to challenge the patriarchal order was Girijabai Kelkar's five-act play, *Purushanche Band* [Men's Rebellion], written in 1913.[109] Located 'somewhere in Hindustan',[110] all the action takes place in a kingdom ruled by a king called Sadhu Singh who, under the influence of a misogynist monk, Vikarananda, drives out all the women, forcing the latter to form their own parallel kingdom and assume all roles, from the queen to soldiers guarding their domain, in order for their society to continue to function. Although it has a fantastical setting, the plot itself is inspired by real-life concerns of Maharashtrian women, such as women's higher education, their need for a degree of economic independence, rights to inheritance and maintenance, and to contemporary issues such

---

[107] For a study of a variety of symbolic inversions in Western societies, see the collection of essays in Barbara Babcock (ed.), *The Reversible World: Symbolic Inversion in Art and Society* (Ithaca: Cornell University Press, 1978).

[108] Susan Friedman has convincingly analyzed how 'the return of the repressed' takes effect in women's narratives; her findings are in keeping with censorship rules through the study of texts by Hilda Doolittle in 'The Return of the Repressed in Women's Narrative', *Journal of Narrative Technique*, 19 (1989): 141–56.

[109] For samples of other women writing in this genre, see Kashibai Kanitkar, *Palkicha Gonda* [The Tassel at the Centre of the Palanquin] (Poona: Kanitkar & Mandali, 1928). Kashibai first published it as a serial in a popular Marathi journal called *Navayug* in 1913.

[110] Even though it was first published in 1913, the second edition, which was reprinted in 1921 and published by Induprakash Press of Bombay, is used here.

as the 'position of women' in the Shastras, the 'nature of womanhood', the institution of marriage, rape within marriage and social status of women. The contemporary flavour to an old-fashioned setting of the play is a curious blend but Girijabai reveals why this was so in the 'Foreword' to the play. Indeed, the inspiration for it lay in a real-life conversation between the author and some of her male friends. When Kelkar argued that men were doing nothing to change the 'condition of women ... because men held women as inferior to them',[111] one of her male friends replied that the demands of contemporary women had made men rebellious. She responded by basing her play on the discussion and appropriating his argument for her title, arguing that

Men blame women for the backwardness of the nation and allege that social reform is stagnating because women refuse to educate themselves. According to them women are ignorant and superstitious but I say this is not an in-born defect of womanhood, in fact, what is happening today is that very few people rise on their own merit, a majority of the population needs to be pushed to improve themselves and this is exactly what men folk do not do—that is, encourage and stand behind women.[112]

By illustrating the chaos that ensues from following her male friend's argument to its logical conclusion, she is able to 'make men realize their duties and recognize their shortcomings'[113] in a form that was accessible to a wide variety of people.[114]

An important aspect to the play is the fact that the chaos is not generated by the women but rather by the king, who heeds Vikarananda's arguments that 'women are the gateway to hell', 'the 'barbed fence around reason', and 'once man gets entailed in her coils he can never escape the cycle of re-birth and never attain salvation'.[115] According to Vikarananda, a relationship with a woman was comparable to housing a cobra and feeding it with sweetened milk.[116] This was not merely an instance of a playwright placing words in a character's mouth; such arguments were often found in the Hindu scriptures widely known and read in Maharashtrian homes.[117] The king succumbs to Vikarananda's exposition on the nature of 'woman' and decides to take the idea to its logical conclusion and rid society of women's 'evil influence' completely, declaring that no man in the kingdom will get a job or be allowed to practice any

---

[111] See foreword to Girijabai Kelkar [Men's Rebellion], p. 1.

[112] Ibid., p. 2.

[113] Ibid., p. 2.

[114] Girijabai had in fact written a book where many of the themes explored in [Men's Rebellion] had been discussed but this work she felt had reached only a privileged few who were educated enough to appreciate it. See *Striyancha Swarga* [Women's Paradise] 2nd edn (Bombay: Parchure Puranik and Co., 1921; 1st edn 1912).

[115] [Men's Rebellion], p. 2.

[116] Ibid., p. 4.

[117] See O'Hanlon's thoughtful treatment of the subject in *A Comparison between Women and Men: Tarabai Shinde and the Critique of Gender Relations in Colonial India* (Madras: Oxford University Press, 1994), pp. 38–49.

profession unless he leaves his wife,[118] and turning ascetic, enters Vikarananda's ashram, much to the distress of the queen. The rest of the male population promptly follow his example and, with the exception of one *sardar* [nobleman], Yashwant Singh, they sign a contract stating that they would not have anything to do with the female sex and drive their wives out. Yashwant Singh, on the other hand, states that only those men who treat their wives as slaves would agree to such a degrading contract and refuses to be part of it; he chooses to resign his post rather than obey for, as he tells the king, his high regard for his own wife would make abiding by the proclamation impossible.[119]

What follows is a state of anarchy in the kingdom of men. There is utter lawlessness; crime increases and there is chaos and confusion. Moreover, Chandrakant, the heir to the throne, receives many petitions by cloth-merchants, goldsmiths and other tradesmen who complain bitterly about the great losses that they have incurred due to the fact that they have lost their main customers, women.[120] More significantly, the efficiency of men in all professions drops considerably, as most of them also have to take on the household chores, and quickly become worn out with the 'dual burden'. The playwright cleverly demonstrates how multitasking, which she seems to suggest comes easily to women, is not the forte of men. This is illustrated by the head gardener's impatient retort to the king's criticisms of the unkempt appearance of the palace gardens and parks; 'How can you expect a man who spends most of the night baking bread and looking after four children to work well throughout the day?'[121] Whilst the men were swiftly buckling under the weight of their duties, the women had swiftly regrouped around their leaders. Whereas Vikarananda had persuaded the king to abrogate some of his responsibilities, the Western-educated *puranika* [female preacher learned in Hindu scriptures], Saraswati Devi, convinces the distraught queen to take control of the female kingdom in her hands. Interestingly, like Vikarananda, she uses holy texts as justification for her arguments, drawing on Lord Krishna's famous discourse in the *Bhagavad-Gita* [part of the epic Mahabharata and considered by Hindus as a holy book] to highlight the queen's responsibility for her subjects.[122] Saraswatibai's assistant is Kumudini, the daughter of a noble who is a modern woman with feminist ideals, and together they open a large number of women's organizations and a hospital for women. In addition, with the queen's blessing, they are able to organize a large number of women's welfare schemes. Depicted as resourceful and enterprising, the women also combat the potential hardships that they face from the

---

[118]   [Men's Rebellion], p. 10.

[119]   Ibid., pp. 25–6.

[120]   Ibid., pp. 67–8.

[121]   Ibid., p. 56.

[122]   It is not uncommon amongst women's subcultures in India to use the epic literature in distinctly female ways in order to subvert authority. For a study of a women's *Ramayana*, see V.N. Rao, 'A Ramayana of Their Own: Women's Oral Tradition in Telugu', in P. Richman (ed.), *Many Ramayanas: The Diversity of a Narrative Tradition in South Asia* (Berkeley: University of California Press, 1991), pp. 114–36.

king's orders to his tradesmen not to have any business dealings with them, by assuming all the responsibilities of merchants, bankers, oil and cloth manufacturers and other tradesmen themselves. The process is completed by the fact that coachwomen appear with whips and female soldiers appear dressed in male attire. In sharp contrast to the men's kingdom, the women's kingdom prospers and is efficiently run.

The success of the women in their new environment demonstrates that, when women assume traditionally masculine roles in public life they function as well as or better than men in public life, challenging the male argument that women were inferior in intellect, reasoning and administrative abilities. As Saraswati Devi states, 'women [are] ... equal ... to men, and if there is difference to be found between the sexes it is merely one that nature endows us with';[123] indeed, in a world without women, the result is disorder and inefficient administration. Moreover, as Saraswati Devi observes, the men's rebellion also forces many women who were previously happy to accept their place in society to reassess their beliefs:

> Men's rebellion has demonstrated to women what the former think of them!! Now the women are enraged because they have come to realize their inferior status. They have also been driven to prove their worth and through their own efforts have gained confidence. It is now firmly impressed on their minds that their progress depends on them alone.[124]

The transformation that some of the women undergo is best seen by the conversion of Janakibai, the wife of a Brahmin priest, who, prior to the king's decree, is a traditional woman who believes in the Hindu notion of a *pativrata*[125] and strongly condemns nonconformist single women, such as Saraswati Devi and Kumudini. However, her world is shattered when, despite this, her husband obeys the Raja's orders and throws her out of the house without as much as an explanation. As she leaves, she bitterly says to him:

> Now your true colours are out. You are a fine man, indeed! What great depths is your love for your wife! What returns for the many years of *seva* [service] rendered to you![126]

Her response to his betrayal is to participate wholeheartedly in the emancipation programmes being pursued by female leaders, thus liberating herself from her previous reliance on men. While some women, such as Janakibai, only accept their new existence after experiencing the painful process of rejection, there are others in the

---

[123] Girijabai, [Men's Rebellion], p. 124.

[124] Ibid., pp. 52–3.

[125] For an extremely detailed study of this prescriptive Hindu notion through an eighteenth-century Sanskrit text, see Julia Leslie, *The Perfect Wife: The Orthodox Hindu Woman According to the Stridharmapaddhati of Tryambakayajvan* (New Delhi: Oxford University Press, 1989).

[126] Girijabai, [Men's Rebellion], p. 32.

group who are not as naive or trusting of their husbands, and welcome the opportunity to prove that they could manage to carry out tasks that they were normally prevented from doing. Indeed, the wives of the soldiers, cooks and gardeners are not too unhappy about their husbands abandoning them; a feeling echoed by the *malin* [female gardener] who says:

> See, we women work so hard. A lot harder than men do. I am the one who plucks the flowers and makes the garlands. Only when it comes to grabbing the salary and spending it on liquor, it is only this area that he (referring to her husband) specializes in. And, if I protest he beats me... serves him right. Now not only will I earn but I will keep it too. I will be rich enough to make my own jewels too.[127]

Although expressed in comic tones, the underlying message is serious. The idea that a woman could earn and spend her own money and that a husband has no right to beat his wife may no longer be novel concepts. However, in nineteenth-century India expressed via the loud tirade of a subaltern woman in a play such ideas were meant to cause uproar amongst the audiences listening to the new-found confident voice of the female gardener. They also led women to reflect on the new changes taking place in their own lives in this period. Using new literary devices such as the light-hearted 'what happens in the dead-of the-night scene?' in a play, Girijabai Kelkar is able to explore themes of sexuality and question patriarchal notions of ownership and right to a woman's body in a way that may otherwise be considered too dark for entertainment.

An example of this is the way in which Kelkar explores the issue of rape within marriage in the play. An incident takes place at the dead of night, when a neighbourhood is woken up by a woman's screams for help. Several policewomen on patrol arrive and apprehend an intruder who has entered a woman's house. The intruder protests that he has not committed any crime as he is in his own house and the woman who screamed for help is his wife. When the bewildered patrol officer questions the woman, however, she replies that, as her husband had broken the marital bond by signing the king's contract, he is now a stranger, meaning that his entry into 'her' house is illegal and his demands for sexual intercourse is deemed as 'molestation'.[128] The intruder is returned to his own realm, where the king punishes him for his transgression.

The women's triumph is completed when the heir-apparent is seriously injured in a car accident and some female passers-by bring him to the women's hospital where he is nursed back to health. When the king hears this news, he comes to the hospital to thank the doctors. What follows is a confrontation between Saraswati Devi and Vikarananda, the holy man who has misled the king.[129] The debate between them is conducted at several levels. Initially, both opponents fall back on the scriptural injunctions delineating the rights and duties of the sexes. Saraswati Devi ably matches

---

127 Ibid., p. 50.
128 Ibid., pp. 78–83.
129 Ibid., pp. 109–23.

Vikarananda's learned arguments; for every example he cites in which women spell doom for men's path to salvation, she provides ten that demonstrate the contrary. At another level, she compares and contrasts the administration in the men's kingdom to that of the women's and highlights the male kingdom's inefficiency. She also lets the men know that every woman in the kingdom 'prefers complete independence' rather than follow men who are under the 'influence of a man with half-baked ideas like Vikarananda'. The monk's credibility is finally destroyed when Saraswati Devi exposes him as her husband who had abandoned his marital duties and left behind his child-bride to fend for herself. The king is now completely convinced of his own folly and of Saraswati Devi's wisdom: he begs her forgiveness, as does Vikarananda. Saraswati Devi's final words of advice to the heir-apparent are that

> God created the sexes and He treats them as equals. They are blessed with equal intelligence and equal rights. If one sex tries to rule the other it will end in chaos.[130]

To this advice, the heir to the throne replies that he would try to ensure that no injustice would take place against the female sex in future.

Although set in a fictional world, the play through the use of role reversals and inversions demonstrates the way in which women were able to exercise their power and protest against an unjust social order in order to gain parity of esteem with men. It is significant that the women of the play do not merely mimic men and male conduct but rather use their newfound freedom to create a place that operates harmoniously. Girijabai's vision shows that both sexes could share equally the joys and sorrows of life; far from hindering men, women were necessary for society to continue to function properly. The revolutionary nature of this view can be seen in the fact that it was twenty years later, when the women's movement was led by prominent nationalists, such as Kamaladevi Chattopadhyaya, that the idea that women were 'equal, but different'[131] became common currency in Indian feminism.

That is not to say that the straightforward tract did not have a place in the dissemination of nineteenth-century feminist ideas. Perhaps the foremost exponent of this art of using role reversals was Tarabai Shinde, who skilfully used analogy and appropriated traditional imagery to expose men's selfishness, and the moral lapses and violations of social decency that they committed, as the following extract shows:

> Savitri, of the *stri jati* [female sex] tracked God himself in order to persuade him to resuscitate her lifeless husband, but no such example is cited in the holy books of a man who appealed to God to give the kiss of life to his dead wife. As soon as a woman loses her husband, she is banged up in the four walls of the prison called home. In a similar fashion, shouldn't men cut off their beards, shave off their moustaches, and go and live in a forest—leading a simple and frugal life, thus expressing their grief on losing their wives? In practice what happens is that, once a wife dies, the widower

---

[130] Ibid., p. 116.
[131] Kamaladevi Chattopadhayaya, 'Women: Past and Present', *Roshni*, December 1948, and her book, *Awakening of Indian Women* (Madras: Everyman's Press, 1939).

marries within ten days of her death. Now, do tell me please, which canny God showed you this path? What applies to women ought to apply to men. How blessed are your virtues that God gave you such *Mokaleek* [freedom of action]?[132]

Tarabai is referring to the legendary story of Savitri (from the epic *Mahabharata*) who, through her intelligence and perseverance, was able to reverse fate itself by convincing the God of Death, Yama, to restore her husband's life, her blind in-law's eyesight and the kingdom that they had lost. By invoking the story, she is able to illustrate the whole gamut of rituals and observances in this divinity's name that Hindu women are required to follow in order to prolong the lives of their husbands in contrast to the irresponsible and uncaring behaviour of men in the same situation. Indeed, she argues that some of the more extreme rituals that women in mourning were forced to undergo, such as *sati*, were, in fact, more suitable for men than women:

> There is more loss and harm done when a woman commits sati rather than when a man. You ask me why? Well, who will look after the children and their well-being? Isn't there a proverb that says, 'Let the roving father die, if he must, but spare the spinning mother.' When the father dies, the mother's life is absolutely necessary because she alone, albeit miserable, will be able to bring up the children.[133]

Tarabai Shinde's approach to the thorny question of *sati* throws doubt on the current historiography, which claims that the nineteenth-century debates on *sati* were conducted solely on the basis of scriptural sanction and the reconstitution of the custom under colonial rule. But women's writings especially by widows show that their discourse on *sati* is less governed by abstract principles and more so, by day-to-day concerns. By reversing the roles, Tarabai questions the right of a man to live a layman's life (one which involves enjoyment and pleasure) after the death of his wife, and also demonstrates the impact of the practice on the welfare of the children, who were deprived of their mother. The irresponsibility of men's behaviour is contrasted unfavourably with that of women's throughout her polemic; comparing ageing women to ageing men, for instance, Tarabai highlights the pathetic and often comical attempts made by elderly men to try and combat the ageing process by using wigs or dyeing their hair, aping youthful styles of dress, wearing gleaming dentures that contrasted sharply with their wrinkled skins and marrying young girls of ten years of age. Faced with such folly, all the author can do is wryly ask, 'Now, how many older women in similar situations do you find adopting such farcical acts?'[134]

Certainly, Tarabai was skilled in what, James Scott, in his influential work on everyday forms of resistance used by poor Malayan peasants against their wealthy masters, termed as 'argument as resistance', where the enemy's arguments are

---

[132]   Tarabai Shinde [Women and Men, A Comparison], p. 8.
[133]   Ibid., p. 20.
[134]   Ibid., p. 11.

first listed and then systematically refuted.[135] She begins by carefully building up the statements contained within the *shastras* and epic writings, faithfully rendering what they say about women and female nature, before fiercely tearing down the edifices that she had reconstructed to expose the male double standards regarding female sexuality and morality that underpin them.[136] She challenges men to produce evidence that justifies the fact that men were allowed to remarry immediately after the death of their wives whilst women were simultaneously forbidden to remarry at all.[137] By constantly showing how terrible and degraded men's behaviour would look if the protagonist was female, she demonstrates how hollow Hindu religious sayings were in regard to women's welfare and highlights the sham *dharma* [set of rules guiding the proper conduct of men] towards women. However, her arguments left her extremely exposed to the criticisms of a hostile male press, who not only destroyed her work but also managed to end her fledgling publishing career. Girijabai Kelkar's method of protest and her choice of writing a play that could be enacted had been much shrewder. Despite, or indeed, because of, the sometimes hostile press (although it is important to note that it received positive views as well),[138] the play attracted large audiences, eager to see what the fuss was about. By cloaking her arguments in humour, irony and paradox—the core elements of the literary technique of inversions within a play— Girijabai was able to get her audiences to swallow what, to many, must have seemed a bitter and unpalatable message. Kelkar's use of the medium of the play allowed her mode of protest to slip from the symbolic to the open, invoking lively debates among the theatre-loving Maharashtrian public.

The use of inversion as a mode of resistance to challenge authority was also a feature of many women's songs, as women's songbooks from the period demonstrate. In a song entitled '*Matari*' [A venerable old lady], for instance, oppressed by a disciplinarian mother-in-law and suspicious husbands, four daughters-in-law, who are initially depicted as infertile and sexually frustrated, proceed not only to indulge their sexual appetites but also take revenge on their husbands and mother-in-law.[139] When the mother-in-law's sons leave the village to attend to some business, they leave strict instructions with their mother not to let their wives out of the house—they cannot even go down to the riverbank to fetch water. Their fear of other men making sexual advances on their wives while they are absent is apparent by the remark they make to

---

[135] James C. Scott *Weapons of The Weak: Everyday Forms of Resistance* (New Haven and London: Yale University Press, 1985), chapter 5.

[136] Tarabai Shinde [Women and Men, A Comparison], especially pp. 2–5, 11, 16–18.

[137] Ibid, p. 10.

[138] In Jalgaon (a small town in Maharashtra where the author stayed for a while), a theatre group called Shri Bharat Drama Company staged it several times; even among the stage artistes, a heated debate took place (see also Preface by K. Kolhatkar to Girijabai Kelkar, [Men's Rebellion], p. 9).

[139] In Vishnu Parashuram Shastri Pandit (ed.), *Strigayansangraha Athava Bayakanchi Ganyi* [A Collection of Women's Songs] (Bombay: Indu Prakash Press, 1882), pp. 103–6.

their mother before they depart: 'You know the ways of the cunning *murari* [Krishna]'.[140] Once they leave, the mother-in-law immediately locks her daughters-in-law in the house, much to their annoyance. However, that very night an old woman calling herself Krishnabai appears at the door, seeking refuge for the night. Krishnabai claims to be on a pilgrimage to Kashi, and is welcomed into the house by the mother-in-law, who confides in her that the daughters-in-law are unable to conceive and asks the old woman to pray on their behalf. The mother-in-law is clearly entranced by her new guest so when, in the middle of the night Krishnabai complains that her body is aching, the mother-in-law sends the daughters-in-law in to look after her. However, the old lady is, in fact, Krishna in disguise and transforms into four handsome young men, who spend the night 'entertaining' the daughters-in-law. At dawn, Krishna smears the mother-in-law's nose with lime-powder (a mark of shame), before disappearing. The folk song concludes by making two significant points: the oppressed daughters-in-law are able to fulfil their sexual desires and bear children whilst the mother-in-law is forced to recognize and come to terms with the bitter fact of her sons' impotency.

The appeal of this particular folk song is demonstrated by the fact that it appears almost unchanged in later compilations in the early half of the twentieth century.[141] Like Girijabai Kelkar's play, it was able to use fantastical situations that allowed it to circumvent male censorship[142] whilst simultaneously expressing several themes that would have been immediately familiar to many women: repressed desire, controlling mother-in-laws and husbands and the idea that, if women could not conceive, then it is somehow their fault; it was unthinkable to directly question men's virility or acknowledge physiological deviations. Along with other songs of this era,[143] it was an important vehicle for women, allowing them to act out forbidden desires, and question the existing order of society in late nineteenth- and early twentieth-century Maharashtra. Like the writings of Tarabai Shinde, and the plays of Girijabai Kelkar, the folk songs not only provided a 'steam valve' for subordinated peoples[144] but also sent a message to the *purush jati* [male sex] that women wished a more just world, based on amicable reciprocity and parity of esteem. It was this heritage that provided later Indian feminists, such as Kamaladevi Chattopadhyaya, a solid foundation upon which to build their vision for female equality in the twentieth century.

---

[140]   Vishnu Pandit, [A Collection of Women's Songs], p. 104.

[141]   The same song is reprinted in the early half of the twentieth century in Parvatibai Gokhale (ed.), *Stri Geetratnakar* [A Collection of Women's Songs] (Poona: Bharat Bhushan Press, 1912), pp. 11–13.

[142]   For another example, see the song 'Vakadi Vat' [A Warped Course] in Parvatibai Gokhale, [A Collection of Women's Songs], pp. 136–7.

[143]   'Sasubaichisamajavani' [Appeasing Mother-in-law], in Shamrao Moroji Naik (ed.), *Strigeetmala Athava Striyanchi Manoranjak Gani* [Collection of Women's Songs or Songs for Women's Entertainment] (Bombay: Jagmitra Press, 1882), pp. 55–8.

[144]   A classic formulation of the 'steam valve' effect demonstrated through rites of rebellion is Max Gluckman, *Order and Rebellion in Tribal Africa* (New York: Cohen and West, 1963).

Accessing Information: Women and the Sources of Knowledge

This chapter has demonstrated the way in which women sought to transform their lives for the better through the modes of assertion or resistance. However, the most popular ways of doing this, such as petitioning the state or enlisting the help of the vernacular press in highlighting instances of injustice, required a degree of education that only certain sectors of society possessed. What is therefore striking is that the archive yields a rich mine of letters and petitions from 'women' belonging to all walks of life. The nature of at least some of the petitions reveals the petitioner to be a woman. Premabai, for example, had requested that her son should be hired by the government so that her family could survive in the absence of her husband who had died in the service of the Raj but when the government responded positively by offering her son a job in the army she turned it down on 'emotional' grounds as her husband, who had been a *subedar* [equivalent to an army captain] had been killed in a skirmish.[145] Another petitioner, Fatmabi, argued that, even though she had remarried, her first husband's pension should continue until the wedding of her daughter from her first husband's marriage, as her second husband had refused to maintain the girl. Her appeal was successful; although, under the Civil Pension Code, pensions lapsed if the widow remarried, in this instance, the Accountant-General found the argument of the widow sound enough to produce a report for the government in her favour.[146] The diversity of these cases indicates that illiterate women would have had access to help from women who were literate or liberal-minded men and knew how the official channels of complaint operated.

One of the ways that women would have developed informal networks to assist them would have been at the *halad kunku* parties that are described in more detail in chapter 3. Even groups that had been ostracized, such as *kalavantins* [female artistes], found *halad kunku* rituals useful to make public statements about their status.[147] The ceremony was also significant for the *kalavantins* in that it allowed them the chance to display their wealth and, by extension, their legitimate place within Bombay society. Govind Madgavkar, a late nineteenth-century contemporary observer, for instance, mentions that, in a *halad kunku* ceremony during her daughter's mock wedding, a fabulously wealthy *kalavantin* distributed silver cups in order to deliberately signal her wealth.[148] In taking this course of action, she was able to buy the silence of her critics by 'gifting' expensive goods and 'cleansing' her property in this munificent act. Indeed, in the *kalavantins'* case, the *halad kunku* rite can also be seen as a 'ritual of resistance' in its own right, an attempt to combat some of the growing prejudices of the Indian middle-classes against this class of

---

[145] Petition by Premabai, 20 March 1885, BJP, 1885, p. 408.
[146] 17 May 1883, JD, 1883, vol. 3, comp. no. 652, MSA.
[147] See chapter 3 for a description and analysis of this women's rite.
[148] Madgavkar, [An Account of Bombay], p. 301.

women.[149] As shown in an earlier chapter, middle class women had given these rituals new functions and used them as forums for publicizing the many social reform activities beneficial for the *bhaginivarg* [sisterhood]. *halad kunku* rituals served as collective self-help agencies and hence can be read as sites of resistance.

However, this was not the only means for women of this period to exchange ideas and thoughts and act on them. Susan Harding, for instance, has studied the relationship between 'gossip' and formation of gender identities among illiterate peasant women in Spain, and argued that it gave women opportunities to think, articulate and organize themselves.[150] Their experiences are mirrored in those of nineteenth-century Indian women, with gossip providing a means of overcoming caste and communal barriers. The number of approaches for legal advice that Cornelia Sorabji, an appeal lawyer in Baroda, received from village women, for instance, never failed to amaze her. She cites a particularly interesting case, which involved an approach from the sister of a woodcutter's wife who had been arrested on false charges of hacking her husband to death. When Cornelia's mother, Franscina, asked how the woman knew exactly who to approach, the woman replied that it was common knowledge that Franscina had a 'ballister (barrister) daughter'.[151] This example demonstrates the way in which daily gossip provided illiterate women with the means to obtain help from other women in times of crisis.[152]

It also provided a means for illiterate women to develop an awareness of political events that were occurring beyond the borders of their village. The Indian press in the late nineteenth century, especially the vernacular newspapers, was increasingly critical of the colonial government. The philanthropic individuals who funded them did not see them as commercial enterprises but rather as conduits to arouse, mobilize and educate nationalists to oppose the Raj. Bipan Chandra notes that the influence of the Indian press went 'far beyond its literate subscribers ... reach[ing] remote villages [where it ...] would then be read by a reader to tens of others.'[153] Moreover, it also provided information on a wide range of social legislation that directly concerned them, namely the Age of Consent and the restitution of conjugal rights. It is this legislation that we will go on to study now.

---

[149] My reading of *halad kunku* as a ritual of resistance is adapted from the powerful conception of Nicholas Dirks's study of the subversive aspects of ritual practice and discourse of the Aiyanar festival in 'Ritual and Resistance: Subversion as a Social Fact', in D. Haynes and G. Prakash, *Contesting Power*, pp. 213–38.

[150] 'Women and Words in a Spanish Village', in R. Reiter (ed.), *Toward an Anthropology of Women* (New York: Monthly Review Press, 1975), pp. 283–308.

[151] Cornelia Sorabji, *India Calling, The Memories of Cornelia Sorabji* (London: Nisbet and Co., 1934), p. 59.

[152] The term 'gossip' here is adapted from both Susan Harding and James Scott's conceptual formation to mean news conveyed about an 'absent third party'; in this context, its power to circulate effectively comes from the fact that the news has 'no author but many retailers'. See also J. Scott, *Weapons of the Weak*, p. 282.

[153] Bipan Chandra et al., *India's Struggle for Independence* (Delhi: Penguin, 1989), p. 103.

Chapter 5

Women, Crime and Survival Strategies in Colonial India

Introduction

As the first two chapters demonstrated, Indian feminists and reformers, whether Christian or Hindu, sought to improve the position of women by campaigning against oppressive traditional practices, such as child marriage and widow remarriage, and educating them to allow them a greater degree of autonomy. However, before this process could be completed, the British government embarked on a period of aggressive intrusion into Indian society by extending colonial law and eroding the legal systems, such as the caste *panchayats* [courts] and village councils, which had traditionally governed Indian life. This left women in a particularly exposed situation: bound by the constraints of traditional society and forced to undertake desperate acts hitherto shown a degree of understanding, they now felt the full weight of colonial law. Traditional institutions had shown greater flexibility because of their more intimate knowledge of the context of actions or 'situational context' deemed 'criminal' by the new British courts.[1] When a more impersonal colonial law, framed at a distance, superseded these, new definitions of crime and criminality emerged. Defined, pursued and prosecuted by the courts as criminals, it was in the second half of the nineteenth century that 'the female criminal' emerged in India.

This chapter explores several key areas in which this process unfolded. The policy of designating certain subaltern groups as belonging to 'criminal classes' had a profoundly negative impact on the women of such communities. Equally, wives who used force to resist brutal husbands through husband poisoning and killing felt the full rigour of the law. Perhaps the most important area in which we see the emergence of the female criminal was in the creation of the 'crime' of infanticide. A product of the

---

[1] In a revisionist approach to Hindu law, Werner Menski has put forth a compelling argument that within customary law, *dharma* (every Hindu's obligation to act appropriately in any given circumstance) was a 'relative' value as it had no absolute notion of 'good' or 'bad' [*adharma*]. Hence, the 'precise definition' of what constituted 'dharma' was dependent on the 'situational context' of the offence. Customary justice was sought in the 'situational context' and not in abstract rules or textual authority, thus giving Hindu law enormous scope for reform and flexibility through millenia. Werner Menski, *Indian Legal Systems Past and Present* (University of London: SOAS Law Department, 1997), occasional paper, no. 3 see especially pp. 1–23.

ban on widow remarriage in Indian society, traditional social mechanisms had been in place to deal with them. The extension of colonial law, before movements of social reform had made any headway, highlighted the mother's responsibility for the act while ignoring the circumstances surrounding it. In each of these areas, the ways in which the law affected women detrimentally will be shown and how women's actions served to highlight their resistance to the pressures thrown up by changing gender relations in the nineteenth century. In tracing the emerging female criminal, we also uncover women as agents in processes of social change under colonialism.

Since the 1970s, increasing numbers of social historians have turned their attention to the subject of crime, a trend which has seen the broadening of definitions beyond the purely juridical to uncover alternative meanings which reflect the social context of infraction.[2] Despite the widening of approaches in the subject of crime in South Asian history, women's perspectives have remained largely absent.[3] Indeed, even in instances when historians have turned their attention to crimes such as *sati* [widow burning] and female infanticide, they have tended to focus on the implications that they had on the development of the colonial state's authority and missionaries and indigenous elites[4] rather than what such acts meant to women themselves.[5] Such approaches not only ignore the ways in which the new notions of crime and criminality that emerged under colonialism often had an adverse effect on many women's lives; by failing to examine the issue from the perspective of these women's lives, they also ignore the fact that many female perpetrators took a different view from the authorities about the actions that they had committed. Acts that, at first glance, appear to be straightforwardly criminal, such as spousal murder or infanticide, take on a very different character when relocated into the context of unequal power relations. By looking at certain forms of behaviour and violent acts by women, classified by the criminal justice system as 'crimes', in the context of changing gender relations, and the way in which they intersected with wider social and political relations in colonial India, this chapter will demonstrate how female crime was often a violent form of resistance, part of a limited range of strategies for survival available to

---

[2] Pioneers in the field are Anand Yang (ed.), *Crime and Criminality in British India* (Tucson: University of Arizona Press, 1985); David Arnold, 'Dacoity and Rural Crime in Madras, 1860–1940', *The Journal of Peasant Studies*, 6/2 (1979): 140–67; David Hardiman, 'From Custom to Crime: The Politics of Drinking in Colonial South Gujarat', in R. Guha (ed.), *Subaltern Studies IV* (Delhi: Oxford University Press, 1985).

[3] Sadly, little has been done to remedy the conspicuous omission of women in studies of crime highlighted by Yang in the introduction to *Crime and Criminality in British India*, p. 23.

[4] Lata Mani, *Contentious Traditions: The Debate on Sati* (Berkeley: University of California Press, 1998); Radhika Singha, *A Despotism of Law: Crime and Justice in Early Colonial India* (New Delhi: Oxford University Press, 1998).

[5] Indeed, the numerous studies of the *sati* seen as 'eternal victim' have now been subjected to a critical review. See Ania Loomba, 'Dead Women Tell No Tales: Issues of Female Subjectivity, Subaltern Agency and Tradition in Colonial and Post-Colonial Writings on Widow Immolation in India', *History Workshop Journal*, 36 (1993): 209–27.

subordinated groups, whether they were battered wives or unhappy widows. It will argue that, far from being a manifestation of a criminal nature, acts of violence by married women, such as poisoning husbands, were often responses to instances of extreme brutality committed by men, which ranged from beating their wives when they were perceived to have done something wrong to branding and cutting their noses if they were thought to have committed adultery. The pressures on widows, although more intangible, were no less acute. Societal prohibitions on remarriages meant that some widows, particularly those who had lost their spouse at a relatively young age, had illicit liaisons, which sometimes resulted in pregnancy. The ensuing dilemma combined with the lack of escape routes for the widow meant that it resulted in infanticide; an act which the colonial authorities viewed with particular abhorrence.

A further area of interest to this study is to reflect on why the state and the judicial apparatus were so concerned with reinscribing crimes, like that of infanticide, on to the social canvas of nineteenth-century Maharashtra, and the functions that this served. In addition, it also examines what motivated indigenous elites to participate in the debates surrounding issues of women's chastity; by doing this, we can move towards an understanding of how power relationships between the state and indigenous groups often proved to be at the forefront of the restructuring of gender relations in colonial India.

Women of 'Criminal Castes and Tribes'

The study of women and crime in India reveals the ways in which the colonial state's imposition of the law could both empower and inhibit women. One group of women adversely affected by the legal system were those who belonged to certain communities that the colonial authorities classified as 'criminal classes'. The Criminal Tribes Act of 1871 effectively stated that responsibility for criminal acts did not just lie with the individual perpetrator but, in some instances, could be extended to their communities as well; an extension that inevitably had a deleterious effect on those women belonging to the 'criminal' tribes.[6] Since caste was so central to British conceptions of India, not only could criminal castes and tribes be identified, further, their 'criminal' disposition was assumed to be entrenched in Indian societal structures.[7] In locating the origins of criminality among such groups, the British began to view the women of 'criminal' communities as accomplices and accessories in the crimes committed by their men

---

[6] The so-called criminal tribes have received a good deal of attention from scholars but the women of such groups have been almost entirely neglected. As well as the articles in the Yang collection, see Sanjay Nigam, 'Disciplining and Policing the 'Criminals by Birth', part I and II, *Indian Economic and Social History Review*, 27/2 (1990): 131–64 and 27/3, (1990): 257–87.

[7] Anand Yang, 'Dangerous Castes and Tribes: The Criminal Tribes Act and the Maga-hiya Doms of Northeast India', in Yang, *Crime and Criminality,* p. 112.

folk, a view that had its roots in British legal procedure.[8] Due to the women's position in the household and the family, early modern English legal commentators had associated women with the crime of receiving stolen goods, and women were therefore often viewed as accessories. However, although they were often viewed as being complicit in the criminal acts that had been undertaken by their spouses, British women were rarely prosecuted, a fact ignored by the colonial authorities in India who found large numbers of women in India guilty of this crime.[9]

This was particularly true of women belonging to tribes such as the Kaikadis and Kaddi Korva which the colonial authorities believed to be engaged in activities such as house-breaking, pick-pocketing on trains or at fairs or dacoity [gang robbery].[10] Traditionally, the Kaikadis were a nomadic tribe whose occupation was weaving reed baskets for domestic purposes; however, some travelogues of the times reveal that they had fallen on hard times and resorted to the newer occupation of acrobatics and street performances in urban centres.[11] The colonial authorities believed that women of these tribes were often active participants in the alleged urban 'crimes' committed by these tribes. Such was their belief in the criminal nature of the members of these tribes that, even if the women had not directly participated, they were viewed as accessories to the crime. Contemporary nineteenth-century independent commentators have noted these injustices visited on female Indian criminals, such as the journalist M.F. Billington, who, after inspecting Indian prisons in the early 1890s and talking to female prisoners, observed that 'an extraordinarily large number of the female offenders [we]re in prison for receiving stolen goods'.[12] Although not entirely free from the colonial practice of stereotyping of 'criminal minds' in certain castes and tribes of India, Billington concluded that 'it is fairer to judge her as a victim to her circumstances than as a law-breaker on her own account'.[13] The women prisoners she spoke to justified their misdemeanours on the grounds that they could not defy their husbands, especially when they often threatened to use brute force if the women did not follow their orders. Women of such classes also suffered greatly when large numbers of men belonging to their caste were arrested and transported. In such circumstances, the lands and homes

---

[8] J.M. Beattie, *Crime and the Courts in England, 1660–1800* (Oxford: Clarendon Press, 1986); R. Gillespie, 'Women and Crime in 17th Century Ireland', in M. MacCurtain and M. O'Dowd (eds), *Women in Early Modern Ireland* (Edinburgh: Edinburgh University Press, 1991), pp. 43–52.

[9] See Beattie, Ibid., pp. 185–90.

[10] M. Kennedy, *Notes on Criminal Classes in the Bombay Presidency* (Bombay: Government Central Press, 1908), pp. 10, 26.

[11] Curiously Pandita Ramabai refers to them as 'gypsies' and 'beggars'. See *United Stateschi Lokasthiti ani Pravasvrit* [The Peoples of United States], (Mumbai: Nirnaya Sagar, 1889), chapter 7. A translation in English is now available. See Pandita Ramabai, (1889), *The Peoples of United States*, trans. and ed. M. Kosambi, (Delhi: Permanent Black, 2004).

[12] Mary Billington, *Women in India* (London: Chapman and Hall, 1895), p. 242.

[13] Ibid.

belonging to the group involved were seized, meaning that women left behind were reduced to living in poverty. Appeals to the state for help in restoring their property were rarely successful; the government, who suspected the property, especially moveable goods, to be stolen goods, often dismissed their claims.[14] It was unsurprising, therefore, that many women from such tribes felt anxious about the future prospects for the security and material welfare of themselves and their families, leading some to take action to improve their situation. In the 1880s, for instance, when the British were making efforts to settle the wandering Magahiya Doms of Champaran in Bihar, it was the female members of the tribe, weary of persecution and being driven out of whereever they settled, that took the initiative and approached the local authorities about "a resting place or employment" to sustain them and their families while their husbands were in jail.[15]

In India, the relationship between poverty and increased crime is well-documented;[16] similarly, female petitioners to the government often show themselves to be driven by the need for stability and the preservation of their material circumstances rather than any other consideration. In many instances, women did not appeal for the lives of their spouses, but instead for the fields or the ornaments that their husbands had possessed before they were arrested. If they lost these, women in these tribes would often face ruin, as the description of the plight of Bhimi and five other women in a petition to the government demonstrates. Revealing their identities as the wives of dacoits, they appealed for the return of ornaments and fields that had been confiscated when their husbands had been convicted, arguing that, otherwise, they and their children faced the 'bitterest pangs of starvation and destitution'.[17] Indeed, even in instances when groups of women made joint petitions for the release of their husbands, it was significant that many of these appeals were made not on the basis of the innocence of the men concerned, but were rather attempts to save themselves and their children from death through starvation.[18]

The changing fortunes of the women of criminal tribes and castes highlights the ways in which women could be the victims of the intrusion of colonialism into indigenous society, not only through the state's imposition of alien legal values, but also their interpretation of gender roles, especially the position of women within the family and community. Nevertheless, despite the fact that colonialism created a new kind of female criminal, women were often able to find ways of using such procedures

---

[14] See the government's resolution to the petition of Ghania and eleven other women, 4 October 1883, Bombay Judicial Proceedings (hereafter BJP), 1883, vol. P/2422, no. 269, p. 103, Oriental and India Office Collection, (hereafter OIOC).

[15] Anand Yang, 'Dangerous Castes and Tribes', p. 122.

[16] David Arnold, 'Dacoity and Rural Crime in Madras', pp. 145–9.

[17] Petition of Bhimi and others, 29 December 1883, Judicial Department (hereafter JD), 1884, vol. 42, comp. no. 267. Maharashtra State Archives (hereafter MSA); see also petition by Crustnabaee and others, 5 April 1870, BJP, 1870, vol. P/442/4, no. 80, OIOC.

[18] Petition signed by 17 wives of dacoits headed by Ghaina, n.d., JD, 1884, vol. 96, comp. no. 267, OIOC.

as appeal to mitigate its most harmful effects on domestic life. This paradox was not just confined to using the executive arm of the state as a 'resource' in resolving domestic property issues, but was also utilized in instances involving physical harm or, in some cases, murder or manslaughter, with women accused of such crimes using the system, which had often led to them finding themselves in such circumstances, to tell their side of the story.

Husband-Poisoning, Wife-Beating and Uxoricide

Cases that involved women accidentally poisoning their husbands when they sought to assuage marriage problems by utilizing traditional remedies provide a stark illustration of one of the ways in which the application of colonial law had a deleterious effect on women who were often seeking to alleviate intolerable circumstances. In India in the nineteenth century, the social position of a wife largely depended on her ability to win and retain the affection and sympathy of her husband. This was the case whether it was a question of maintaining a balance in power relations with a co-wife or mother-in-law or even with regard to commanding respect both within the marital home and in the community at large. The importance of receiving love and affection from their spouses to female happiness is reflected in the disproportionate amount of space that Marathi fiction, treatises that examine gender relations and women's magazines meant for female consumers give to the issue, with folk-tales and women's songbooks depicting the sadness and anxiety of those unlucky women who failed to do so.[19] Given the emphasis on achieving happiness through marriage, it is therefore predictable that those women who had less than perfect marriages would turn to any means they could to rekindle their relationship. It was quite common for wives in dysfunctional marriages to try and improve the situation by administering aphrodisiacs; an action that often had a tragic outcome.[20] While some courts recognized that such acts were purely misadventure and correspondingly sentenced women to relatively short prison terms of a few years, others women were treated much more harshly. Akku, for example, was sentenced to transportation for life. She appealed, arguing:

> I did not knowingly administer poison to my husband. As my husband did not like me I mentioned the circumstance to a neighbour named Ramu bin Babaji who told me that he would give some substance to me and that if I administered the same to my husband

---

[19] (Compiler unknown), *Striyan Va Mulikarita Sangeet Sundar Gani* [Songs of Women and Girls] (Ratnagiri: Damanskar, n.d.), pp. 100–101; Vishnu Parashuram Shastri Pandit (ed.), *Strigayansangraha Athava Bayakanchi Ganyi* [A Collection of Women's Songs] (Bombay: Indu Prakash Press, 1882), pp. 128–9.

[20] Basavi, who had asked her father to give her 'some medicine which would bring back the love of her husband', was supplied with some poisonous substance. Her husband survived but she was sentenced to five years rigorous imprisonment. See JD, 1885, vol. 38, comp. no. 764, MSA.

with food, my husband would start to like me ... Had I known that the powder was a
poison and that it was injurious to life, I would not have done so.[21]

In spite of this plea the petition was turned down.

Such instances were not confined to the administration of aphrodisiac potions;
'medicines' that women, in particular those in poorer or rural areas, administered to
their husbands to alleviate their illness frequently proved to be fatal.[22] The use of
chemicals such as arsenic and lead or curative drugs in the form of herbs, oils and
seeds came through knowledge of medicines passed on through generations.
Reproductive rituals, even in contemporary India, reveal the knowledge and
recommend the use of a range of kitchen-based herbs and dietary items to enhance
fertility.[23] Women's songbooks refer to the cycle of reproduction with an amazing
accuracy of detail and precision as well as giving advice on parturition and other topics
pertaining to reproduction.[24] In rural communities knowledge of folk medicine was
transmitted orally. The trial of Veni is illustrative of the widespread use and practice of
folk medicine, which sometimes resulted in accidents. Veni had mixed some herbs
with her husband's meal to cure him of epileptic fits, but he had unfortunately become
ill as a result of the medicine he had consumed. The courts showed little mercy towards
her, and she was tried and sentenced to five years' rigorous imprisonment.[25] Neither
was any clemency shown towards elderly women, usually mothers and great aunts,
whose concern for the health of their family members resulted in them committing acts
that, with hindsight, only exacerbated the situation rather than lessen it. In 1880, for
instance, a Parsi mother-in-law was sentenced to nine months' rigorous imprisonment
for branding her daughter-in-law, despite the fact that she claimed that she had only
done it in order to cure the girl of a nervous disorder.[26] A similar lack of clemency was
shown to Savitri, who had given her daughter some medicine to help her get rid her of
syphilis and thus save herself from disgracing her in-laws. However, in her anxiety, she
forgot to tell her daughter to apply it externally, meaning that, when she took it orally,
the daughter was poisoned. Even though the daughter recovered, her mother was
transported for ten years despite the fact that she had given it to her daughter in good

---

[21] Akku's petition, 20 November 1890, JD, 1890, vol. 70, comp. no. 174. MSA

[22] Pandita Ramabai, *Stri-Dharma Niti* [Prescribed Laws and Duties on the Proper
Conduct of Women] 3rd edn (Kedgaon: Mukti Mission Press, 1967; 1st edn 1882), pp. 74–
5.

[23] Seetha Anagol, 'When Treatment Fails', in Kanthi Bansal, (ed.), *Practical Approach
to Infertility Management* (New Delhi: Jaypee Medical Publishers, 2004), pp. 610–14.

[24] 'Gane Garbhakhand Varnan' [Songs on Pregnancy and Birth], in (compiler unknown), *Songs of Women and Girls*, pp. 67–70 and 74–81. Also songs on 'Dohale' [The
Longings of Pregnant Women] and 'Palan' [Childbirth Rites] in Shamrao Naik (ed.),
Strigeetmala athava Striyanchi Manoranjak Gani [Collection of Women's Songs or Songs
for Women's Leisure] (Bombay: Jagmitra Press, 1882), pp. 62–77.

[25] Proceedings of the case of Veni v. Dew Ramji in JD, 1881, vol. 46, comp. no. 793,
MSA.

[26] Petition of Dhunbai, 28 March 1880, JD, 1880, vol. 49, comp. no. 354, MSA.

faith.[27] Whereas traditional legal systems such as caste panchayats and village councils had shown flexibility and understanding in such circumstances, the British judicial system showed no such mercy. This meant that, although many feminists and women reformers, as chapters 1 and 2 demonstrate, were tackling such ignorance and superstition through education programmes, many well-intentioned women were subjected to the harsh penalties imposed by the colonial courts.

Whilst these women had unintentionally harmed or, in some instances, killed their loved ones out of a desire to ease their suffering, however, other women clearly administered herbs and potions with the unmistakeable intent to murder their husband. With the caste panchayats effectively rendered powerless, divorce forbidden for higher-caste Hindus and separation for other classes only permissible in the rare occasions that the man gave his permission, most women, as the previous chapter demonstrates,[28] were left with no legitimate means of escaping from their misery. The desperation that some women, especially child-wives, often felt when trapped in disagreeable or abusive marriages drove some to poison their husbands, often as much a protest against their natal families as their repulsion towards the spouse which guided their violent dissent;[29] a strategy also employed by some women whose misery had driven them to seek solace in extramarital liaisons.[30] The violent actions that these women committed against their spouses could therefore be viewed as a means of resistance, with poisoning proving a particularly popular stratagem as it did not involve direct confrontation against a physically superior opponent. Even those who employed other methods, such as Ambi kom Dhavji, who was hanged after she killed her husband with a sickle, tended to act when their partner was asleep.[31] In a climate which often sanctioned punishing women by cutting off their noses, branding[32] or wife-beating, it is hardly surprising that many women trapped in such a position eventually resorted to such desperate measures.

Indeed, wife-beating was not only common in nineteenth-century India but there is some evidence to suggest that its prevalence in certain communities was on the increase. If this is indeed the case, it could be that it was caused by the changing notions of identity and power relations in late nineteenth-century India, a theory that is expounded upon at length by Tarabai Shinde, who appears to argue that the

---

[27] Imperatrix v. Savitri, JD, 1884, vol. 46, comp. no. 1352, MSA.

[28] See section entitled 'Right to Remarriage and Custody of Children' in chapter 4.

[29] See the case of Mohona kom Mahadu whose desperation can be measured by the fact that she refused to appeal against her sentence of transportation for life, in JD, 1883, vol. 87, comp. no. 1088, MSA.

[30] See petition of Changi, 4 January 1870, JD, 1870, vol. 59, comp. no. 1277; and the petition of Chanda kom Bala, 1 June 1889, JD, 1889, vol. 5, comp. no. 2825, MSA.

[31] For details see *Mahratta*, 27 July 1895, Native Newspaper Reports (hereafter NNR).

[32] Four-fifths of the cases that came up for enhancement of penal sentences were about violence towards women. 'Return of cases in which sentences have been enhanced by the High Court on review, reference or appeal from 1 Jan. 1878 to 10 Sept. 1885' (hereafter 'Return of cases'), JD, 1885, vol. 99, comp. no. 532, MSA.

phenomenon was due to the fact that women were becoming more rebellious and finding the concept of *stridharma* [women's duties], an already impossible abstract ideal, even more difficult to follow as Indian men aligned with the Raj and forged new forms of domination over women, whilst simultaneously excluding women from enjoying the benefits of foreign rule.[33] Redefined norms of behaviour among caste groups undergoing change could certainly affect women harshly. In the Satara district, for example, it was reported that wife-beating and branding were increasing at such an alarming rate that they had become the norm, with the *kunbis* [agricultural castes] actually considering them an 'act of manliness'.[34] Yet, although the cases were increasing, the pain that the women felt when subjected to such acts did not diminish, with individual cases showing the degree of cruelty inflicted on some abused wives. Yamaji Tulsiram, for instance, was accused of causing grievous hurt to his wife with a hot iron, with the transcript describing how 'the accused ... tied up his wife to a beam and branded her in six places, her breasts, between her buttocks and the calves of her legs'.[35] In another case, Balabhai Rajubhai chopped off his wife's arm and leg in an attempt 'to correct her behaviour'.[36] His justification turned out to be untrue, with the townspeople testifying at the trial that his wife was, in fact, a chaste woman and that Rajubhai used to beat her savagely on a regular basis, causing her to run away to her father's house.

Another social institution that greatly impacted on the lives of many women was the continued practice of the custom of polygamy, which often resulted in wives competing to secure the attention of their husband, particularly if they happened to be his second or third wife. In such an atmosphere, it was unsurprising that squabbles often arose, and that the animosity between different wives occasionally spilled over into violence, as the case of Kashi illustrates. Accused of attempting to murder her co-wife, Baji, and Baji's daughter by poisoning them, Kashi made the following plea for mercy:

> I am scarcely advanced in years or experience, being nearly only twenty-five years of age. My caste is polygamous and I had the misfortune to have had the complainant as a rival wife of my husband. Would that the system of polygamy never have existed in

---

[33] *Stridharma*, she suggests wryly, boiled down to the grisly detail of the servile wife asking her husband, after he had beaten her black and blue, whether he needed his arms massaged lest his hands hurt him from the effort of thrashing her. See Tarabai Shinde, *Stripurushtulana athava Striya va Purush Yant Sahasi kon he Spasta Karun Dakavinya-karita ha Nibandh* [Women and Men, A Comparison or an Essay Showing Who is More Wicked] (hereafter Women and Men, A Comparison), ed. S.J. Malshe, 2nd edn (Bombay: Mumbai Marathi Grantha Sangrahalaya Publications, 1975; 1st edn 1882), pp. 1–2.

[34] *Vritta Sudha*, 4 March 1893, NNR. See Jim Masselos' study of patterns of behaviour in Bombay households which enumerates a number of punishments inflicted on adulterous wives by their spouses, 'Sexual Property/Sexual Violence: Wives in Nineteenth-Century Bombay', *South Asia Research*, 12/2 (1992), pp. 81–99.

[35] Proceedings of the case are in 'Return of cases', 1885, MSA.

[36] JD, 1884, vol. 30, comp. no. 24, MSA.

India or that I was never born in a polygamous society; I have now to leave not only my native land and my dearest relations but I have now to leave behind two infant sons to the mercy of any wife that my husband fancies to take ...[37]

However, despite her pleas and the fact that the evidence used to prosecute her was entirely based on Baji's statement that her daughter had died after consuming some food, an assertion which both assessors in the case found highly suspect, Kashi was convicted of attempting to poison Baji and her daughter. Despite the fact that the evidence was far from conclusive—indeed, either Baji herself or Purshotram, the father, could equally have caused the death—the prevalence of such cases was enough to convince the judge of her guilt.

The often bleak state of Maharashtrian domestic relations, however, did not always result in women committing such desperate acts. Indeed, whilst the authorities punished those women who attempted to readdress the injustices that they suffered on their own harshly and without consideration for their individual circumstances, they also acted against those men who took it up on themselves to punish their wives by mutilating or disfiguring them in acts such as branding, whipping and cutting parts of the body. The state considered all forms of mutilation and disfigurement such as branding, whipping and cutting parts of the body as a threat to its own monopoly of physical authority. Such acts of violence by one individual against another were considered crimes by the state and the perpetrators were to be brought to justice. Some abused women were able to exploit the law and assert their will in order to ensure that their tormentor had been properly punished. Some women were even successful in their petitions to get the sentence on their aggressors enhanced from one year's rigorous imprisonment to seven years transportation, although others were not so fortunate.[38] The patriarchal nature of the judiciary meant that some judges showed sympathy towards men who committed violent acts towards women, especially when errant husbands showed what was termed as 'genuine remorse'.[39]

Indeed, mitigating factors were often taken in account even if uxoricide had been committed; whilst female murders were sentenced without mercy, the same criminal justice system was quick to recognize the mitigating circumstances surrounding a man's murder of his wife, even when the possible provocation, such as a wife

---

[37] Details in JD, 1885, vol. 35, comp. no. 378, MSA.

[38] For a successful case, see the proceedings of the sentence on Krishna bin Sakha in 'Return of cases', 1885. Conversely, in the case of Govinda's wife, after her husband abused her by cutting her nose, she complained to the District Commissioner when her husband was acquitted, and the government agreed with the Magistrate that an appeal to the High Court was uncalled for. See the proceedings in the case of Imperatrix v. Govinda in JD, 1880, vol. 17, comp. no. 5782, MSA.

[39] For example, Hari Sakharam was imprisoned for only three months hard labour after he had disfigured his wife by cutting her nose, which he admitted, was done in 'a fit of jealousy'. In JD, 1881, vol. 49, comp. no. 1252, MSA.

committing adultery, was often inconclusive.[40] Judicial records of uxoricide cases reveal that male offenders were given shorter terms of imprisonment based on 'extenuating circumstances', which arose as a result of the husband suffering from a sudden 'fit of passion'. Therefore, although in some ways the legal system provided an outlet for abused women to obtain justice, it is clear that the colonial state not only recognized but also largely reinforced a deeply entrenched patriarchal society[41] that favoured the rights of men over women. Even on the rare occasions that it did show clemency to women, such as shortening the sentences of some women convicted of poisoning their husbands, it did not do this out of compassion for the women convicted but rather in order to uphold the values of Hindu society and family discipline, as the case of Veni v. Dew Ramji illustrates.[42] The judge remitted a portion of Veni's sentence (from transportation to five years' hard labour), but only on the condition that she secured a bond that meant that, in effect, she would remain under the protection of her husband for the rest of her life.

The punishments that were imposed under the Indian penal code were extremely harsh and made no allowances for ordinary female convicts. Women convicted of serious crimes, such as murder, forgery and arson, faced capital punishment (although this could be converted to transportation for life if their appeals were successful) whilst the sentences for less serious offenders varied from rigorous (hard labour) to simple imprisonment. The philosophy of punishment underpinning the criminal justice system in nineteenth-century India echoed that of the metropolitan state. This is most apparent with regard to the maintenance of the death penalty and the frequent use of mercy through an elaborate system of appealing and petitioning to the executive authorities.[43] Female juvenile offenders and pregnant female convicts were treated with more care; female convicts under eighteen were not transported to the penal colonies until they reached their majority whilst pregnant female convicts were not hanged until they had

---

[40] See, for example, the widely reported case of the Crown Prince of Udaipur (also known as the 'Chhota Udeypur case'), who had murdered his wife because he suspected she might have committed adultery. This case came is interesting because it reveals how unanimously the Indian language press sympathized with the offender. Similar cases reported often in the press lauded the man's actions on the grounds that it was 'in keeping with the Indian notions of morality and honour'. See *Dnyan Prakash*, 23 October 1880, NNR; *Bombay Samachar*, 23 October 1880, NNR.

[41] See judgement passed by the Sessions Judge on Bhola, 22 June 1879, JD, 1880, vol. 45, comp. no. 632, MSA. See the case of Bhikia bin Dharma, who had murdered his wife and her lover yet had his sentence reduced from capital punishment to transportation for life when he petitioned the courts, 19 August 1881, BJP, 1881, vol. P/1796, no. 2010, OIOC.

[42] JD, 1882, vol. 137, comp. no. 1098, MSA.

[43] For the functions of the criminal justice system in eighteenth-century England, see Douglas Hay 'Property, authority and the criminal law', in D. Hay et al., *Albion's Fatal Tree: Crime and Society in Eighteenth-Century England* (London: Penguin, 1975), pp. 17–63.

delivered their child. Female criminals who were deemed to be 'lunatics' were also treated differently and confined to asylums rather than sent to prison.

These changes in penal practice were intrinsically linked to the changing balance of power in the relationship between the state and the individual, with the state increasingly seeking to control the individual by imposing limitations on the way in which they conducted themselves, even in the apparently private realm of the domestic sphere. The men and women who were directly affected by them did not, however, meekly accept such controls, and they contested them using various methods. Indeed, even when they were sanctioned, women often continued to resist the state's attempts to subdue them; there are several recorded instances of women in prison rebelling against treatment that was designed to humiliate or degrade them. Although the reasons for these women resisting prison discipline varied,[44] one case that illustrates what motivated these women to continue to defy the authorities even when they had been incarcerated was the rebellion of the women in Ratnagiri Jail in 1885. The catalyst was a high-caste female inmate who, at her trial, complained to the trial magistrate that the inmates were ill-treated and had also been tortured. Her claims resulted in the vernacular press launching a campaign that ultimately led to a high-level inquiry being set up to investigate the events in the jail.[45] By seeking a joint petition from the female prisoners, the inquiry found that women who were members of high castes had been ordered to do scavenging work. Because of their status, they had refused and went on a hunger strike; the prison's response was to 'put [the women] in stocks' and forcibly feed them. In order to ensure that such a situation did not arise again, the inquiry recommended that sweeper caste female convicts be employed to carry out sanitary work.

Underpinning the women's resistance was a fear of what would happen to them upon release if they did carry out tasks that were contrary to their status. Kashi Bhandari, for instance, argued that the state owed her fifty rupees because she had been obliged to do scavenger's work in prison which meant that, upon her return home after her release, her husband refused to remain with her and the village people excluded her from the caste; 'my poor father had therefore to borrow 50 rupees, to defray the expenses for the ceremony of bringing me back to the caste'.[46] Such concerns were not

---

[44] On prisoners in India, see Anand Yang, 'Disciplining Natives: Prisons and Prisoners in Early Nineteenth-Century India', *South Asia*, 10 (1993): 29–45; for women prisoners during the nationalist period, see Kamala Visweswaran's study of the gendering of prison attire in 'Small Speeches, Subaltern Gender: Nationalist Ideology and its Historiography', in S. Amin and D. Chakrabarty (eds), *Subaltern Studies IX* (New Delhi: Oxford University Press, 1996), pp. 99–112.

[45] Petition by 'Sitaram Gangaji and one hundred and forty-eight other Marathas, Bhandaris and Guraos, inhabitants of Ratnagiri', 18 January 1886, JD, vol. 33, comp. no. 659, MSA. A summary of it was published in several Indian language newspapers like the *Subodh Patrika* and *Maharashtra Mitra*, 15 April 1886, NNR.

[46] Petition by Kashi kom Bhikoo Bhandhary, 7 March 1886, to the Governor-in-Council, JD, 1886, vol. 33, comp. no. 659, OIOC.

just confined to Indian women; the rationale behind rioting by female convicts in England during 1853 and 1859 against the conversion of their sentences from transportation to imprisonment[47] was similarly based on a fear of the treatment that they would receive upon release; hence, the preference for Australia where they felt they could at least start life afresh. Although the Indian female prisoners could not forge an entirely new life for themselves in the same way, by protesting against their treatment and making judicious alliances with the local press and others within the native population, they could at least ensure that prison authorities respected the caste rules that governed the female convicts' lives, thereby improving their chances of being reintegrated into their communities when they were released.

Women asserted their right to live their lives in the best way known to them when they found their lives unbearable, equally they maintained their right to select from the limited choices of resistance available to them. However, the state had made devastating inroads into the domestic lives of Indians and had begun to exercise immense control over the body of the female in various ways. A more general resistance to it by women was imminent as will be examined in the next section.

Distinguishing 'Female Infanticide' from 'Infanticide': The Emergence of the 'Female Criminal'

In 1876, Dinbai, a Parsi widow reputed to be from a 'respectable family' in Bombay, was charged with infanticide when the death of her newborn child was brought to the attention of the police. The High Court sentenced both Dinbai and the midwife who carried out the act to death. In April 1881, Vijayalakshmi, a Brahmin widow aged twenty-four, was convicted of killing her newborn illegitimate infant and was also sentenced to death.[48] Both instances generated a massive amount of public debate after Indian language newspapers published the growing number of convictions for the crime of infanticide. In 1872, statistics revealed that 406 women were tried for the offence in the North-West Provinces, while in the Bengal, Madras and Bombay Presidencies, the corresponding figures were 197, 77 and 15 convictions respectively;[49] ten years later in 1886, the corresponding figures for these provinces were 227, 309, 373 and 203 respectively. The figures for Bombay Presidency were comparatively lower but still saw a dramatic increase from 15 to 203 cases in the same period.

In previous chapters, we saw how the emerging female intelligentsia took note of these trends and drew up programmes of action to improve the plight of women.

---

[47] See Michael Ignatieff, *A Just Measure of Pain: The Penitentiary in the Industrial Revolution, 1750–1850* (New York: Macmillan, 1978), pp. 138, 203–4.

[48] All the correspondence between the Governor-in-Council and the Judges, petitions by Vijayalakshmi and extracts from newspapers are to be found in J.D, 1881, vol. 46, comp. no. 1036, MSA.

[49] These figures are taken from a table showing the statistics for convictions of infanticide in five provinces from 1870–84, in *Mahratta*, 25 June 1887.

Noting the government's tendency to arrest women for this offence and the duplicitous attitudes of their own men folk, some Maharashtrian women were sufficiently moved, like Tarabai Shinde, to write general treatises questioning contemporary gender relations whilst others began to form women's organizations to agitate for reform.[50] On the 11th of June, 1883, the Arya Mahila Association, a prominent women's organization of Bombay Presidency, argued for a home for abandoned wives and destitute widows to be established. Appealing to the Governor of Bombay on the issue, the leader of this Association complained that, in recent years, the crimes of abortion and infanticide had been solely attributed to women:

> ... it does not enter the mind of anyone that a great share of this sin rests on the shoulders of men. The whole blame of the matter is being thrown on women alone, even though the men that do it know the common saying that it requires two hands to clap...[51]

Fully aware of the complicity of Indian men in such crimes, feminists of the time initiated similar self-help organizations; in the next three decades, the Maharashtrian feminists went onto found other women's organizations, such as the Mukti Mission and the Seva Sadan, which were similarly designed to ameliorate the suffering of vulnerable Indian women and provide them with a place of sanctuary.[52]

When looking at this type of infanticide, it is important to distinguish between this and the more widely studied phenomenon of female infanticide, where *female* children were killed because of certain societal customs. With infanticide—defined as the murder of a newborn infant—the sex of the child was not an issue: it occurred when either male or female children were born out of wedlock, more often than not to widows or unmarried girls. The British had targeted female infanticide with varying degrees of zeal from 1795.[53] During the East India Company's rule, 'female infanticide' had been identified as an act arising out of a pernicious Hindu custom practised rampantly by Rajput clans of Northern and Western India, although it was recognized that the practice existed elsewhere too. Hence, efforts were targeted at dissuading Rajputs from the 'custom' through a range of incentives.[54] The emphasis on

---

[50] Vijayalakshmi's case was widely reported in Maharashtrian newspapers. Tarabai Shinde says in the Preface of her tract [Women and Men, A Comparison] that her treatise was a vindication of the slander to which widows like Vijayalakshmi were being subjected to everyday and also to expose the real criminals.

[51] Petition of Arya Mahila Association, 11 June 1883, to 'Hon'ble Sir Bartle Frere Saheb Bahadoor', n.p., Institutional Collection of Mukti Mission (hereafter ICMM).

[52] See chapters 2 and 3.

[53] A well-researched social history of the crime of female infanticide in Gujarat and Rajasthan focusing on British policy is available in Lalitha Panigrahi, *British Social Policy and Female Infanticide in India* (New Delhi: Munshiram, 1972), p. 18. See also K.B. Pakrasi, *Female Infanticide in India* (Calcutta: Indian Editions, 1970).

[54] The Infanticide Act of 1870 aimed at a more rigorous curtailing of the practice. The emphasis here was on prevention and deterrence through the provisions of the act, which included

working with communities to eradicate such practices continued throughout the early half of the nineteenth century, with the 1830s in particular seeing the British encourage the indigenous population to participate in the reform of Indian social mores.[55] However, infanticide was subsequently recognized as a 'general' crime affecting all parts of India, hence it was dealt with under the terms of the Criminal Code of 1860 with the consequent emphasis less on prevention than on bringing the perpetrators to justice. Under these terms, the killing of children was dealt with as murder for which there were the much greater penalties of rigorous imprisonment, transportation to penal settlements and death by hanging.

It is relevant to understand how and why the legal shifts occurred in the definition and penalties for the crime of 'female infanticide' from the early nineteenth century to the practice of largely 'infanticide' in the latter half of the nineteenth century. Panigrahi and Saxena's studies of female infanticide in Gujarat and Rajasthan show that the crime was traced by the East India Company officials to Hindu customs and therefore male heads of households and village authorities were vested with the responsibility of reporting the crime as well as they were subject to punishment for breach of laws.[56] However, the shift in the judiciary's perceptions of the perpetrator of the crime and the reconfiguring of Indian female sexuality as one marked by depraved maternal instincts, endorsed by indigenous social reformers, singled out the mother as the sole perpetrator of the crime. Hence, for the authorities, by the late nineteenth century, the most obvious culprit in cases of 'infanticide' was the mother herself, and punishment centred on her alone, rather than on the family or community as in the case of 'female infanticide'. As a result of this new turn, we see the emergence of a new female criminal: the infanticidal woman.

One of the main lines of enquiry here is to examine the imperatives and priorities by which the courts vested responsibility for the offence of infanticide in women. Lalita Panigrahi has argued with regard to female infanticide that British motives were based on a humanitarian concern for life.[57] The fact that the emphasis remained on prevention rather than punishment would seem to be consistent with this view. There can be no doubt that this was a concern in the move to deal with infanticide also. After all, infanticide had no supporters and was condemned by indigenous society as well. With infanticide, however, unlike the Age of Consent,[58] the impetus for intervention came from the British. It is therefore at the Raj we must look if we are to explain this purposeful intrusion into Indian society. Part of the answer lies in changing British

---

the taking of censuses, the registration of births, marriages and deaths, and punishment in the form of fines for the individuals and communities involved. Once the act was committed, only then was imprisonment, transportation and in rare cases, death for the killer of the child awarded. See Panigrahi, Ibid., pp. 140–43, 146–54, 173.

[55] Ibid.

[56] Ibid., chapters 4 and 5; R.K. Saxena, *Social Reforms: Infanticide and Sati* (New Delhi: Trimurti, 1975), chapters 1 and 2.

[57] Panigrahi, Ibid., p. 191.

[58] See next chapter.

notions of state power. Whereas in the 1830s, the last great period of social intervention, the British had tried to change India in a spirit of cooperation with indigenous society, however, the latter period was characterized by a spate of 'aggressive legislation' based on the belief that 'a benighted people had to be compelled towards the light.'[59] The British conception of authority was an exclusive one, which combined both power and the notion of 'moral influence'—the idea that the Raj was the ultimate definer of appropriate social behaviour.[60] While the Rajput's practice of female infanticide posed no direct threat to British power, in being so conspicuously at odds with British conceptions of morality its existence undermined authority by suggesting the impotence of the colonial state.[61] Fitzjames Stephen served as Law Member of the Government of India from 1869–72 and was closely involved with the passage and implementation of the Infanticide Act. Stephen argued that it was necessary for the Government of India to interfere with Indian practices in order to suppress crimes, which were considered 'abominable' according to European standards of morality.[62] Introducing the Bill in January 1870, John Strachey argued that it was the duty of the Government '... to declare that it would not suffer any longer the continuance of these horrible practices ... and that it would put forth the whole of its power for their repression'.[63] It was this binding of moral influence so closely to the authority of the Raj that assured intervention. The passing of the Infanticide Act signalled the government's intent to outlaw practices, which were so critically in conflict with its moral standards, and this included infanticide as well as female infanticide. Female infanticide had previously been the most obvious target of the legislation but, as the state developed a more effective and systematic control apparatus, it increasingly uncovered infanticidal acts that were not committed in order to fulfil peculiar 'local' customs or because of the baby's gender but by mothers acting on their own initiative. Typical of this was this case of Vijayalakshmi, whose actions were uncovered when the police carried out operations that were initially designed to uncover instances of female infanticide that were believed to have taken place in her village of Olpad, near Surat. To the judges who presided over such trials, such instances represented the inconsistency of a policy that expended great energy in the prevention of female infanticide but tolerated infanticide.

The close association of moral influence with authority may have remained purely abstract were it not for other developments related to the changing nature of the colonial state. After 1860, the British established a more effective and systematic control apparatus with the adoption of the Criminal Code in 1860 and the

---

[59] Eric Stokes, *The English Utilitarians and India* (Oxford: Oxford University Press, 1959), p. 269.

[60] Sandria Freitag, 'Collective Crime and Authority in North India', in Yang, *Crime and Criminality*, p. 141.

[61] Ibid., p. 157.

[62] Panigrahi, *British Social Policy*, p. 147.

[63] Female Infanticide Bill, 14 January 1870, cited in Panigrahi, Ibid., p. 148.

reorganization of the Indian police.[64] The expansion of the colonial state through an extension of the law went hand in hand with new techniques of governing which revealed its developing sophistication.[65] As the colonial state made a more successful claim to a monopoly of legitimate physical force, the less reliant it became on the direct use of force to maintain its rule. Surveillance in the form of information gathering became an increasingly important tool in the maintenance of rule. The modernizing colonial state was able to carry out a more effective monitoring of the population. This resulted in unprecedented levels of intrusion into, not just the Indian home, but also, in the reproductive life of Indian women. By the 1870s the Bombay government had introduced a system of information-gathering for the detection of infanticide through the systematic registration of pregnancies by unmarried women and widows, the investigation of unusual deaths of infants, close checks on the movements of midwives and prostitutes and boosted by promises of rewards and promotions to police officials.[66]

Judicial Discourse and the Creation of the Infanticidal Woman

The prosecution and trial of infanticidal women was to generate a compelling body of knowledge about Indian female sexuality, and it is argued here that such claims to knowledge about Indian female sexuality served significant political functions for the colonial government. Indeed, even if such knowledge does not entirely explain the government's motives in dealing with infanticide, it is indisputable that the discourses on female sexuality in the 1870s and 1880s formed a nexus that helped define the power relations between the colonizer and the colonized. Infanticide provided the authorities with exemplary narratives of the superiority of the civilized West over that of the depraved sentiments and debased civilization of the East, as Fitzjames Stephen's justification for outlawing such practices demonstrates:

> The introduction of the essential parts of European civilization into a country densely peopled, grossly ignorant, steeped in idolatrous superstition, unenergetic, fatalistic, indifferent to most of what we regard as the evils of life, and preferring the repose of submitting to them to the trouble of encountering and trying to remove them.[67]

---

[64] Freitag, 'Collective Crime and Authority', p. 146.

[65] For the changing nature of the colonial state, see Patrick M. McGinn, *Maintaining the Mask: British Governance and Indigenous Resistance in India* (forthcoming).

[66] This system of surveillance had started as part of the operations for the suppression of female infanticide in Gujarat. See D.D. Wilson, *History of the Suppression of Infanticide in Western India* (London: Smith, Elder and Co., 1855), pp. 115, 125. For a broader study of information gathering and surveillance system, which made empire possible see Chris A. Bayly, *Empire and Information: Intelligence Gathering and Social Communication in India, 1780–1870* (Cambridge: Cambridge University Press, 1996).

[67] Cited in Panigrahi, *British Social Policy*, p. 147.

Judges contrasted the behaviour of Indian women who gave birth out of wedlock to Western women who had been forced to remain single,[68] concluding that, whilst Western women in this situation would devote their energies to philanthropic tasks as reparation, Indian women displayed no contrition. Despite the fact that 61 percent of infant deaths under the age of one in nineteenth-century Britain were attributed to disguised forms of infanticide,[69] judges instead chose to focus on what they saw as the Indian woman's inability to feel maternal affection and their lack of control over instincts that Western society considered base in civilized society; as Justice West's assertion shows:

> ... the accused must have known when she indulged her lust, or yielded to the indulgence of the lust of someone else, that these dire consequences might follow; and what was the value, either morally, or from any point of view of sensibility which was sufficient to make a woman destroy her own offspring, but which was not sufficient to guard her against the indulgence of her lust.[70]

Such attitudes differed greatly from those displayed by many judges to Indian women trapped in the same situation earlier in the century. Whereas in the first half of the nineteenth century, judges showed considerable sympathy for the circumstances that often drove Indian widows to commit such a desperate act, after 1870, the courts showed no such mercy. This was not to say that the practice was any more acceptable in the first half of the nineteenth century; in Britain, legislation introduced in 1803 imposed harsh punishments on single women who were found guilty of concealing pregnancies and the births and deaths of their illegitimate children,[71] and harsh penalties were also in place for women who committed the same crime in India. However, judges in the earlier period would often show greater mercy towards the accused, as the outcome of Goorningowa's trial for infanticide in 1847 demonstrates. Instead of sentencing her to transportation, the usual punishment for such acts, Mr Tagore, the session judge, asked the government to consider the case, recommending that they showed clemency towards her. The government accepted his judgement, with Mr Gibbs, a member of the Governor's Council, declaring that

---

[68] The expansion of empire had led to an exodus of men leaving behind a 'genteel surplus' in Victorian Britain giving rise to increasing numbers of spinsters. A fascinating study of such women who went to colonies in search of adventure or 'husband hunting' is in Geraldine Forbes, 'In Search of the 'Pure Heathen': Missionary Women in 19th Century India', *Economic & Political Weekly*, 30/17 (April 26, 1986): WS 2–8.

[69] Lionel Rose, *Massacre of the Innocents: Infanticide in Great Britain, 1800–1939* (London: Routledge and Kegan Paul, 1986), pp. 5–14.

[70] Proceedings in the case of Vijayalakshmi, JD, 1881, vol. 46, comp. no. 1036, pp. 239–40, MSA.

[71] Mark Jackson, *New-Born Child Murder: Women, Illegitimacy and the Courts in Eighteenth-Century England* (Manchester: Manchester University Press, 1996).

> In England, even cases of this kind are leniently dealt with—I have always felt great pity for uneducated Hindu widows whose law is supposed to prevent their remarriage, and whose religion as they understood [sic] it, places a very slight moral restraint on their actions.[72]

As a result of this judgement, Goorningowa received the relatively lighter punishment of seven years' rigorous imprisonment.

This example of relative mercy would have been unthinkable after 1870, with judges now arguing that Indian widows were no more victims of their circumstances than other women in the world who found themselves in the same situation, a view expressed by the judges in the 1881 Vijayalakshmi case, Justices Pinhey and West, who asked:

> Was a woman who was prevented from marrying a second time to be distinguished from thousands and millions of women, who in civilized Europe, on account of the great preponderance of the female sex, were prevented from marrying?[73]

For the judiciary, Vijayalakshmi's widowhood was outweighed by the fact that she had previously enjoyed conjugal rights before widowhood came upon her. In addition, she had given birth to children whilst she was married, meaning that her maternal instinct had also been satisfied prior to losing her husband. Given these circumstances, the judges believed that the only plausible explanation was that her naturally depraved nature, exacerbated by the restrictions imposed on her by a superstitious, tradition-bound society, had led her to commit a terrible act. Whilst Justice West acknowledged, 'If the caste prohibition to remarry encouraged infanticide the caste ought to withdraw it',[74] there was no clemency shown towards the woman who had committed the act; she was regarded as the sole perpetrator and the full weight of punishment therefore fell on her shoulders alone.

Yet, although the force of the punishment was now solely concentrated on the female perpetrator, it was intended that its impact would reverberate beyond individuals and influence Indian society at large, making it more amenable to British rule. Not only did the laws against infanticide represent a significant attempt to bring Indian legislation into line with that of nineteenth-century Britain, British judicial structures provided an effective mechanism of exercising power over the Indian population. Moreover, the pursuit of infanticidal women meant that the police now had a disciplinary function in addition to their role as the auxiliary of justice, which allowed them to enter a space that had previously been closed to them: the Indian home. The colonial authorities sanctioned and encouraged the judiciary and the police to speak openly about the previously closed realm of female sexuality. This necessitated the continuous registration and observation of Indian women; this information, combined

---

[72] Cited in the resolution of the Governor-in-Council in regard to the Vijayalakshmi case, in JD, 1881, vol. 46, comp. no. 1036, MSA.

[73] Ibid., p. 242.

[74] Ibid., p. 343.

with the formidable body of negative knowledge about Indian female sexuality that was formed during discussions of what led some mothers to murder their infants, provided a potent argument that could be deployed by the British authorities in claims to rule.

The relatively high number of cases of infanticide[75] that the authorities claimed to identify also provided them with the opportunity to challenge indigenous practices and mores that they did not agree with, most notably the prohibition of widow remarriage. By the time that Justice West had pronounced his judgement on Vijayalakshmi, The Widow Remarriage Act of 1856 was practically viewed by the judiciary in this period as a dead letter and it was placing significant pressure on Indian society to permit widows to remarry. One way of doing this was to retain the death penalty for women convicted of infanticide. In doing this, the judiciary hoped to place pressure on Indian society to permit widows to remarry, a point made explicitly by the Governor of Bombay:

> That the crime of child murder especially by widows is prevalent is notorious and publicly admitted. It is to be hoped that the miserable results of the enforced celebacies [sic] of widows, whether infant or not, is attracting extensive notice in the native community and will in time and by degrees work out the abolition of the social law.[76]

This strategy of cultural control demonstrates the way in which the colonial authorities were employing any means available to them to coerce the Indian castes to adopt British norms of domestic and social life. Such an intervention by the colonial state into the private lives of the Indian people posed a significant challenge to the beliefs and authority of Indian men, and thus it was inevitable that they were soon drawn into the debate over infanticide and began to posit their own solutions about how to resolve it.

Female Unchastity as a Crime: Indigenous Society, Caste and the Control of Female Sexuality

The publication in 1876 of statistics on convictions for infanticide presented an irrefutable challenge to indigenous reform groups, and considerable opposition to the practice developed among Indians in the towns of Bombay, Poona, Ahmedabad and Sholapur. One of the most articulate representatives of Indian male opinion on the subject was Sir T. Madhava Rao who, using his influential position as the Dewan of Baroda, pressed the government to review its law on infanticide. Rao's views gained wide support in both the Indian and English language press and were frequently cited in the newspapers well into the 1890s; moreover, his treatise, 'Considerations of the Crime of Infanticide and its Punishment in India', appeared in a London periodical in

---

[75] At the time of Vijayalakshmi's trial the judges argued it was four per week.

[76] Governor's note on Sangowa kom Gurshidapa, 16 June 1881, JD, 1881, vol. 46, comp. no. 1036, p. 125, MSA.

1876, winning sympathy from liberal Britons and educated Indians abroad.[77] He argued that infanticide was committed by young widows who, denied the right to marital life by caste rules, and being youthful, could not overcome their passions and instincts. This led to conception and delivery in secrecy and ultimately the crime itself. The motive, as he understood it, was not, like so many other crimes, driven by profit. Rather, the mother's dread of social opinion was so great that her natural affection for the child was suppressed, leading her to sacrifice its life in order to escape censure. Thus, he argued, 'her respect for social opinion is *much stronger* [sic] than even her affection for her child'.[78] The suggestions of Madhava Rao were considered but not accepted by the government and there was no amendment of the law. After 1879, however, every case of infanticide that reached the High Court was referred to the local government for reconsideration on appeal.

Public discussion of the issue took on an added urgency after the trial of Vijayalakshmi in 1881. The High Court's refusal to reduce the sentence of death for Vijayalakshmi led to a variety of responses by Indians, although there were certain common strands. No reformer or traditionalist denied its existence, but argued that it was, in fact, an extremely rare occurrence. Secondly, there was a unanimous consensus with the British observations on the nature of Indian female sexuality: that the Indian widow was lustful and that she alone committed the crime, and completely ignored the role of men behind the scenes. 'Female chastity', traditionally interpreted as a 'virtue', became an acrimonious issue between the dominant groups in the infanticide debates. While colonial administrators had no doubts about the uncontrolled sensuality of Indian women, the desirability of chastity—that is, female chastity—was one issue that all male groups involved in the debates agreed upon. However, in the eyes of Indian male reformers, the woman's crime was 'unchastity' rather than 'infanticide' itself. They therefore urged the government to sentence the woman to rigorous imprisonment as a just penalty for the loss of her 'virtue' rather than sentence her to death. An astute and skilful lawyer, Sir Madhava Rao argued that, by passing down a sentence of capital punishment nothing was gained as the woman in question had no time for remorse, nor was it a cautionary tale to other women, because the latter had no access to newspapers and did not witness public executions. Instead, he urged the government to keep such women alive in jail. This would make them the subject of talk among female members of the public and eventually, when released, they would still serve as an example to society as a whole.

In both the Dinbai and Vijayalakshmi cases, the judges questioned the moral probity of women who, according to them, had enjoyed marital rights, borne children, and yet continued to indulge their passions. Indian male reformers interpreted the colonial discourse on Indian widows' morality or lack of it as a slur on the Hindu religion and those who were defending its high standards of morality. This placed Hindu reformers in a peculiar position. By acknowledging that the crime of infanticide had taken place, but arguing that it should be the initial act of gratifying unbridled

---

[77] See *Journal of the National Indian Association*, 65 (May 1876): 131–7.

[78] Ibid., p. 133.

passions, rather than the murder of the child born of the act that should be punished, they were, in effect, agreeing with the view that Hindu widows were inherently unchaste. They tried to circumvent contradictions in their arguments by blaming Hindu widows and not Hinduism and placing responsibility for the crime on them alone. The debates over infanticide in Maharashtra clearly demonstrate the way in which indigenous elite groups collaborated in shifting the gaze of the law on to the Indian female as the sole offender. Indian men argued that Hindu widows had to be distinguished from Western women because of their differences in education, and in mental, moral and social training; it was women's ignorance of the Shastric injunctions against this crime that led them to equate immorality only with public scandal, and their illiteracy that caused them to think that 'being found out' was 'the essence of wrong doing'.[79] Women's fragmented awareness of the importance of the concept of women's chastity in the *shastras*, based on a belief that it was the evidence of the act, rather than the act itself, which was wrong, meant, some male reformers argued, that the women were driven to commit such acts, despite that fact that it went against true Hinduism and morality.[80] It was also suggested that widows committed such violent acts in a temporary state of insanity;[81] with some arguing that the natural maternal instincts were clouded after the birth of a child 'when the mother's mind must have been in a more or less demented condition'.[82] In portraying infanticide as a product of female unchastity, and in highlighting the infanticidal woman's state of mind, Indian men therefore shifted responsibility away from Hindu religion, men and society and placed it solely on the women's shoulder, thereby contributing significantly to the picture that was being painted of the 'wicked' infanticidal woman during this period. The fact that Tarabai Shinde singles out this central argument by placing the notion of 'wickedness' in the title of her treatise is indicative of the significant breakthrough that is achieved within Indian feminist consciousness of the times through the Vijayalakshmi case trials.[83]

Contemporary debates emphasize the fact that the body of the Hindu widow was assumed not only to belong to the Indian male but also to the caste and religious community into which she was born. In 1876, the question of infanticide received heightened attention among indigenous reform circles when Dinbai, a Parsi widow belonging to a 'respectable family' of Bombay, was sentenced to death for infanticide. The Parsi press widely publicized her case and agitated relentlessly on her behalf until her sentence was commuted to three years' simple imprisonment.[84] There were striking similarities between this campaign and the one pursued by influential Brahmins from

---

[79] Extract from the *Times of India*, 27 May 1881, attached to another appeal by Vijayalakshmi, in JD, 1881, vol. 46, comp. no. 1036.

[80] *Subodh Patrika*, 4 June 1881, NNR.

[81] Petition of Poona Sarvajanik Sabha, 5 June 1881, JD, MSA.

[82] *Times of India*, 27 May 1881.

[83] Tarabai poses a question in her title asking 'who is more wicked, Men or Women?' See footnote 33 of this chapter.

[84] *Jame Jamshed*, 16 December 1876, NNR.

Poona, Bombay, Kolhapur and Sholapur in the case of a Brahmin widow who was found guilty of the same act. Indian men were waking up to the fact that the British courts, as their actions in the case of Vijayalakshmi demonstrated, were treating high-caste widows without any regard to their status. The importance of this in Indian eyes is exemplified by the memorial of the Poona Sarvajanik Sabha, petitions by the residents of Sholapur and Bombay and the treatise of Sir Madhava Rao; all of which uniformly reflect a preoccupation with caste affinity. In the public memorial by the Poona Sarvajanik Sabha, the most widely circulated and publicized reaction of the educated middle-class Maharashtrian male, the Sabha declared to the Governor-in-Council that

> ... it had been moved to take action in this matter solely from the fact that Vijayalak-shmi's case is a typical one, representative of a large number of similar cases, in which the present state of the law often conflicts with the national sense of justice.[85]

This submission was characterized by a careful differentiation between infanticide committed by Brahmin widows and customary Hindu practices. Furthermore, in their submission, a distinction was drawn between the Brahmin crime and the type of female infanticide practiced by Rajput communities, whose origins, he argued, were marked by a cold-blooded, premeditated murder of legitimate infants that were sanctioned by a customary right. On the other hand, the petitioners continued, Brahmin widows were driven to abandon or kill illegitimate infants born to them due to the great sense of guilt and shame that weighed heavily on their minds. To draw parallels between the two and to infer that infanticide was a general practice among Brahmins, and argue that it was necessary to make an example of it, was therefore totally unjustified.[86] The distinction that high-caste Indian males drew between widows from Brahmin castes and other widows is demonstrated by the fact that when, in 1881, sixteen widows belonging to the non-Brahmin castes such as Kunbis, Mahars, Lingayats, and Banias were convicted of infanticide and sentenced to transportation for life, their trials received no publicity in the Indian language press and no leading reformers campaigned on their behalf. Whereas popular opinion, as represented by the Indian language press and urban public associations such as the Poona Sarvajanik Sabha, urged compassion on the grounds that the law did not have popular consent, it appeared that it had limits as to which classes and castes of women it included.

In general, the discursive trends discernable amongst the Hindu male public seemed to prefer alternatives to widow remarriage, in particular the amendment of the penalty for infanticide, rather than the introduction of measures that would ease and pave the way for widow remarriage. According to Sir Madhava Rao, widows committed infanticide in order to hide their unchastity, as the infant was the only evidence of their immoral behaviour, and therefore they had to be punished. He recommended that the woman should be:

---

[85] Petition from Sarvajanik Sabha, Poona, 5 June 1881, JD, 1881, vol. 46, comp. no. 1036, MSA.

[86] Ibid., p. 221.

punish[ed] ... by making her suffer that pain—that very pain which she *most* dreaded. Sentence her publicly, send her to gaol publicly, keep her there publicly, and let her suffer the pain of shame which she had dreaded so much. Would not that be a sufficiently deterring punishment?[87]

There was no call for a stringent law to apprehend male participants in this crime. Nor did Indian men (apart from the non-Brahmin leader, Jyotiba Phule) pursue social means of combating the problem, such as opening foundling homes or homes for widows; it was female reformers like Pandita Ramabai who would later take the initiative in these areas. What is striking here is that a life-and-death question to one sex appears to have been mere rhetoric to the other. Indian male reformers' concern over gender-based issues like infanticide went no further than polemics. In fact, both Sir Madhava Rao and the public memorial of the Poona Sarvajanik Sabha stressed that, until 'nationalist feelings' on widow remarriage changed, no action could be taken in this direction. As far as widow remarriage was concerned, Hindu men wanted the status quo to continue. Hindu male opinion did not argue for the promotion of widow remarriage or the enactment of new laws to prosecute the offending parties involved in every infanticide case. Instead, their rhetoric hinged on amending the legislation that set the penalty for women convicted of this charge, so that it would be more in line with 'national feeling' on the subject.

Traditional legal institutions always had to balance the desire to exert authority against the need to maintain local harmony. The British use of indigenous structures of power, whether through informal methods of control or Mughal legal institutions, militated against the exercise of authority. With the formalization of the law through the judiciary and the police, there were fewer and fewer constraints on the exercise of authority through the law. A more impersonal law, framed at a distance, was impervious to local checks and balances. This had serious and probably unforeseen implications for British rule. Whereas before, the application of the law was negotiated locally, now a more generalized law gave rise to a more generalized process of negotiation, carried out in the press and in petitions to government. The British therefore now had to contend with 'national feeling' over the application of the law that threatened to progress from a critique of the law to a critique of British authority itself. Any immediate threat to the state was forestalled, however, by the fact that indigenous society was less concerned with critiquing colonial authority than with confronting the threats posed to the Hindu religion and dealing with the caste and gender concerns which the infanticide issue had highlighted.

Simply by concentrating on the dual nature of female sexuality—chaste/virtuous in opposition to unchaste/infanticidal—the dominant discourses of the colonial authorities and Indian elites exonerated men from the responsibility of parenthood outside marriage and diverted attention from female poverty by instead focusing its attention on notions of 'shame' and 'honour' for Brahmin widows. The circumstances

---

[87] 'Considerations of the Crime of Infanticide', p. 134.

surrounding the act of infanticide and the nebulous role of women in it were therefore obscured. By contrasting the colonial penal approach with older customary practices towards infanticidal women, the next section will demonstrate how the creation of the infanticidal woman resulted in the general position of Indian women deteriorating even further. Later, through the retrieval of more than a hundred petitions by female offenders, an attempt will be made to reconstruct the act of infanticide in its social context. The voices of these resisting women did not significantly alter their sentences nor did they play a role in shaping the dominant discourses that defined them. Their significance instead lies in the fact that they present a conspicuously different picture of who committed infanticide and what their motivations were from those created by Indian male and colonialist discourses.

Assigning Responsibility: the Creation of the Infanticidal Woman

The infanticidal woman was a creation of colonialism, emerging clearly after the passing of the Infanticide Act in 1870. Whereas, in cases of female infanticide, the practice of killing newborn females in certain communities, responsibility was assigned to the leaders of the groups involved, in cases of infanticide, the blame was exclusively assigned to the woman. It was not that infanticide itself was new, but rather the innovation lay in culpability—the blame had been shifted from the collective, male-led community to the female individual. The rendering of what was a complex situation into one of simple apportioning of blame was what distinguished colonial law from customary practice. Furthermore, as we can see from the previous section, Indian men not only condoned this shift, they helped to reinforce it.

Whether infanticide was considered a serious crime in precolonial Indian society with penalties commensurate with those of the British is doubtful. Nor was blame focused exclusively on the woman. Male offenders in infanticide cases were sometimes readmitted into the caste after a ritual purification ceremony that was accompanied by a small monetary fine.[88] The scope and legitimacy of the courts under Peshwa rule (pre-British rulers in Western India) was always limited in such matters. Adulterous wives were punished and under the Peshwas, Brahmin women were especially singled out for their 'unchaste' behaviour. Even then, one finds that the punishment tended to be a fine based on the financial circumstances of the woman, although Brahmin women who were made pregnant by low-caste men were irrevocably excommunicated from the caste. But even here, the worst fate that the offender faced was being driven off the precincts of the village or town. However, there are no recorded instances of women who aborted foetuses or committed infanticide being punished severely.[89] Local

---

[88] The Arya Mahila Association reported one incident in Kolhapur when a man was readmitted in his caste after a payment of twenty rupees. See its petition to Sir Bartle Frere, 11 June 1883, n.p., ICMM.

[89] See V.S. Kadam, 'The Institution of Marriage and Position of Women in Eighteenth-Century Maharashtra', *Indian Economic and Social History Review*, 25/3 (1988): 362.

communities through their involvement in caste and village councils more usually dealt with infanticide, and this was the situation, which the British encountered when they first began to display an interest in the issue. A case involving exclusion that occurred in 1868 was narrated by Savitribai Phule, who appeased the enraged Mahar [untouchable] community of her village by taking away a young Mahar girl who had an illegitimate child by a Brahmin priest to Poona.[90] The flexibility of customary law, based as it was on a consideration of the facts and circumstances of every case, with due regard to local usages and scriptures (texts) only sought as a residual source of legal guidance, has been the subject of comment by a great number of legal scholars.[91] Legal scholarship in this area seems to agree that the Anglo-Indian laws, 'a conglomerate of precedents built on nebulous textual authority' and embodied in the Code of Criminal Law represented by the Indian Penal Code (1860), were received with 'silent non-acceptance', if not downright hostility, by the general population.[92] Legal historians endorse that, in the nineteenth century, official law and customary practice continued to jostle alongside each other, often coming into direct conflict as the former unsuccessfully tried to outlaw the latter.

However, the best guide to contemporary notions on how crimes of infanticide were treated is the Indian public response to the British convictions of infanticidal women. Although they were anxious to point out that the *shastras* considered infanticide a terrible sin visiting the sinner with severe punishment, in practice, popular Hindu opinion, as expressed in articles in the Indian language press and men's petitions, revealed a more tolerant approach to the crime. Even though Hindu religion and morality mores placed powerful restraints on widows' conduct, lapses had tended to be tolerated by society as long as the widow concealed the fact of her unchastity. Following on from this, contemporary Hindu opinion seemed to have a pragmatic view of the subject, as this statement, made by the residents of Sholapur in a petition to the government on the subject of Vijayalakshmi's prosecution, demonstrates:

> The Criminal Law of the Country so far as it affects the crime of Infanticide by Hindu widows is opposed to the national sense of justice and the prevalent Public opinion is unanimous that so long as widow marriage is forbidden by the caste rules amongst Hindus, it is positively cruel to visit such occasional lapses from moral rectitude as that by Vijayalaksmi with severe penalty.[93]

---

[90] M.G. Mali, *Krantijyoti Savitribai Jotirao Phule* [The Revolutionary Savitribai Jotirao Phule] (Kolhapur: Asha Prakashan, 1980), p. 87.

[91] J.D.M. Derrett, *Religion, Law and the State in India* (London: Faber, 1968); A.C. Banerjee, *English Law in India* (New Delhi: Abhinav, 1984).

[92] Menski, *Indian Legal Systems*, p. 37; also Vasudha Dhagamwar, *Law, Power and Justice: The Protection of Personal Rights in the Indian Penal Code* (New Delhi: Sage, 1992), pp. 9–10.

[93] Daji Dhalchand Gujar et al. to the Chief Secretary to Government, 25 July 1881, JD, 1881, vol. 46, comp. no. 1036, MSA.

Moreover, as the case of Bai Rupli demonstrates, customary practice offered the potential for flexibility. When Bai Rupli fell pregnant with the baby of her late husband's eldest brother, the caste *panch* [court] gave them permission to marry. It was only when he subsequently abandoned her and fled the village before they could be married, that another one of her brothers-in-law, Asha Dwarka, killed her to prevent her from bringing shame on her late husband's family.[94] Had she continued to live, she not only would have put the whole family's social relations with the rest of the community at risk, as such liaisons were regarded with ridicule, but could have left them facing a wide range of social sanctions, including excommunication, termed as 'social death' by many petitioners. Even wealthy, powerful and high-caste Indian families were at risk of losing their social status within the community if one of them fell pregnant out of wedlock. Caste councils were aware of the fact that often families participated actively and perhaps ordered the killing of illegitimate children but the local knowledge and practices of local communities was not accessible to English judges placed as they were hundreds or thousands of miles away from the far-flung scene of the crime.

Even if a family could have borne the social stigma, there were also economic reasons why Hindu joint families generally refused to rear an illegitimate child, even when the child was born from a blood-tie within the family. If a Brahmin widow already had children from her marriage, the question of inheritance rights would surface, as illegitimate children were known to contest for property.[95] In a largely agricultural economy where large joint families depended on land for a living, this was seen as a serious economic threat. To prevent such an occurrence, the joint family often took it upon itself to kill the newborn infant, more often than not without the consent of the mother.[96] Infanticide was therefore not necessarily always a singular act by the mother but a collective act by her joint family; a fact disregarded by the British legal system when it defined infanticide as the 'case of a woman killing her illegitimate child directly after birth'.

Certain gender-based inequalities were built into the laws governing punishment with an inherent assumption that the mother was the main murderer in this act. Male participants in the deed could only be charged, under Section 303, as an abettor to the secret disposal of the body. The mother, on the other hand, could be charged separately under three sections: Section 301—culpable homicide amounting to murder; Section 302—exposure and/or abandonment of the child; and Section 303—secret disposal of

---

[94]   JD, 1880, vol. 50, comp. no. 917, MSA.

[95] Sudha Desai, *Social Life in Maharashtra under the Peshwas* (Bombay: Popular Prakashan, 1980), p. 88; See also Raymond West and Johann Georg Buhler (eds), *A Digest of Hindu Law*, Book I (Bombay: Education Society Press, 1867) especially Introduction and chapter 6.

[96] The head of the household, usually the father-in-law and sometimes older relatives like great-uncles, took such decisions. See the proceedings in the case of Sangowa kom Gursidapa, JD, 1881, vol. 46, comp. no. 996, pp. 115–31; also the proceedings in the case of Thaku, JD, 1882, vol. 52, comp. 1525, pp. 414–15, MSA.

the body. Despite the fact that Section 302 does make reference to the 'parent', it was only used against the father in a very small number of cases where they were actually charged. Furthermore, when, in 1883, a problem arose over the disposal of a body by a third party with or without the mother's tacit consent, the court ruled that the mother was to be held responsible in all such cases.[97] The essential principle governing the law appears to have been that only the mother had a motive for committing child murder; there was no enactment that recognized that the father of the child would have had a motive in assisting or committing the deed himself in order to escape detection. This meant that even the system of detecting such acts was weighted against the mother; while village police officials were trained to keep a close check on the movements of pregnant women and women who had recently given birth, with midwives made responsible for reporting the births and deaths of newborn female infants, their men folk escaped such scrutiny.[98] The information-gathering service itself shows a bias towards letting off men from any kind of culpability.

This was despite the fact that, as women's petitions from the time demonstrate, it was not always the mother who committed the crime; the petitioners in these instances implicate fathers-in-law, brothers-in-law, their lovers, village *Patils* [Heads] and even stepsons. Indeed, if the woman could get witnesses, she could successfully reveal the true criminal. This happened in the case of Tukki kom Siddappa, a prostitute, who was successful in implicating the village headman, despite the fact that he was shielded by the village sepoy and the head constable, by getting the midwife and her assistant who attended Tukki's delivery to testify on her behalf, resulting in Tukki's sentence being reduced from transportation to five years' rigorous imprisonment.[99] The way that the penal code was framed forced the mother on the defensive, which meant that, if she implicated someone else, she had to provide the evidence for it. This clause that demanded evidence of proof made it difficult for women to implicate male offenders, as it was very unlikely that a woman who had recently delivered a child would have had the opportunity to observe anything happening around her. This is demonstrated by the fact that, except for one case of a stepson transported for life, there were only five cases of men being arrested for abetting the crime in sixteen years of the Bombay Presidency. Even in these cases, all five men were acquitted and discharged on the grounds of insufficient evidence.

---

[97] From 'Want of provision in the law for punishing such crimes as the prevention of the crime of exposing and abandoning infants', in JD, 1883, vol. 56, comp. no. 720, MSA.

[98] The enrolment of the midwife as an informer was a legacy from the Company's regulations to suppress female infanticide. Panigrahi notes that a system of rewarding alert midwives was instituted in some extreme cases. *British Social Policy*, chapter 4.

[99] JD, 1882, vol. 44, comp. no. 950, MSA.

The Perspective of the Infanticidal Woman: A Question of Survival

Indigenous male elites and the colonial authorities argued that Hindu widows were killing their newborn illegitimate infants because of the shame and loss of honour that this involved. However, when we examine the motives of the women themselves, we see motivations more complex than a simple fear of social opinion. Indeed, for most infanticidal women it appears to have been a question of survival. For a Brahmin widow, living in a large joint family, raising an illegitimate child was impossible; such an act would have been abhorrent to Hindu custom. Abortion and infanticide alone offered escape from such a situation. Although begging and prostitution appeared to be further options for a woman in such circumstance if she chose to rear the child, they were impossible choices for wealthy Maratha and Brahmin widows who, having led a protected and sheltered life with minimal dealings with the outside world, were like orphans themselves when thrown out on to the streets. The only option that they had was to choose between their own life and that of the illegitimate child. The decision, when it happened to be the woman's, was thus always reduced to a question of survival. At the other end of the social scale, the most important motive for women was their ability to feed themselves and the child. Many cases of infanticide were reported during years of famine and plague. Sometimes a whole household disappeared in a plague-ridden town, leaving behind women who, reduced to stark poverty, were forced into terrible decisions. Moreover, as the petitions demonstrate, these decisions were usually made in a traumatized state of mind, with the women debilitated by lack of food or sickness or both.[100] Many women under such intolerable strain took their own lives as well; many reports of infanticide that had occurred in these instances are also accompanied by reports of the mother's suicide. Reporting on the 'New Arrangements in regard to the Relief Works of the Current Famine', in 1877 *The Bombay Samachar* commented:

> Particularly women with one or more children cannot maintain themselves and their young ones. If the mothers try to feed their children, half-starving themselves, the children soon become orphans; if they neglect them, the latter fall victims to starvation.[101]

However, despite the fact the women in such circumstances who were brought to trial explained the nature of their quest for survival in their petitions at great length, their views and experiences were dismissed and no clemency was shown towards them.

The two vital support systems for a woman were her natal home when unmarried and, after marriage, the family of her husband. Withdrawal of such protection was a catastrophe for a woman, both economically and psychologically. Section 302 of the Indian Penal Code describes infanticide as 'Exposure of child by parent with intention

---

[100] See the proceedings in the case of Mamti in JD, 1880, vol. 45, comp. no. 942, MSA.

[101] Reported on 10 March 1877, NNR.

of wholly abandoning it'. However, in all cases of abandonment by mothers of newly born infants or of children, the mothers themselves had also been abandoned. Infanticidal women had often been abandoned by parents, brothers or sisters, husbands, or, in the case of widows, by lovers and relatives. Even if they had not been abandoned, many were terrified that their families would find out and abandon them or punish them in even worse ways; Petawwa, an eighteen-year-old girl, delivered a child out of wedlock at her sister's house and admitted that she had killed it as she was afraid that her mother and brother, with whom she normally lived, would beat her to death if they found out about her pregnancy and also because she feared 'the dishonour to herself if the matter became known to the public'.[102]

Desertion of wives seems to have been a common practice, especially among the lower castes in Maharashtra and sometimes among the Marathas. It was usually a consequence of a new marriage or favours shown to mistresses and rarely due to economic reasons such as droughts or famines. Desertion of wives by husbands or of widows by their lovers was also accompanied by factors such as abandonment by family, ill-treatment and violent behaviour towards women by kith and kin, acute poverty and a failure to secure gainful employment. Gunga, a twenty-year-old Mahar, stated in her petition:

> I was a widow but was kept by Dirya Mahar in his house, who had promised to marry me. I had intercourse with him and was big with child. Subsequently he turned me out of his house. I told him that I had the child by him and asked him where I was to go.[103]

She was eventually forced to seek shelter in her sister's house, where she was made to feel unwelcome since she had borne an illegitimate child, which was referred to as a 'scandal'.[104]

A crucial test for the survival of the infant was the ability of the deserted wife or abandoned widow to find employment. Lower-caste women could find employment in the construction industry, but employers often discriminated against mothers with suckling infants and pregnant women. Many cases of such discrimination come to light in the criminal records by female petitioners as well as in newspaper reports. It is therefore not surprising that the women who eventually threw their children into wells or tanks, and sometimes went on to kill themselves, did not do this immediately after the birth of their infants but after a fortnight, a month, or even a year or two, depending on when they reached their nadir. Chandra kom Kundoo stated that she had been abandoned by her second husband before being dismissed by her employer as she was in an advanced state of pregnancy, and then turned out of the house of her sister, with whom she had sought refuge, by her brother-in-law.[105] In Gungi kom Krishna's case, the child died of neglect as her mother-in-law and brother-in-law sent her back to the

---

[102] JD, 1887, vol. 76, comp. no. 298, MSA.
[103] JD, 1887, vol. 40, comp. no. 1179, MSA.
[104] Ibid., MSA.
[105] JD, 1882, vol. 52, comp. no. 1419, MSA.

relief works the fifth day after her delivery. Ill and undernourished, she told the Court she did not have enough milk to suckle the child.[106] There are, therefore, instances of deserted women who, in spite of their poverty, illness and unemployment, would have been willing to look after their children if their natal home had offered some support.[107]

Scholarly works on infanticide often cite status as a determining factor in the commission of the act.[108] A great number of the Brahmin widows quoted status as an important motive for committing the act, although it was only one among a range of considerations. Women such as Vijayalakshmi claimed that being a Brahmin had been an obstacle to finding employment elsewhere.[109] Brahmin widows could only be employed in the houses of Brahmins and only then in the capacity of menial outhouse work in order not to violate notions of pollution, so integral to the caste system. It was a formidable choice for a Brahmin widow who had led a sheltered life, and it would have meant a great lowering in the standard of living. More significantly, it meant a precarious existence. Material conditions were ultimately crucial factors because, even those who said it was fear of social opinion knew that, if their unchastity was made public, they would be denied the shelter of the home, whether natal or marital, and would invite the wrath of the caste or village. Status was therefore in direct correlation with the economic prospects for a Brahmin widow. In the case of lower-caste women, desertion and poverty, abandonment by the husband, sickness and impoverishment or famine and unemployment, or a combination of several factors led them to make painful decisions such as infanticide, sometimes combined with suicide. Both the Brahmin and lower-caste widows had only sexual value to their lovers. Once it turned into reproductive value, women of both classes were rejected and denied any form of shelter or privileges. Infanticidal women in the nineteenth century, whether elite (Brahmin) or subordinate (Mang or Mahar), in caste terms, were undeniably the lowest in the gender hierarchy.

Not even if an infanticidal woman had conceived her baby as a result of rape, was any mercy shown, despite that the fact that petitions reveal that Indian women, especially widows, were vulnerable to this form of violence, with many instances of widows being raped by a member of a vast network of relations within the joint family reported; in some cases, the kinship tie was as close as a father-in-law or brother-in-law. When Sangowa, widow of Gursidapa of Kaladgi, conceived after being raped by one of the joint family members of her husband's family, her father-in-law forced her to commit infanticide by threatening to throw her out of the house if she failed to carry out the act. He was convicted merely of burying the body of the child and sentenced to

---

[106] JD, 1890, vol. 107b, comp. no. 138, MSA.

[107] For example, in the case of Baya who stated that she would not have abandoned her child if her mother had given her shelter JD, 1881, vol. 47, comp. no. 1301. MSA

[108] For a study of notions of 'shame' and 'honour' as determinants in the act of infanticide in rural Mediterranean society, see Stephen Wilson, 'Infanticide, Child Abandonment, and Female Honour in Nineteenth-Century Corsica', *Comparative Studies in Society and History*, 30 (1988): 762–83.

[109] Vijayalakshmi's petition, 21 June 1881, JD, 1881, vol. 47, comp. no.726, MSA.

three months; Sangowa was transported for seven years.[110] Moreover, without the symbolic and real protection of the husband, lower-class widows were as vulnerable as widows of higher-castes. Rakhuma, a day labourer, confessed that she had been waylaid while working in a paddy field by a man belonging to her caste a few months after the death of her husband, and that, as a result of this 'forcible intercourse', she had borne a child. She also stated that she had not aborted the foetus because she had one surviving child by her deceased husband whom she loved and wanted to take care of, as the child had no one aside from her. The death of her child borne of rape, she insisted, had been due to malarial fever.[111]

Petitions reveal the pitiful dilemmas of widows who had been raped by very close members of the husband's family, such as a brother-in-law. The notion of pollution attached to widows was exacerbated if they were found to have conceived due to rape. Unwilling to incur the wrath of the family by naming the person involved, the widow usually murdered the newly-born infant in the hope that, by getting rid of the evidence of the rape, she would be retained in the family, although, in many cases, they did not even have a say in the matter. In 1885, Rakhuma kom Bala was transported for ten years in spite of her claims that she had been forced to commit the crime under the pressure from her husband's family. Raped by her brother-in-law after the death of her husband, she was told by her father-in-law that the reputation of the family would be in jeopardy if the town came to know of the rape and was thus persuaded to commit the act. Sentencing her to ten years' transportation, the Governor commented:

> ... the case is a bad one of its kind—for the woman's only excuse for killing the child was that she was afraid of being turned out of caste.[112]

The legal interpretations did not consider the circumstances of Rakhuma's conception or the instigators behind the act but only her role in the commission of the act.

It seems clear that women alone understood the crucial links between infanticide and the survival of the mother concerned. A shared sense of a subordinate status and experience is seen in many cases of infanticide that came in front of the colonial courts. Very often, midwives, grandmothers, aunts, friendly neighbours' wives or female friends rallied around women who were pregnant with an illegitimate child; their involvement is demonstrated by the number of elderly women, including grandmothers, who were arrested for administering medicines to daughters with a view to causing a miscarriage,[113] or charged with murder, abetting murder, or of disposing of the child's body. Despite the fact that the grandmother was often a relatively elderly

---

[110] JD, 1881, vol. 46, comp. no. 998, MSA.

[111] JD, 1885, vol. 33, comp. no. 1282, MSA.

[112] JD, 1885, vol. 53, comp. no. 601, MSA.

[113] See the proceedings in the case of Saipi kome Sonda, sentenced to 10 years' rigorous imprisonment for procuring medicines in order to induce abortions, JD, 1882, vol. 60, comp. no. 865; see also the case of Bhima who inserted a 'medicated twig in the private parts of Ganga' in order to help the latter abort, JD, 1885, vol. 99, comp. no.532, MSA.

lady of fifty or sixty years, and they were usually acting out of a desire to prevent their daughter being humiliated and excommunicated by the caste and village *panchayat* [councils] for conceiving as a result of coercion by a close relation, the law treated them as harshly as the mothers themselves.[114] Nevertheless, some women continued to act to protect the daughter from the wrath of the family or caste, revealing the solidarity that existed between some Indian women and, it could be argued, even displaying a rudimentary feminist consciousness. A similar trend of assisting female relatives had been noted by Judith Tucker in her study of nineteenth-century Egyptian women; by carrying out what Tucker refers to as acts of resistance within the home, women often attempted to assist those female members most in need.[115]

Paying the Penalty: Punishing the Infanticidal Woman

We can therefore see that, both in terms of assigning responsibility for the killing of an infant and with regard to the circumstances that drove infanticidal women to act in the way that they did, the phenomenon of infanticide was a complex one. However, the intricate web of factors that contributed to the crime were largely lost when deciding on punishment because Section 109 of the Indian Penal Code presented peculiar problems of interpretation to the judiciary in the Bombay Presidency. It was often taken to also include crimes that were not necessarily straightforward infanticide, meaning that women who should have been tried under different laws were instead subject to its strictures. It failed, for instance, to make any provision for married women, especially *savatis* [second wives] who killed legitimate children; a failure that led to further confusion about its inability to distinguish infanticide from infanticide accompanied by suicide. In times of desperation, for instance, some housewives seem to have been driven to throwing themselves and their children into rivers, tanks and wells. Wife battering, neglect and ill treatment were the main motives behind such desperate acts of suicide and infanticide, as this petition by Basawa kom Basapa shows:

> I lived happily with my husband Basapa until he married Chanawa by Pat ceremony. Chanawa always quarrelled with me on some pretext or other. My husband treated me very cruelly ... and turned me out of his house. I returned home again but they kept me starving. Having lived in this way for fifteen days I requested him to make some arrangement for my maintenance. He and my co-wife, however, began to beat me and drove me out of the house. They struck me with an iron ladle and the mark left by it is still visible on my chest. I could not live any longer without food and being disgusted with my existence in this world my head turned and I could not see what to do ... Being

---

[114] For instance, Madivalowa's appeal was rejected by the Governor who stated that, 'Only mothers killing infants directly after birth are considered by the government'; JD, 1890, vol. 104, comp. no. 238, MSA.

[115] Judith Tucker, *Women in Nineteenth-Century Egypt* (Cambridge: Cambridge University Press, 1985), p. 135.

unable to bear it any longer, I took my child and went to a well and threw myself into it with the child, not knowing the consequences of what I was going to do.[116]

When a co-wife was involved, women were often driven to commit infanticide along with suicide, as they were convinced that their children would not get a fair chance.[117] Such cases were dealt with by the Governor-in-Council under the category of 'derangement of senses' compounded by ill treatment. Sentences were commuted from transportation for life to ten or seven years' hard labour but never less than five years. The lack of distinction between the various kinds of situations giving rise to this offence led to infanticidal and suicidal women being harshly treated by the criminal justice system.

Neither did the law consider the material circumstances of women arrested for infanticide. As we have seen, Indian elites petitioned strongly in cases of Brahmin widows. For women belonging to lower castes and classes such as Kunbis, Mahars or Mangs convicted for this act, however, the chances of escaping transportation were slim, and they had to fight hard to have their sentences remitted. Kesar, a widow and a victim of a famine-stricken area, for instance, was convicted of the murder of her eighteen-month-old child. In her petition, she stated that she had been reduced to great distress after the death of her husband, as she had to maintain her mother-in-law as well as the child and herself and could earn little or nothing by her labour. Moreover, her husband's relatives could give no assistance as they themselves were in a similar financial situation. She pleaded that she committed the act under great provocation and, in order to relieve the distress she felt at her inability to feed the child and relieve its suffering. Her petition was rejected on the grounds that:

> ... it is usual to commute a sentence for a widow who had killed her child in the agony and excitement of childbirth but not for a widow who kills her legitimate child one and a half years after its birth. Her only excuse offered is poverty. Dangerous to commute as lower classes are tempted to free them from responsibility.[118]

It is clearly evident from the case of Kesar that the judiciary was informed by Victorian stereotypes of classism and elitism. Equally, many of the infanticide cases were fraught with ambiguity and the courts dealt arbitrarily with them. Furthermore, none of the legal guidelines made allowances for natural infant mortality caused by sickness and the undernourishment of the mother and child. When, for instance, Durgi, a 20-year-old Mang offender, pleaded, 'Not Guilty' to the charge, she stated:

> I took care of the child for three months, supporting myself all the while by begging. Then I became ill with fever and the child also became ill, suffering from itches that

---

[116] JD, 1890, vol. 70, comp. no. 279, MSA.

[117] See proceedings in the case of Sakrowa kom Bhimapa, J.D, 1882, vol. 52, comp. no. 1069, MSA.

[118] JD, 1887, vol. 76, comp. no. 298, MSA.

produced large blotches on its body .... When I became ill, we suffered much for want of food and shelter and the child being very young and ill died as a consequence.[119]

Despite her testimony and the fact that the postmortem report recorded no signs of violence against the child, the High Court disbelieved her as the child was born out of wedlock; proof, in the judge's idea, that she had killed it out of shame. As a Mang, Durgi had no such constraints placed on her by her caste and kin but the law of infanticide was governed so strictly by ideas of 'licit' and 'illicit' intercourse and 'legitimate' and 'illegitimate' children that such assumptions were made even when they didn't apply.

Such strict interpretation of the law also failed to make allowances for women affected by malarial fever or other debilitating sicknesses who naturally miscarried or gave birth to stillborn infants. There are many instances of women protesting their innocence on these grounds; most of these appeals, however, failed on the grounds that 'there ought to be contrition on confession as a basis for an appeal to the clemency of Government', and not a justification for the act. As infanticide was judged to be a crime resulting from shame, the penal code was based on the idea of obtaining a 'confession' from the accused. It is therefore not surprising that, when we come across two or more petitions, they follow the bizarre format of a plea of 'Not Guilty' in the first trial, sometimes 'Not Guilty' in the second, then finally, in the third petition, include a plea for clemency that contains a confession to a crime which may or may not have been committed. When judges pointed out the contradictions in such appeals, an amazing number of women simply replied that jailors, relatives or friends advised them that, until they pled guilty, their sentence would not be remitted.[120]

The penal code was, however, not necessarily set in stone. Debates on the issue within indigenous society led to changes in penal measures that, in turn, reflected the tensions that existed between the judiciary and the executive. In 1881, the judges who sentenced Vijayalakshmi departed from the policy of recommending cases to the government for mercy as four other similar cases had been reported in the same week; an increase which was believed to be a direct result of the government's leniency. Justice Pinhey noted the reasons for the change in the policy thus:

Transportation for life is the best possible fate these unfortunate women can experience. They are defiled and outcasted for life by their incontinence and their subsequent crime. Under no circumstances and after no lapse of time can they be received back into their families on terms of equality. If they are transported and behave well they will in time earn qualified freedom and eventually amongst a new people and in a new country be able to form new domestic ties.[121]

---

[119] JD, 1880, vol. 100, comp. no. 23, MSA.

[120] See the proceedings in the case of Rakhmin of Ratnagiri, JD, 1887, vol. 76, comp. no. 298, MSA.

[121] Proceedings in the case of Sangowa kom Gursidapa, JD, 1881, vol. 46, comp. no. 996. MSA

Besides, he ended optimistically, the obnoxious customs of Hindu India would be absent in the Andamans, which would, naturally, remove the motivation for infanticide and therefore serve as a guarantee that she would not commit the crime again.[122] However, the disciplinary function appropriated by the judiciary proved to be unacceptable to the government. Tremendous pressure was applied by Indian elites and finally the Governor compromised. He stated that the judges appeared to have dealt with the Vijayalakshmi case more from an abstract point of view rather than with any real appreciation of the actual circumstances of a Hindu widow. Vijayalakshmi's sentence was therefore reduced to five years' rigorous imprisonment.[123] The politicization of the Vijayalakshmi case was clearly seen in the orders of the government that from 1881 onwards no statement of reasons was to accompany remission of sentences on infanticidal women and no response was to be given to the public memorial of the Poona Sarvajanik Sabha.[124]

The question of 'choice' rose again in 1884 in the case of Baya, a seventeen-year-old girl convicted of infanticide where Sir James Fergusson, Governor of Bombay Presidency, once more raised the question of transportation of teenage convicts to the Andamans. Agreeing with the judges, he felt that it was more merciful to transfer infanticidal women to penal colonies.[125] Such benevolent feelings on the part of the Governor were actually matters of urgent concern to the state, with prison arrangements jeopardized by the dwindling numbers of female convicts, as the extract of a letter to the Home Department from the Superintendent of Prisons at Port Blair shows:

> ... the number of convicts in the female jail at Port Blair is rapidly decreasing, and if a larger number of females are not transported than has been done during the past three years, it will be impossible to carry out the system of permitting male convicts to marry, and to carry on the weaving manufactory which is productive of large savings to Government ...[126]

The Government of India, however, refused to modify the rule that barred female convicts serving short-term sentences from being transported to the isles. Despite this, the Governor of Bombay found a way of circumventing this by simply increasing the sentences of transportation to seven and ten years and positing it as a choice to be given to women convicted of infanticide. After June 1884, a woman convicted of infanticide was lured towards the penal colonies with the promise that:

---

[122] Ibid., MSA.

[123] JD, 1881, vol. 46, comp. no. 1036, MSA.

[124] Ibid., MSA.

[125] JD, 1884, vol. 41, comp. no. 229, MSA.

[126] 'Letter from Col. T. Cadell, Superintendent of Jails, Port Blair and Nicobars, to Secretary, to the Government of India, Home Dept., 23 November 1886', JD, 1886, vol. 37, comp. no. 1456, MSA.

... she will be made to work for a few years, and then probably *be allowed to marry a ticket-of-leave convict,* [sic] and be exempted from further punishment, though she will be obliged to remain in the Andamans.[127]

The authorities therefore combined benevolence with astute policies and made further use of the Indian female body in the service of the colonial state. One might, as a result, have expected shiploads of Indian women to be transported, but this did not happen. A case of bigamy took place in the Andamans and was reported in the newspapers; consequently, the incentive of marriage was removed from the choice offered to female offenders. Quite a few of the women convicted of infanticide were abandoned wives and so a second marriage was beyond their reach. Besides, not a single female convict between 1884 and 1890 opted to go to the Andamans, despite all the incentives offered to them. Many of the women simply stated that they had no wish to remarry and many more said that they had children from their first marriages whom they could no longer see if they went to the penal settlements.[128] In 1890, this system of offering the 'choice' of going to the penal colonies was discontinued and the government reverted to reducing sentences to a term of rigorous imprisonment.

Campaigns by Brahmin elites about the fate of Brahmin women convicted of infanticide also had a clear impact on the actions of the judiciary; indeed, the bias in favour of the Brahmin widow was so great that it influenced all of the courts' decisions in cases involving Brahmin widows after 1881. When a Brahmin widow was convicted of infanticide after this date, it was standard practise for judges to commute sentences of transportation for life to a period of imprisonment on the grounds that Brahmin widows were forbidden to remarry.[129] The preferential treatment of this group had a negative impact on the way in which the court treated low-caste widows; Kondi kom Shivappa, a Mahar widow aged thirty, for instance, did not have her sentence of transportation for life commuted to five years' rigorous imprisonment because Justice West thought that '... the prisoner has not the excuse of palliation that might be urged in her favour as were a Brahmin widow'.[130] Gender issues were thus intimately linked to caste in reformist debates, and this bias informed the decisions of the courts right up to the end of the nineteenth century.

As we have seen, in colonial discourse the Indian widow was identified with sensuality. She was described as a person who gave vent to 'backward instincts' and had no control over her passions. In colonialist eyes, it was important to control this sexuality as it represented a danger to human life. Moreover, Indian views on female sexuality highlighted the 'temporary insanity' of infanticidal women, thereby

---

[127] From 'Modification of the order of the Government of India in sending women convicted of infanticide and sentenced to transportation for seven years or more to the colonies', in JD, 1884, vol. 41, comp. no. 229, MSA.

[128] See the statement by Gangu kom Tukaram, JD, 1884, vol. 68, comp. no. 765; also the statement by Huseinbi kom Imam Saheb, JD, 1885, vol. 53, comp. no. 601, MSA.

[129] See also the proceedings in the case of Banabai kom Bhiwraj, JD, 1890, vol. 107A, comp. no. 138, MSA.

[130] Ibid., MSA.

inadvertently drawing the state's attention to it and giving them ample space to introduce medico-judicial mechanisms designed to control the biological perversions of mothers beset with murderous obsessions.[131] This trend can be seen from the 1880s onwards when the state took upon itself the task of keeping a close watch over all suicides and infanticides following parturition and devised a rational technology to rectify it. In the 1880s, lunatic asylums in Bombay Presidency were admitting women convicted of attempted suicide, infanticide or both whilst, in 1890, the directors of the asylums in Colaba, North Kanara and Nasik complained that they had no more space to accommodate female convicts and drew the state's attention to the need to build new asylums for this purpose.[132]

The combination of medical measures and judicial powers reconstructed the female psyche in terms of a hysterical condition. The deranged woman throwing herself and her child down a well or the ill-treated wife exposing her child in a field was invariably examined for hereditary epilepsy; the fever-racked, undernourished *kunbi* cultivator who committed infanticide was supposed to have committed the act in a state of ungovernable passion and unsoundness of mind; the woman who had supposedly committed infanticide due to post-puerperal mania—all of them filled the lunatic asylums of the Bombay Presidency. The assumptions that the state made in its provision of lunatic hospitals to correct these women brought unprecedented problems, especially in the case of women convicted of infanticide committed during post-puerperal mania.[133] The families to which these women belonged did not always appreciate the interventionist nature of the judiciary; despite the fact that it was, in most cases, a temporary condition and women were freed once they were declared to be of 'sound mind', not many families accepted them back into their homes; Tulsa kom Lakshman, for instance, who was released three months after her conviction, was refused entry by her own husband.[134] There are also many cases of infanticidal women being examined for epileptic fits and, after being released from the asylums, facing similar problems with their families.[135] These refusals were not merely due to the fact that the woman had been in an asylum but was also a result of the security demanded by the government under Section 475 of the Criminal Procedure Code, which placed an unwelcome responsibility on the family.[136]

---

[131] Mark Jackson has argued that the creation of 'puerperal insanity' as a novel disease to be placed in a separate category gave way to the nineteenth-century perception of newborn child murder as a 'predominantly medical issue'. See *New-Born Child Murder*, p. 128.

[132] JD, 1885, vol. 60, comp. no. 322, MSA.

[133] A more accurate description of this condition as understood in medical parlance today is postnatal depression.

[134] 'Proceedings in the case of Tulsa kom Lakshman', BJP, 1885, vol. P/2651, no. 618. MSA

[135] JD, 1882, vol. 98, comp. no. 1181, MSA.

[136] Ibid., MSA.

Not even age was taken into account when passing sentences on infanticidal women, with the law treating young girls arrested for infanticide in the same way as older women convicted of the same act. Yenki kom Phakira, a seventeen-year-old girl, was sentenced to be hanged by the Sessions Judge of Belgaum under Sections 109 and 302. On appeal, the government reduced the sentence to transportation for life with the convict being sent to the Andamans on her attaining eighteen years of age.[137] Such harshness sometimes resulted in local residents lodging protests against such judgements, with, for instance, the inhabitants of Ahmednagar presenting a petition against Judge Wedderburn's conviction of a fourteen-year-old girl, Ameerabee. They argued that the sentence of transportation for life was an extremely severe one for a young girl protesting:

> ... the object of the Legislative (sic) in punishing such offenders is to give a warning to persons in the position of the person sentenced against committing like offences. This punishment will not serve as a lesson to children of eight or nine years old ...[138]

However, in spite of their protests, the girl's sentence was not commuted. Indeed, there is no evidence to show whether such juvenile offenders were sent to reformatory homes, as was the case with male children. On the contrary, the sentence of transportation for ten years or more meant, in effect, a lifetime in the Andamans, which showed that no mercy was shown towards juvenile female offenders for this type of crime.

This chapter has analyzed how notions of crime and criminality that the state attributed to certain women's acts and types of behaviour resulted in both the material conditions and social status of women undergoing a significant deterioration, but the very same historical processes also resulted in a heightened feminist consciousness. Movements of collective *bhaginivarg* [sisterhood] solidarity and action which had begun over the Vijayalakshmi trial were to continue, and how women contested the representations of both colonial and indigenous discourses and successfully used the legislative and judicial apparatus in bettering their own lives will be examined in the next chapter.

---

[137] JD, 1883, vol. 87, comp. no. 707, MSA.
[138] JD, 1880, vol. 146, comp. no. 104, MSA.

Chapter 6

Women as Agents:
Contesting Discourses on Marriage
and Marital Rights

Introduction

A prominent social reformer, N.G. Chandavarkar, reported the contents of a conversation between an eminent Hindu lawyer and a *kunbi* [cultivator] client of his. The lawyer asked the peasant what he thought of British rule. The *kunbi* replied:

> … it is a very good Government indeed—we live so much in peace and security. But there is one evil to which it has led. Under former rulers, one could govern one's wife, but now the moment you beat your wife, she runs up to a magistrate.[1]

That conjugal relations should feature so prominently in the cultivator's assessment of the Raj is highly indicative of a wider discussion on the 'home' and the 'domestic' taking place in late colonial India. Both the awareness of the movement for self-assertion that had begun among women which the peasant noted with disquiet, and the way in which the main subjects of the debate, Indian women, were absent from the dialogue between Indian men and the colonial authorities is reflected with clarity in the agriculturalist's response quoted above.[2] In the long historiography on the Age of Consent, which stretches back to the 1970s, scholars have analyzed the nature of this dialogue and the motivations of the *male* participants;[3] Charles Heimsath and Geraldine Forbes, for instance, studied the issue of social reform as expressed in the

---

[1] Narayan G. Chandavarkar, *The Speeches and Writings of Sir Narayan G. Chandavarkar*, ed. L.V. Kaikini (Bombay: Manoranjak Grantha Prasarak, 1911), p. 21.

[2] In an early formulation of this chapter in 1992, I had made a case for seeing women as agents by comparing and contrasting the oppositional narratives of women to that of the colonial and Indian male discourses on the issue of child marriage. See Padma Anagol-McGinn, 'The Age of Consent Act (1891) Reconsidered: Women's Perspectives and Participation in the Child Marriage Controversy in India', *South Asia Research*, 12/2 (1992): 100–118.

[3] Early works on the subject of child marriage are Prem Narain, 'The Age of Consent Bill (1891) and its Impact on India's Freedom Struggle', *Quarterly Review of Historical Studies*, 10/1 (1970–71): 7–21; Rajendra Singh Vatsa, 'The Movement Against Infant Marriages in India 1860–1914', *Journal of Indian History*, 49 (1971): 280–95.

Age of Consent debates in order to understand how nationalism grew and why Indian elites undertook the project of 'modernizing' the nation.[4] More recent scholarship, however, has turned its attention to highlighting the connections between gender categories and gender relations and the structures of colonial power. For these scholars, discussions of women and social reform served to further colonialist agendas.[5] Himani Bannerji has claimed that the annexation of civil society in India was undertaken in a 'hegemonic' fashion via social reform as expressed through the child marriage debates at the time of the passing of the 1891 Act.[6] In a similar vein, Mrinalini Sinha has argued that the British used 'social reform as a test of native masculinity—a handy stick with which to beat Indian nationalists.'[7] Indeed, 'the imperial and the national' discourses not only frames the politics of gender but, according to Sinha, are also 'constitutive' of its very meaning.[8]

This privileging of the politics of colonialism and nationalism has led scholars to miss the real dynamic of change in gender relations. Male anxiety was not a product of the entry of the colonial state into the private sphere as some scholars have maintained. It stemmed from the increasing recourse of Indian women to colonial structures, principally the law, as a means of renegotiating conjugal relations. The movement for self-assertion that had begun among women, which the peasant's observation so clearly revealed, had vast repercussions that went beyond Maharashtrian society. As the above quotation indicates, it was women's agency, especially their increasing resort to colonial law, that was seen as an unwelcome innovation by the male public. The critical moment of realization for Hindu men came when a Hindu wife, Rukhmabai, a product of the emerging feminist movement, defied the court's injunction to join Dadaji, her husband, after he brought a suit for restitution of conjugal rights.[9] Defiant

---

[4] Charles Heimsath, 'The Origin and Enactment of the Indian Age of Consent Bill, 1891', *Journal of Asian History*, 4 (1962): 491–504; Geraldine Forbes, 'Women and Modernity: The Issue of Child Marriage in India', *Women's Studies International Quarterly*, 2 (1979): 409–19.

[5] See Mrinalini Sinha, *Colonial Masculinity: The 'Manly Gentleman' and the 'Effeminate Bengali' in the Late Nineteenth Century* (Manchester: Manchester University Press, 1995); Himani Bannerji, 'Age of Consent and Hegemonic Social Reform', in C. Midgley (ed.) *Gender and Imperialism* (Manchester: Manchester University Press, 1998), pp. 21–44.

[6] Banerji, 'Age of Consent', Ibid., p. 21.

[7] Sinha, *Colonial Masculinity*, p. 142.

[8] Ibid., p. 172.

[9] Since the publication of my article in 1992, exhaustive accounts of Rukhmabai's activities in Maharashtra and Britain have appeared. All of them however, either emphasize the ever-widening grip of the colonial discourse or the importance of Rukhmabai's case for the formation of nineteenth-century metropolitan discourses of femininity rather than the agency of Indian women. See Meera Kosambi, 'Gender Reform and Competing State Controls Over Women: The Rukhmabai Case (1884–88)', *Contributions to Indian Sociology*, 29/1, 2 (1995): 265–90; Sudhir Chandra, *Enslaved Daughters: Colonialism, Law and Women's Rights* (New Delhi: Oxford University Press,

acts by such women set in train a fierce rearguard action by Indian men. So intense was the perceived threat from women that former stalwarts of progressive opinion joined conservative Maharashtrian groups in opposing reform.[10] In fact, in Bengal, as Tanika Sarkar has shown, the Bengali orthodoxy clearly understood that the battleground for the confrontation between the ruler and ruled had shifted from the public arena to the private sphere of the domestic social arrangements that were represented by conjugal relations and were using 'defence of tradition' as a 'political strategy' in order to protect their last bastion of autonomy: the home.[11]

In the crucial decades prior to the 1890s, the centrality of the restitution of conjugal rights and women's recourse to the colonial courts galvanized progressive elements in the Indian elite to call for marriage reform. By concentrating on women's agency, while taking into account the Indian male reformist, revivalist and the colonialist discourse, I shall argue that, if the Hindu patriarchal system felt it was under siege, this was engendered not so much by the claims of the unreserved masculinity of the foreigner, but *from the real threat of their womenfolk acting as agents of their own destiny*. This chapter therefore begins by showing how considerable numbers of women were accessing the courts to renegotiate conjugal relations in the late nineteenth century. Though these actions galvanized some male reformers, like M.G. Ranade, to call for marriage reform, they brought forth a formidable rearguard action on the part of Indian men who sought the assistance of the colonial authorities in their attempt to stem the growing threat posed by female autonomy. Despite a clear attempt to exclude them from the debates that their actions had initiated, Indian women counterattacked by vigorously contesting the male and colonialist discourses that attempted to define them. It will be shown that, through their actions and interventions in debates about female sexuality, women's public participation reveals that a clear sense of *bhaginivarg* [sisterhood] informed an emerging feminist movement in late nineteenth-century India.[12]

1998); Antoinette Burton, 'From Child Bride to "Hindoo Lady": Rukhmabai and the Debate on Sexual Respectability in Imperial Britain', *American Historical Review*, October (1998): 1119–46.

[10] Some staunch liberals turned conservative during this agitation, like Sir T. Madhava Rao and Dr K.R. Kirtikar, who wrote vitriolic articles condemning her action.

[11] Tanika Sarkar, 'The Hindu Wife and the Hindu Nation: Domesticity and Nationalism in Nineteenth-Century Bengal', *Studies in History*, 8/2 (1992): 213–35; see also 'Rhetoric Against Age of Consent: Resisting Colonial Reason and Death of a Child Wife', *Economic and Political Weekly*, 28/36, 4 September 1993, 1869–78.

[12] The different ways in which the feminist concept of *bhaginivarg* developed is discussed in chapters 2 and 3.

The Restitution of Conjugal Rights: British Law and the Empowerment of Indian Women

The history of suits for the restitution of conjugal rights in India reveals that women were ready to use British law as resource to improve their position and assert their rights in marriage. In a pattern which would be further developed in the late nineteenth century, it also reveals that Indian male recognition of the empowering nature of colonial law was quickly followed by successful attempts to check its effectiveness by lobbying the colonial authorities. Restitution of conjugal rights was the only relief offered by British law to all Indian communities in cases of marital disharmony, whether they were Hindus, Muslims, Parsis or any other religious community;[13] suits for the restitution of conjugal rights were unknown in precolonial India. Scripture-based Hindu law did not sanction it, although customary laws did incorporate less formal ways of dealing with marital disputes. The concept of restitution of conjugal rights was, in fact, an importation from English ecclesiastical law. Blackstone's summary of this legal suit in Britain allowed suits for the restitution of conjugal rights to be brought whenever either the husband or the wife was 'guilty of injury or subtraction, or lives separate from the other without any sufficient reason in which case they will be compelled to live together again.'[14] Although the law governing the restitution of conjugal rights was grafted onto the existing Indian Penal Code in the nineteenth century with little modification,[15] the form that it subsequently took in this period was wholly controlled and shaped by Indian interpretations of marital rights and obligations.

For Indian Parsis and Muslims, marriage was regarded as a contract; for Hindus, however, it was a religious union, although it was not a sacrament according to ecclesiastical law as the Christian tradition defined it, because Hindu men continued to take second and third wives or keep mistresses. Furthermore, these ties were not forged between consenting adults as arranged marriages, especially in the period under study, were often agreements between families, not agreements between the couple themselves. Indeed, the notion of consent often did not arise, as the spouses were usually betrothed as children if not infants. Importing the concept of restitution of conjugal rights and applying it to Hindus was therefore entirely inappropriate; as lawyers and judges continually pointed out during this period, suits for the restitution of conjugal rights did not formally constitute part of any of the major religions in India, despite the fact that all of them did make reference to the broad duties involved in cohabitation. In cases of severe disagreements between couples, the most common practice was for the wife to voluntarily flee to her natal family or be driven to seek their help by the husbands. In the 150 case studies conducted for this study, separation had

---

[13] Paras Diwan, *Law of Marriage and Divorce* (Allahabad: Wadhwa and Co., 1991), p. 283.

[14] Cited in Rukhmabai, *Indian Law Reports* (hereafter *ILR*), 10 Bom. 312, 1885.

[15] 'The Indian Divorce Act, 1869', section VII, clause 32, reproduced in Diwan, *Law of Marriage*, p. 749.

normally already taken place before the cases came up in court, with women often recounting their tales of gratitude to members of their extended families for care and maintenance.

In the mid-nineteenth century, Indian law recognized two kinds of matrimonial suits for the purpose of obtaining conjugal rights. The first was for Restitution of Conjugal Rights (Act XV of 1877, Schedule II, article 35), available to both parties, that is, husband and wife. But the second was restricted to the husband claiming the society of his wife, namely, recovering his wife from a person harbouring her with ill-intent (Act XV of 1877, Schedule II, Article 34). Sections 259 and 260 of the Code of Civil Procedure of 1882 provided comprehensive regulations for the execution of decrees of both suits. Section 260 of the revised Code of 1877 provided that, if a spouse refused to comply with a decree given in a suit of restitution of conjugal rights, then he or she could be dealt with by imprisonment or attachment of property, or by both. These decrees interfered extensively with customary law and, in the later nineteenth century, were arbitrarily used against women. Formerly, women could seek the help of the extended family in cases of violence against them by husbands, but the wording of Section 259 meant that the extended family could not interfere, especially if the person 'harbouring' her was a distant relative; for example, an uncle instead of a 'parent'. Section 260 also worked against women with a little property in the form of *stridhan*. However, it is a testimony to women's resilience and determination that they increasingly resorted to the first form of suit, restitution of conjugal rights, knowing full well that the husband would rather agree to a maintenance grant than give up the privilege of making polygamous arrangements.

The origin and history of ecclesiastical jurisdiction reveals clearly that suits for restitution of conjugal rights had been entertained from the first introduction of English law in India. Matrimonial disputes amongst the various settlers of Bombay had been frequently brought and uniformly heard in the Supreme Court of Bombay (from 1823 to 1856) and prior to this, the Mayor's Courts (until 1823) that preceded the Supreme Courts. The Recorder's Court of Bombay lists a total of eight cases heard from 1800 to 1856; two were from the Armenian community, five from Parsis and one from a Muslim couple. It is a point worth noting that seven out of the total of eight cases of suits for the restitution of conjugal rights were brought by the wives against their husbands.[16] The wives demanded that the husbands should take them back and treat them with 'conjugal kindness'; if they refused, alimony should be provided to them. In six of a total of seven cases heard in the recorder's Court of Bombay between 1800 and 1856, the court granted alimony to the wives. This inventory of facts crystallizes the manner in which the British courts were upholding the right of the Indian wife for a maintenance grant in the case of a failed marriage and were holding men to their

---

[16] The eighth was a warring Muslim couple disputing the validity of the marriage. These statistics are compiled from E.F. Moore, *Reports of Cases Heard and Determined by the Judicial Committee and the Lords of Her Majesty's Privy Council on Appeal from the Supreme and Sudder Dewanny Courts in the East Indies* (Bangalore: Richmond F. Hayes, 1858) (hereafter *Moore's Indian Appeals*).

marital duties. This situation was not to the liking of Indian patriarchs and soon the winds of change were to blow with the rise of Indian lawyers speaking on behalf of their male clients who wished to engage in polygamous relations or keep mistresses without their rebellious wives getting any kind of maintenance from them.

In 1856, the Privy Council was to hear the most celebrated case in the history of the restitution of conjugal rights. This was Ardaseer Cursetjee v. Perozeboye, a dispute between a Parsi couple from Bombay. Ardaseer's astute Indian lawyer brought a suit challenging ecclesiastical jurisdiction over Indians.[17] The set of arguments proposed by the Bar in London reveals a great sensitivity towards safeguarding the rights of Indian women. A point in case is the set of arguments used in defence of the wife, Perozeboye, by Charles Jackson. He argued against exercising ecclesiastical jurisdiction over Hindus, Muslims and Parsis and for suits to reinstate conjugal rights amongst Indians to be refused. However, he also argued that women should have access to legal remedy in cases of gross marital neglect by husbands by adapting the law of alimony. He further demonstrated that wives and husbands could not be forced to cohabit together as the notion was anomalous to Asian marriage laws; furthermore, it was only Christian marriages that treated the woman as part of the man (Canon law considered a man and his wife as one person), thus meaning that the case could only be dealt with by ecclesiastical courts and not by the civil courts. In India, no such principle existed in either Islamic, Hindu or Zoroastrian laws, meaning, he argued, that in such instances 'Native married women are *feme soles* and the Supreme Court at Calcutta treat them so'.[18] According to this reasoning, Ardaseer was guilty on three counts, of having forcibly evicted his wife from the house, refusing to take her back and having failed to maintain her—all these facts of abandonment and cruelty meant that there was nothing 'to prevent his wife from bringing an action against her husband for damages, or a suit for a maintenance past and present.'[19]

The force and conviction of these arguments were enshrined in the final judgment given by the Right Hon. Lushington of the Privy Council who upheld Jackson's argument that the Courts in India, on the ecclesiastical side, should not entertain such suits, but that the British state was obliged to provide legal remedies to subjects in suits arising in matrimonial matters; Perozeboye was therefore directed to apply for adequate

---

[17] 'Ardaseer Cursetjee v. Perozeboye, 12 and 14 April 1856', Ibid., vol. 6.

[18] 'Feme sole' is better understood in relation to its sister concept the 'feme covert'. In nineteenth-century English law the wife was regarded as the 'property of her husband' because the doctrine of coverture declared that the legal personality of the woman was merged in her husband's after marriage. A 'feme covert' often referred to a married woman who could not alienate her property, including that which had come to her before marriage, nor sign contracts, or make a will without the consent of her husband. However, a degree of autonomy was embedded in the term 'Feme sole' which was defined as 'A wife with a separate estate could deal with *that* [sic] property as if she were unmarried, or what the law called a *feme sole*.' This quote and information is from Mary L. Shanley, *Feminism, Marriage and the Law in Victorian England* (Princeton: Princeton University Press, 1989), pp. 25–6.

[19] Ibid., p. 372.

relief in a civil court against her husband. Two facts emerge forcefully in this history of the legislation on the restitution of conjugal rights that were to have far-reaching implications and consequences. Early nineteenth-century cases show that suits for restitution were brought by wives against neglectful and cruel husbands in the hope that, if they were not taken back, at least the court would grant them maintenance rights. In the precedent created by the Ardaseer case, we also find that British legal experts were reluctant to apply ecclesiastical laws to the Indian situation; moreover, the gendered arguments also reveal their anxiety to create safeguards for the protection for married Indian women. Since marriage in India was deemed more a contract than a sacrament, wives were encouraged to apply on the equity side of ecclesiastical courts for maintenance and alimony from uncaring husbands. After this groundbreaking case, in which the Privy Council ruled that ecclesiastical law could not be strictly applied to non-Christian suits for restitution of conjugal rights, these cases increasingly came to be entertained on the civil side of the courts in India. The early history of conjugal relations, especially case law as it emerges in modern India, demonstrates that it is difficult to sustain the view that 'English law was an instrument of oppression'.[20]

Instead, the argument here is that, in the late nineteenth century, English law as interpreted by Indian legal scholars and reformers becomes a tool for oppressing women and was a creation of Indian male agents with little assistance from their British counterparts who were mostly pressurized by the 'trial' of Indian newspapers into consenting to Indian orthodox opinion. Firstly, the Privy Council judgement that Indian marriages were more contractual rather than sacramental in character was turned on its head by Indian legal experts, who argued the reverse; that Hindu unions were religious and hence sacraments and it was actually Christian ones which were more contractual in nature. Following this new definition of Hindu marriages, the Privy Council's understanding and ruling of Indian wives's status as *feme soles* was overturned by conservative Indians, who redefined the position of Indian wives as *feme covert* and bound the Hindu woman in the person of the Hindu male (that is, her husband). Secondly, the early law enshrined in Privy Council rulings had instituted restitution of conjugal rights as a marital remedy to 'protect' the 'rights' of wives. By subverting the emphasis on to 'duties' of wives in the later nineteenth century, Indian elites overturned the implications of this legal remedy. Originally acting as a force for the empowerment of Indian women, British law was manipulated by Indian male elites who successfully contrived to turn it into a source of women's oppression.

A Rebellion of Wives: Legal Action against Marital Injustice

If Indian wives were quietly exercising their rights in the courts to maintenance and alimony in cases where there was gross neglect of conjugal duties by husbands, as a result of the national publicity over what became known as the 'Rukhmabai case',[21] the

---

[20] Amongst a host of scholars see in particular Sudhir Chandra, *Enslaved Daughters*.

[21] For details on her life and work see Appendix.

1880s were to bring changes in the marital remedies available to warring couples. For good reasons, the Rukhmabai case became one of the most publicized legal disputes of the later nineteenth century, and it was to have far-reaching consequences. Out of the contentious debates over the restitution of conjugal rights and divorce in the Rukhmabai case, there arose the greatest social reform issue of the nineteenth century, the child marriage controversy. Rukhmabai argued that she was a victim of the institution of child marriage and that, in the absence of the consent of the two parties, her marriage ought to be declared null and void. This provided an opportunity for Indian liberals to start a discussion about raising the marriage age for girls, a dialogue which culminated in the major social legislative enactment of the century—the Age of Consent Act of 1891. The Government of India had consistently refused to entertain the idea of interfering in the domestic areas of their Indian subjects when Behramji Malabari, a Bombay social reformer and journalist, beseeched the government to change the law in his 'Notes on Infant Marriage and Enforced Widowhood In India' in August 1884.[22] The consistent points emerging in favour of noninterference in the official replies to Malabari until 1890 hinged on the government's insistence that 'the battle of social reform must be first fought by those whom it immediately concerns'; that 'the impulse must come from within, not from without'.[23] It would take six years of campaigning, including a trip to London in which he sought to win influential allies, for Malabari to finally persuade a reluctant government to intervene. Given the absence of any evidence that the government initiated it, the argument that the Age of Consent issue was a 'hegemonic social reform issue', imposed by the colonial state, is a grossly flawed reading of the archive on the subject by some contemporary scholars.[24]

Rukhmabai's case came to public attention in 1884 when Dadaji Bhikaji filed a suit for the restitution of conjugal rights in the Bombay High Court. At the age of twenty, Dadaji had been married to Rukhmabai who was then eleven years old. The marriage had not been consummated as Rukhmabai reached puberty back in her mother's home and not much later the marriage broke down irrevocably as the family elders fought amongst themselves. Rukhmabai was heiress to a modest fortune from her natural father, Janardhan Pandurang, on the remarriage of her mother, Jayantibai, to Dr Sakharam Arjun.[25] Dadaji's contention was that his in-laws coveted Rukhmabai's inheritance and had therefore contrived to keep the

---

[22] In *Infant Marriage and Enforced Widowhood in India: Being a Collection of Opinions, For and Against, Received by Mr B.M. Malabari from Representative Hindu Gentlemen and Officials and Other Authorities* (Bombay: Voice of India Press, 1887).

[23] See the correspondence of officials especially Hon'ble Sir Auckland A. Colvin to Malabari, 15 July 1884; 15 September 1884; and 26 September 1884. Also Hon. Sir Stewart Bayley, to Malabari, 7 July 1884 amongst others. Ibid.

[24] See for instance Bannerji, 'Age of Consent', in C. Midgley, *Gender and Imperialism*, pp. 21–44.

[25] Jayantibai lost claims to her first husband's property as the Widow Remarriage Act of 1856 disallowed remarried widows from inheriting their previous husband's property. See Lucy Carroll, 'Law, Custom and Statutory Social Reform: Hindu Widows' Remarriage Act of 1856', *Indian Economic and Social History Review*, 20/4 (1983): 363–88.

spouses apart.[26] He alleged that Rukhmabai was completely under the influence of her mother and grandfather, despite the fact that, at the time of the suit was filed, Rukhmabai was over 26 years old, and Dadaji had not claimed marital rights from his wife for 15 years. Rukhmabai claimed that it was Dadaji's inability to earn an honest livelihood, his immoral life style, his refusal to educate himself and his poor health [he was in the intermediary stage of tuberculosis], which prevented her from joining him. She also explained the various occasions on which her acute aversion towards him had been formed:

> He abused my relatives including my mother in language, which was shameful. He set at defiance the efforts made by my father and grandfather to educate him and took to ways which a woman's lips cannot utter. Mr. Dadajee [sic] went through every course of dissipation till my aversion for him was firmly settled.[27]

Significantly, Rukhmabai did not stress the factor of incompatibility, but instead placed her emphasis on complaints that an average traditional Hindu family could relate to, such as the life-chances of a bridegroom and his economic prospects. She pointed out that, even a caste panchayat would agree, on the basis of textual precepts, that a man had to provide for his wife in order to claim her person because Hindu marriages were contractual in nature as the arrangement had been made between the family elders rather than by her as a child-bride or Dadaji as a young groom. An interesting shift in the male debates on Hindu tradition was the highly selective process of picking up those points of objection from Rukhmabai's statements that diverted the debate from the *duties of a husband* to that of the *duties of a wife* and inverting her statement that her marriage was *more contractual* in character than *sacramental*.[28]

The case took four years and two legal suits to reach a final resolution; one in the High Court, and the other in the Appellate courts. A third was filed in the form of a defamation case, but when Dadaji was advised about the certainty of losing the case (in the first two hearings witnesses were not called, and decisions were made merely on the basis of abstract principles or legal tenets, while in the third, witnesses were called and they supported Rukhmabai's allegations), he agreed to an out-of-court settlement. The terms of this settlement were that, apart from all legal costs, a sum of Rs. 2000 was to be paid by Rukhmabai to Dadaji.[29] The resolution of the case through an informal financial transaction goes a long way to explain the cold rationale behind suits for the restitution of conjugal rights in colonial India, indicating that Hindu marriages were anything but 'holy' and 'unbreakable' unions.

---

[26] 'An Exposition of Some of the Facts of the Case of Dadaji vs. Rukhmabai', in *Law Tracts* (Bombay: Advocate of India Press, 1887), pp. 1–13.

[27] See 'Rukhmabai's reply to Dadajee's "Exposition",' 29 June 1887, Ibid., p. 3.

[28] The emphasis is mine.

[29] Mohini Varde, *Dr Rukhmabai: Ek Arth,* [Dr Rukhmabai: A Saga] (Bombay: Popular Prakashan. 1982), chapter 9.

Between the 19th and 21st of September 1885, the High Court maintained that no civilized government would force a wife against her will to live with her husband and thus declared Rukhmabai, in refusing conjugal rights to her husband, to be a free agent.[30] The controversy that followed this decision during the next three years in Maharashtra resulted in fierce debates being conducted in the English and Indian language press. The case of Rukhmabai touched some of the innermost concerns of the Hindu world; namely, who controls female sexuality? Did it belong, as Rukhmabai's later defiant stand insisted, to the woman, or did it belong to the Indian male or the ruling powers? The discursive trends within the ensuing indigenous debates revolved round 'Hindu law versus British law', with Indian men arguing that reference to the textual injunctions on the primacy of male authority over women in India could provide the only legitimate means of resolving the question. Dadaji appealed against Pinhey's judgement and, in the second hearing, the judges were put under a great deal of pressure by the indigenous press, who expressed extreme hostility to the idea of Rukhmabai being released from her conjugal obligations. The traumatized British Judges dubbed the crucial three years in which the legal battle was fought as a 'trial by newspapers.'[31] And the decision was reversed in the second hearing. Rukhmabai's biographer records that she courted imprisonment rather than join her husband.[32] The government was put in a strange position whereby the defiant gesture of Rukhmabai meant incarcerating her which was deemed by the British public in India, as well as Indian liberals, 'as repugnant to modern ideas'.[33] Therefore, in 1887, the Government of India put forth a proposal to amend Section 260 of Article 14 of the Code of Civil Procedure, 1882, relating to the execution of decrees for the restitution of conjugal rights and divorce.[34] The proposal wished to streamline the Indian legislation to follow the amended British law. Several of the proposal's provisions were quite radical; firstly, a 'decree for restitution of conjugal rights shall not be enforced by process against the person', which effectively meant that a Hindu wife could no longer be 'bodily [handed over] into the hands of the husband'; secondly that, 'when the application is made by the wife, the Court may order that, in the event of the decree not being

---

[30] Judge Pinhey's Minute in 'Dadaji Bhikaji v. Rukhmabai' (*ILR*), 9 Bom. 530, 1885, pp. 345–9.

[31] The phrase is telling in its ironic stand that Rukhmabai never had a real chance of winning justice in the courts of law due to the highly politicized nature of the case.

[32] Rukhmabai spent a day in prison according to her own testimony to a friend. In Varde, [Dr Rukhmabai], p. 62.

[33] See 'Letter containing a proposal for amending the provisions of Section 260 of the Code of Civil procedure, 1882, dated 30 March 1887'. Enclosure in the correspondence from Secretary to Government of India to all administrations regarding 'Suggested Amendment of Section 375 of the Indian Penal Code decree for restitution of conjugal rights.' File 1313, L/PJ/6/283, 1890 (hereafter 'Suggested Amendment').

[34] See 'The proposed amendment of Section 260 of C.P.C. so far as its provisions relating to conjugal rights', in JD, 1888, vol. 4, comp. no. 235 (hereafter 'Proposed Amendment').

complied with the respondent shall make payments as for alimony.' Thirdly, if the application was by the husband, then the court could order the property of the wife to be settled for the benefit of the petitioner and their children. And, finally, noncompliance with the decree was deemed as 'desertion'; a suit for judicial separation could be instituted and, where the husband was also found guilty of adultery, the wife could petition for the marriage to be dissolved.[35] The first provision, which mitigated an Indian man's command over his wife, the third provision, which was to be disputed on the grounds that many wives were too poor, and the last provision, which effectively recognized divorce, all, as we shall see presently, enraged the Indian male public.

Fourteen leading judges and civil administrators in the Bombay Presidency were requested to give their opinions; no women were consulted on an issue that directly concerned their welfare. An analysis of the emotive response of Indian opinion towards this judicial initiative is crucial to understanding the popular perceptions of marital relations in India at this time, as well as demonstrating how women's self-determination and autonomy was perceived by Indian men. In the first hearing of the Rukhmabai case, Justice Pinhey had declared that Rukhmabai could not be held responsible for her marital obligations because she was a minor at the time of the marriage and the marriage had not been consummated. However, the vernacular Press took the view that consummation was not a criterion for absolving a marriage because a Hindu marriage was a 'sacrament' and not a 'contract'. Besides, if Pinhey's arbitration were carried a little further, then "ninety nine percent of Hindu marriages would be null and void" as most of these marriages were contracted when both parties were below the age of consent.[36] *Native Opinion*, a popular paper and bastion of conservative opinion under the powerful editorship of one of the most formidable legal experts of the Bombay Presidency, V.N. Mandlik, used other arguments that allow us to easily gauge the popular notions of Hindus. The decision of the court aimed to achieve no less than a revolution in Hindu marital law. Furthermore, it caused anxiety in the whole Hindu community, which had all along believed that their marriage relations were governed by their own ancient laws. Only cruelty, it insisted, provides a wife with justifiable grounds for refusing to live with her husband; incompatibility was not a sufficient reason. According to the newspaper, therefore, Pinhey was not 'interpreting' the law but 'legislating' and therefore subverting the principles that had traditionally governed Hindu society.[37]

At this juncture, it is crucial that we do not overlook the fears expressed by the Indian male public regarding the government's imminent grant of autonomy and rights to Indian women. Male anxiety predated British legal interventions and stemmed directly from resistance campaigns by Indian women. Rebellion against the oppressive atmosphere of the husband's home formed a substantial part of the civil and criminal cases of the colonial courts in the nineteenth century. There are

---

[35] 'Suggested Amendment'.

[36] *Indu Prakash*, 10 October 1885, Native Newspaper Reports (hereafter NNR).

[37] Ibid.

many instances when the Court of Small Causes fined a father-in-law or husbands for inflicting grievous bodily harm on the person of the wife or daughter-in-law. The most common form of chastisement inflicted on wives and daughters-in-law were branding and cutting off the tip of the nose.[38] The reason attributed for such brutalities was the newfound rebellious nature of women. Mahipatram Rupram, an influential social reformer, gave graphic details of how a recalcitrant wife was dealt with in Western India, '... we sometimes see in the mofussil towns and villages a husband seizing his reluctant wife in a public street by her hair or hand, and dragging her to his house amidst the admiration of his spectators.'[39] Hindu men acted in the belief that the husband was authorized to the use of personal chastisement to exact obedience from the wife.

Court cases as well as newspaper reports reveal other forms of resistance by women who found themselves in incompatible marriages. Suicide and the killing of a husband or co-wife were some of the most common means of ending a marriage, but proved to be more a source of misery than of happiness. Women resorted to such forms of resistance because of ill treatment and neglect by husbands or relatives; newspapers often reported the death of women by suicide due to quarrels with their husbands, or due to extreme ill treatment.[40] British magistrates confirmed the resistance put up by several child-wives when they poisoned their husbands after the latter had successfully claimed a decree for restitution of conjugal rights.[41] A contemporary feminist, Pandita Ramabai, added adultery by both men and women to the list of offences resulting from the Indian style of marriage. She expressed the opinion that many virtuous wives committed suicide because they could not win the affection of wayward husbands, and that many women turned to extra-marital affairs to find love due to the neglect of their spouses. The end result was often uxoricide. Pandita Ramabai did not hold either partner responsible for such acts, but considered them to be a result of a marriage system that denied both the choice to marry and dissolve the marriage when conjugal relations broke down irretrievably.[42]

In the nineteenth century, considerable obstacles stood in the way of women attempting to redress marital injustices. Ill-treated and abandoned wives fortunate enough to have the support of parents or the extended family looked to the civil courts to intervene and resolve marital disputes. As divorce was disallowed under the British

---

[38] See chapter 4.

[39] A confidential reply by Rao Bahadur Mahipatram Rupram to A. Shewan, Acting Under-Secretary to Government, 6 August 1887; in 'Proposed Amendment'. Maharashtra State Archives (hereafter MSA).

[40] For example, on 30 June 1885, *Times of India* reported that Vithee, a 19-year-old labourer's wife, committed suicide. A postmortem revealed death due to opium poisoning; the reason given was 'quarrels with husband'. Two days later, the same paper reported the suicide of Munjoobai, a 15-year-old wife of a dock labourer. The same means were cited as well as the same reason for suicide.

[41] Letter by J.W. Walker, 6 September 1887, 'Proposed Amendment', MSA.

[42] Pandita Ramabai, *Stri-Dharma Niti* [Prescribed Laws and Duties on the Proper Conduct of Women], 3rd edn (Kedgaon: Mukti Mission Press, 1967; 1st edn 1882), p. 70.

interpretation of Hindu law, women resorted to the strategy of seeking the dissolution of their marriages on technical points of law. For example, a suit by a Hindu mother, as the guardian of her infant daughter, in favour of a declaration that the alleged marriage of the daughter with the defendant was null and void, was held to be a suit of a civil nature and was adjudicated upon.[43] Similarly, there were attempts to set aside marriages which had already taken place on various grounds for reasons such as the bride had been given away by her mother and not her father, or by her stepmother when her paternal grandmother was alive, or because she had been married to a person belonging to a different caste or that her husband had married a second wife and had previously agreed that, when such a marriage occurred, the first marriage should be considered dissolved.[44] Non-Brahmin wives also sought divorce, but due to the operation of the colonial reinterpretation of Hindu law, it was increasingly difficult for women to exercise this option.[45]

If we judge by statistics alone (see Table 6.1 below) the cases which annually came before the civil courts in the Bombay Presidency (including subordinate, district and high courts) between 1881 and 1885 consisted of 727 suits for enforcing decrees for the restitution of conjugal rights and 81 suits for the dissolution of marriages. The latter were usually between Christian husbands and wives, while the former involved Hindus and Muslims. Not all of these suits were by deserted wives seeking legal remedies to their dysfunctional marriages. Guardians and parents of young girl-wives brought quite a few of these cases to the court in their anxiety to protect them; presumably they followed the technical route described in the previous paragraph.

Table 6.1 Numbers of civil suits for enforcement of marriage contracts and the dissolution of marriages in the Bombay Presidency, 1881–1885

Year	Subordinate Judge' Courts		District Courts		High Court	
	Enforcement	Dissolution	Enforcement	Dissolution	Enforcement	Dissolution
1881	120	4	11	4	2	8
1882	123	6	12	1	3	2
1883	106	5	29	4	4	8
1884	135	10	10	4	2	6
1885	155	12	12	5	3	2
Total	639	37	74	18	14	26

(Source: Letter from Rao Bahadur Mahadeo Govind Ranade, Poona, to the Chief Secretary to Government, Bombay, 19 September 1887, Judicial Department, 1888 [Acts], vol. 4, comp. no. 235, MSA.)

---

[43] See the letter of Dayaram Gidumal, Acting Assistant Judge, Ahmedabad, to the Secretary to Government, 15 September 1887, 'Proposed Amendment', MSA.

[44] Ibid., p. 173.

[45] See chapters 3 and 4 for details.

Given the factors that militated against women seeking legal redress, it is surprising that so many cases came to court. Achieving a remedy through civil courts was not a popular method, especially for women who had very few resources or did not know that Act XV of 1877, Schedule II, provided an unwilling wife the option of serving six months' imprisonment in a civil jail instead of acquiescing to fulfil her conjugal duties. Mahipatram Rupram, a district judge, recorded that *vakils* [pleaders] never provided this vital information to female clients, despite the fact that they were forfeiting at least one source of income.[46] Furthermore, Rupram shows how it was only the wide publicity given to the Dadaji v Rukhmabai case in the vernacular newspapers that alerted the public in the remoter parts of Maharashtra to the fact that a wife could actually choose imprisonment in preference to the company of her husband. The anxiety of Indian male lawyers to restrict women's access to knowledge that could potentially have empowered them speaks volumes of their fear of women undertaking independent action. It is also an indicator of their desire to maintain the status quo that privileged men by containing the legitimate claims of rebellious wives in a society where the traditional power networks were being eroded as the colonial courts grew in influence. A by-product of this was the empowerment of women, who increasingly sought the British law courts which were determined to uphold the popular perception that that the Raj stood for the 'rule of law' and justice. It was precisely the Maharashtrian women's acts of assertion that led to a backlash from the indigenous male population.[47]

An interesting trend in the assertive acts of women is that many female clients preferred to use the criminal courts, as they were less expensive and more effective than the civil courts. Maharashtrian wives were also aware of the fact that, even if they applied for restitution of conjugal rights and won the case, the civil courts could not in a practical sense enforce their decree. By practicing polygamy, a husband could always informally defy court orders by taking new wives and ignoring or maltreating his previous wife.[48] In their replies to the government regarding changing the laws that governed suits over the restitution of conjugal right and separation, Mahipatram Rupram and M.G. Ranade pointed out that even illiterate women knew that they could obtain payments as alimony from their husbands by applying to a Magistrate;[49] moreover, many of these applications were likely to be successful. Between 1881 and 1885 (see Table 6.2 below), a total of 2,874 wives brought cases against their husbands before the criminal courts of Bombay Presidency, demanding redress in the form of maintenance payments for the ill-treatment that they had suffered.

---

[46] See his letter dated 6 August 1887, 'Proposed Amendment', MSA.

[47] Ibid.

[48] See the reply of Tirmal Rao Venkatesh Inamdar, retired judge, Court of Small Causes, Dharwar, 14 August 1887, in 'Proposed Amendment'.

[49] Testified by the peasant's quotation at the start of this chapter.

Table 6.2 Maintenance suits filed in criminal courts in the Bombay Presidency, 1881–1885

Year	Persons Accused	Persons Convicted	Persons Acquitted
1881	423	314	109
1882	447	332	115
1883	462	359	103
1884	735	382	352
1885	807	389	418
Total	2874	1776	1097

(Source: As for Table 6.1).

Not all of the suits listed in Table 6.2 were brought by adult wives; some of the cases were lodged by the parents of neglected child-wives. The statistics were compiled by M.G. Ranade, a celebrated social reformer and seasoned legal expert, who argued that 'the large majority of the cases under chapter thirty-six are undoubtedly due to the neglect of marital duties by husbands towards their wives'.[50] He uncovered considerable evidence of women's dissatisfaction with contemporary marriage laws; moreover, he recognized that they were not inclined to see the status quo continue, especially when they perceived the Raj as a good government that looked after its subjects irrespective of gender. Ranade's close observations and his everyday interactions in the courts led him to become a prominent advocate of divorce, although he stood alone and unsupported by his fellow reformers.

Given indigenous and colonialist constructions of the Indian woman as passive, even a few isolated cases of women resorting to the courts would be highly significant. Yet the statistics on matrimonial disputes are considerably higher. If we combine civil and criminal cases, thousands of women every year sought legal redress to improve the quality of their domestic lives in the Bombay Presidency. Contemporary Indian men were quick to realize the subversive nature and veiled implications of the assertive acts of women. When we understand the constraints on women actually bringing a case to court, it is clear that Indian women were resisting a system of marriage that perpetuated maladjusted conjugal unions; in other words, what we witness during this period amounts to a great rebellion of wives against ill treatment or abandonment. By signalling autonomy and self-determination, the women's actions led to the resident patriarchs of nineteenth-century India formulating a formidable and negative response. The significance of this wives' rebellion needs to be understood if we are to properly assess the nature of debates set off by the Rukhmabai and age of consent controversy.

---

[50] Reply by Rao Bahadur Mahadev Govind Ranade to The Chief Secretary to Government, 19 September 1887, 'Proposed Amendment', MSA.

A Question of Ownership: Indian Male Discourse on Marriage and Female Sexuality

Through the rational and deliberate exercise of free will, discontented wives increasingly used the colonial courts to get recalcitrant husbands to acknowledge their marital duties and obligations. This did not go unnoticed by Indian men. The catapulting of the Rukhmabai case onto the national scene provided an instance for indigenous male agency to curb the power of Indian women. In a bid to oppose radical change in Indian marriage arrangements, Indian men applied immense pressure on the government, arguing that the Rukhmabai case was an exception to the rule. However, as we have seen from the court cases, there is plenty of evidence to suggest that Rukhmabai's agency in resolving her unhappy marriage was far from an isolated case. Instead, her case ought to be seen as symptomatic of a much broader and more general feeling of discontent among Indian wives who increasingly sought the judicial arm of the state to assert their claims and hold their husbands responsible for marital commitments.

Indian men used arguments about 'tradition' to legitimize their claims over female sexuality; in doing so, they were able to play on the British state's sensitivity towards Indian 'religion' and religious matters. By selectively quoting the pronouncements of Manu, Acharkhand, Panini and Mitakshara in the *shastras* men attempted to justify their arguments of what the supposed duties of women to family and state should be and, in doing so, demonstrate their right to authority over women. They caricatured woman's 'nature' as weak, fickle and inherently irrational, and argued that it was these traits which caused wives to rebel against their husbands. The way in which they used the *shastras* can be seen in examples such as the lengthy diatribe submitted to the *Times of India* in response to Rukhmabai's letters, which described her behaviour as 'irresponsible' and 'insolent'.[51] The writer argued that Rukhmabai was deluded about the options open to an Indian woman. According to him, the *shastras* identified only four classes of women; the first were intensely devoted to God, the second were intensely devoted to husbands, the third were equally divided between devotion to God and to their husband, and the last were solely devoted to their husbands, believing them to be incarnations of God. Of these, only the first group could renounce their responsibility to their husband; the second category committed *sati* [widow-burning], the third remarried after the death of the first but lived intensely for a second husband as though the first had never died, and the last led an exemplary life of chastity after the death of the first. 'No other possibilities for women in Hindu life existed other than these four', he asserted, arguing that, as Rukhmabai belonged to none of these categories, she was transgressing ancient laws.[52]

Moreover, Hindu religious authorities, whose opinions were solicited by the government on the restitution of conjugal rights and divorce, developed similar arguments regarding the nonperson status of Indian wives. Referring to ancient texts to prove that women had no decision-making or, taking powers, Narayan

---

[51] Cited in Varde, [Dr Rukhmabai], p. 42.

[52] Ibid.

Shastri Gokhale argued that the *kanyadan* [giving away of the virgin bride] ceremony, an essential marriage rite, represented, '...the doing away of one's ownership in a thing and then creating therein the ownership of another, and thus is created the ownership of the receiving party in the girl that is given just as in the case of the cow etc ...'[53] The notion that a wife represented a 'nonperson' or 'object', whose status was comparable with a cow was a stark illustration of the extent to which he believed a woman should not be granted agency in marital matters. Hindu law did not grant women essential freedoms, he argued, as the nature of Indian womanhood was 'fickle', which meant that wives quarrelled with their husbands and would leave them on the slightest pretext for other men. Furthermore, he added, the functioning of the state would be adversely affected as men would not be able to carry out their duties effectively if women were not 'properly controlled' by 'bodily chastisement',[54] the only means that inconsistent wives would understand. He warned that, if the state abolished imprisonment for the execution of the decree for the enforcement of restitution of conjugal rights, it would ultimately be the loser. By invoking the *shastras* and combining it with the idea that change amounted to a threat to the state, he had developed an argument deliberately designed to directly appeal to British sensibilities.

In demarcating gender roles, the most popular tenet taken from the ancient past was the notion that a woman's place was at home and her personality should be completely merged with her husband's. 'Obedience', they argued was a wife's prime duty towards her husband. The first hearing of and decision on Rukhmabai's case, which had upheld her rights, was interpreted as upholding a woman's disobedient act, and supporting her defiance of her supreme Lord and master—her husband. Disobedient wives, Indian men argued, were being encouraged by the state to rebellious and defiant acts that were wrecking homes and ruining families all over India. They alleged that labouring-class women were disrupting the domestic life of the countryside by constantly appealing to courts for maintenance or damages from husbands on grounds considered by men to be frivolous.[55] Male opinion, as expressed in newspapers, argued that British laws were subverting Hindu tradition by awarding a 'premium to disobedient wives'.[56]

In the Rukhmabai case, the colonial state had initially upheld Indian women's claims to autonomy. However, B.G. Tilak's agitation on behalf of the traditionalist school put pressure on the Government to re-hear the case, with the episode providing him one of the earliest issues to attack the reformist school led by M.G. Ranade. The

---

[53] Narayan Shastri Gokhale, 16 August 1887, in 'Proposed Amendment'.

[54] Ibid.

[55] An editorial in the *Bombay Gazette* expressed anger at women demanding redress through courts by citing cases where wives had successfully won damages for ill treatment. A woman who had secured maintenance of Rs. 250 and had the court dissolve her marriage on account of her husband suffering from leprosy was discussed at length in the press. From Varde, [Dr Rukhmabai], p. 43.

[56] *Sind Times*, 12 March 1887, NNR.

core of his argument lay in the fact that, besides being indefensible on moral grounds, the whole case had been judged on legal premises that, he argued, were incorrect as ancient Hindu law did not recognize female autonomy; according to this argument, a woman's consent was not necessary for a marriage to be validated as long as the proper rituals had taken place. Therefore, to rule that Rukhmabai was now a free woman on the basis that she had been married as a minor without her consent meant that no marriage in India was valid as almost every marriage in India was a child marriage.[57] His arguments, with their legal precision and brilliance, appealed not only to conservatives but to liberals as well. Even liberals amongst the Indian educated public were concerned that increased leniency would remove the existing deterrent to disobedient wives, a phenomenon that was perceived to be a growing social problem in India. A prominent leader of the movement for higher education of women and one of the founders of the Poona High School for Girls, S.P. Pandit argued on the basis of using popular opinion as a 'plebiscite' for bringing legal changes. According to him, even though Hindu law did not prescribe imprisonment for a recalcitrant wife and the code that empowered the court to do so was imported from English canonical law, contemporary opinion, as revealed in the discussions of the press, approved this move[58] despite the fact that it was alien to Hindu law. Imprisonment, he agreed, was a punishment that a rebellious wife deserved and 'the orthodox public considers the law about the imprisonment as a very valuable warning to wives.'[59] Female sexuality and its regulation was, according to him, a matter for men alone to decide and, if a foreign law could assist this process, Indian patriarchs were happy to utilize it.[60]

Reformers and conservatives were united in their hostility to divorce in India. In their responses to the government's call for amending the law on the restitution of conjugal rights, more than half of Indian reformers and conservatives replied that, although imprisonment was a foreign concept, it had to be retained as a means of imposing discipline as women had no capacity for attachment, as few owned property. Indeed, aside from M.G. Ranade, every Indian male luminary who was called on to give his opinion on the introduction of divorce firmly opposed it. Many of them argued that the Rukhmabai's case ought to be used as a warning to the larger community of women of a wife's proper behaviour, suggesting that a display of leniency would revolutionize marital arrangements and reduce the moral standards of Indian society to that of the dissolute West.[61] Women's agency as witnessed in their seeking legal redress in the colonial courts of nineteenth-century India terrified the Indian patriarchy, resulting in their increasingly aggressive reaction about how a woman should behave

---

[57] B.G. Tilak, *Kesari*, 4 October 1884.

[58] Shankar P. Pandit, 22 September 1887, 'Proposed Amendment', MSA.

[59] Ibid.

[60] In a thoughtful essay on the Bengali opposition to the Age of Consent, Tanika Sarkar has argued convincingly that Indian men were tutoring the colonial government about effective 'patriarchal management'. See 'Rhetoric Against Age of Consent', 1869–78.

[61] Nineteenth-century Indian discourses on sexuality also created a stereotype of the 'decrepit' Western morality.

within a marriage and their justifications for controlling women's sexuality. It was thus not passivity of the Indian women but its polar opposite—their agency—that had galvanized Indian men into taking action against them.

Disobedient Wives as a Threat to Society: Judicial Discourse on Marriage and Female Sexuality

In the year following Rukhmabai's first hearing, the Indian media relentlessly pursued what the judges complained was a 'trial by newspapers'. However, when the views of the British judges themselves are scrutinized, we see how Indian conservatives had strongly influenced the minds of British legal commentators. They also converged with the government's views, as seen in Justice Farran's decision in the second suit, which entirely reversed the first judgement on Rukhmabai's case. In his Minute, Farran ruled that, as Rukhmabai had been married in a consensual Hindu marriage ritual, her defiant action demonstrated 'a great contempt of the Hindu law'.[62] Farran's decision was a product of the judicial discourse on the amendment of procedural law governing conjugal rights and the question of divorce and demonstrated the way in which it had succumbed to the constant haranguing and bullying tactics of the indigenous press.

Of the many arguments put forth by the Indian orthodoxy, the one that caught the imagination of the judiciary was the one that focussed on the potential threat that disobedient wives posed to both society and, by extension, to the state. The authoritative sixty-page treatise produced by Justice Raymond West provides a fine illustration of how the judiciary responded to this idea of unruly wives terrorizing the husband, family and the state.[63] It proved to be the most authoritative judgement that was produced and was the one consulted by all other judges when considering the proposed Amendment of the Act. Each judge ended his own Minute by heartily agreeing with West's arguments.[64] A powerful argument on the whole issue of restitution of conjugal rights was built up by West, who took the decision that it was best to adhere to the principle of noninterference at the cost of the female's right of self-will. He argued that, if sanctions and procedures in restitution of conjugal rights were changed to accommodate females' free will, Hindu society would descend into chaos and law and order would break down, as it was only Hindu religious laws controlling the chastity of women that prevented universal licentiousness from prevailing. He also referred to the texts on Hindu law in order to demonstrate that, in the 'less-civilised' India, a woman actually became a part of the husband's subcaste, as she left her father's *gotra* on her marriage. Therefore, if the husband showed 'sustenance and kindness', in turn the wife would show 'subordination and obedience', meaning that the regulation of duties could then be 'in a great and useful measure defined and enforced by the State'.[65]

---

[62] His judgement is reprinted in *Times of India*, 4 March 1887.

[63] Minute by Justice Raymond West, 5 August 1887, 'Proposed Amendment', MSA.

[64] Ibid.

[65] Ibid.

Besides upholding patriarchal Indian society, judicial discourse successfully usurped political functions and effectively became repressive by elevating the concept of 'duty' over that of 'rights'. The duties of a woman were towards the man and the man's towards society and society's towards the state. West's treatise did consider in some detail the customary laws, which allowed for *kadimod* [separation] and *ghatasphot* [divorce]. However, no British legal expert was in favour of giving them importance as it conflicted directly with the court authority's ever-widening hold over civil society. Customary laws, he opined, could not be, '...extensively replaced without great risk of disintegration of the indigenous family system and of the whole scheme of society that rests upon it'.[66] Because he saw the task of the judiciary as promoting an 'ordered society' and combating the threat of 'social chaos', it was inevitable that the rights of women to assert themselves would be discarded.

Both the indigenous elites and judicial discourse shared the same opinions on the 'nature' of lower classes and castes and their attitude towards sex and sexuality. Indian elites held lower-caste women to be 'wild and passionate', a view shared by Victorian judges. A popular misconception held that the lower-class males bought wives for a certain price and, if the law failed to regulate the behaviour of these women, they would neglect their husbands to indulge their lovers. It was therefore important, as West had argued, 'to protect the marital rights of a labouring man who needs the services of his wife', so that he could function better and participate fully in the economy.[67] By upsetting their marriage structure, not only would licentiousness become endemic but crimes of violence would result wherein the rural masses would take coercive measures themselves rather than go to court. Any system of marriage, whether sacred or contractual, he asserted, could have detrimental effects on individual women, but the very existence of society demanded it. Women, he felt, could gain immensely from the institution of marriage as long as they did not breach any recognized social relations and laws. Thus, in his opinion, the state was only guarding the 'social integrity' of Indian society.

Finally, and somewhat contrarily, judicial discourse succumbed to the Orientalist notions of a submissive Indian womanhood. Justice West, for example, ignored the reality he saw every day in the courts when he romanticized the feelings of Indian women on marital relations in ways that reveal how thoroughly he had absorbed indigenous male discourse on womanhood. To him, an Indian woman:

> ... looks on herself as created and given by the Gods to be the completion of her husband's life, and never for a moment questions the divine ordinance ... a Hindu woman would look on it as a kind of sacrilege to claim equality with her husband.[68]

---

[66] Ibid.
[67] Ibid.
[68] Ibid.

The image of a self-effacing wife, ready to respond to every call of her husband no matter how disagreeable, implied that a woman could never desire to be an agent, a theory furiously refuted by Tarabai Shinde in her analysis of *stridharma* [women's duties] as practised by Maharashtrian women in the nineteenth century.[69] In any case, within the legal discourse, the Indian woman had become a subject without agency. West qualified this statement by adding that Western notions and education could probably train a Hindu girl, '... to a higher sense of her own rights and capacities, but she cannot sincerely embrace this creed of freedom, equality, and wedlock of souls, and at the same time remain sincerely a Hindu.'[70] In other words, in order to be a good 'Hindu' woman, the Indian wife had to become a nonperson. An Indian wife was one who acted in the family's interest, drained of any self-interest, self-will or self-awareness. What we notice from a study of the history on marriage reform regarding execution of decrees for restitution of conjugal rights and its related issue of separation and divorce was that the British lawyers had turned completely about-face between the time of the Ardaseer v. Perozeboye case in 1856, when they had deemed an Indian wife be treated as a *feme sole* on the basis of the Indian marriage being a 'contract', and the Rukhmabai case in 1885, when they judged Indian women to be nonpersons and Indian marriage to be a 'sacrament'. This shift can be directly traced to pressures brought to bear on the colonial state by Indian male opinion. In fact, indigenous sections decided what constituted appropriate Indian female behaviour, and the judiciary and the government then ultimately provided the mechanisms to uphold it.

The picture that emerges is of a colonial state buffeted by various strains of indigenous discourse. It therefore seems wholly illogical to portray the debates on the restitution of conjugal rights and divorce as a hegemonic enterprise of the British state in India. In any case, the fact that a Hindu woman was now defined as a nonautonomous person meant that the indigenous and judicial discourse on female sexuality trapped Hindu women in a textual representation of what a Hindu woman *ought to be* rather than *what she was*.

It was precisely the danger of remaining a 'representation' that made Maharashtrian women insist on 'experience' as the primary category of analysis in their delineation of the position of Indian women; it is these perspectives that we examine now.

---

[69] Tarabai Shinde argued instead that *stridharma* was an ideal prescribed within Hindu texts but could not be practised by contemporary Maharashtrian wives as their husbands did not behave in a manner that deserved such devotion. See *Stripurushtulana Athava Striya Va Purush Yant Sahasi Kon He Spasta Karun Dakavinyakarita Ha Nibandh* [Women and Men, A Comparison or an Essay Showing Who is More Wicked], ed. S.J. Malshe, 2nd edn (Bombay: Mumbai Marathi Grantha Sangrahalaya Publications, 1975; 1st edn, 1882), pp. 1–9.

[70] Minute by Justice West, 'Proposed Amendment', MSA.

The Creation of a Counter-Discourse: Women on the Institutions of Child-Marriage and Family

In a previous section, it was demonstrated that Indian men selectively recalled the ancient past through the *shastras* and constructed a discourse on the deportment of wives and wifehood by fixating on their *duties* alone regardless of their rights. By comparing and contrasting male to female discourses, the next two sections will show that women shifted their focus from the *shastras* of the olden days to concentrate on the *present* that was constructed through the cumulative experiences of contemporary women. I shall argue that, by stepping away from the misogynistic *shastras* which they had come to learn were major obstacles in achieving the female autonomy and self-improvement outlined in chapters 2 and 3, women were able to counter male arguments on the institution of child marriage and the related issue of arranged marriages. In the late 1880s, having benefited from the emerging women's movement in Maharashtra and taking confidence from the collective solidarity of women of all religions and caste backgrounds, namely the *bhaginivarg* and European feminists, they effectively managed to alter the focus of the debate on child marriage from one of 'age' to a more complex one involving 'consent' as well, lobbying firmly for state intervention on a issue that they realized had great implications for women's welfare.

Between June and September 1885, Rukhmabai published a series of letters in the *Times of India* on the subjects of infant marriage and enforced widowhood. Her case, as we have already seen, elicited a strong response from Indian males. Indian women engaged in an equally vociferous display of *bhaginivarg* [sisterhood], campaigning in the press and through women's organizations. The discussions generated amongst women on this issue did not stop with the passing of the Act in March 1891 but continued in the women's press right up until the time came for the next round of negotiations in the 1920s. Rukhmabai's predicament was immediately taken up by the women's organizations in Maharashtra and a Rukhmabai Defence Committee was formed which included prominent European and Indian women leaders as well as some sympathetic men who held a liberal disposition.[71] Rukhmabai was initially hesitant about using her own name, fearful of the repercussions on the *bhaginivarg* [sisterhood]. Instead, she adopted the pseudonym of 'The Hindu lady'. However, she changed her mind in 1887, when the press spread scurrilous rumours that a man in fact composed the 'The Hindu Lady's' letters.[72] During the same period, Behramji Malabari wrote a treatise addressing marriage reforms; his action prompted reformers from all provinces of India to give their support to the Age of Consent Bill. Rukhmabai had followed the progress of his propaganda and was prompted to express her own views on the subject. While acknowledging the gratitude of Indian women for his exertions, she constructed a gendered critique for the abolition of child marriage that was startlingly different from that of Malabari. At the time of the

---

[71] Details are in Varde, [Dr Rukhmabai].

[72] In 'Rukhmabai's reply to Dadajee's "Exposition"', *Law Tracts*, pp. 9–10.

publication of her letters, the case was heard in the Bombay high court; the court's decision came three weeks after the publication of her second letter on 'Enforced Widowhood'. In the first letter on 'Infant Marriage' she stated that she was, '... one of those unfortunate Hindu women, whose hard lot it is to suffer the unnameable miseries entailed by the custom of early marriage. This wicked practice has destroyed the happiness of my life.'[73] However, her observations were also drawn from the lives of her female friends and were therefore formulated according to the cumulative experiences of actual women. Rukhmabai did not resort to the courts out of simple individual self-interest; her action was a result of her consciousness of *bhaginivarg* [sisterhood], developed through her participation in the activities of organizations such as Arya Mahila Samaj and the Prarthana Samaj. The Maharashtrian women's movement in the late nineteenth century enabled Rukhmabai to observe and relate with women who possessed a fairly developed consciousness on women's rights.[74] Drawing strength from this *bhaginivarg,* she stated that the institution of child marriage cut across caste and class considerations and adversely affected all age groups and both sexes, although 'women', she concluded, were its 'greatest victims'.[75] According to her, infant marriage presented a persistent obstacle to the psychological development of a female child, stultifying her personality by denying her higher education. The way that Indian marital relationships were structured, she claimed, cramped women's ability to freely express their views and robbed them of any initiative.

This sense of *bhaginivarg* is also apparent in the activities of other women. The debate in the press over legislation on the restitution of conjugal rights and separation were issues that women began to engage with and write about in their correspondences with each other. Their writings confirm Rukhmabai's analysis of marital relations. A consideration of women's perspectives on this important question reveals that humanitarian and feminist concerns motivated women to agitate against the custom of child marriage. The unhappiness and terror of a child-wife, the strain in conjugal relations that led to many wives committing suicide, the death of women in their prime due to early motherhood and widowhood; all of these were seen as the terrible consequences of early marriage. Women's views stood starkly contrasted with men's in respect of this issue. A great number of women considered ill-treatment and incompatibility as the main effects of child marriage and as issues for redress. In the years leading to the passing of the Act, they hotly debated the issues surrounding child marriage and arranged marriages in women's journals and newspapers.

There was unanimity of opinion amongst women about child- and arranged marriages causing conflict between couples.[76] Women considered the lack of conjugal

---

[73] Rukhmabai, 'Infant marriage', *Times of India*, 26 June 1885, p. 4.

[74] See chapters 2 and 3 for details on nineteenth-century women's organizations.

[75] Rukhmabai, 'Infant marriage'.

[76] 'Eka sushiksit stri kadun' [By an educated lady], 'Gulabbai ani Shevatibai yancha bodhpar samvad' [Instructive debates between Gulabbai and Shevatibai], *Arya Bhagini*, June 1891, 52–3.

felicity between couples as a direct result of the Indian institution of marriage. The prevailing system of arranged marriages without heed to the preference of the boy or the girl, the act of demanding dowry and the young age of the couple were considered to be the principal reasons for marital disharmony, finally causing unhappy wives to rebel. Women felt that mutual love and affection was very difficult to cultivate within the limits of an imposed contract of arranged marriage. The chances of a learned man being married to a woman who was uninterested in sharing his intellectual pursuits or an intelligent girl being prevented from pursuing further study due to early marriage or the whims of her husband were equally high. Either way, women recognized that such marriages could only result in bitter acrimony. This was amply proved by the case of Rukhmabai who was married to a man who shared no common interests with her; their childhood betrothal was sufficient to ruin both their lives. Women recognized that, whenever such a mismatch occurred, a woman bore it silently as no options were offered to her, while a disgruntled husband sought solace outside the marriage, either through remarriage or by resorting to mistresses or prostitutes. It is therefore unsurprising that women showed a strong preference for adult marriages and choice in marriage rather than arranged marriages. Moreover, as they believed that domestic strife was due to the unhappiness and discontent of young wives, they came up with the radical suggestion that choosing a spouse should not only be the man's prerogative but the female should also be consulted.[77] This was the main reason why a revival of *swayamvar* [the ceremony by which a woman chose her spouse in an open competition between male suitors] supposed to have existed in the Vedic times, was enthusiastically called for, rather than an uncritical nostalgia for the 'golden age'.[78] It is important to distinguish the adherence to a Vedic past by nineteenth-century Indian feminists arising out of a concern for granting 'choice' of partners in marriage from the 'new women' of current Hindu fundamentalist groups whose political agendas and programmes are tinged with communalism.[79]

Given the absence of divorce, women argued that there were many extenuating reasons explaining why wives deserted their husbands, committed suicide or homicide. Even though, with good reason, women hesitated about writing explicitly on the subject of divorce, the statistical analysis of the previous section reveals many abandoned or neglected wives sought separation and maintenance for themselves and their children. In marked contrast to Malabari's proposals, Rukhmabai recommended divorce as the primary means of resolving domestic tensions within a marriage that had broken down irrevocably.[80] At the height of conservative reaction from indigenous quarters, Indian women advocated some radical measures that represented a potential revolution in Indian conjugal affairs.

---

[77] Ibid.

[78] Indian women's interpretation of 'golden age' theories is in chapters 2 and 3.

[79] 'Women and Religious Nationalism in India', in A. Basu (ed.), *Bulletin of Concerned Asian Scholars*, 25/3 (October–December 1993).

[80] Rukhmabai, 'Infant marriage', p. 4.

The issue of child marriage was considered to be central to the deplorable condition of Indian women. Most women writing at this time were relating their own personal experience of such a marriage, capturing vividly the tension and anxiety felt by a child-wife. Physical and mental immaturity was considered as a major cause of maladjusted behaviour in the home of the in-laws. One of the main preoccupations of educated women was to find a resolution to this problem. Most agreed that no girl below the age of 15 should be given in marriage, thereby ensuring that she properly understood the institution of marriage as well as what was expected of her in the new environment of her in-laws.[81] A traumatized child-wife often became a rebellious one and usually faced a great deal of hardship in her in-laws' house, to the extent that many were driven to commit suicide. It was agreed amongst women that an underage girl-bride simply could not adjust to the rigorous discipline of her in-law's home, an experience graphically described by Kanthabai Tarkhadkar in the following extract:

A young girl blossoms in the warmth of her parent's home and like a streak of lightning glows in the loving company of her siblings. Here, she has no clue to the notion of what a husband is or for that matter—an in-law. Alas! The days of fun and frolic draw to a close when she reaches maturity. She is suddenly transported to the *karagriha* [prison] called married life and then her condition is so pathetic that even *Saraswati* [Goddess of Learning] would be at a loss of words to describe it. How can one expect a child to love a stranger as her husband? How can she understand how to behave with her sisters-in-law who constantly prey on her like tigresses? She is then referred to as obstinate, uncaring and insolent and soon she becomes a subject of abuse. That's why, although alive she is as good as dead, for the benefit of one's society and country. Surely ninety percent of women are facing this situation.[82]

The problems of a child-wife were compounded by the lack of support they received from their husbands. Women realized that child-wives were often married to teenage husbands who were too young to fully comprehend the feelings of alienation that their wives experienced. In addition, because of their age, they were unable to exercise any real authority in the home and prevent their wives from being ill-treated.[83] Women reformers were aware of the helplessness of younger males due to their financial dependence and hierarchical forms of control in a tightly structured patriarchal institution, and therefore also campaigned for a ban on child marriages on the grounds that young men would also continue their education uninterrupted and marry only

---

[81] Anandibai Lad, 'Lavkar lagna karnyache chal' [The custom of early marriage], *Arya Bhagini*, March 1886, 3–6; Kanthabai Tarkhadkar, 'Striyanchi sthiti' [The condition of women], *Arya Bhagini*, April 1892, 26–9; Rukhmabai, 'Infant marriage', Ibid.

[82] Kanthabai, Ibid., 26.

[83] Rukhmabai's letter, Ibid., p. 1; Lakshmibai Dravid, ''Lahanpani Lagne va Strishikshan' [Child Marriage and Women's Education], in *Deshseva Nibandhmala* [Essays in Service of the Nation] (Pune: Vijayanand Press, 1896), pp. 22–3; Kanthabai, Ibid., p. 27.

when they were old enough to look after their wives' welfare, independent of the interference of their elders.

A prominent Marathi journal, *Masik Manoranjan*, interviewed various women activists of Maharashtra who had participated in the Age of Consent agitation. Kashibai Kanitkar, an important member of the Arya Mahila Samaj, asserted that 99 percent of marriages were unhappy, and argued that raising the Age of Consent would correct this sad state of affairs. Although not all women resorted to divorce, many felt like doing so, she stated, because they felt deceived by marital arrangements in which they were not consulted.[84] She argued that no girl should be below the age of fourteen and no boy below the age of twenty at the time of marriage; in addition, both the sexes should have freedom to choose their partners so that if the marriage broke down, 'they will not point fingers at others but at themselves'.[85] Kashibai's views stemmed from the observation that only adults could shoulder the responsibility of maintaining the important institution of marriage.

Another key argument against early marriage was the subsequent neglect of a girl's education.[86] According to feminists of the time, widening a girl's horizons of knowledge through a sound school education would help her to comprehend marriage better. As Tarabai Nabar put it:

> The responsibility of looking after a home ensures that she remains uneducated and her life passes by in utter ignorance. Her illiteracy also means that she does not know about household management or how to conduct conjugal relations. There will be a wedge in their relationship if the husband is considerably older than her. If he is unable to secure a loving companionship from her, he will go to mistresses and ruination of the man follows while the wife is thrown into a well of misery. Child marriage has all these negative accompaniments.[87]

With child marriage, a woman lost out in three vital ways: First, she lost the opportunity for self-development and acquiring the skills that would enable her to manage a household. Secondly, because of her ignorance of the nature of the conjugal relationship, she would be unable to fulfil all her wifely duties. These first two factors inevitably led to the marital bond breaking down irretrievably.

One of the core reasons for attacking the institution of child marriage was its obvious link to early widowhood.[88] The terrible change that a woman underwent as a widow was known to every Maharashtrian woman and was often described in women's

---

[84] In Sarojini Vaidya, *Shrimati Kashibai Kanitkar: Atmacharitra Ani Charitra* [Mrs Kashibai Kanitkar, Autobiography and Biography] (Bombay: Popular Prakashan, 1979), p. 231.

[85] Ibid., pp. 231–2.

[86] See chapter 3 for more details.

[87] Tarabai Nabar, 'The Evil Effects of Child marriage', *Maharashtra Mahila*, May 1901, 235.

[88] See section titled 'The Question of Widowhood and State Intervention' in chapter 3 for more details.

literature and journals. Interestingly, women acknowledged and accepted the physical needs of the female sex.[89] Feminist writers asked the parents of female children whether they preferred continuing the custom of child marriage or to live with the loss of their reputation. Since a child-wife faced the prospect of widowhood, the chances of her being involved in clandestine relations was higher and likely to lead to the occurrence of criminal acts such as infanticide and the family losing their social status.[90] Instead of focusing on controlling a widow's sexuality (as the male discourse did), they addressed the origins of early widowhood, linking it directly to child marriage. Maharashtrian women were in the forefront of demands for child marriage to be abolished; after the passing of the Age of Consent Act, many of them urged Indian states like Baroda to adopt it too. One of the main reasons they gave was to lessen the number of child-widows.[91]

Women's discourse on child marriage and its effects clearly establishes their humanitarian and feminist concerns. If we turn towards the male discourse on the Age of Consent, a totally different picture emerges. In his 'Notes' Malabari painted a powerful picture of a society ravaged by incapable adults and sickly children, over-population and poverty; all factors which led to epidemics breaking out. He argued that child marriage was a catalyst for, '... the breaking down of constitutions and the ushering of disease. The giving up of studies on the part of the boy-husband, the birth of sickly children, the necessity of feeding too many mouths, poverty and dependence ...'[92] The state, he insisted, had to address the question purely on economic grounds, otherwise 'over-population in poverty',[93] would occur. In the late nineteenth century, fears of racial degeneration and public health were powerful arguments in the discourse of the indigenous sections that were attempting to reform cultural practice. Even enlightened reformers and staunch friends of women, such as M.G. Ranade, held a similar view. Ranade asserted that early marriage led to early consummation, and thus to:

> ... the physical deterioration of the race, that it sits as a heavy weight on our rising generation, enchains their aspirations, denies them the romance and freedom of youth, cools their love of study, checks enterprise, and generally dwarfs their growth, and fills the country with pauperism, bred of over-population by weaklings and sickly people, and lastly, that it leads in many cases to all the horrors of early widowhood.[94]

---

[89] Ibid., and chapter 4.

[90] Kanthabai, [The condition of women], *Arya Bhagini*, p. 28.

[91] Editorial, *Maharashtra Mahila*, June 1901, 243–4.

[92] Behramji M. Malabari, 'Notes on infant-marriage and enforced widowhood', *Selections from the Records*, Government of India, Home Department, V\23\49\223, p. 3, OIOC.

[93] Ibid., pp. 3–4.

[94] Letter dated 12 February 1885, From 'Papers Relating to Infant Marriage and Enforced Widowhood in India', *Selections from the Records*, p. 92.

Male discourses concerned themselves with the collective good, whilst women gave precedence to the individual well-being, physical and mental, of the woman involved;[95] men tended to give scant consideration to the disastrous effects of child marriage on the life chances of the girl. On other vital questions of women's education, social liberals used Social Darwinist arguments. Dr K.R. Kirtikar, for example, the President of the Pathare Prabhu Reform Society and a Surgeon at Grant Medical College, argued in many lectures that the only reason why a woman was entitled to education was because she was the 'Mother of the Indian race', and hence needed to have a good grounding in health and hygiene in order to raise robust children.[96] Such arguments show that, in their approach to gender-related reform issues, men appear to be less liberal reformers than 'nationalists'. It is little wonder, therefore, that women showed distrust of male reformers and their rhetoric.

The failure to acknowledge gender inequalities in marital relationships is starkly exposed in another trend within male discourse. The majority of liberal and conservative opinion argued that women themselves were active proponents of the institution of child marriage and opposed all reforms; moreover, widows themselves did not want remarriage and therefore legislation did not need reform as the changes would evolve more slowly over a passage of time.[97] Some prominent Indian officials considered child marriage to be a recent phenomenon due entirely to 'the whims of females...who not only put up, but compel their male members to bring about infant-marriages...'[98] For the noninterventionist or 'reform from within' group, women in India were conservative by nature. They imbibed the ideology of Hindu tradition, first in their parents' homes and then in the in-laws' meaning that, by the time they reached middle age, they personified orthodoxy themselves. Therefore, the only way of modernizing Indian society, they argued, was not *by legislation but by educating women*.[99]

Tarabai Shinde's emphatic invective that all social reform societies were 'fake' and the work of male reformers as much use as a 'spare tit on a goat' therefore appears to ring true when we consider Indian men's position on state intervention.[100] Indeed, even Malabari did not initially invoke the aid of the Legislature on the issue of child marriage except in a benign form. He proposed that the government offer a system of incentives and disincentives that would include suggestions such as 'no married [male]

---

[95] Editorial, 'Social Reform', *Arya Bhagini*, June 1891, 49–52; and Tarabai Nabar, 'Bal vivahache dushparinam' [The Evil Effects of Child Marriage], *Maharashtra Mahila*, May 1901, 234–6.

[96] K.R. Kirtikar, *An Address on the Occasion of the Second Anniversary of the Saddharma Samaj of Thane* (Bombay: Native Opinion Press, 1883), pp. 25–6.

[97] See the replies sent by Atmaram Pandurang, Dr Vishram Ramji Ghollay, Veerchund Deepchand amongst many others. In 'Papers Relating to Infant Marriage', *Selections from the Records*.

[98]   Tirmal Rao Venkatesh's opinion, 30 December 1884, Ibid., p. 55.

[99] The best representatives of this school are Pandurang Balibhadra, Narayan Bhikajee and Dr Amroot Chobhe, Ibid.

[100]   Tarabai Shinde, [Women and Men, A Comparison], p. 18.

student shall be eligible to go up for University examinations, five years hence', and the public sector 'may prefer the unmarried to the married, all other qualifications being equal'.[101] As will become clear in the next section, in complete contrast to men, Maharashtrian women emphatically advocated state intervention and persuaded the government to pass the legislation on the Age of Consent.

Women's Counter-Discourses and Participation in the Age of Consent Bill Debates

An important change discernible in the women's movement of the late 1880s and 1890s was the role of the women's press in raising feminist consciousness on these issues. This was achieved by engaging with mainstream discourses on the institution of child marriage and related themes, such as the role of the state in bringing relief to disempowered sections of society or specific proposals for tackling infant marriage and widowhood. The general lack of concern shown by Indian men for women's suffering within child marriages angered women, galvanizing them to write to Marathi journals contesting the arguments thrown up by men. Women followed the debates closely and expressed opinions on all the major issues raised. A significant concern in women's literature was the institution of marriage and how and why this structure maintained absurd customs. The reasons for the existence and continuance of child marriage proposed by them were radically different from those of men. Within the feminist discourse, there is no engagement with the Shastric injunctions on the primacy of the *garbhadhana* ceremony[102] [literally, the 'gift of the womb', or the ritual to initiate conception] that characterized the dominant male discourse. Instead, women highlighted financial considerations on the part of the boy-groom's parents, the anxiety of the girl-bride's parents on behalf of their daughter due to the low status accorded to the female sex and the sentimental ties between families which often allowed betrothals to take place when the groom, and bride-to-be were in their infancy. These concerns paved the way for the shift in women's arguments from the focus on 'age' to 'consent' of the boy and girl in marriage arrangements.

In contrast to men, women argued firmly for state intervention in regulating marital reforms. As shown in the previous chapter, Maharashtrian women had criticized the state when it had introduced legal changes that adversely affected infanticidal women; however, on the issue of child marriage, they recognized the need for government support. The *bhaginivarg*'s studied cynicism and contempt for male 'reformers' and the reform movements they led was underpinned by their implicit belief in the efficacy of the colonial government. The majority of Maharashtrian women were sceptical of male reformers' intentions in bringing about changes that would affect women's lives

---

[101] Malabari, 'Infant Marriage in India, Paper I', in *Infant Marriage and Enforced Widowhood*, p. 2.

[102] For the significance of this *samskara* [ritual] for Hindu women see K.M. Kapadia, *Marriage and Family in India* (London: Oxford University Press, 1955), pp. 132–5.

in a positive manner. Referring to the male reform movement as a 'sham', Tarabai Shinde repeatedly acknowledged the various actions of the colonial government in improving the position of women and called for further interventions by the state in order to curb the 'wicked ways' of Indian men. After male replies to the Malabari proposals were published, women wrote profusely to express their chagrin, not at the 'opinions of old-fashioned, credulous and the God-fearing older generation'—this, they could comprehend—but with the 'opinions of young learned men who aped modern ideas only in dress and diet but were actually worse than the conservatives'.[103] It was the essential conservatism of Indian men, whether educated or uneducated, that led to Indian women's belief that it was imperative that the state intervene.

Women drew attention to the 'reform from within' group of Indian liberals who were opposed to legislation on the grounds that change would occur in a natural fashion within Indian society only when they achieved self-government. Indian women protested that this was only an argument for those who really wished for the status quo to continue. 'Sati', argued one lady, 'would never have been abolished, left to the Indian people, but was the greatest favour done by the British government, for saving thousands of lives of women from the agonies of the fire'.[104] They urged the government to display the same firm conviction over the issue of the age of consent. Women's expressions and enthusiasm for the Age of Consent Bill reveal that they viewed the colonial state as an empowering resource in contrast to Indian men who saw state intervention in a wholly negative light. Contemporary scholarship from postcolonial and Subaltern perspectives has portrayed the state as a hegemonic instrument of repression on this issue. However, many of the authors concentrate wholly on deconstructing metropolitan discourses on masculinity and race, almost neglecting women's voices completely, and it is therefore unsurprising that their conclusions are skewed.[105] By studying the viewpoints of women on the child-marriage controversy, it is impossible to maintain the view that the colonial state was interventionist and hegemonic.

The vernacular print literature of nineteenth-century Maharashtra was an important vehicle for constructing gender identities. One prose genre, *stricharitra* [portrait of women] by misogynistic male writers, was particularly significant.[106] Conservative groups in Poona had written and enacted *stricharitras* in connection with the Age of Consent Bill.[107] Much of the material in these plays contained sensational portrayals of women who had remained unmarried due to the enactment of the bill. Women's journals began a protest against this vilification of the female sex by mainstream

---

[103] Editorial, 'Social Reform', *Arya Bhagini*, June 1891, p. 51.

[104] 'By an educated lady', [Instructive debates], *Arya Bhagini*, July 1891, pp. 60–61.

[105] For a critique of the deterministic agendas of post-colonial scholarship, see Sumit Sarkar, 'Orientalism Revisited: Saidian Frameworks in the Writing of Modern Indian History', *Oxford Literary Review*, 16 (1994): 204–24; and Tanika Sarkar, 'Rhetoric against Age of Consent', pp.1869–78.

[106] See chapters 2 and 3 of this book.

[107] 13 June 1891, NNR.

society. *Bhamini Prakash*, a women's journal based at Poona and edited by Chimabai Kadam, was among the first to protest against these attacks. Women wrote articles condemning men for writing such slanderous stories and also attacked conservative newspapers like the *Pune Vaibhav* and *Shri Shivaji* that published letters under female pseudonyms containing obscenities and indecent allusions in their opposition to the bill.[108] Of greater importance, however, was this journal's role in complaining to the government about the character assassination of women and the negative portrayal of women present in this form of literature. *Bhamini Prakash* requested the government to take action on two issues: firstly, to provide stricter guidelines to curb the activities of irresponsible vernacular newspapers and, secondly, to stop 'Dramatic Groups' from performing plays on the Age of Consent theme.[109] They also brought to the attention of the government the fact that men in higher education, such as the male students of the various government medical colleges in Southern Maharashtra, were participating in these performances. They requested that the government expel students if they failed to withdraw from performing in such slanderous plays.

They also sought support from British feminists, both for guidance and in mobilizing public opinion, even if this support did not turn out to be entirely altruistic. In nineteenth-century British India, it has been argued that European medical men were effectively performing the function of maintaining the image of physical and moral superiority of the ruling race.[110] The European medical woman was also perpetuating the same function. Much of the medical evidence selectively cited by Indian women in support of the agitation came from imperial female doctors who gave fiery lectures on the enervating effects of child marriage on the Indian race.[111] Indian women, however, emphasized the maternal mortality figures to argue against child marriage. Women's reliance on the imperial female and the colonial government reflects significantly their loss of faith in indigenous circles. It was not just European women doctors who provided vital support to Indian women at this time; during the height of the legal battles fought over the restitution of conjugal rights controversy, hundreds of British women sent Rukhmabai letters of sympathy and also monetary aid that had been raised through fund-raising in Britain.[112] European women's unconditional support and solidarity with Indian women on the question of marriage reforms questions the postcolonialist contention that the imperial project was an unmitigated one of violence and exploitation.

---

[108] *Bhamini Prakash*, summarized in 13 June 1891, NNR.

[109] Ibid., 20 June 1891, NNR.

[110] David Arnold, 'Medical Priorities and Practice in Nineteenth-Century British India', *South Asia Research*, 5/2 (November 1985): 167–83.

[111] Dr Pechey-Phipson, *Address to the Hindus of Bombay on the Subject of Child Marriage* (Bombay: Times Press, 1890).

[112] Rukhmabai's biographer has conducted an in-depth study of British women's campaigns. See Varde, [Dr Rukhmabai], especially chapters 8, 11, 12 and 13.

Public Participation of Women's Organizations and Lobbying Tactics

Women's organizations became crucial bodies for the popular participation of women in the Age of Consent debates. Leading newspapers reported the work of a Women's Committee made up of prominent British and Maharashtrian women in support of the Age of Consent Bill in Bombay in the middle of 1890.[113] In London, Millicent Fawcett lobbied through the Indian National Association, calling for the government to take legislative action as an 'act of conscience'.[114] Thus, the first memorial sent by women from the Bombay Presidency was accomplished with the assistance of British feminists from Bombay and London. This memorial was addressed to the Queen, and was signed by two thousand Maharashtrian women. Due to the intensely hostile atmosphere surrounding the debates, their identity remained confidential and only the social position and caste of the signatories was revealed.[115] The memorialists drew the government's attention to 'the necessity for legislation in the interests of child-wives and other female minors'. They argued that 'the criminal law in India may be so altered as to protect at least girls under fourteen from their husbands as well as from strangers'.[116] The petitioners pointed out the absurdities and anomalies in the criminal law of 1860, which fixed the age of consent for British girls at twelve and for Indian girls at ten. They pointed to the anomaly in the law, whereby a girl of eighteen could not validly consent to grievous harm to her person but could be subjected to rape. Similarly, a girl less than twelve could not validly consent to the removal of jewels on her person, but she could to 'the theft of her honour'.[117] They finally argued that the Queen's 'keen maternal interests' in her subject people would influence her to take action to redeem the status of her weakest subjects—the womanhood of India, treating them on a legislative par with their British counterparts.

Basing their arguments on the information supplied to them by female European doctors in India, Indian feminists argued that girls in India normally did not attain maturity before fourteen. Dr Edith Pechey-Phipson was a highly respected member of the colonial elite in Bombay and oversaw the operations of several hospitals for women and children in Bombay Presidency. Together with Maharashtrian women she

---

[113] Lady Reay and Dr Pechey-Phipson comprised the British representatives and Indian women were Rukhmabai Modak, Pandita Ramabai and Rukhmabai.

[114] *Induprakash*, 22 December 1890, 3.

[115] Many of the leading newspapers published this memorial verbatim. See *Mahratta*, 14 December 1890 and *Induprakash*, 6 October 1890.

[116] 'Memorial of 1600 women of India to her Gracious Majesty Queen Victoria, Empress of India', sent by W. Lee Warner, Secretary to Government of Bombay, 30 December 1890 in 'Papers relative to the Bill to amend the Indian Penal Code and the Code of Criminal Procedure 1882', extract from the *Abstract of the Proceedings of the Council of the Governor-General of India* (hereafter *Proceedings*), April 1891, P/3951, Appendix n. 13, British Library (hereafter BL).

[117] Memorial of 1600 women of India, *Proceedings*, ibid.

conducted a tireless campaign on the issue.[118] She produced voluminous evidence to counteract the assertions of European and Indian medical men that girls in India reached puberty much earlier than European girls. In fact, she argued, 'a Hindoo girl of fifteen is about the equal of a British child of eleven instead of the reverse'.[119] European women doctors took special interest in the child marriage controversy. They spoke with an authority on female reproduction that was based on their professional practice as well as their personal friendships with Indian women. European female doctors from many parts of India came together to compile evidence gathered from their practices to prove that child marriage resulted in maternal mortality and child retardation; their findings were integrated into an important petition to the government.[120] European female doctors specifically stated that the custom of child marriage had an adverse effect on the fertility of Indian men and women.

Indian women's campaigning reached its peak between the despatching of the first memorial in December 1890 and the deliberations of the Viceregal Council on the bill in March 1891. At least eight women's meetings were held in Western India and one was held in Bengal to consider aspects of the bill, pass resolutions and write new petitions. In Calcutta, under the leadership of Mrs Ghosal, a private meeting of Hindu women passed a unanimous resolution in favour of the bill.[121] Attendance at these meetings ranged from 75 to 250; almost all of them took place in urban places like Bombay, Amravati, Poona and Ahmedabad and were comprised entirely of educated, middle-class women. Two types of public participation are evident among women. They joined either as members of caste or religious-affiliated women's bodies or under the umbrella of secular women's organizations. Examples of the former are the Native Christian Women's Society, the Zoroastrian Women's Club and the Bene-Israelite Women's Organisation.[122] Illustrations of the latter type are the Aryan Ladies Association, Bhagini Samaj and the Arya Mahila Samaj. While women successfully adopted the new form of agitation of holding public discussions and submitting memorials to the government, they condemned the recruiting techniques of their male counterparts.[123] An important strategy for them was to inform the government of unscrupulous practices used by anti-legislationists. The orthodoxy in Maharashtra felt the threat posed by women's meetings. Writing in the *Kesari* and *Mahratta,* Tilak, the leader of the opposition, acknowledged the unity of women over the bill but tried to

---

[118] On Edith Pechey-Phipson's life and work, see Padma Anagol, 'Phipson, (Mary) Edith Pechey- (1845–1908)' in H.C.G. Matthew and B. Harrison (eds), *Oxford Dictionary of National Biography*, (Oxford: Oxford University Press, 2004), <http://www.oxforddnb.com/ view/article/56460>.

[119] Pechey-Phipson, *Address to the Hindoos*, pp. 2–3.

[120] See Memorial of Lady Doctors in India, signed by Monelle Mansell and 49 others, 22 September 1890, *Proceedings*, Appendix A15.

[121] Reported in *The Statesmen* and reproduced in *Induprakash*, 16 February 1891.

[122] Bombay's Jewish women participated in these campaigns under the leadership of a prominent midwife of this period, Rebecca Simeon. For her life and work see Appendix.

[123] For details, see Anagol-McGinn, 'Age of Consent Act (1891) Reconsidered', 114–15.

dismiss and belittle their memorials.[124] Some conservative vernacular papers declared that anti-legislationist groups would break the influence of liberal women by organizing their wives and sisters to hold counter-meetings.[125] There are no reports of such meetings taking place, but such claims indicate the intense fear of the orthodoxy on seeing the passionate demonstrations and campaigns conducted by women.

The unprecedented traditionalist group's agitation against the bill brought women from different faiths together and united them on an issue which they saw as a gendered one; their sense of *bhaginivarg* is clear. In one such meeting, while arguing a case for firm commitment and unity of women, the speaker said, 'the question concerns *our* most vital interests rather than of *men* [sic]'.[126] Likewise, a woman writing with the authority of a 'mother of several children' said that allowing a husband to have sexual intercourse with a prepubescent wife was an outrageous act. Further, she added, 'Women as a sex, were subject to and underwent far more excruciating pains and miseries and risks of the worst kind happening in child-bearing, than man, the opposite sex, had ever conception of …'[127] She therefore cautioned against listening to male views, as they had no idea of what women went through, and argued that men indulging in premature cohabitation should be severely punished.

Women turned the age of consent issue into a case unique to the *stri jati* [female sex] where the experience of women was privileged over textual interpretations offered by men. Feminists of this period objected to the romanticization of Indian womanhood and drew the attention to it in sharp criticism. The *Subodh Patrika* had reported the views of the famous Indologist, Max Mueller, on the issue of child marriage. He had idealized Indian marriages, stating that love and affection was generated in infant marriage through the sheer act of the child-spouses growing up in the same home, implying that harmony and domestic bliss were integral aspects of such arranged marriages. The women's periodicals, which engaged in a debate on the contemporary question of child marriage, roundly condemned such romantic expressions, with the women's magazine *Arya Bhagini* criticizing him for his lack of firsthand experience of India and his reliance on a purely text-based knowledge of the East thus:

> Max Mueller sahib [sic] is going to live abroad forever. He has no first hand knowledge of the domestic life of an average Indian or of the behaviour and conduct of our men. Therefore the statements made by Saheb are not applicable uniformly to every one of us. Among child marriage cases only around 4 or 5 couples out of hundred live in a state of mutual love and harmony. Whilst 90 couples out of a hundred do not

---

[124] 28 February 1891, NNR; Also *The Mahratta*, 6 December 1890, NNR.

[125] *Pune Vaibhav*, 13 December 1890, NNR; Other vernacular newspapers which condemned women's meetings and participation were *Jagad-hitechchu*, *Vartahar* and *Hindu Punch*, reported in 7 March 1891, NNR.

[126] Under 'Correspondence, Poona News', 2 March 1891, *Induprakash*, 22 December 1890, 4.

[127] *Induprakash*, 8 December 1890.

experience this state of love and affection instead there is constant bickering and quarrelling in the home.[128]

It is important to recognize how *reality* as opposed to *idealism* and *context* over *text* are strategies successfully used by women in colonial societies to combat the many untruths told about women and female sexuality in the child marriage controversy. It is also impossible to disregard 'experience' as a category of analysis because it was on the basis of individual and collective interaction of the 'self' and the 'outer world' and their continuous engagement with social reality that Maharashtrian women became feminists; ultimately, it was experience that prompted them into consciousness-raising acts.[129]

We begin to understand the differential participation of Indian women under the leadership of their own women leaders when we compare the first memorial drafted with the help of British feminists addressed to the Queen to the later petitions. In the first memorial, under the guidance of British women, the minimum age of consent for girls was set at 14 years. But when no response was received by February 1891, women leaders such as Rukhmabai Modak and Dhaklibai Sukthankar reasoned that this was probably rejected by the government on grounds that it was unrealistic. Therefore, in all future petitions, they instead pleaded for the age-limit to be 12 years.[130] The second difference is discerned in the construction of arguments for raising the age of consent. While the first memorial was legalistic and concentrated on the anomalies of the penal code, the later petitions present the issue as one concerning the female sex. The five 514 petitioners from the Arya Mahila Samaj argued that the misrepresentations against the bill were by male oppositionists but as far as women were concerned, 'The feeling in favour of the Age of Consent Bill among the female classes is indeed very general wherever the object of the Bill is correctly understood.'[131] Thus, their petition made the case that, not only did the issue exclusively concern the *stri jati* but also that it had the consent of the women of Maharashtra. The tone of the later petitions was also marked by a caution that was absent in the first memorial; this was designed to appease and win over the opposing sections of men to the Act. While some petitions requested guarantees against the misuse of the criminal process by vesting it in magistrates alone, others asked a less severe punishment in the case of

---

[128] 'By an educated lady', [Instructive debates], *Arya Bhagini*, September 1891, 78–9.

[129] See the introductory chapter for a fuller discussion of how subjectivity is constructed through experience.

[130] Petition from the Aryan Ladies Association, Poona, by 65 Hindu ladies and 23 Bene-Israel ladies, in *Proceedings*, p. 32, and the 'Petition of certain Parsi and native Christian ladies of Poona', 23 February 1891 to His Excellency The Governor-General of India, signed by 128 Parsi ladies and 83 Indian Christian ladies', in *Proceedings*, Appendix A 12.

[131] A petition from Dhaklibai Sukthankar, Secretary, Arya Mahila Samaj, Bombay, 4 March 1891 to K.L. Nulkar accompanied with Memorial of 514 native ladies of Bombay and Poona, *Proceedings*, Appendix A18.

husbands guilty of breaching the Act.[132] Indeed, judging by the penalties for the husband, if found guilty of breaching the Act,[133] the government seems to have taken on board some of the suggestions of these women petitioners

This study has pointed to the role of women as agents in changing social legislation that affected their well-being in the broader arenas of marriage and family. The question that remains is why were Maharashtrian women the most vocal in making their views known?[134] An obvious feature that differentiates Maharashtrian women's consciousness and movement for women's rights from that of women in other regions was the way in which they built separate female institutions in the late nineteenth century that enabled their collective voice to be heard. Whether they were based on religion like that of Zoroastrian women or secular ones like the Arya Mahila Samaj, the organizations had strong leaders who gave women the confidence to speak out. Controlled by women and conducted in the Marathi language, the Maharashtrian women's press also provided a forum for increasing awareness of the issues affecting women, as well providing them with a sounding board. However, there were certain external factors that also contributed to the fruition in feminist consciousness in Maharashtra. The social reform movement took a different course in Maharashtra from that of Bengal;[135] the specific instance of the Age of Consent debate provides a good illustration of this. In Bengal, the debate was based on the control of female sexuality and therefore centred on the sexual nature of Bengali women.[136] On the western coast, however, in the hands of B.G. Tilak and for reformers like K.T. Telang, the debate became a nationalist issue to prove that social reform precedes political reform. The lines on which debate was conducted by indigenous discourses necessarily sharpened the differences for women. The debate by women on the age of consent was marked by a clarity of thought which was sharpened by the fact that they realized it was a gender issue rather than a national or a religious one. Women therefore did not resort to the scripture-based arguments used by conservative and radical reformers alike but instead

---

[132] A memorial adopted by 60 high-caste Hindu women from Ahmedabad, reported in *Times of India*, 25 February 1891, p. 5.

[133] When the Act was passed, the penalties for a husband were far less severe. For example, he could be tried by the District Magistrate rather than be arrested and investigated by the police. He could be sent to jail for a period of time and his offence was a bailable one, but escaped harsher penalties such as transportation for life.

[134] The existing historiography on the Age of Consent Bill debates within Bengal has so far neglected to study the question of agency amongst Bengali women.

[135] The social reform movement in Bombay was more circumspect and less revolutionary than the Bengali one; however, its very cautious nature made the Bombay reformist activities more practical and found readier public acceptance than the fiery Bengali one which, as the fortunes of the Brahmo Samaj demonstrate, broke away and lost its popular base. Other details of these variations are in Charles Heimsath, *Indian Nationalism and Hindu Social Reform*, p. 14, 86–7 and 104–8.

[136] Dagmar Engels has argued that the age of consent debate was a reflection of two opposing views of sexuality as represented by the Bengali and the British, 'The Age of Consent Act, 1891', *South Asia Research*, 3/2 (1985): 107–34.

concentrated on the pain and suffering caused to child-wives and mothers, arguing that 'consent' of the spouses was important; this necessarily involved raising the 'age' at which they were to wed.

In late nineteenth-century Maharashtra, a regional discourse with strong 'Maratha' nationalist elements was emerging. There is evidence of the pains to which Maharashtrians went to distinguish themselves from Bengal. After the publicizing of the Phulmani case when a Bengali husband killed his prepubescent wife in the act of intercourse, Bengal was presented as a culturally backward region of India by Western Indian vernacular newspapers. Even the progressive groups in Western India cited the speeches of R.C. Mitter or Sir Stuart Bayley and believed the many allegations regarding Bengali female sexuality. Their rationale (also the beginning of a powerful stereotype) was that, in a region like Bengal where *purdah* was rife, and women were not allowed to look at men other than their close blood relations, it was only natural that Bengali women were full of sexual thoughts and craved for the company of their husbands before puberty.[137] In contrast, Maharashtrian women were *purdah*-free and the region's cultural practices made consummation of marriage before puberty an exception. Significantly, this argument was to be found among significant numbers of both legislationists and anti-legislationists in Bombay. Given the advanced state of movements for political and social reform in Maharashtra, it is not surprising that women's politics also developed rapidly in that region. The tone and colour of the indigenous debates in Maharashtra indicates that women were free from defending their sexuality, allowing them to participate on equal terms with men. This notion is demonstrated by the arguments used by female petitioners who agreed that consummation of marriage before the girl reached the age of twelve was indeed rare in Maharashtra but the government had to recognize the existence of the practice in other Indian regions and make provisions against it.[138]

The significance of women's participation in the Age of Consent debates lies in their counter-discourses, which wove three clear strands of argument: firstly, the fact that infants or children (be they of either sex) did not provide their consent to betrothal and marriage, leading to incompatible marriages and the girl-wife becoming maladjusted as she was raised in the alien environment of her in-laws; secondly, the non-sympathy of the boy-husband who could barely understand his own rights let alone his wife's; finally, they pointed to the nature of Indian marriages as 'contracts' and how they were cold and calculating arrangements between families. All these factors, they argued, simply compounded the misery of the Indian wife and effectively prevented her from developing and improving herself. Such arguments were a powerful force in proving to the government the correctness of intervening in the domestic arena to uphold women's rights. Although women called for the reconstitution of conjugal relations, the dominant discourses erased their voices from the mainstream deliberations on the restitution of conjugal rights and divorce. In the

---

[137] *Sudharak*, in 24 January 1891, NNR; *Subodh Patrika*, in 21 February 1891, NNR; *Indian Spectator*, in 14 February 1891, NNR.

[138] Petition from Secretary, Arya Mahila Samaj, Bombay, *Proceedings*, Appendix N.

case of the Age of Consent debates, however, women were able to contribute and impress their views more effectively.

The generation of bodies of knowledge about the Indian woman arose in reaction to a clear and unambiguous demonstration of female agency in resolving marital disputes through appeals to the criminal and civil courts. Female agency was therefore not something that had to negotiate and contest already existing colonialist and indigenous discourses, which attempted to define and limit them. Social historians have referred to the latter half of the nineteenth century as the 'era of civil litigation' as it had the greatest number of suits by Indians in British law courts of the time.[139] What has been demonstrated here and in previous chapters is how Indian women also came to call on the courts for the resolution of all problems, marital, inheritance, property and employment. This newfound and assertive move by Indian women is precisely what the peasant cited at the beginning of this chapter complained about to the Indian lawyer and is understood to represent a crucial moment in marking the changes in gender relations as a 'result' of British rule. Formidable as these reactive male constructions were, they did not go uncontested. Women created an oppositional discourse which sought to challenge colonialist and indigenous male discourse on the issue of conjugal rights and in the construction of a gendered critique of the institutions of arranged and child marriages. Previous scholarship has focussed *solely* on the contest between colonial and male discourses on the female body. This chapter has highlighted the participation of women in these debates and, in doing so, located Indian women's early participation in public forums in the nineteenth century much earlier than previously supposed.

---

[139] David Washbrook, 'Law, State and Agrarian Society in Colonial India', *Modern Asian Studies*, 15/3 (1981): 649–721.

Chapter 7

Indian Feminism and Its Legacy: A Concluding Note

This book explored the challenges posed by Indian women to male hegemony in colonial India in the period 1850 to 1920. Its objectives were twofold: First, to provide an account of the development of feminism in Indian society and secondly, a gendered rereading of modern Indian history. By placing gender or relations between women and men at the heart of Indian society and politics, the book has endeavoured to make visible a long but hidden tradition of feminist thought and politics and has tried to reconfigure our understanding of modern Indian history.

This study has argued that the nature of Indian women's feminism was a complex and varied one. Nineteenth-century Indian feminists worked towards social and domestic reform informed by a discussion of the oppression of the *stri jati* [female sex]. Certain core issues bond women together irrespective of caste and class differences. Women's perceptions on a range of issues were drawn upon to show the commonalties between them as well as the feminist distinctiveness of the women's movement. Key to this has been an awareness of women as a specific group—*stri jati* and a concept of sisterhood—*bhaginivarg*. In the nineteenth century, Indian women possessed the defining feature of a 'feminist': the awareness and expression of ideas about the roots of women's subordination and a desire to remedy it. This book has argued that a concept of sisterhood developed among women, born of an awareness of the hostility of men to the improvement of women's lives. The constant attacks on women by male conservatives led to the coinage of the term *bhaginivarg* [sisterhood]. This was a crucial step in the formation of feminist consciousness whereby women began to perceive themselves as a collective. This solidarity cut across caste and religion as evinced by the way in which Hindu women rallied round Pandita Ramabai when she came under attack by male conservatives and was manifested in their bold call on the government over the child marriage controversy (1891), arguing that the state alone could help oppressed groups such as women and children. Such actions by women helped develop a stronger and more widespread sense of *bhaginivarg* in the late nineteenth century that encompassed Parsi, Jewish, Hindu and Christian women.

The development of feminist consciousness in nineteenth-century India demonstrates that historical processes cannot always be studied as unilinear trajectories. The search for continuities from the colonial past to the present in the case of women's history can prove a futile one.[1] The struggle for women's rights, like many other social movements, was eventually subordinated to the needs of the greater nationalist struggle. In this process, the advances and achievements of earlier women were lost by the peculiar alignments made between feminism and nationalism during the 1930s and 1940s. There were several reasons for this. Christian feminists had made a clean break with the Indian past by rejecting Hinduism on the basis of a gendered approach to religion. They had fruitfully applied the 'welfare' and 'mission' rhetoric of Christianity to assert themselves in breaking with traditional roles and legitimating their entry into public professional roles. Their refusal to belong to any one church as well as their rejection of clerical mediation along with funding from non-Indian sources had given them autonomy to create a unique brand of Indian feminism and also provide leadership to the women's movement. However, Christian feminist leaders were able to sustain women's interests only as long as the active phase of the reform movement lasted. Their alignment to mission Christianity, which at this time equated Christianity with civilizing values and modernizing impulses with the West, meant that they denounced nationalism and its growth. Eventually, it had two effects. Firstly, it prevented them from effectively countering the nationalist ideologies of the early twentieth century with new strategies for enrolling women into their movement that had hitherto promised emancipation with conversion. Secondly, it paved the way for Ramabai Ranade's leadership, who in due course marginalized Christian feminists with a take-over of the women's movement.

Although Hindu women questioned Hinduism and Hindu customs and rituals, unlike their Christian counterparts, they did not reject it. This meant working within the structures of Hindu society and its limitations. As demonstrated in chapter 3, several Hindu feminist leaders overcame the hindrances of working within Hindu society through a strategy of assimilation and accommodation. Separate female institution-building programmes by women were to prove to be the vehicle for the movement of Hindu women's embracing of modernity and in the development of the Maharashtrian women's movement. First, it enabled women to mobilize in pursuit of the goal of their own welfare. Secondly, it contributed immensely to the transformation of women's public roles. This was made possible by the astute leadership of the far-sighted women who founded these organizations. Their feminism, which embodied the ability to 'assimilate and accommodate', kept the larger Hindu society's criticism of their programmes to a minimal level. In the period 1870 to 1920, when men did not accept women as equals, the creation of a separate public sphere was probably the only viable

---

[1] Due to the constraints placed on women in the past, feminist thought has developed in 'jumps' and 'starts'. One generation of feminist scholars has not led to another taking off where the former left but beginning all over again—a process traced by Gerda Lerner which she terms, 'generations of wasted talents'. Gerda Lerner, *The Creation of Feminist Consciousness: From the Middle Ages to Eighteen-Seventy* (New York: Oxford University Press, 1993), see 'Introduction'.

political strategy giving their leaders greater autonomy in management and policy-making, while providing their individual members the strength that only numbers and a common platform could offer. The idea of a separate but public sphere of activity was no doubt an astute solution for Hindu women desirous of effecting changes in women's lives within the constraints of Hindu society. Ultimately, however, it was to restrict the growth of an independent women's movement. In the early twentieth century the anxiety of women regarding the safeguarding of their interests took on an urgency due to the almost certain victory of the 'political reform before social reform' argument. Separate female institutions, such as the Seva Sadan, in attempting to maintain the focus on women's interests, did not allow its members to participate in political organizations associated with nationalist activities. The very nature of these institutions meant that separate female organizations were not able to fulfil all the aspirations of their members. Further, the discussion of Hindu women's engagement with the 'golden age' theory undertaken in chapter 3 showed that they were not only unwilling to break with the past, but approved vigorously of the reconstituted images of Indian womanhood. Their uncritical appraisal of the Hindu past was a contrast to their Christian sisters, and gave rise to several problems. While the representation of Indian womanhood taken from the Vedic past was indeed a glorious one (allegedly women had equal rights with men measured by criteria such as the absence of sati; that they were educated, had choice in marriage and remarriage), Hindu feminists made no efforts to distinguish the functions of their own representations of Indian womanhood from that of nationalists and religious revivalists. Thus, it can be seen how women were attracted to the redrawn images of Indian womanhood presented to them by Gandhi since they resembled so clearly their own leaders' representations of Indian womanhood and came with the added incentive of equal participation in the forbidden arena of political movements.

It is the contention of this book, however, that nineteenth- and early twentieth-century feminism in Maharashtra under the guidance of dynamic female leaders was far more radical and visionary than the women's movement in a Gandhi-inspired nationalist movement. Hindu women's attack on the *shastras* [Hindu prescriptive texts] is the most important marker in their progression towards feminism binding them into a community of women with common interests born of the peculiar disadvantages not shared by their men folk. Even within as fragmented an enquiry as a 'letter to an editor' it was made clear that a large number of Hindu women struggled to understand the sources of knowledge production about *stri* [woman] and *strivarg* [womanhood]. Women in the nineteenth century were 'subjects' striving to understand how women became the 'object' of men's knowledge. Many of them realized that women's oppression arose from men's writing of religious books that gave legitimacy to a whole range of misogynist views and actions. Many of the gender critiques were published as articles in newspapers, furious letters of vindication or books or as petitions to the government. What is discernable is that women's writings themselves constitute resistance so far as contesting traditional notions of what constituted moral and immoral behaviour for both men and women. Women asserted quite clearly that if the contemporary state of morality was in ruins this was not just because of unrealistic expectations from women, but also due to the fact that men themselves were less than shining models of exemplary conduct.

Unlike utopian feminist writers, Indian women did not yearn for a gender-free world. They saw two sexes, with differing bodies and roles in reproduction, and differing degrees of physical strength and hence advocated complementary roles. As long as women possessed exclusive rights to reproduction, their lives would be differently structured than those of men, who occupy a different physiological, cultural and sociopolitical space. On this basis, they argued, women were to be treated with the same respect as men. This was not a form of essentialism by these early feminists because they did not believe that biology is destiny (in fact the utopias in women's literature have women performing all the roles of men) nor did they think that women were bound by a 'universal character or nature'.[2] Equality is not mistaken, as some American feminist thought seems to imply today, with 'sameness'.[3] Women's demands were not for women to be 'as men' but for a more relational and complex set of attributes for women. To be more explicit, Indian feminists advocated a world where women gain the same respect, dignity and justice for the labours they perform, however different they may be from men. For the turn of the century Indian feminist, feminism meant empowering women to realize their full potential as women without impediments: it was not about making women the 'same as men'. Late nineteenth-century and early twentieth-century women's organizations like the Vanita Samaj and the Seva Sadan did not consider older values of motherhood and nurturing as incompatible with the new values of ambition and individual initiative. Moreover, female identity was not imbued with shame or inferiority but was a source of pride. They celebrated femininity as a privilege granted to women over men. Even their symbolic role-reversals in literature demonstrated that they held a world-view wherein men and women did not compete but were equals. This 'equality in difference' theory was what nineteenth-century Indian feminists bequeathed to their sisters who followed the paths set for them in the early twentieth century. With this in mind, it is easier to understand the standpoint of prominent Indian women of the later nationalist period of the 1930s and 1940s who ferociously differentiated Indian from Western feminism as one not marked by male-hatred.

In the history of modern India, patriarchy was already well entrenched and institutionalized. It was well defended by both religious strictures and enforced by the priestly classes via the laity. However, it was forced to engage in continuous reinvention and reinforcement due to the impact of colonialism. It is within this

---

[2] As Karen Offen puts it succinctly, 'essentialism' has 'to do with philosophical arguments about a common "nature" of "woman," not with "physiological realities..."' *European Feminisms*, p. 15.

[3] Karen Offen shows how European feminisms differed from American feminism in this respect: see Ibid.

context we see the rise of Indian feminism where the primary claim made by the *bhaginivarg* was expressed as a broad, comprehensive claim for the equal rights of women. These claims spilled over specifically in demands for the end of maligning women and womanhood in print [*stricharitra*], for educational opportunity and for access to knowledge for its own sake; for economic self-reliance and for creative self-expression; for a revision of man-made laws that disadvantaged women in property and inheritance and restricted their mobility; towards the achievement of these goals they seized the opportunities provided by female leadership for participation in women's organizations.

This study has also analyzed the informal methods of assertion and resistance of ordinary women in colonial India. Although it is not possible to quantify or track the influences of the formal women's movement on the informal activities of women, yet it is clear that the number of women seeking the help of the British government through petitioning or more directly the law courts in resolving inheritance and property disputes, marriage, right of physical mobility and employment reveals that their awareness of their rights and civil liberties was far greater than assumed in the historiography. If the lineament of Indian feminism was demonstrated through educated middle class women's formal entry into women's organizations, the informal methods of agitation and everyday forms of resistance discussed in the latter half of the book has proven the case for a more widespread effect of the women's movement in consciousness raising as well as action on the part of Indian women.

An analysis of the development of the Indian women's movement highlights several issues. The more traditional women were awakened over their need to cope with the changes brought by urbanization and the changing needs of the emerging middle class. The more progressive among them developed a clearly feminist perspective by relating to the everyday misery of belonging to the *stri jati*, be it a child-wife or widow. However, the meeting point of the two was that together they constructed a critique on the 'condition of women' based on either their own personal experiences or the everyday existence of their *bhagini* [sisters]. This analysis of the condition of the *stri jati* bonded Hindu women together. Another remarkable feature of nineteenth-century Indian feminism was that women's discourse on social reform was based on humanitarian ideals, rather than the arguments used by male social reformers who constantly sought the sanction of the *shastras* for it. The differences in the arguments proposed by male reformers from their female counterparts also highlights the inescapable conclusion that it would be an affront to call Hindu women reformers' function a 'mediating role' in late nineteenth- and early twentieth-century Maharashtra. Far from it, their constant contestations of men's role in holding women back as well as their separate women's organizations reveal an independent and assertive role in which men played a minimal part.

Historians of the subaltern school have focused on giving the life of a subaltern meaning, but this has hardly included the greatest and most subordinated of all people in India—women. This monograph has not only given their lives meaning and told their history in their narrative but additionally we are now in a position to observe subaltern perceptions of the Raj. One of the richest insights into how the colonial state was viewed by subordinated groups is provided through a study of women's assertion and resistance. Fear, submission and deference—the more readily associated reactions of Indian women towards their menfolk are missing when it comes to their attitudes to the state. Whilst claiming recognition of their rights, women appeal to the state as the supreme arbiter of justice. Women's adulation of the Raj and their firm belief in the state's will to do good can be read as a sign of how the state was utilized as a tool to counteract patriarchal injustices. The Raj is seen as a humanitarian resource and the final arbiter—certainly in Girijabai Kelkar and Tarabai Shinde's conception of state, wherein the state is registered as the sovereign authority, far more so than the patriarchal head of household. The greatest impact women's crusades in the late nineteenth century had can be discerned in their persuasion of the government in legislating in favour of women. By illustrating the insensitivity of men and the double standards embedded within men's thinking on sexuality, the resulting outrage stimulated the movement well into the twentieth century for legal reform, for the case of women doctors and for women's suffrage.

Contemporary historians can only understand the legacy that twentieth-century Indian women inherited from their immediate predecessors by *studying the nineteenth century in its own right*. The connections between the Mukti Mission of Pandita Ramabai, the Anti-Temperance Society of Shevantibai Nikambe and Soonderbai Powar, are immediate and noticeable with the thought and work of Sarojini Naidu, Kamaladevi Chattopadhyaya and Annie Besant. Equally, the much-acclaimed SEWA or Self Employed Women's Association movement in Western India in the latter half of the twentieth century had its precursor in the early cooperative and cottage industry movement that the Seva Sadan of Ramabai Ranade represented. Indian feminists of the nineteenth century had reinvented and reworked the old concept of *dhandharm* [Philanthropy] and given it a new meaning encompassing the more pressing and new needs thrown up by migration and urbanization. Rescue work and the notion of bettering the lives of their *bhaginivarg* stimulated all of these campaigns, and none of them more so than the movement for the legal protection of women and children. Loopholes in the law existed and which women were quick to take advantage of, such as the Watandari Act studied in chapter 4. The participation of women in moral reform campaigns of the late nineteenth century demonstrated that they wanted a complete re-haul of Indian family relations and a transformation of the relations between the sexes within the home and outside. And the women's press of the nineteenth century played an intimate and indispensable part in awareness raising and provided the much-needed experience for early twentieth-century editors of women's journals. Any issue of the women's journal *Arya Bhagini* of the late nineteenth century resembles an issue of the contemporary women's magazine *Manushi* in its animated spirit of writing, concerns and argumentative tone. Even if the direct influence of the nineteenth-century magazine on its sister-concern of the twentieth century cannot be tracked, yet, their feminist and humanist problems remain the same.

It is a matter of conjecture whether Indian culture and society in the nineteenth century was more or less patriarchal than in other ages. But what seems clear is that Indian culture, especially the gritty, fertile and impassioned Maharashtrian society, became more conducive to feminist complaint and criticism and this was made possible by the modernizing impulses and the contingencies thrown up by the social reform movements of the late nineteenth century. Feminist impulses expressed themselves through robust leaders and women's organizations initially before being taken up individually by women at large. By the feminist critiques they wrote or plays enacted, the demands of feminists forced opponents to come to the fore and defend their antifeminist stands, thus exposing their prejudices and stereotypes about gender whilst enabling women to counter them. Equally the colonial state was made more receptive to the challenges thrown by feminists either on their own or as a result of their influencing the larger male body.

It has often been pointed out that feminist claims are primarily political claims and arise in—or respond to—particular sociopolitical historical settings and pose explicit demands for change. Gender and sex are not the only categories or determinants of historical change but also caste, class and race within colonial India. Thus, at the heart of the arguments running through this book is one which claims that the history of feminism in nineteenth-century India must be understood as part and parcel of the cultural, economic, political and social history of modern India. This book has told a story of Indian feminism—a story of individual and collective struggles of women to better their position, of their advances and setbacks and successes and failures. This is by no means a celebratory account of unblemished feminist heroines. Indeed, it recounts at times the painful story of how middle class women ruthlessly trod over their less fortunate lower class companions in pursuit of more narrow aims. Nevertheless, if there is a tale of advancement, then it is told in unconventional ways, delineated through resistance—through petitioning, reinterpreting rituals as support groups and literature and the more conventional ways of forming organizations, resolving disputes in courtrooms and influencing men in positions of authority that women had genuine grievances which were just and needed redressal and that striking changes had to be made in the laws, institutions and practises that governed relations between the sexes.

Indeed, in Maharashtrian society, the particular brand of feminism that arose from within the fabric of the social reform movement and the contingencies of colonialism had some significant successes, not least when their advocates have forced the upholders of patriarchal arrangements, whether religious or secular, to defend their views, to make their arguments explicit, and to launch repeated if not wholly effective counteroffensives. Women conducted searches in their own country's traditions for the means to achieve gender justice and selectively chose from the scrambled discourses of modernity. It is this feature of selection, amalgamation and negotiation that gives Indian feminism of the nineteenth century its uniqueness. Nineteenth-century Indian feminism is akin to what is happening in the Arab world today, where secular, Islamist and 'Muslim' feminists work alongside each other and imply fluid boundaries between them. However, for Arab women today, the crucial issue remains regarding what they 'borrow' or 'reject' out of their negotiation with Western discourses on feminism and how selective they are, regarding choices from their own traditions and histories. [4]

This study began with a critique of the dominant paradigm that has overshadowed Indian gender and women's history, namely, the uncovering of patriarchy. This hegemonic narrative, it was argued in the Introductory chapter, has marginalized the question of women's agency and swamped the scholarship interested in it. In contrast to the dominant paradigm this work has shown how Indian women negotiated the colonial world, questioned or adapted to it when necessary and ultimately made sense of it. In doing so, Indian women demonstrated that they were agents in terms of their own lives and that their actions went into the shaping of modern Indian history. One goal of this book has been to recover a buried account of feminist thought and action from India and outline its legacy. It has been claimed that 'amnesia', rather than 'lack of history, is feminism's worst enemy today.'[5] If we wish to understand the resilience of Indian patriarchy today as it reinvents itself in various forms we need to understand how it was resisted in previous generations so that the new generation springs new bargaining strategies for a better negotiation with patriarchy.

---

[4] For a discussion of contemporary Arab brands of feminisms see A. Karam, 'The Dilemma of the Production of Western Knowledge in Western Academic and Islamist feminism', <http://artsweb.bham.ac.uk/mdraper/transnatsufi/Research_Papers/Karam.html> (undated) and Heba Ra'uf, 'Rethinking Secularism: Rethinking Feminism', <http://www.islamonline.net/English/contemporary/2002/07/Article01.shtml>.

[5] Karen Offen, *European Feminisms*, p. 17.

Appendix

A Note on Women Reformers, Writers and Feminists

Many of the women covered in this note were known by their first names such as 'Rukhmabai' or had titles attached such as 'Godavaribai Pandita' and 'Anasuyabai Pandita'. Consequently, it seemed appropriate to arrange these biographical portraits alphabetically according to their first names rather than their surnames.

Anandibai Joshi (1865–1887)

Anandibai came from an elite land-holding family of Western India. Her father doted on her and gave her a good education at home. She married Gopal Vinayak Joshi in 1874, and travelled with him all over India as he worked in the Postal Department. When she was fourteen years of age she gave birth to a child that died ten days later. Anandibai considered her child's death to be a result of incompetent medical care and this largely influenced her to train as an obstetrician later when she took up medicine for a career. She graduated from the Woman's Medical College of Pennsylvania in March 1886 and in June 1886 was appointed to the position of Physician-in-Charge of the Female Wards of the Albert Edward Hospital, Kolhapur. Anandibai was erudite and was as familiar with the works of Macaulay, Edwin Arnold and Goldsmith as she was with Manu and Kalidas. A reformer at heart, she held the priesthood of India in contempt for having corrupted the national life of India and considered the West to be a harbinger of good for Indian womanhood. She believed that every man and woman had to be self-reliant and economically independent. One of the questions she answered in an album preserved in Mrs Carpenter's works captures Anandibai's outlook. The question in the book read: 'What is your *bete noir*?' to which she had written 'Slavery and dependence'. Anandibai succumbed to a chest infection and died on 26 February 1887 before she could take up the post at the Kolhapur Hospital.

Anasuyabai Pandita (1830–1929)

Anasuyabai's father, Siddheswar Maharaj, was an acclaimed scholar-priest at Pandharpur. He educated Anasuyabai in Sanskrit and at a young age she competed with male scholars and won the title of 'Pandita' in Kashi (Varanasi). Knowing well that it would be difficult to find a groom for his exceptionally gifted daughter her father married her to his own disciple, Nana Dixit. Anasuyabai's daughter Parvatibai Degaonkar enrolled the services of her mother in the cause of the women's organization, Saraswati Mandir at Sholapur. From the1890s to 1920s, she acted as a fund-raiser for Saraswati Mandir in Southern Maharashtra, providing sterling service to the cause of women's education and welfare. By profession, Anasuyabai was a *kirtankar* [religious discourse-giver]. Exceptionally good at delivering religious discourses, she made a successful living out of it. A contemporary of Pandita Ramabai, she displayed a similar mastery of Sanskrit texts and Hindu religious scriptures. In the late 1870s and early 1880s, she was much sought after by both the orthodoxy and reformers.   In her outlook Anasuyabai represents the ultimate paradox of nineteenth century India. She believed that traditional India held enough opportunities for gifted women to express themselves and was sceptical about the uses of 'modern' education. In her personal life, it is alleged that she had inverted gender roles completely. Her reformist friends record that Anasuyabai thought that she equalled Dnyaneshwar and Tukaram (medieval Maharashtrian poet-saints) and treated her husband with disdain and looked down upon her mother-in-law as a servant. Every morning, her husband and mother-in-law would bow to her and attend to her every whim, playing a role that was normally reserved for the traditional Indian wife.

Chimabai kom Lakshman Kadam (dates unknown)

Hired by the School Textbook Committee in Maharashtra, Chimabai was the first woman cartographer of modern India. She produced maps of India as well as continents and other countries around the world. The following are attributed to her: a map of Europe, Asia, Africa and an Atlas of the world. She was occasionally also commissioned to draw maps of Maharashtra's districts and major towns and cities such as Bombay, Poona and Satara. The print runs varied between 80 and 1000 copies, and their dates indicate that this work was carried out between the 1880s and the 1900s. The names of cities and rivers are in the Marathi language. The Oriental translator, fully aware of her gender, does not merit her work for a more in-depth discussion other than listing the maps as the: 'Work of a female artist' in the *Catalogue of Books printed in the Bombay Presidency starting from the Quarter Ending 30 September 1867 to Quarter Ending 31 December 1896* (see chapter 3).

Cornelia Sorabji (1866–1954)

A second generation Christian and the fifth daughter of Rev. Sorabji Kharsedji Langrana and Franscina (see below), Cornelia Sorabji is representative of a colonial subject of the nineteenth century whose 'hybrid' identity was formed through the encounter between Imperial Britain and colonial India. Cornelia was one of her mother's first pupils in the newly opened Victoria High School in Pune from where she matriculated and from then onwards is a story of outstanding performances from passing exams with merit to winning prizes and scholarships. She was awarded the BA degree in 1888 and took a teaching assignment in an all-male college (Gujarat College) of Ahmedabad. In 1889, she joined Somerville Hall, Oxford University in the hope of earning a law degree. From 1889 to 1923 is a saga of trials and tribulations she faced from a jealously guarded, exclusively male profession such as the law represented in Victorian Britain. Although she was allowed to sit the exams and gain the degree of Bachelor of Law in Oxford and yet another law degree in Bombay, she was prevented from practising law until she had been called to the Bar. As a result of the Sex Disqualification (Removal) Act of 1919, and when the Bar finally threw open its doors to women in 1922, she became a member of the Lincoln's Inn in 1923. In 1904, she finally landed a job in India as a Legal Advisor to the Court of Wards. She worked in this position for a further thirty years giving legal advice on property and inheritance matters to aristocratic women, especially widows and child-wives in Eastern India. In 1909, the government honoured her with a Kaiser-i-Hind medal. A prolific writer, the books *India Calling* and *India Recalled* contain her reminiscences. She also wrote numerous children's stories and acted as a social commentator on India's problems for leading nineteenth-century British magazines such as *Nineteenth Century and After* and *National Review*. She was a 'New Woman' of her era (a term she would have hated but was used by her male peers in the Lincoln Chambers) since she represented self-reliance and single-mindedly pursued a career. Despite her anti-suffragist and anti-nationalist stance, she had, ironically, crossed both gender and race boundaries and embraced Victorian imperial culture in pursuit of becoming an imperial citizen.

Franscina Santya Sorabji (1833–1905)

A Hindu convert to Christianity, Franscina was adopted by Lady Georgina and Sir Francis Ford at the age of 12. As self-proclaimed Orientalists, her adoptive parents ensured that she received an eclectic education. Despite an 'English' upbringing and education she was nevertheless brought up to feel proud of India. She married Kharsedji Sorabji in 1853. In the 1860s when her husband was managing his Industrial School in Nasik she went out to villages as a catechist. In 1876, she started a unique educational experiment in Poona under the name of Victoria High School, which was the first school in India run by an Indian for Eurasian children of both sexes. She opened four more schools for Indian children, which were ably managed by three of her daughters. In 1886, under the auspices of the Zenana Bible and Medical Mission, she visited England in order to raise money for her schools. She was an important witness for the Hunter Education Commission of 1883. As a pioneer educationalist, her help and advice were sought after by many including

Pandita Ramabai. She combined a passionate loyalty to the Queen with a spiritual allegiance to Christianity. She believed that British rule was beneficial for India. Her influence as a feminist on her own daughters was such that all six of them broke traditional boundaries both in their choice of professions and marriage.

Girijabai Kelkar (1886–1980)

This remarkable Hindu feminist was married into a family of illustrious Marathi literary figures; although her mother-in-law did not support her forays into the public arena, Girijabai's husband, Madhavarao Kelkar sympathized with her aspirations and encouraged her to seek a profession in Marathi literature. A prolific writer, she promoted Marathi language and literature. She wrote and lectured extensively on all aspects of women's lives and rights. In the early twentieth century she opened a women's organization called Bhagini Mandal at Jalgaon. She was President of the All India Hindu Mahila Parishad in 1935. She held complex views on the nature of women's oppression, which are expressed in her literary works, such as *Purushanche Band* [Men's Rebellion] and *Striyancha Swarga* [Women's Paradise]. She wrote the play *Purushanche Band* to counteract the effects of the vilification of Indian women in the play *Striyancha Band* [Women's Rebellion] by Khadilkar. Her memoir titled *Draupadichi Thali* provides rich details on her life and impressions. (See chapters 3 and 4 for an analysis of her work and the bibliography contains a list of her main works).

Godavaribai Pandita (dates unknown)

Details on her personal life are scarce but it is obvious that as a writer she was well known to the Maharashtrian public in the late nineteenth century. She came from an orthodox Brahmin family and was married to an educated man at the age of 11, under whose tutelage she learnt Marathi and English. A prolific writer, she produced several novels, an advice manual, and books on culinary and home management for women in Marathi and became a literary celebrity in Poona. She admired the scientific framework that formed the basis of Western knowledge but was unwilling to accept it as 'superior' to Indian ones. For example, despite adopting what she considered to be admirable features of English cooking, such as the use of weights and measures and the principles of hygiene, overall, she viewed it as merely the 'science of making soups'. Her patron was the royal family of Baroda, to whom she dedicated her cookery manual. She urged women to seek an education and participate in public life, citing herself as an example of how a woman could retain her womanliness and be a chaste, dutiful wife and mother despite also possessing the trappings of modernity. (See chapter 3 and bibliography for her main works).

Kashibai Herlekar (1874–1936)

Born in 1874 to Narayan Vishnu Deo and Sagunabai Deo, Kashibai was fortunate in having schoolteachers as her parents. Her mother Sagunabai taught Ramabai Ranade and in return was housed in the vicinity of Justice Ranade's mansion in Shukravarpeth, Poona. When Kashibai was merely four years old, Sagunabai was employed as the tutor to the Queen of Baroda on a salary of 60 rupees per month along with accommodation. In 1884, Kashibai won a prestigious scholarship given by the Baroda State to pursue further education in Hujur Paga High School for Girls, Poona. In 1889, Kashibai passed the English Sixth Standard in flying colours but her marriage at this time to a person uninterested in her education was to have disastrous consequences on her future. However, with the help of the *bhaginivarg* [sisterhood] at the time rendered by women like the Sorabji sisters and Miss Hurford she passed the matriculation exam in 1895. She was a prolific writer contributing many articles to the women's press of the time on topics such as widowhood, the institutions of arranged and child-marriage and women's education. She wrote under the pen name of 'Suvasini'. From 1890 onwards she served in the post of headmistress of a school in Baroda. In the early part of the twentieth century she gained many accolades and was feted by the reformist circles in Western India when as a representative of the Baroda State she spoke at the Indian Social Conference, Indian Women's Conference and the 'Winter Series' of Lectures in Bombay organized by prominent social reformers of the time.

Kashibai Kanitkar (1861–1948)

Born into a wealthy Brahmin family and married to Govind Vasudev Kanitkar at the age of nine, she had no formal education but learnt to read and write Marathi, Sanskrit and English at home. Extremely well read, she mastered many Hindu religious, scientific and historical treatises. She expressed a desire to translate J.S. Mill's *Subjection of Women*, which had a powerful impact on her values and beliefs regarding womanhood. Despite strong opposition from her husband, she became a Theosophist. A staunch feminist, she believed that women's oppression stemmed from male dominance and strongly supported the women's movement of her time. She wrote several novels, short stories and essays, all of which dealt with women's issues. A contemporary of Girijabai Kelkar, she wrote a strikingly similar novel using the same genre of a woman's utopia titled *Palkicha Gonda* [The Tassel at the Centre of the Palanquin]. See chapters 3 and 6 for more details.

Krupabai Khisti nee Sathianadhan (1862–1893)

Born at Ahmednagar on 14 February 1862, her parents, Haripant Khisty and Radhabai, were among the earliest Brahmin converts in the Bombay Presidency.

Her father died early and she was brought up by her mother, a Bible-woman, and educated at home. When she was 12 years old, she was sent to an American mission school in Bombay where it was soon found that she was far ahead of the highest class. Noting her precocious intellect, the missionaries offered her the option of studying further. By then, Krupabai had already decided to be a doctor so she was sent to the Madras Medical College, which had opened its doors to women, and came top of the class in her first year. In her second year, however, Krupabai's health started to fail and she was forced to discontinue her studies. She went on to marry Samuel Satthianadhan, a Cambridge-returned Indian Christian, but died at the early age of 31. In her own time, she was widely known and had a national and international audience for her writings. A prolific writer, her known writings are around twenty essays, two full-length novels and innumerable poems. She was hailed as India's first female novelist and poetess writing in the English language. Her novels are compared to Jane Austen due to her eye for detail, the satirical voice she adopts and their exposure of the domestic hypocrisies of the time. Of interest are her feminist critiques, exposition of white racism, the wry delineation of and missionary mentalities and her criticisms of the English-educated Indian middle classes. (See chapter 2).

Lakshmibai Deshmukh (1866–unknown)

Lakshmibai Deshmukh, alias Maisaheb, was born in 1866 in the village of Linvgoa, in Sholapur district, Maharashtra. She came from a well-known and well-to-do family of Sardar Apte. At the age of six she was married to Laxmanrao, alias Appasaheb, the youngest son of the radical reformer Rao Bahadur Gopal Hari Deshmukh, popularly known as 'Lokahitavadi'. Appasaheb, Lakshmibai's husband, was in the Civil Service and was posted in 1895 to Sholapur as its first Indian Collector. Like many other Maharashtrian feminists of her time, Lakshmibai learnt about women's subordination through observation and experience. She admitted that not knowing how to read and write posed great difficulties in her day-to-day household management, which made her eager to learn English, Marathi and accounting. In 1895, she found like-minded women in Sholapur such as Parvatibai Degaonkar, Kashibai Kanitkar and Lakshmibai Kirloskar and together they founded the remarkable women's organization—Saraswati Mandir. Lakshmibai Deshmukh was a 'doer' by nature rather than a writer or thinker. By her privileged position in Maharashtrian social circles she was able to influence other women of her time by example.

Lakshmibai Dravid (dates unknown)

Her biographical details remain obscure but it is clear that she was a contemporary of Pandita Ramabai and Tarabai Shinde. Her work *Deshseva Nibandhamala*

[Essays in Service of the Nation] published in 1896 was the first economic critique of imperialism by an Indian woman. The tract is a fragmented exploration in many ways, but clearly expresses nationalist aspirations and urges women to stop using foreign goods and instead support indigenous traders and industries through the use of *swadeshi* or Indian-manufactured products. Whilst she critiqued Western interpretations of Indian history she believed in the 'Golden Age' of the Orientalists and theories that blamed India's decline on Muslim rule. Lakshmibai Dravid must be considered a pioneer in many ways despite her religious intolerance. Her work is unique not just for Maharashtra but for nineteenth-century India because it is the first tract by an Indian woman on government and taxation, devaluation of the rupee and de-industrialization, language politics and the cow protection movement.

Lakshmibai Kirloskar (1871–1914)

Lakshmibai was born in Vammannahalli near Hubli (now in North Karnataka) in a well-known family called Tembe. At the age of ten she was married to Raosaheb Kirloskar. Her education began in her in-laws home under the watchful eye of her husband, a man of liberal ideas. Gifted with a phonetic memory, Lakshmibai quickly learnt Marathi, Sanskrit and English and maintained a highly successful public profile with the image of a very able housewife and daughter-in-law to the elite family of Kirloskars. In her adult life she became a *kirtankar*, rendering the hymns of Moropant and Mukteshwar on a regular basis to the public in Sholapur. The annual reports of the women's organization in Sholapur claim that she gave all her earnings from the profession of a *kirtankar* for funding the Saraswati Mandir's multifaceted activities. Having borne seven children, she had learnt through personal experience the difficulties women faced through the institution of early marriage and its obstacles to women's education and professional aspirations. Under her dynamic leadership Saraswati Mandir became Southern Maharashtra's premier women's organization in the 1910s. She added a further dimension to the Saraswati Mandir's profile by opening a Kanyashala [School for Orphaned Girls] around the turn of the century. Her contemporaries remember her for her first rate oratory especially in front of all-male audiences on topics such as 'Why do men tread on women's rights?', 'The necessity of women going beyond *chool ni mool* [kitchen and kid] ', 'The evils of child marriage', and 'On the professional training and education of widows,'. She has been credited with the invention of the *Mushti Fund* in Sholapur (see chapter 3 for details).

Lakshmibai Tilak (1868–1936)

Lakshmibai Tilak was a first-generation Hindu convert to Christianity. Born in 1868, she married a highly intelligent but eccentric poet, Narayan Vaman Tilak, in

1879; he went on to embrace Christianity in 1895. It would not be far from the truth to say that Lakshmibai's personality was completely formed by the trauma of adjusting to this event, and the wrath of her extended family heaped on her husband. Her trials, tribulations, attempts at suicide, subsequent reconciliation with her husband and her own decision to become a Christian in 1900 are all powerfully expressed in her autobiography. Her memoirs are now an integral part of the canon of Marathi literature due to the use of humour as a literary weapon in order to express intimate details of Indian social life and also her conversational style of writing. Literary critics regard her as one of the modern Marathi writers of her time. However, it remains unstudied by historians, despite the fact that it contains a wealth of information on critical issues of social and cultural history of the nineteenth century such as the public health issue of plague, inter-caste relations, domestic and conjugal relations, the urban–rural divide and so on. Some extracts from her Marathi memoirs titled *Smriti Chitre* [Recalled from Memory: My Life] relating to her conversion were translated and published by Josephine Inkster in 1950 as *I Follow After*.

Mary Bhor (1865?–1913)

Daughter of Rao Saheb Ramji Gangaji Bhor and a second-generation Christian, she took advantage of her English education and fairly liberal background provided by her parents. She had obtained a teacher's training certificate from London and in her capacity as headmistress she had travelled widely in the Bombay Presidency. In the 1890s, she held a highly paid appointment as a governess to the Princesses of Baroda. She became the Lady Superintendent of the Poona Female High School around 1905. She wrote a travelogue in English called *My Impressions of England* (Poona, 1900) and a Marathi novel, *Pushpakarandak* [Basket of Flowers: A Homily], in 1890. The novel is relatively free from a commentary on the relative merits or demerits of Hinduism and Christianity, yet a juxtaposition of one-dimensional characters such as the 'good and virtuous Shanta' and the 'bad prostitute Sundrabai' places it firmly in the canon of nineteenth-century Marathi literature when the novel as a genre was still in its formative phase.

Parvatibai Athavale (1870–unknown)

Born in 1870 at Devrukh to a poor Brahmin family, she was married off at the age of 11 and was widowed at 21. Her life was transformed when her widowed sister Bayabai married D.K. Karve. Bayabai brought her to Poona and encouraged her to study. At the age of twenty-eight she trained to be a teacher but her natural aptitude for oratory led her to become a full-time fundraiser of the Hingne Widows' Home, which Karve founded in 1897. Her boundless energies enabled the Hingne Widows' Home to maintain sixty widows through her own fundraising activities.

She believed that widows should not wait for deliverance but act. She also campaigned incessantly for a ban on *keshavapan* [tonsure ceremony] to which Hindu widows were subjected. She was one of the few Hindu women leaders who would not mince words with foot-dragging male reformers. At the age of 46, she travelled to America to learn about the American women's movement and addressed prominent women's organizations such as the Sorosis Club in New York. She disliked Indians who mimicked the West blindly. Instead she asked women to learn organizational skills, discipline and methods from Westerners and apply them to typically Indian problems. In 1928, she wrote a memoir in Marathi that was subsequently published and translated by Justin Abbott under the title *My Story*. Written with a male colleague's help, it portrays her in a conventional cast and fails to capture her radical nature. In order to gauge her true views, I would suggest to readers that they read her public speeches and what she wrote in the women's press at this time (see chapter 3).

Pandita Ramabai (1858–1922)

Born in a Chitpawan Brahmin family of Mangalore district, Karnataka, her father Ananta Shastri Dongre, taught at the Peshwa's court where he was impressed by the Sanskrit knowledge of the Peshwa's wife. He taught his wife, Lakshmibai, who, in turn, taught Ramabai. In 1875, Ramabai accompanied her parents on their wanderings round India, and her parents died in the famine of 1877. Ramabai was a child prodigy and by the age of 12 had committed to memory 12,000 verses of the ancient Sanskrit scriptures. In Calcutta, at the age of twenty, she was drawn into the reform circles and, in an open competition with male pandits, won the title of 'Pandita Saraswati'. In 1879 she married a non-Brahmin Bengali, Bipin Behari Medhavi, and moved to Silchar (Assam) for 19 months; her daughter Manoramabai was born there. In 1880, her husband died in a cholera epidemic and she went back to Bombay. Fluent in Marathi, Kannada, Hindi, Bengali as well as Sanskrit, in later years she mastered Greek, Latin and Hebrew and in 1882, she learned English with Ramabai Ranade in Poona. It was at this time that she also amalgamated her Ladies Association with other women's groups, bringing them together under the rubric of a single organization called the Arya Mahila Samaj. The earnings from her first book in Marathi, *Stri-dharma Niti* [Advice Manual on the Duties and Conduct of Women], funded her travel to England, where she stayed with the Wantage Sisters and learnt Christian theology and converted to Christianity in 1883. For a while, she held the Chair of Sanskrit at the prestigious Cheltenham Ladies College before travelling to America where, between 1885 and 1887, she studied the kindergarten system of education. Meanwhile, her vision for the liberation of Indian women had crystallized and she lectured extensively to draw attention to the pitiable condition of Indian women and the need to emancipate them. Her next book in English, *The High-Caste Hindu Woman*, a powerful feminist tract, captured the imagination of a wide cross-section of the American public, from Quakers to Evangelicals, and 65

'Ramabai circles' were formed; an elected board from these, called The American Ramabai Association coordinated their activities. Pandita Ramabai was awarded the Kaiser-i-Hind medal by the Indian government in recognition of her services to Indian women. She died in 1922. A selection of her works is now available in Meera Kosambi (trans. and ed.), *Pandita Ramabai in Her Own Words* (New York: Feminist Press, 2000). Also see, Pandita Ramabai, *The Peoples of United States* (1st edn 1889), M. Kosambi, trans. and ed., (Delhi: Permanent Black, 2004).

Ramabai Ranade (1862–1924)

Married in 1873 to Mahadeo Govind Ranade, an extremely influential reformer of Western India, Ramabai Ranade's potential as an original thinker and activist was only realized after the death of her husband in 1901. She was the key figure in the Seva Sadan, one of western India's most spectacularly successful philanthropic institutions. Three of her achievements deserve special mention: for initiating a movement for the compulsory education of girls in Maharashtra; successfully campaigning for the enfranchisement of Indian women as well as their representation on the Legislative Council; and her protest against the indentured system of labour in British colonies. Her liberal politics was probably the key to her extraordinary success in many of the campaigns she led (see chapter 3) Ramabai wrote an autobiography in Marathi in 1910, titled *Amchya Ayushyatil Kahi Athavani* [Memoirs of Our Life Together], which rightly became an instant classic for capturing beautifully her life after meeting her husband and their personal, spiritual, emotional and intellectual journey through life together. This vignette captures wonderfully the vicissitudes faced by couples in the social reform movement of the nineteenth century and their struggles in mixing and matching the scrambled discourses of modernity with tradition. A very able translation was made available by Kusumavati Deshpande in 1963 and published by the Government of India as *Ranade: His Wife's Reminiscences.*

Rebecca Simeon (1859–1904)

Rebecca's maiden name was Seema Ghosalkar. Born in the Bene-Israelite community of Alibag, Seema was sent to a missionary school by her father, Subedar Ghosalkar. In 1875 she chose to marry Benjamin Simeon, a friend from her schooldays. After her marriage, she came to be known as Rebecca Simeon. Rebecca showed an interest in gaining a medical education and enrolled in the Grant Medical College's Midwifery Class. Having passed her exams she started a private practice in Bombay, which attracted a great number of women patients from all classes. With her reformist husband Benjamin she opened an organization in Bombay called Niti Prasarak Mandal in 1882, which had close links with Jyotiba Phule's Satyashodhak Samaj. Rebecca was well known in her time for philanthropic activities, oratory and writings. She wrote many books and articles in Marathi in relation to children and women's health. Her main works, *Kutumba Mitra* [A Family Friend: Manual on Medicine], first published in 1878 and *Sooin* [The Midwife], published in 1879, received much attention from the Marathi press and public and reveal a combination of knowledge and use of conventional medicine such as Ayurveda and also new techniques taken from alleopathy. (see chapters 3 and 6).

Rukhmabai (1862–1953)

If Caroline Norton had drawn the attention of the British public to the whole issue of women's subordinate status in marriage through a highly sensationalized campaign, pressurizing the Parliament to revise the matrimonial laws of the time, Rukhmabai began a similar high-profile campaign in the late nineteenth century in India and subsequently in Britain. Rukhmabai was born in 1862 to Jayantibai and Janardhan Pandurang Savle, members of an affluent Maratha caste of Bombay. When she later remarried, Jayantibai brought all her children from her first marriage, including Rukhmabai, to live with them and appointed an English tutor to educate them. Dr Sakharam Arjun, Rukhmabai's stepfather, was an eminent surgeon and a prominent figure in the social reform circles of Bombay. In 1887, Rukhmabai catapulted to notoriety when she openly defied the court's injunction to join her husband and denied him conjugal rights (see chapter 6 for details). Rukhmabai subsequently went to England to train as a doctor, returning to India in 1895 with a medical degree. She went to Surat (in the present state of Gujarat) to practice medicine to avoid any future scandals. She worked for the welfare of women and children in Surat and Rajkot for the next 22 years and was awarded the Kaiser-i-Hind medal for her tremendous work in the field of medical care and relief of women. In 1917 she retired, and she died at the age of 91. Her marriage to Dadaji was never annulled in court. Instead it had the nature of the old Maratha custom of *kadimod* [separation] rather than g*hatasphot* [divorce]. Although she is not reported to have had any other partner, her husband Dadaji Bhikaji had remarried in 1899. Although separated from her husband Rukhmabai never stopped wearing the traditional symbols of a married Hindu woman, and when Dadaji died in 1904, she formally adopted the clothes of a widow.

Salubai Tambwekar (dates unknown)

Salubai, the wife of Bhau Saheb Tambwekar, came from a wealthy background. Salubai's bold forays into the Marathi literary world indicate that her life spanned the mid and late nineteenth century. She was a promising novelist who tried her hand at transforming the more fantasy-based themes of Marathi literature with the newer forms of romantic comedy borrowed from the English novel that was met with hostility. Her first novel, *Chandraprabhaviraha* [Heartache of Chandraprabha on her Separation from her Beloved] was published in 1873 in Poona. This novel's theme was a perfectly acceptable and highly visible genre in Marathi literature of the time, namely, the pining of a woman besotted with thoughts of her beloved from whom she had the misfortune of being separated. The other novel, titled *Hindustanatil Tara* [Indian Princesses], and published in 1895, was about princesses being captured by giants and rescued by dashing merchant princes adept in the art of sorcery and was received with lukewarm enthusiasm. Salubai's first novel appeared in the 1870s but her second novel came as late as the mid-1890s. She perhaps took the criticism seriously though she was not discouraged from publishing again.

Savitribai Phule (1831–1897)

Savitribai's importance as an educationist, woman's rights activist, scholar and poet of the late nineteenth century has only recently come to light due to the superb work of Marathi scholars such as Prof. M.G. Mali, who has edited her collected works. The information here has been culled from Mali's Marathi biography of her published in 1980, *Krantijyoti Savitribai Jotirao Phule* [The Revolutionary Savitribai Jotirao Phule]. She was born in 1831 and married to Jyotiba Phule at the age of nine (1840). Along with her husband she pioneered the rehabilitation of *mang-mahars*—the untouchable castes of Western India. Together, they provided sterling service in the cause of women's emancipation and five schools are credited to her and her husband. Four of them were meant for the education of women and girls and one was for *mang-mahar* children opened in and around Poona in the 1850s. Savitribai braved a great deal of criticism and ostracism from mainstream Maharashtrian society which harassed her and her family for transgressing gender and caste boundaries and boldly proclaiming the ills of Indian society and the need for equality between humans.

Shewantibai Nikambe (dates unknown)

Her life spanned the latter half of the nineteenth and early twentieth centuries. Although little is known about her early life, she was a well-known second generation Christian and played an active role in missionary activities in England and America. She was a headmistress of a girls' school run by the Students' Scientific and Literary Society of Bombay but quit in 1890 in order to open her own school called the Princess Girls High School. Apart from her educational enterprises she was a literary figure in her own right and published a novel in the English language titled *Ratanbai: A Sketch of a Bombay High Caste Hindu young wife* in 1895, which made her famous within her own lifetime. The novel is interesting, not only for the way in which it shows how the institution of child marriage stunts the mental and physical development of girls and boys, but also for its insights into Bombay's urban character, and how this milieu gave rise to ignorance and superstition among women. She was also associated with the Indian temperance movement and was Secretary of the organization Striyanchi Madhyanishedhak Sabha [Women's Anti-Drink Society].

Soonderbai Powar (1856–1921)

She was the daughter of Ramachandra and Ganderbai, a first-generation Christian couple who originally came from wealthy high-caste families. As a child she accompanied her parents as they preached the Gospel in rural parts of Maharashtra and thus learnt a great deal about popular Hinduism. Up to the age of twelve, her father and a Sanskrit tutor taught her at home, and, at the age of 14, she taught English to the wife of the Deputy Collector of Sasvad. She soon expressed a desire to be a *zenana* teacher; her parents therefore sent her to Bombay to acquire the necessary education. For several years she dabbled in nursing and teaching but did not enjoy the work and went back to teaching in *zenanas* [women's secluded quarters]. She differed radically from Western missionaries in her methods of instruction. The first booklet written by her, *Is Zenana work a failure?*, was intended to provide encouragement to disheartened missionaries. She was well known in Britain for her anti-opium crusade. In 1883 she met Pandita Ramabai and was so impressed by her learning and courage that, when Ramabai moved her school Sharada Sadan from Bombay to Pune, Soonderbai left *zenana* work and accompanied her. For seven years, she was Ramabai's 'right-hand'; when the latter's work was placed on a stable footing, she left the Mukti Mission and opened a Zenana Training Teacher's School in Poona. This school flourished on funds she had secured by her travels in England, Scotland and Ireland. She wrote many tracts, amongst which the book *Hinduism and Womanhood* most clearly expressed her views on women's issues.

Tarabai Shinde (dates unknown)

With a life that spanned the latter half of the nineteenth and the early twentieth centuries, Tarabai Shinde was born in a prosperous dominant warrior peasant community (Marathas). Her own family formed part of the elite of Buldhana, a small town in Varhad province of Central India and her father, Bapuji Hari Shinde, was a reformer and member of the Satyashodhak Samaj; Tarabai Shinde's own work is mentioned in Jyotiba Phule's (prominent non-Brahmin leader of the time) larger works. Tarabai was the only female child and was indulged by her father who taught her Sanskrit, English and Marathi. Her main work, *Stripurushtulana* [Women and Men, A Comparison] was published in 1882 with a print run of 500 copies; the hostile reception it received from the Maharashtrian press meant that she never published again. Her contribution to the development of the Marathi language in terms of linguistic innovations and the importance of her tract as a 'feminist' critique of gender relations in nineteenth-century India remains to be fully assessed. A translation of her work is now available. See Rosalind O'Hanlon, *A Comparison between Women and Men: Tarabai Shinde and the Critique of Gender Relations in Colonial India* (Madras: Oxford University Press, 1994).

Vithabai Chaudhari (1850–unknown)

Born into a Brahmin family in Poona in 1850, she was educated by her father against the wishes of her mother and grandmother. She trained to be a teacher, although she really wanted to enter the medical profession and knew five languages. She met Mary Carpenter and was inspired by her. She served as a headmistress of girls' schools in various towns of the Bombay Presidency. She was interviewed by the members of the Education Commission of 1883 to sound out her views on the problems besetting female education in India. Vithabai believed that female teachers laboured under various disadvantages and ought to be given more incentives than male teachers.

Yashodabai Joshi (1868–1948)

Born to an elite Brahmin family of Abhyankar. In 1874, she married Vishwanath Moropant Joshi, a social reformer and nationalist who later became the most popular legal practitioner from Amravati. Yashodabai began her education at her in-law's home at the age of seventeen. She is one of the finest examples of an Indian feminist who learnt through experience. Her autobiography, written in 1940, and not originally meant for publication, is not only full of rich detail about her work to promote 'women's progress', but also contains a fearless critique of contemporary society. She also founded a premier women's organization called Vanita Samaj in 1892 in Amravati. Influenced by Pandita Ramabai and Ramabai Ranade, it is likely that the women's movement she led in Central Maharashtra was modelled on the Arya Mahila Samaj of Poona (see chapter 3 and bibliography). Yashodabai's daughter Manikbai Bhide published her mother's memoir in 1965, calling it *Amchi Jeevanpravas*, and recently her grandson, V.V. Bhide brought out an English translation of the same titled *A Marathi Saga: Yashodabai Joshi* (Roli Books, 2003).

Bibliography

Primary Sources

The bibliography contains an exhaustive list of English and Marathi primary source materials, which went in the making of this book. Although secondary sources are not listed here, they can be easily tracked through the 'Index'. The 'Index' contains names of all authors cited in this book. The full reference of every secondary source can be found in the main chapters of this monograph whenever it is cited for the first time.

I   Unpublished Material

1   *Government Archives: Oriental and India Office Records, British Library, London*

Government of India, Bombay Education Proceedings, Part (A), 1870–1910.
Government of India, Bombay Judicial Proceedings, Part (A), 1870–1920.
Government of India, Bombay Legislative Proceedings, Part (A), 1870–1920.
Government of India, Bombay Military Proceedings, Part (A), 1850–1910.
Native Newspaper Reports, Bombay Series, 1860–1917.

2   *Government Archives: Maharashtra, Bombay*

Education Department, Part (B), 1870–1920.
General Department, Part (B), 1870–95.
Judicial Department, Part (B), 1870–1910.
Legislative Department, Part (B), 1870–1915.

3   *Manuscript Sources*

Mrs Sarojini Chawalar's Private Collection, Dharwar
Huzur Paga School Collection, Poona
Institutional Collection of Mukti Mission, Kedgaon, Maharashtra
    Pandita Ramabai Papers
        Petition of the Arya Mahila Association to 'Hon. Sir Bartle Frere Saheb

Bahadoor', 11 June 1883 (handwritten manuscript), unpaginated
'Story of Jivi and others' (typed manuscript), unpaginated
Rajas Dongre's collection in Mukti Mission, Kedgaon, Maharashtra
Oriental and India Office Collections, British Library, London
Private papers of Cornelia Sorabji, MSS.Eur.f.165, Seva Sadan Collection, Seva Sadan, Poona

4 *Unpublished Theses and Articles*

Bose, Amina, 'American Missionaries' Involvement in Higher Education in India in the Nineteenth Century,' Ph.D. thesis, University of Kansas, 1971.
Michel, Martina, 'The Sarda Act, Political Strategy and Trends in Discourse in the Child Marriage Debate in India during the 1920's', M.A. dissertation, University of Hannover, July 1989.
Pearson, Gail, 'Women in Public Life in Bombay City with Special Reference to the Civil Disobedience Movement', Ph.D. thesis, Jawaharlal Nehru University, Delhi, 1979.
McCarthy, Patrick, 'Should Restitution of Conjugal Rights Become Part of a Uniform Civil Code of India?' M.A. thesis, School of Oriental and African Studies, London University, July 1986.
Raeside, Ian, 'Agarkar, Apte and The Kanitkars', unpublished paper.

II Published Material

1 *Newspapers and Periodicals (English)*

Cheltenham Ladies College Magazine, Mukti Mission Library, Kedgaon.
The Indian Antiquary, School of Oriental and African Studies, London.
Journal of the Indian National Association, British Library, London.
Mahratta, Kesari and Mahratta Office, Poona.
Mukti Prayer Bell, Institutional Collection of Mukti Mission, Kedgaon.
Pan-Anglican Papers (London, 1908), Institutional Collection of Mukti Mission, Kedgaon.
Panch Howd Magazine, Mukti Mission Library, Kedgaon.
Roshni, Centre for South Asian Studies, Cambridge.
Times of India, British Library, London.
The Woman's Herald, Fawcett Library, London.

2   *Official Publications and Reports*

'Act No. XIV of 1868. An Act for the prevention of certain contagious diseases passed by the Governor General on the 17th April 1868', *Acts passed by the Government of India, (1835–1917)*, Maharashtra State Government Archives, Bombay.

Administration Report on the Civil Hospitals and Dispensaries under the government of Bombay, 1882 (Bombay: Government of Bombay, 1882).

Annual Report of the American Ramabai Association (Boston, 1885–1910), Institutional Collection of Mukti Mission, Kedgaon.

Annual Report of the Director of Public Instruction in the Bombay Presidency, (1880–1910), Maharashtra State Archives, Bombay.

Catalogue of Books Printed in the Bombay Presidency, 1867–1950, Quarterly Lists (Bombay: Department of Public Instruction), Oriental and India Office Collections, British Library, London.

Copy of the Report to Marquis of Salisbury by Miss Mary Carpenter on Prison Discipline and on Female Education in India, dated 7 September 1876. Oriental and India Office Collections, British Library, London.

Diamond Jubilee Souvenir, Poona Seva Sadan Society, 1909–1969 (Poona: Seva Sadan Society Press, 1970).

Indian Law Reports (Bombay Series, 1875–95), (Madras: Law Reports Office), School of Oriental and African Studies, London.

Malabari, B.M., 'Notes on infant-marriage and enforced widowhood', in *Selections from the Records*, V/23/49/223 (Government of India, Home Department, 1887).

Moore, E.F. *Reports of Cases Heard and Determined by the Judicial Committee and the Lords of Her Majesty's Privy Council on Appeal from the Supreme and Sudder Dewanny Courts in the East Indies* (Bangalore: Richmond F. Hayes, 1858).

Pandita Ramabai Centenary Souvenir, 1858–1958 (Bombay: S.M. Adhav, 1958).

Report of the Indian Education Commission, 1882–1883 (Calcutta: Government of India Publication, 1883), Oriental and India Office Collections, British Library, London.

Richey, J.S., *Selections from Educational Records*, Part II (Calcutta: Bureau of Education, 1922).

Silver Jubilee Album of the Seva Sadan Society containing Review and Report of the varied activities of the Society at its headquarters in Poona and at its outside branches, 1935 (Poona: Seva Sadan Society Press, 1936).

3   *Newspapers and Periodicals (Marathi)*

Abalamitra, Mumbai Marathi Grantha Sangrahalaya, Mumbai
Arya Bhagini, Shasakiya Vibhagiya Granthalaya, Pune
Balikadarsh, Huzur Paga School, Pune
Dnyanodaya, Centre for South Asian Studies, Cambridge

Grihini Ratnamala, Shasakiya Vibhagiya Granthalaya, Pune
Grihini, Mumbai Marathi Grantha Sangrahalaya, Bombay
*Induprakash,*Centre for South Asian Studies, Cambridge
Kesari, Kesari and Mahratta Office, Pune
Maharashtra Mahila, Mumbai Marathi Grantha Sangrahalaya, Bombay
Saubhagyasambhar, Pune Marathi Granthalaya
Simantini, Mumbai Marathi Grantha Sangrahalaya, Bombay
Strisadbodhachintamani, Mumbai Marathi Grantha Sangrahalaya, Bombay
Strishikshanchandrika, Mumbai Marathi Grantha Sangrahalaya, Bombay
Subodh Patrika, Jawaharlal Nehru Library, University of Bombay, Kalina Campus
Swadesh Bhagini, Pune Marathi Granthalaya, Pune
Vividhadnyan Vistar, Jayakar Library, University of Pune

4   *Books (Marathi)*

Ambabai (alias Lakshmibai Siddhaye), *Padya Sangraha* [Collection of Hymns] (Bombay: Indian Printing Press, 1888).

Anandibai, *Anandibaikritpancharatnageet* [Composition of Anandibai on Hindu Theology, Philosophy and Devotional Subjects], 2nd edn (Bombay: Ganpat Krishnaji, 1896; 1st edn 1870?).

Agarkar, G.G. *Agarkar Vangmaya, Khand Ek* [Collected Works of Agarkar, Vol. 1] (Mumbai: Marathi Grantha Sangrahalaya, 1992)

Baba Padmanji, *Yamuna Paryatan* [Yamuna's Rambles], 4th edn (Bombay: E.V. Padmanji, 1937).

Bal, V., *Kamalaki* [Aunt Kamala] (Bombay: Mauj Prakashan, 1972).

Bhave, L.D., *Ganapatiche Ganen va Striyanche Nashibacha Dakhala* [Songs in Praise of God Ganapati and Musings on the Fate of Women] (Poona: Siddhi Vinayak, 1895).

[Compiler unknown], *Striyan va Mulikarita Sangeet Sundar Gani* [Songs of Women and Girls] (Ratnagiri: Damanskar, n.d.).

Dharadhar, Y., *Sutachya Vina Kamachen Pustak* [Manual on Weaving Cotton Clothes] (Bombay: Nirnaya Sagar, 1898).

Gadre, B.G., *Shimga* [Holi Festival] (Bombay: Subodha Patrika Press, 1884).

Godavaribai Pandita, *Pakdarpan athava Maharashtriya Swayampakashastra* [Cookery Manual or Maharashtrian Culinary Science] (Poona: Dnyan Chaksu, 1893).

Godavaribai Panditina, *Rangavallika athava Rangoli ani Leni Kadnyachi Pustak* [Art of Rangoli and drawing Figures using Coloured Powders and Dyes] (Bombay: Bombay City Press, 1889).

Gokhale, P. (ed.), *Stri Geetratnakar* [A Collection of Women's Songs] (Poona: Bharat Bhushan Press, 1912).

Bhagvat, N.H., *Hunda Prahasan* [A Farce on Dowry], 2nd edn (Poona: Sudhakar, 1887).

Inamdar, R.I., *Striyakarita Manoranjak Ganyacha Pustak* [Poetry for Women's Entertainment] (Pune: Shivaji Press, 1884).

Joshi, Y., *Amchi Jivanpravas* [Our Life Together] (Poona: Venus, 1965).

Kanitkar, K., *Palkicha Gonda* [The Tassel at the Centre of the Palanquin] (Poona: Kanitkar and Mandali, 1928).

———, *Sou. Dr Anandibai Joshi Yancha Charitra* [Biography of Mrs Dr Anandibai Joshi], 2nd edn (Poona: Kanitkar and Mandali, 1912; 1st edn 1889).

Karve, A., *Maaze Puran* [My Autobiography] (Bombay: Keshav Bhikaji Dhavale, 1944).

Karve, D.K., *Atmavritta* [Autobiography] (Pune: Hingne Budruk, 1928).

Kashibai, *Sangita Sitashuddhi* [The Purification of Sita in Verse] (Bombay: Nirnaya Sagar, 1897).

Kelkar, G., *Grihini Bhushan, Pushpahar, Bhag Dusra* [Guide-books for Women, Part Two, A Garland of Flowers, Part Two] (Jalgaon: Babaji Press, 1921).

———, *Shri. Sou. Girijabai Kelkar Yanchi Adhyakshiya Bhashane* [The Presidential Speeches of Mrs Girijabai Kelkar] (Dhule: Maag Prakashan, 1957).

———, *Purushanche Band* [Men's Rebellion], 2nd edn (Bombay: Indu Prakash Press, 1921; 1st edn 1913).

———, *Striyancha Swarga* [Women's Paradise], 2nd edn (Bombay: Parchure Puranik and Co., 1921; 1st edn 1912).

———, *Draupadichi Thali* [A Memoir] (Place of publication unknown: G.L. Thokal Publications, 1959).

Kirloskar, S., *Amrita Vruksha: Saraswati Mandir, Sholapur, 1895–1970* [The Nectar Tree: Saraswati Mandir, Sholapur 1895–1970] (Pune: Kirloskar Press, 1970).

Lokahitavadi, *Lokahitavadi Vangmaya* [Collected Works of Lokahitavadi] (Mumbai: Marathi Grantha Sangrahalaya, 1990).

Madgavkar, G.N., *Mumbaiche Varnan* [An Account of Bombay] ed. N.R. Phatak (Bombay: Mumbai Marathi Granthasangrahalaya, 1961; 1st edn 1863).

Madgavkarin, B. (comp.), *Muli va Striyansathin Fugadya, Kombada, Jhima, Pinga, Ithyadi Manoranjak Ganen va Khel* [Fugdi, Kombada, Jhima, Pinga and other Entertaining Songs and Games for Women and Girls] (Bombay: Jagadishwar Press, 1885).

Mainabai, *Urnavyuti athava Lonkarichi Vina* [Manual on Knitting Woollen Clothes] (Poona: Shivaji Press, 1886).

Mali, M.G., *Krantijyoti Savitribai Jotirao Phule* [The Revolutionary Savitribai Jotirao Phule] (Kolhapur: Asha Prakashan, 1980).

Naik, S.M. (ed.), *Strigeetmala athava Striyanchi Manoranjak Gani* [Collection of Women's Songs or Songs for Women's Entertainment] (Bombay: Jagmitra Press, 1882).

Pande, L. *Maharashtracha Kartrutvashalini* [Able Ladies of Maharashtra] (Pune: Teacher's Ideal Publishing House, 1953).

Pandit, V.P.S.P (ed.), *Strigayansangraha athava Bayakanchi Ganyi* [A Collection of Women's Songs] (Bombay: Indu Prakash Press, 1882).

246   *The Emergence of Feminism in India*

Pandita Ramabai, *Stri-Dharma Niti* [Prescribed Laws and Duties on the Proper Conduct of Women], 3rd edn (Kedgaon: Mukti Mission, 1967; 1st edn 1882).

——, *United Stateschi Lokasthiti ani Pravasvrit* [The Peoples of United States] (Mumbai: Nirnaya Sagar, 1889).

Patwardhan, G., *Chakoribaher: Ek Atmakathan* [Beyond the Courtyard, An Autobiography] (Poona: Sadhana Prakashan, 1974).

Pathare Reform Association, *Marriage of Hindu Widows, advocated by the Pathare Reform Association of Bombay: With an Epitome of the History of Bhim Raja, Founder of the Race of Pathare Prabhus*, 2nd edn (Bombay: Indu Prakash Press, 1869; 1st edn 1863).

Phadke, B., *Marathi Lekhika: Chinta ani Chintan*, [Women Authors in the Marathi Language: History and Criticism] (Pune: Sri Vidya, 1980).

Phatak, P., *Shikshantagnyan Tarabai Modak* [The great Educationist, Tarabai Modak] (Bombay: Majestic, 1981).

Sanzgiri, R., *Sutachi veenkam shiknache pustak* [The Art of Crochetting] 2nd edn (Bombay: Gopal Narayan, 1902; 1st edn 1891).

Shinde, T., *Stripurushtulana athava Striya va Purush Yant Sahasi kon he Spasta Karun Dakavinyakarita ha Nibandh* [Women and Men, A Comparison or An Essay Showing Who is More Wicked], ed. S.J. Malshe, 2nd edn (Bombay: Mumbai Marathi Grantha Sangrahalaya Publications, 1975; 1st edn 1882).

Shirke, A., *Sanjvat* [The Evening Lamp] (Bombay: Mauj Prakashan, 1972).

Shrimant Sagunabai (alias Tai Saheb Pant Pratinidhi), *Vatasavitri Akhyan* [Legend of the Divinity Savitri] (Satara: Pandurang Sakharam Kashikar, 1888).

Tambwekar, S.B.B., *Chandra Prabha Viraha* [Heartache of Chandra Prabha on her Separation from her Beloved] (Poona: Vithal Sakharam Agnihotri, 1873).

——, *Hindustanatil Tara* [Indian Princesses] (Poona: Jagadhitechchu, 1895).

Tilak, B.G. *Samaj va Samskruti* [Society and Culture], vol. 5, from *Samagra Tilak Agralekh* [Collected Works of Tilak] (Pune: Kesari Prakashan).

Umakant, *Kai Shri Ramabai Ranade* [The Great Ramabai Ranade] (Bombay: Hind Mahila Pustakmala, 1925).

Vaidya, D.G., *Prarthana Samajacha Itihas* [The History of Prarthana Samaj] (Bombay: Publisher Unknown. 1950).

Vaidya, S., *Shrimati Kashibai Kanitkar: Atmacharitra ani Charitra* [Mrs Kashibai Kanitkar: Autobiography and Biography] (Bombay: Popular Prakashan, 1979).

Varde, M., *Dr Rukhmabai, Ek Arth* [The Saga of Dr Rukhmabai] (Bombay: Popular Prakashan, 1982).

Yelwande, P. and Yelwande, S.K., *Mausa Paka Nishpatti* [Manual on Cooking Meat Dishes] (Poona: Chitrashala, 1883).

5   *Articles (Marathi)*

Anon., 'Garib, Madhyam, va Shrimant Striyani Apaplya Yogyate Pramane Upayogi Asave' [Appropriate Occupations for Lower, Middle and Upper-class Women], *Arya Bhagini*, April 1890, 31–4.

———, 'Saraswat Gaud Brahmanache Swami ani Stripunarvivaha' [The Leader of the Saraswat Gaud Brahmin Community and Widow Remarriage], *Arya Bhagini*, October 1891, 80–81.

———, 'Eka Brahman Striyen Stri Shikshanavar Vyakhyana' [A Brahmin Woman's Essay on Women's Education], *Arya Bhagini*, February 1891, 20–23.

———, 'Amchya Kithyek Vedgal Chali Rithi' [Some of Our Foolish Traditions]', *Maharashtra Mahila*, October 1901, 156–8.

———, 'Mulana Devi Kadnyachi Avashyakata' [The Necessity of Vaccination for Children], *Maharashtra Mahila*, April 1901, 170–73.

———, 'Matari' [A Venerable Old Lady] in V.P.S. Pandit, ed., *Strigayansangraha athava Bayakanchi Ganyi* [A Collection of Women's Songs] (Bombay: Indu Prakash Press, 1882), pp. 103–6.

———, 'Vakadi Vat' [A Warped Course] in P. Gokhale, ed., *Stri Geetratnakar* [A Collection of Women's Songs] (Poona: Bharat Bhushan, 1912), pp. 136–7.

———, 'Sasubaichisamajavani' [Appeasing Mother-in-law], in S.M. Naik, ed., *Strigeetmala Athava Striyanchi Manoranjak Gani* [Collection of Women's Songs or Songs for Women's Entertainment] (Bombay: Jagmitra Press, 1882), pp. 55–8.

———, 'Gane Garbhakhand Varnan' [Songs on Pregnancy and Birth], in *Striyan va Mulikarita Sangeet Sundar Gani* [Songs of Women and Girls] (Ratnagiri: Damanskar, n.d.), pp. 67–70, 74–81.

———, 'Dohale' [The Longings of Pregnant Women], in S.M. Naik, (ed.), *Strigeetmala Athava Striyanchi Manoranjak Gani* [Collection of Women's Songs or Songs for Women's Entertainment] (Bombay: Jagmitra Press, 1882), pp. 62–70.

———, 'Dohale' [Cravings during Pregnancy], *Strisadbodhachintamani*, September 1881, 32–3.

———, 'Shriharitalika' [Shriharitalika Ritual], *Saubhagyasambhar*, 1 (1902): 14–17.

———, 'Palan' [Child-birth Rites] in S.M. Naik, (ed.), *Strigeetmala Athava Striyanchi Manoranjak Gani* [Collection of Women's Songs or Songs for Women's Entertainment] (Bombay: Jagmitra Press, 1882), pp. 71–7.

———, 'Grihinicha Anubhav' [Experiences of a Housewife] in *Grihini*, all issues of 1888 and 1889.

Athavale, P., 'Dipushtachi Ghaan' [Stench from Temple Lamps], *Saubhagya Sambhar*, November 1905, 75–7.

'Arya Mahila', 'Samsarathlya Goshti' [A Story of a Home], *Maharashtra Mahila*, July 1901, 16–18.

Bhor, M., Book Review of Rukmini Sanzgiri's *Sutachi Veenkam Shiknache Pustak* [The Art of Crochetting] in *Karmanook*, 21 November 1896.

Desai, A.P., 'Striyas Uttam Shikshan Kontha? Bhag Dusra' [Which is the Most Appropriate Curriculum for Women? Part Two], *Maharashtra Mahila*, September 1901, 122–8.

Degaonkar, P., 'Shri Saraswati Mandir' [Saraswati Mandir], *Maharashtra Mahila*, May 1901, 226–9.

Dravid, L., 'Lahanpani Lagne va Strishikshan' [Child Marriage and Women's Education] in *Deshseva Nibandhamala* [Essays in Service of the Nation], (Pune: Vijayanand Press, 1896), pp. 22–8.

Editorial, 'Shri Saraswati Mandir: Nibandhmala' [An Essay on the Women's Institution, Saraswati Mandir], *Maharashtra Mahila*, October 1901, 170–71.

———, 'Mahilecha Uddhar', [Women's Welfare], *Maharashtra Mahila*, all issues between 1900–1903.

———, 'Samajik Sudharana' [Social Reform], *Arya Bhagini*, June 1891, 49–52.

———, 'Eka Brahman Striyen Stri Shikshanavar Vyakhyana' [A Brahmin Woman's Essay on Women's Education], *Arya Bhagini*, February 1891, 18–23.

'Ek Kulvadhu' [An Upper-class Housewife], Letter dated 26 July 1890, to 'Kartri' [Woman-editor], *Arya Bhagini*, August 1890, n.p.

'Eka Sushiksit Stri Kadun' [By an Educated Lady]., 'Gulabbai ani Shevatibai Yancha Bodhpar Samvad' [Instructive Debates between Gulabbai and Shevatibai], *Arya Bhagini*, all issues between 1886–1892.

'Ek Gaud Saraswat Brahmani Stri' [A Gaud Saraswat Brahman Lady], 'Punarvivaha' [Remarriage], *Arya Bhagini*, July 1891, 63–5.

'Ek Saraswat Gaud Brahmani Stri' [A Saraswat Gaud Brahman Lady], 'Saraswat Gaud Brahmanachya Swamiche Prakaran' [Public Announcement of the Head of Saraswat Gaud Brahman Community], *Arya Bhagini*, October 1891, 84–6.

Gadekar, A.R., 'Prapanchikas Shahanpanachi Avashyakata' [Prudence and Wisdom as Essential Attributes of Domestic Life], *Strisadbodhachinatamani* [Women's Advice Manual], September 1881, 2–4.

Goa, S., 'Anathbalikashram' [Orphanage for Girls], *Saubhagyasambhar*, 2 (1904): 33–6.

Kanitkar, K., 'Samrajyasatthekhali Stri Shikshanachi Pragati' [Progress of Women's Education under Imperial Rule], *Vividhadnyanvistar*, April 1912, 552–61.

———, 'Purvichya Stri ani Hallicha Stri' [Indian Women of the Past and Present], *Subodh Patrika*, 8 May 1882, 7.

———, [Book Review] of Parvatibai Chitnavis, *Amchya Jagacha Pravas* [Our Travels around the World], *Vividhadnyanvistar*, March 1916, 20–26.

Kanthabai, 'Condition of Women', *Maharashtra Mahila*, April 1892, pp. 29–31.

Kashibai, 'Women's Duties', *Maharashtra Mahila*, October 1901, p.178.

Kelkar, G., 'Hindu Samajatil Strishikshanache Pudildyaya', [The Aims of Education of Women in Hindu Society], *Grihini Bhushan, Bhag Dusra, Pushpahar* [Guide-books for Women, Part Two, Garland of Flowers] (Jalgaon: Babaji Press, 1921), pp.10–17.

Kelkar, G., 'Tarunpidi va Samajik Sudharana' [The Younger Generation and Social Reform], *Grihini Bhushan, Bhag Dusra, Pushpahar* [Guide-books for Women, Part

Two, Garland of Flowers] (Jalgaon: Babaji Press, 1921), pp.72–84.

Kelkar, I., 'Adarsh Hindi Striyanchi Kartavya' [Duties of the Ideal Indian Woman], in *Balikadarsh*, April 1936, 30–32.

Killedar, R., 'Strivargavar Khota Arop' [False Accusations against Women], *Maharashtra Mahila*, September 1901, 110–11.

Kibe, K., [Book Review] of Kashibai Kanitkar, *Dr Anandibai Joshi Yanche Charitra* [The Biography of Dr Anandibai Joshi], *Vividhadnyanvistar*, March 1916, 14–20.

———, 'Samaj Chitra, Number Ek: Balavriddhavivaha' [Picture of our Society, Number One: Marriage of an Old Man with a Young Girl], *Vividhadnyanvistar*, September 1911, 113–19.

Kirloskar, K., 'Striyanchi Kartavya Karmen' [Women's Duties], *Maharashtra Mahila*, October 1901, 171–8.

Lad, A., 'Lavkar Lagna Karnyache Chal' [The Custom of Early Marriage], *Arya Bhagini*, March 1886, 3–6.

———, 'Lagnyachi Chali' [Marriage Customs], *Arya Bhagini*, March 1886, 1–3.

Lad, M., 'Dagine' [Jewellery], *Arya Bhagini*, September 1891, 80–81.

———, 'Pandita Ramabai', *Arya Bhagini*, August 1891, 68–9.

———, 'Jyotish ani Shakun' [Astrologers and Omens], *Arya Bhagini*, July 1891, 57–9.

'Ek Vidhawa Mulgi' [A Widowed Girl], *Arya Bhagini*, May 1892, 34–5.

Mankar, R.B., 'Dindi' [Torch-bearer], *Arya Bhagini*, September 1890, n.p.

Mantri, J., 'Striyanchi Prasuti ani Tatsambandhi Upchar' [On Delivery and Related Subjects], *Maharashtra Mahila*, February 1901, 70–85.

Mitra, M., 'Prachin Striyanchi Marathi Kavita' [The Marathi Poetry of Women of Ancient India], *Maharashtra Mahila*, October 1903, 230–38.

———, 'Striyancha Unnatisambandhichi Prayatna' [Schemes and efforts made in the Direction of Women's Progress], *Maharashtra Mahila*, all issues of 1901, 1902, 1904.

———, 'Naval Vishesh' [Special News], *Maharashtra Mahila*, all issues of 1901, 1902, 1903.

Nabar, T., 'Bal Vivahache Dushparinam' [Evil Effects of Child Marriage], *Maharashtra Mahila*, May 1901, 234–6.

Nadkarni, C., Letter dated 28 July 1890 from Thana to the 'Kartri' [Woman-editor], *Arya Bhagini*, August 1890, n.p.

Nagarkar, B.B., 'Varishta Pratiche Shikshan: Pandita Ramabai va Umabaiyancha Samvad' [Higher Education: A Debate between Pandita Ramabai and Umabai], *Grihini*, February 1888, 169–76.

Namjoshi, V., 'Sushiksit Bandhuna Anath Bhaginichyavatinen Vignyapathi' [An Appeal from Helpless Sisters to their Educated Brothers], *Maharashtra Mahila*, August 1902, 84–9.

Nerurkar, D.N., 'Katkasar' [Thrift], in *Strishikshanchandrika*, May and June 1900, 131–5.

Phadnis, L., 'Striyanchi Durbalata' [Women's Physical Weakness], *Maharashtra Mahila*, September 1901, 131–4.

Sheti, R., 'Stri Shikshana Sambandhi Matbhed' [Difference of Opinions on Women's Education], *Arya Bhagini*, August 1890, 90–96.

Shingane, K., 'Plague Campatil Hakeekat' [What Took Place in the Plague Camp], *Maharashtra Mahila*, February 1901, 86–91.

Tarkhadkar, K., 'Striyanchi Sthiti, Bhag Ek' [The Condition of Women, Part One], *Arya Bhagini*, April 1892, 26–9.

——, 'Striyanchi Sthiti, Lagnatil Khandani va Bhat Mandalicha Paise Upatnyacha Thata, Bhag Dusra' [The Condition of Women, Punitive Exactions of the Priestly Class during Marriages and their Methods of Extraction, Part Two], *Arya Bhagini*, May 1892, 96–100.

Tarkhadkar, T., 'Strishikshan', [Women's Education], *Arya Bhagini*, October 1891, 81–2.

Vaidya, S., 'Vegvegli Sadye Ani Pragat Marga' [Differing Methods and Paths of Progress], in *Ramasmriti* [In Memory of Ramabai Ranade], (Poona: Seva Sadan Society Press, 1984), pp. 49–55.

Primary Sources: Books and Articles (English)

Athavale, P., *My Story: The Autobiography of a Hindu Widow*, trans. J. Abbott, (New York: G.P. Putnam and Sons, 1930).

Balfour, M.I., and Young, R., *The Work of Medical Women in India* (Oxford: Humphrey Milford, 1929).

Bhor, M., *Some Impressions of England* (Poona: Dnyan Chaksu Press, 1900).

Billington, M.F., *Women in India* (London: Chapman and Hall, 1895).

Burke, M.L., *Swami Vivekananda in America: New Discoveries* (Calcutta, Advaita Ashram, 1958).

Butler, C., *Pandita Ramabai Sarasvati: A Pioneer in the Movement for the Education of the Child-Widow of India* (London: Fleming Revell, 1922).

Carpenter, J.E., *Life and Work of Mary Carpenter* (London: Macmillan, 1879).

Chandavarkar, G.L. (ed.), *A Wrestling Soul: Story of the Life of Sir Narayan Chandavarkar* (Bombay: Popular, 1955).

Chattopadhayaya, K., *Awakening of Indian Women* (Madras: Everyman's Press 1939).

——, 'Women: Past and Present', *Roshni*, December 1948.

Dall, C.H., *The Life of Anandabai Joshee* (Boston: Roberts Brothers, 1888).

Dadaji, B. *An Exposition of Some of the Facts of the Case of Dadaji v. Rakhmabai* (Bombay: Advocate of India Press, 1887).

Deodhar, I. 'Progress of Indian Women', *Diamond Jubilee Souvenir of the Poona Seva Sadan Society, 1909–1969* (Poona: Seva Sadan Press, 1970), pp. 18–22.

——, 'This I remember', *Diamond Jubilee Souvenir of the Poona Seva Sadan Society, 1909–1969* (Poona: Seva Sadan Press, 1970), pp. 27–38.

Dyer, H.S., 'Preface' in Soonderbai Powar, *Hinduism and Womanhood* (London: Christian Worker's Depot, n.d).

Elwin, (Rev. Father), *Thirty–Four Years in Poona City: Being the History of the Panch Howds Poona City Mission, India* (London: Mowbray and Co., 1911).

Enthoven, R.E., *The Folklore of Bombay* (Oxford: Oxford University Press, 1924).

Farquhar, J.N., *Modern Religious Movements in India* (New York: Macmillan, 1915).

Forbes, G. (ed.), *Shudha Mazumdar: Memoirs of an Indian Woman* (New York: Sharpe, 1989).

Gedge, E.C. and Choksi, M. (eds), *Woman in Modern India* (Bombay, 1929).

Ghugare, S., *Renaissance in Western India: Karmaveer V.R. Shinde* (Bombay: Himalaya, 1983).

Goreh, N.N.S., *A Rational Refutation of the Hindu Philosophical Systems*, trans. Fitz-Edward Hall (Calcutta: Christian Tract and Book Society, 1862).

———, *Four Lectures Delivered in Substance to the Brahmos in Bombay and Poona* (Bombay: Education Society Press, 1875).

Joshi, A., *A Speech by a Hindu Lady* (Bombay: By a 'well-wisher', 1882).

Kaikini, L.V. (ed.), *The Speeches and Writings of Sir Narayan G. Chandavarkar* (Bombay: Manoranjak Grantha Prasarak, 1911).

Karve, D. K., 'A Living Testimony', *Pandita Ramabai Centenary Souvenir, 1858–1958* (Bombay: S.M. Adhav, 1958), n.p.

———, 'Pandita Ramabai', *Young Men of India*, June 1922, pp. 302–5.

Kennedy, M., *Notes on Criminal Classes in the Bombay Presidency* (Bombay: Government Central Press, 1908).

Khare, B.H., *How is Woman Treated by Man and Religion?* (Bombay: Nirnaya Sagar Press, 1895).

Kirtane, D.V., *Madhav Govind Ranade,* vol. 1 (Bombay: Manoranjak Grantha Prasarak Mandali., 1906).

Kirtikar, K.R., *An Address on the Occasion of the Second Anniversary of the Saddharma Samaj of Thane*, 20 July 1883 (Bombay: Native Opinion Press, 1883).

Kishwar, M., 'Trying to Live by Her Principles', *Manushi*, 48 (1988): 30–31.

Kittredge, G.T., A *Short History of the Medical Women for India Fund of Bombay* (Bombay: Publisher unknown, 1889).

Leslie, J. (ed. and tr.), *The Perfect Wife: The Orthodox Hindu Woman According to the Stridharmapaddhati of Tryambakayajvan* (New Delhi: Oxford University Press, 1989).

Lutzker, E., *Edith Pechey-Phipson, M.D.: The Story of England's Foremost Pioneering Woman Doctor* (New York: Exposition Press, 1973).

MacNicol, N., *Pandita Ramabai* (Calcutta: Association Press, 1926).

Mandlik, N.V. (ed.), *Writings and Speeches of the Late Honourable Rao Saheb Vishwanath Narayan Mandlik* (Bombay: Native Opinion, 1896).

Mankar, G.A., *A Sketch of the Life and Works of the Late Mr. Justice M.G. Ranade* (Bombay: Caxton Press, 1902).

Mitchell, Mrs Murray, *Sixty Years Ago* (Edinburgh: MacNiven and Wallace, 1905).

Mueller, G. (ed.), *The Life and Letters of the Right Hon. Friedrich Max Muller*, vol.2, (London: Longmans, Green and Co., 1902).

Naik, J.P. (ed.), *A Review of Education in Bombay State, 1855–1955* (Bombay: Asia Publishing House, 1958).

Nikambe, S.M., *Ratanbai: A Sketch of a Bombay High Caste Hindu Young Wife* (London: Marshall Bros., 1895).

Nurullah, S., and Naik, J.P., *A History of Education in India during the British Period* (Bombay: Macmillan, 1955).

Padmanji, B., *Once Hindu: Now Christian, The Early Life of Baba Padmanji, An Autobiography*, trans. J.M. Mitchell (London: Nisbet and Co., 1890).

Pandita Ramabai, 'Account of the Life of a Hindoo Woman', *Cheltenham Ladies College Magazine*, 12 (Autumn 1885): 138–46.

Pandita Ramabai, 'Indian Religion', *Cheltenham Ladies College Magazine*, 13 (Spring 1886): 106–18.

———, 'Woman's Religion as Taught by the Hindu Shastras', *Mukti Prayer Bell*, September 1906, 24–8.

———, *A Testimony*, 6th edn (Kedgaon: Mukti Mission, 1964; 1st edn 1907).

———, *A Short History of the Kripa Sadan, or Home of Mercy*, 6th edn (Kedgaon: Mukti Mission Press, 1964; 1st edn 1908).

———, *The High-Caste Hindu Woman* (London: George Bell, 1888).

Parasnis, D.B., *Poona in Bygone Days* (Bombay: Times Press, 1921).

Pechey-Phipson, E., *Address to the Hindus of Bombay on the Subject of Child Marriage* (Bombay: Times Press, 1890), Tracts/799, British Library, London.

Powar, S., *Hinduism and Womanhood* (London: Christian Worker's Depot, n.d.).

Raghunathji, K., 'Bombay Dancing Girls', *The Indian Antiquary*, 13 (1884): 165–78.

Rakhmabai, 'Rakhmabai's Reply to Dadajee's "Exposition"', in *Law Tracts* (Bombay: Advocate of India Press, 1887).

———, 'Infant Marriage', *Times of India*, 26 June1885, p. 4.

Ranade, M.G., *The Miscellaneous Writings of the Late Hon'ble Justice M.G. Ranade* (Bombay: Manoranjan Press, 1915).

Ranade, R., *Himself: The Autobiography of a Hindu Lady*, trans. K. Gates (New York: Green and Co., 1938).

———, *Ranade: His Wife's Reminiscences*, trans. K. Deshpande (New Delhi: Government of India Publications, 1963).

Rao, M.T., 'Considerations of the Crime of Infanticide and its Punishment', *Journal of the National Indian Association in Aid of Social Progress in India*, 65 (May 1876): 131–7.

Richter, J., *A History of Missions in India* (Edinburgh: Oliphant and Co., 1908).

Row, R. R., *Women's Right to Salvation* (Madras: Hindu Press, 1887).

Sarkar, T. (tr. and ed.), *Words to Win: Amar Jiban* (Delhi: Permanent Black, 2003).

Sathhianadhan, K., *Miscellaneous Writings of Krupabai Satthianadhan* (Madras: Srinivasa Varadachari and Co., 1896).

———, *Kamala: A Story of Hindu Life* (Madras: Srinivasa Varadachari and Co., 1895).

———, *Saguna: A Story of Native Christian Life* (Madras: Srinivasa Varadachari and Co., 1895).

Satthianadhan, S., *Sketches of Indian Christians Collected from Different Sources* (London: Christian Literature Society for India, 1896).

Shah, A.B. (ed.), *The Letters and Correspondences of Pandita Ramabai* (Bombay: Maharashtra State Board for Literature and Culture, 1977).

Sherring, M.A., *The History of Protestant Missions in India* (London: Trubner and Co., 1875).

Sorabji, C., 'Social Relations—England and India', *Pan-Anglican Papers* (London: publisher unknown, 1908), pp. 1–4.

———, *'Therefore', An Impression of Sorabji Kharsedji Langrana and his Wife Franscina* (London: Oxford University Press, 1924).

———, *India Calling: The Memories of Cornelia Sorabji* (London: Nisbet and Co., 1934).

Storrie, K., *Soonderbai Powar: A Noble Worker for Indian Womanhood* (London: Pickering and Inglis, n.d.).

Stree Shakti Sanghatana (ed.), *We Were Making History: Life Stories of Women in the Telengana People's Struggle* (London: Zed, 1989).

Tharu, S. and Lalitha, K. (eds), *Women Writing in India, 600 B.C. to the Present*, vols I and II (New York: The Feminist Press, 1991).

Tilak, L., *I Follow After: An Autobiography*, trans. Josephine Inkster (London: Oxford University Press, 1950).

———, *From Brahma to Christ*, trans. and ed. Stacy Waddy (London: Lutterworth, 1956).

Vidwans, M.D. (ed.), *Letters of Lokmanya Tilak* (Poona: Kesari Prakashan, 1966).

West, R. and Buhler, G.B. (eds.), *A Digest of Hindu Law*, Book I (Bombay: Education Society Press, 1867).

Wilson, D.D., *History of the Suppression of Infanticide in Western India* (London: Smith, Elder and Co., 1855).

Index